Surrealism, Bugs Bunny, and the Blues

Selected Writings on Popular Culture

Franklin Rosemont

Edited by Abigail Susik and Paul Buhle

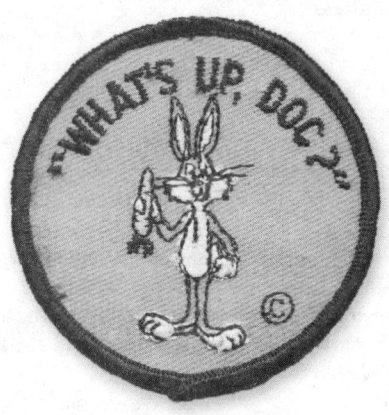

PM

Surrealism, Bugs Bunny, and the Blues: Selected Writings on Popular Culture
© 2025 Abigail Susik and Paul Buhle
This edition © 2025 PM Press

All rights reserved. No part of this book may be transmitted by any means without permission in writing from the publisher.

ISBN: 979-8-88744-086-6 (paperback)
ISBN: 979-8-88744-092-7 (ebook)
Library of Congress Control Number: 2024939657
Cover by John Yates / www.stealworks.com
Cover and title page image: Franklin Rosemont, *Secret of Hegel*, 1968, displayed at *Surrealist Exhibition*, Gallery Bugs Bunny, Chicago, October 27–December 8, 1968, collaged paper, with sewn patch from title page added in 2008 on the occasion of the forty-year anniversary of Gallery Bugs Bunny held at the Heartland Cafe, Chicago. Collection of Abigail Susik.
Interior design by briandesign

10 9 8 7 6 5 4 3 2 1

PM Press
PO Box 23912
Oakland, CA 94623
www.pmpress.org

Printed in the USA.

Praise for *Surrealism, Bugs Bunny, and the Blues*

"There isn't much Franklin Rosemont did *not* know, but what he knew he knew from the inside out. I noticed this in the first few months of our decade-long friendship and collaboration. Whether it is the politics of working-class culture, jazz, rock, blues, hoboes, comics, cinema, ecology, psychoanalysis, poetry and poets, art and artists, Chicago and Paris, or surrealism and surrealists, he saw things from inside the belly. He read, listened, and felt from a warm, churning, vulnerable place and turned the experience into prose with such elegance and clarity, it hit you in the pit of your stomach. Gut punch or tickle attack, either way you're left breathless. Don't take my word. Start on page 1."
—Robin D.G. Kelley, author of *Thelonious Monk: The Life and Times of an American Original*

"Ahead of the game yet unapologetically behind the curve, Franklin Rosemont's writings on popular culture have always been needed. But they seem to be required reading now, more than ever. Without recourse to humor, irreverence, and play, how else is the current moment to be outlived? The editors have done a stellar job of drawing together gems from his prodigious output, originally spread across countless volumes, tracts, pamphlets, and posters. They don't need any polishing, but this volume makes them shine somehow brighter."
—Joanna Pawlik, author of *Remade in America: Surrealist Art, Activism, and Politics, 1940–1978*

"However much the ruling ideas of a society come from its ruling class, such dominance does not extend to our dreams. In this marvelous book, the great surrealist writer, artist, and rebel Franklin Rosemont captures across an incredible terrain the ways in which the wild, the funny, the insurgent, and the uncanny animate what is loved in popular culture. He shows how the imagination, collective and individual, challenges miseries, conformities, and oppressions and finds its audience."
—David Roediger, author of *History Against Misery*

For Paul Garon

Contents

Acknowledgments

Franklin Rosemont's collaborators, Penelope Rosemont and Paul Garon among the most sustained, surely encouraged his fascination in subjects related to popular culture. But it would be fair to say his indulgent parents, Henry and Sally Rosemont, encouraged the boy to pursue his eclectic interests and inspired him through their own lives and work—his mother as a sometime local radio star, his father as a leader of unionized typesetters in Chicago.

For our part, as editors, the texts themselves incited our interest, and Tamara Smith and Ramsey Kanaan provided generous assistance for our project. We are also grateful to David Roediger, Robin D.G. Kelley, and Joanna Pawlik for their enthusiasm and support. From Paul Buhle: Special thanks go to my fellow editors of *Cultural Correspondence*, who, more than anyone else, pushed me in the direction of investigating popular culture's subversive potential. From Abigail Susik: Thanks to my coeditor, Paul Buhle, for his friendship and collaboration and for an example of an academic life merged with an activist existence; my son, Vaughn Lawrence Browning, for sleeping in long enough stretches for me to assemble this manuscript; Paul Garon (1942–2022), whose love of the blues and whose gentle presence permanently altered the surrealist horizon; and Penelope Rosemont for infecting so many of us with contagious elephants.

"Long Live Krazy Kat! Long Live the Surrealist Revolution!"

Franklin Rosemont's Search for Surrealist Affinities

Abigail Susik

In 1975, Paul Buhle and David Wagner cofounded *Cultural Correspondence* (*CC*) (1975–83), a periodical devoted to the exploration of the revolutionary potential of certain forms of popular culture. The editorial board's hopes for the future of the publication were explicitly stated on the first page of the first issue: "Perhaps *CC* will become a journal in time or perhaps only a way of advancing the notions of a cultural front within a resurgent Socialist movement" (fig. 1).[1] Such a nascent initiative of concertedly extracting the socialist political content of the broader "cultural front" had roots in Buhle's prior collaborations. In 1967, Buhle had founded the Students for a Democratic Society (SDS)–affiliated journal *Radical America* (*RA*) (1967–99). In disparate guest-edited issues this journal frequently sought to bridge New Left activism with an exploration of youth culture, avant-garde collectives (like surrealism), and contemporary media such as comics.

With the launch of *Cultural Correspondence* in the mid-1970s, however, Buhle and Wagner took what they saw as the potential radicalization of popular culture as their new journal's primary focus. They sought fresh possibilities for discovery within everyday life in the face of what Buhle later called "the collapse of the New Left."[2] The purview of *Cultural Correspondence* emphasized American topics and included "comics, popular music, good mass-market films, interesting television, and factory-made hallucinogenics" along with blue-collar histories, Americana, popular literature, dance, and, over time, a staggering array of other species of cultural manifestations.[3] Contributors to *CC* were known to "condemn the manipulative qualities of commercial culture"

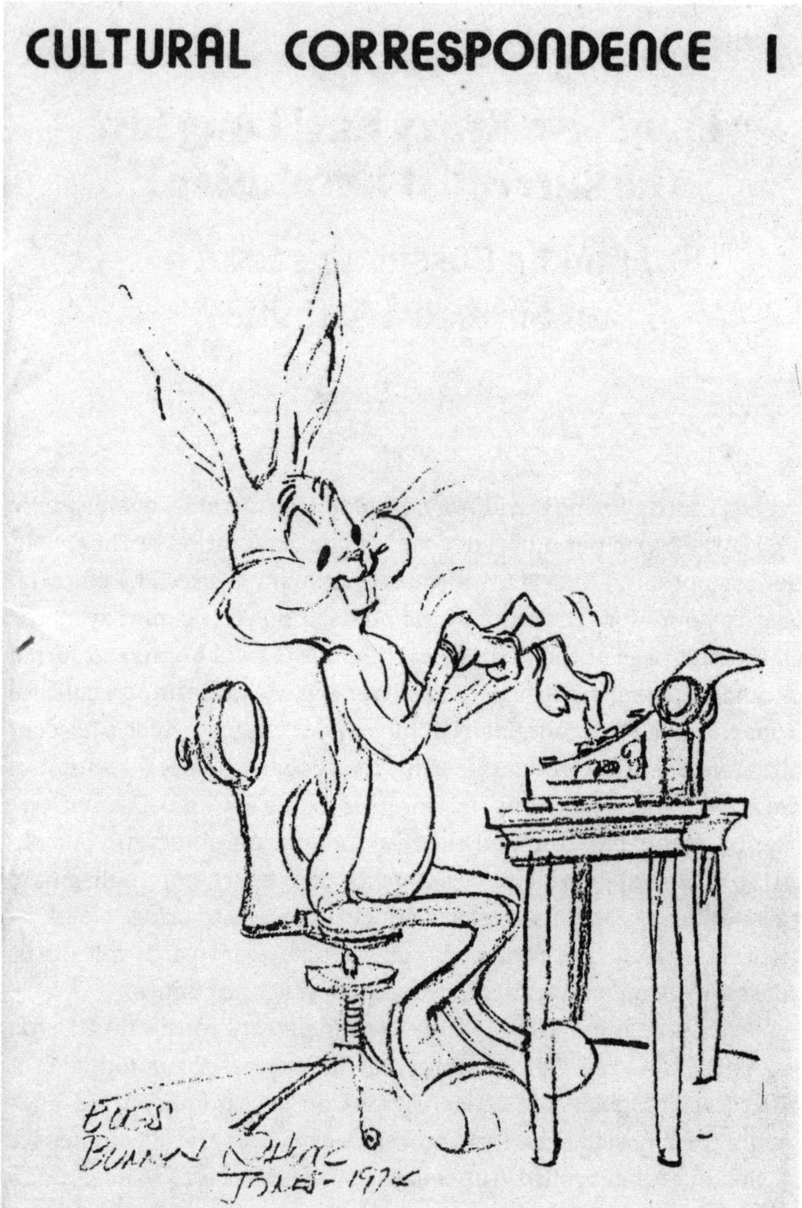

CULTURAL CORRESPONDENCE 1

Fig. 1. Front cover of *Cultural Correspondence*, no. 1, August 1975. Author's collection. Courtesy of Paul Buhle.

and at the same time "vehemently reject nearly all of what has passed for Marxist (or liberal or conservative) orthodoxy on popular culture."[4] In advance of Dick Hebdige's popularization of the term *subculture* in his 1979 book *Subculture: The Meaning of Style* (which in itself was indebted to sociologist Stuart Hall's mid-1970s work on subculture), *CC* was articulating a prescient theory of underground reclamations of dominant media by both survivors of the Sixties New Left and the emergent youth culture.

The cultural hermeneutics of Mikhail Bakhtin and Walter Benjamin offered a clear way forward in this endeavor, according to Buhle. However, Frankfurt School critical theories about the inauthenticity and false consciousness of capitalist consumerism and the culture industry by the likes of Theodor Adorno and Max Horkheimer were seen as relegating Marxist socialism to an "increasingly archaic shell."[5] The editors of *Cultural Correspondence* disagreed that the vernacular culture of everyday working people had become extinct in the machinations of mass culture. They sought to refute Adorno in particular. Theirs was a subtle optimism that, like Marx's idea about the possibilities for the socialization of labor, the realms of leisure and consumption might also be willfully adapted—or appropriated—for socialist purposes.[6] The editors believed the masses had the means of responding in a catalytic way to mass culture by learning from it and subsequently reshaping it for their own purposes. In this spirit, the communities that formed around *RA* and *CC* looked to the life and work of the Marxist and pan-African historian C.L.R. James as a counterpoint to critical theory approaches to popular culture. They were indebted to his argument for the spontaneous appearance of advanced social relations and forms of self-expression in the lives of the working class under capitalism.[7]

As a key contributor to both *Radical America* and *Cultural Correspondence*, Franklin Rosemont (1943–2009) shared some of these viewpoints about popular culture with Buhle and his editorial boards. However, Rosemont's highly idiosyncratic confidence in the persistence of moments of vernacular authenticity in the people's response to commodity culture past and present was the result of his background and individual inclinations rather than an explicitly socialist or theoretical point of view—although certainly Rosemont's own close and early attention to the work of James influenced his thoughts on this subject over time.[8] It might be said that Rosemont's interest in socialism coincided early on with his attraction to popular culture.

It was only starting in the mid-1960s that Rosemont began an in-depth analysis, synthesis, and critique of the work of one Frankfurt School dialectician, Herbert Marcuse, which by the 1970s resulted in Rosemont's correspondence with the German-American philosopher. This epistolary exchange also prompted their extended debate about what Rosemont insisted was the revolutionary potential hiding within dominant or bourgeois cultural forms, entities that Marcuse deprecatingly called signs of "affirmative culture."[9] For Marcuse, affirmative cultural forms encouraged individual versus collective attainment, and this atomization was a problem for the growth of revolutionary consciousness. Contrary to Marcuse's views, Rosemont's lifelong tendency toward a syndicalist, worker-focused orientation permitted him to argue otherwise. Through direct action interventions in daily revolutionary practice, certain forms of authentic popular culture, such as modern types of folklore or proletarian culture and various methods of creative workplace and artistic sabotage, could activate insurgent impulses on a collective basis. In this sense, Rosemont's largely autodidactic approach (he had no high school or college degrees, having only attended two years of college) to his subjects as a member of the working-class intelligentsia might be cast in Gramscian terms as a decisively counterhegemonic activity.[10] His predilection for popular culture was deployed in a derailment of the pacifying power of ruling-class ideologies and fosters in their place the spread of proletarian consciousness and culture.

Already a decade in advance of his dialogues with Marcuse, Rosemont was steadfast in his admiration for certain phenomena that qualified as folkloric, homespun, regional, or sometimes lowbrow American fare. Several strands of experience and predilection established the foundation for Rosemont's profound lifelong interest in diverse categories of popular and nondominant culture—what ultimately amounted to a vast personal archive of beloved sources and artifacts, far too myriad to catalog completely here. He championed particular types of popular music; he preferred jazz, blues, and proletarian songs but also, for a period in his life, certain examples of rock 'n' roll (the Velvet Underground did not make the cut). He was also known to enthuse over cartoons; comics; examples of genre fiction such as horror; self-taught artists; working-class humor, poetry, and games; hobo lore; selections in cinema and dance; histories of popular radicalism, the labor movement (and culture), and utopianism; and Americana or local histories of Chicago. According to Chicago surrealist Hal Rammel, who contributed to Rosemont's 1979 double special issue of *Cultural Correspondence*, "Surrealism and Its Popular Accomplices," Rosemont's interests ranged widely, including the following list of objects and writers who were "surrealists in spite of themselves": "the detective novels of Fredric Brown (*Night of the Jabberwock*, 1950), Harry Stephen Keeler, Irving Phillips's single-panel gag strip *The Strange World of Mr. Mum*, C.C. Beck and *Captain Marvel in the Land of Surrealism* (1948), Charles Addams's cartoons, children's toys (spinning tops), the strange life story of Wisconsin's Alfred Lawson, and so much more."[11]

Rosemont's capacious popular culture sensibility continually attracted friends, comrades, and collaborators, such as the San Francisco–based writers Nancy Joyce Peters and Philip Lamantia, who traveled to Chicago in 1976 for the Marvelous Freedom World Surrealist Exhibition, in itself an elaborate demonstration of Chicago surrealist vernacular culture commitments. Along with City Lights Books cofounder and poet Lawrence Ferlinghetti, Peters and Lamantia were enthusiastic supporters of Rosemont's "Surrealism and Its Popular Accomplices" special issue a few years later. Of their 1976 encounter with Peters and Lamantia, Penelope Rosemont recalled, "Among the things we discussed were comics, music, and movies.... Cthulhu, Clark Ashton Smith, *Fantômas*, and Godzilla. Nancy talked about an essay she was working on, 'Backyard Bombs and Invisible Rays: Horror Movies on Television,' which we later published in 'Surrealism and Its Popular Accomplices.'"[12]

Rosemont's conviction in the power of the people to craft a repurposed and sometimes radicalized version of culture even in the face of advanced capitalism's endless production of kitsch and canned novelty was significantly influenced by his background. His blue-collar upbringing in Chicago combined with his precocious teenage discovery of the Beat Generation and international surrealism to forge a remarkably distinctive attitude about the possibilities for the *détournement*, or rerouting, of mass culture by everyday individuals. Such a premise held out for the inevitability of the infiltration of mainstream culture by subversive currents. He was also raised with a keen awareness of the working-class history and culture of his home city, Chicago. His father was a longtime veteran activist in the International Typographical Union and a leader of the 1949 newspaper strike at the *Chicago Tribune*. His mother was a minor radio personality and president of a musicians' union for women.[13] The Rosemont family lived in a milieu of radical unionists and bohemians.

Rosemont's love of language from an early age first encouraged him to seek out Beat poetry during high school, the study of which eventually led him to a revelatory encounter with traces of the international avant-garde. Accidentally discovering surrealism at the age of fifteen in 1959, Rosemont realized poetry's potential for fomenting a sense of the ridiculous. It was the line "Elephants are contagious" (Les éléphants sont contagieux), the fourth entry in Paul Éluard and Benjamin Péret's 1925 collaborative text "152 proverbes mis au goût du jour," that Rosemont read in translation in the 1956 edition of Lillian Herlands Hornstein's *Reader's Companion to World Literature*. Around that time, this same phrase was encountered by another local high schooler, Penelope Bartik, Rosemont's future wife and collaborator.[14] Contagious elephants, which Éluard and Péret had updated and transformed from a bourgeois commonplace to a surrealist "taste of the day" (mis au goût du jour), proved catchy enough to spark an entire lifetime of surrealism studies for both Franklin and Penelope Rosemont. Of their acquaintance, their mutual love of the meeting ground between popular culture and radical politics, and their social milieu in 1960s Chicago, Penelope Rosemont later explained:

> Our love of comics brought us together. That and the fact that we both knew who Louis Lingg was. Franklin knew about him because of his time in the Illinois Labor History Society. I knew about him from reading Algren's *Chicago: City on the Make*. Algren referred to Haymarket martyr Lingg as "practicing reckless politics in Chicago." One of the most popular of the Haymarket anarchists among the Solidarity Bookshop group, in the 1880s Lingg frequented beer gardens not far from the Solidarity Bookshop location. Haymarket's Albert Parsons was a printer, both my grandfather and Franklin's were printers and owned their own shops—mine in Altgeld's Unity Building

in Chicago, Franklin's on Rosemont Place in San Francisco. The idea of making books came naturally.

We got into long conversations about Bugs Bunny, Scrooge McDuck, Little Lulu, and Micky Mouse. The greatest Bugs Bunny story was "The Magic Sneeze"; the greatest Scrooge McDuck, "The Seven Cities of Cibola"; the greatest Little Lulu, "The Ghost Train"; and the greatest Mickey Mouse, "Phantom Blot." Later, I realized that "Phantom Blot" was the kid's version of the great French series *Fantômas*.

Bernard Marszalek would join in relating oddball skits from *Mad* magazine. Bernard copied the style of *Mad* magazine for his high school newspaper that he self-published and passed around. It was snatched by a Christian Brother and it caused him to be kicked out of the college prep program. He was grateful, since as a result he could skip Latin.

Tor Faegre admired Scrooge's adventures in the land of Tra-la-la. Every Sunday we took the bus down to Maxwell Street, bought comics to sell cheaply at Solidarity. We also bought Marvel comics there, seeking out the Hulk and Madame Medusa. This made the shop popular with the grade school kids in the school across the street. But we also bought back the comics for ourselves—the ones we had a few years ago given away (we missed them terribly). We amassed an entire room full of comics that visiting kids would disappear into.[15]

After dropping out of high school, Rosemont proceeded to hitch-hike and motorcycle across the United States, living in San Francisco's North Beach for a period in 1960 in search of surrealists and beatniks.[16] By the spring of 1961, he returned to Chicago from the Bay Area and enrolled at Roosevelt University, where he soon met a leftist and race-diverse group of students. This cohort included John Bracey Jr., Penelope Bartik, Larry and Dottie Decoster, Robert Green, Lionel Bottari, Bernard Marszalek, Simone Collier, Torvald Faegre, Joan Smith, and Scott Spencer, all of whom participated in some fashion in events and phenomena that predate but partly determine the emergence of Chicago surrealism in 1966. The key points of contact for their group were Roosevelt University's Anti-Poetry Club (c. 1962–64), the Solidarity Bookshop/Industrial Workers of the World (IWW) branch

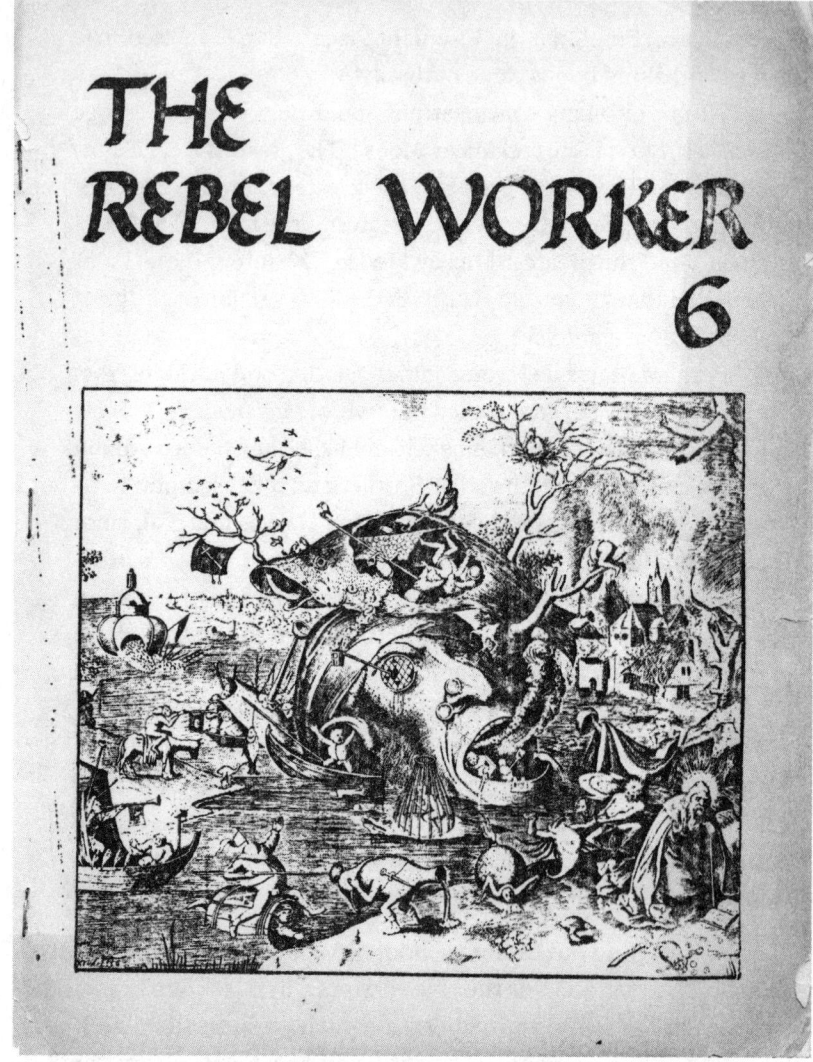

Fig. 2. Front cover of the *Rebel Worker*, no. 6, May 1966. Author's collection. Courtesy of Penelope Rosemont.

office in Lincoln Park (1964–68), and the IWW journal the *Rebel Worker* (nos. 1–7, 1964–66) (fig. 2).[17] Having already studied surrealism extensively in Chicago libraries by 1961, Rosemont experienced a deepening identification with this movement that exerted a palpable influence on several members of his community. The final issues of Solidarity Bookshop's *Rebel Worker* increasingly featured surrealist content alongside the journal's ongoing valorization of the struggle for civil rights,

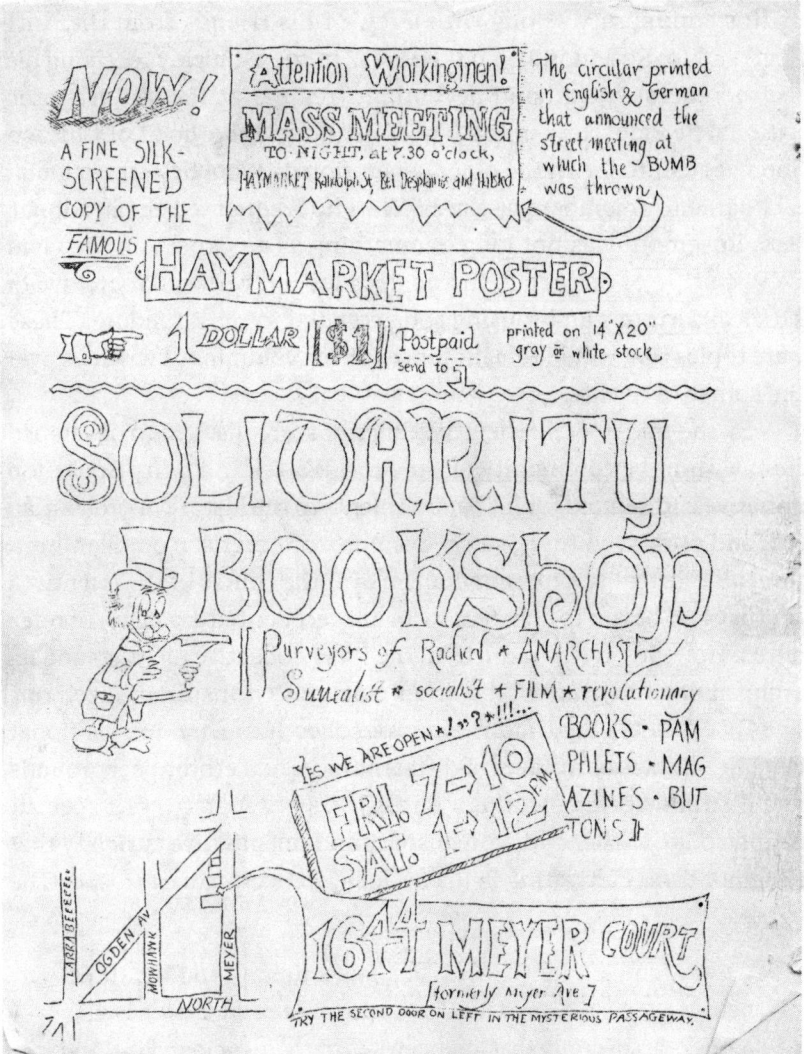

Fig. 3. Back cover of the *Rebel Worker*, no. 7, January 1966. Author's collection. Courtesy of Penelope Rosemont.

workplace sabotage, wage-labor abolitionism, and the right to be lazy, as well as a countercultural take on rock 'n' rollers, comic strips, and poetry by workers on the factory floor (fig. 3).[18]

It was undoubtedly the group's involvement in the IWW as well as their participation in a range of protest causes and collegiate studies in anthropology with African American scholar St. Clair Drake that provided the most concrete commonalities between members of this community. Along with a few of his friends from the Anti-Poetry Club, Rosemont joined the IWW in 1962, quickly receiving his red membership card and becoming a regular at the union's international headquarters in the Lincoln Park neighborhood of Chicago. Soon acquainted with the older generation of Wobblies—the popular nickname for members of the IWW—who frequented the headquarters, Rosemont was not long in emerging as an expert on the vivid IWW culture of direct action and decades-old vernacular archive of satirical cartoons and rousing songs related to rebel folklore. These were topics that would remain central in his voluminous writings over the course of his life.[19]

By the mid-1960s, when the Chicago surrealist group developed from within the community of the *Rebel Worker*/Solidarity Bookshop initiatives, Rosemont's joint commitments to the history of proletarian folk and protest cultures, select examples of American popular literature, and surrealist experimentalism over the course of the twentieth century had begun to cohere into an unprecedented amalgam of references. However, it was more than the IWW collective memory and its archival documentation of worker culture that inspired Rosemont. The IWW's "One Big Union" ethos of collectivism and internationalism, its embrace of workers of different races and ethnic backgrounds, and its unification of workers across lines of separate craft specialization spoke to the kind of inclusivity and imaginative curiosity that Rosemont was cultivating in his outlook. Reflecting in retrospect, he wrote:

> We recognized the IWW as "Joe Hill's union" and the direct heir of 1880s "Chicago Idea" anarchism—a fundamentally anti-authoritarian group that left open lots of room for individual and small-group improvisation; the only group in which we could develop our wide-ranging inclinations: to rethink revolutionary theory, to explore the subversive possibilities of popular culture, and above all to pursue our passion for *poetic action*: that is, for *life as adventure*. We knew that IWW perspectives had a place for all these, and that no other group would even tolerate them.[20]

A conscious synthesis, integration, and transformation of chosen fragments from the existing sphere of culture at large became Rosemont's means of salvaging meaningful aspects of everyday life in the postwar world and fostering a transformative consciousness that might bring about positive social change, whether incrementally or explosively. Art historian Joanna Pawlik has characterized Rosemont's reconstructive approach to history as a performative and "hystericizing" process, by which "the Chicago group aimed to recover the latent Surrealist content in centuries of US culture."[21] Perhaps more than any other factor in Rosemont's life, it was the specific fusion of IWW inclusivity with the surrealist practice of electing predecessors and touchstones from a diffuse horizon of nonsurrealist examples that resulted in what he called, in the quote above, his exploration of the "subversive possibilities of popular culture." Certain facets of mostly American popular culture might be harnessed in service of the surrealist revolution. For example, in a letter to Buhle from the spring of 1968, Rosemont discussed an in-progress essay that compared American literary traditions with American blues music. He described that he was writing "a long study of the U.S. 'underground' poetic tradition, of little known poets and other writers whose significance in the light of surrealism will be seen to be immense: Benjamin Paul Blood, Clark Ashton Smith, Charles Brockden Brown, blues-singers like Robert Johnson, Peetie Wheatstraw, and J.B. Lenoir."[22]

Yet Rosemont's desire to find evidence of inadvertent surrealism in pre–World War II American culture began years earlier. In 1962, Rosemont sent a letter to André Breton in Paris, declaring his intention to publish the surrealist journal *Arsenal* as a collaborative effort between Chicago and the Paris group. In 1963, Rosemont and Larry Decoster visited Leonora Carrington, Alberto Gironella, and Fernando Arrabal in Mexico City, as well as Claude and Gibbsy Tarnaud, Eugenio Granell, Nicolas Calas, and others in Manhattan. It was not until their trip to Paris in 1965–66 that Franklin and Penelope Rosemont became fully ensconced in contemporary surrealist lifestyles and activities. Their repeat exposure to the Eleventh International Surrealist Exhibition, *L'Écart absolu* (Absolute deviation), which opened on December 7, 1965, at La Galerie l'Œil on rue Séguier, and their immediate involvement with the Paris surrealist group facilitated a swift inculcation. Given his avidity for the oeuvre of Breton, Rosemont was already familiar with surrealism's predilection for self-electing precursors and proclaiming disdain for historical figures. This was seen in the surrealist group's infamous list of favored and embargoed writers,

LISEZ :	NE LISEZ PAS :	LISEZ :	NE LISEZ PAS :
Heraclite.	Platon.	Lautréamont.	Kraft-Ebbing.
	Virgile.		Taine.
Lulle.	St Thom. d'Aquin.	Rimbaud.	Verlaine.
Flamel.		Nouveau.	Laforgue.
Agrippa.	Rabelais.	Huysmans.	Daudet.
Scève.	Ronsard	Caze.	
	Montaigne.	Jarry.	Gourmont.
Swift.	Molière.	Becque.	Verne.
Berkeley.		Allais.	Courteline.
	La Fontaine.	Th. Flournoy.	M me de Noailles.
La Mettrie.		Hamsun.	Philippe.
Young.		Freud.	Bergson.
Rousseau.	Voltaire.	Lafargue.	Jaurès.
Diderot.			Durckheim.
Holbach.			Lévy-Brühl.
Kant.	Schiller.	Lénine.	Sorel.
Sade.	Mirabeau.	Synge.	Claudel.
Laclos.		Apollinaire.	Mistral.
Marat.	Bern. de St Pierre.	Roussel.	Péguy.
Babeuf.	Chénier.	Léautaud.	Proust
Fichte.	M me de Staël.	Cravan.	d'Annunzio.
Hegel.		Picabia.	Rostand.
Lewis.		Reverdy.	Jacob.
Arnim.	Hoffmann.	Vaché.	Valéry.
Maturin.		Maïakovsky.	Barbusse.
Rabbe.	Schopenhauer.	Chirico.	Mauriac.
A. Bertrand.	Vigny.	Savinio.	Toulet.
Nerval.	Lamartine.	Neuberg.	Malraux.
Borel.	Balzac.		Kipling.
Feuerbach.	Renan.		Gandhi.
Marx.			Maurras.
Engels.	Comte.		Duhamel.
	Mérimée.		Benda.
	Fromentin.		Valois.
Baudelaire.	Leconte de Lisle.		Vautel.
Cros.	Banville.		Etc., etc., etc...

Fig. 4. Untitled tract ("Lisez/ne lisez pas"), collective surrealist declaration, from a catalog of surrealist publications by Librairie José Corti, 1931.

"Lisez/ne lisez pas" (Read/do not read), which circulated in 1931 (the document echoed Breton's overview of literary proto-surrealists in the 1924 *Manifesto of Surrealism*) (fig. 4).[23] Diderot, Hegel, and Marx were endorsed, while Plato, Voltaire, and Bergson were proscribed. Verne and Balzac, the most popular of the writers listed in the two columns, were relegated to the more densely populated "do not read" column (although at many other times in surrealism's long lifespan, Verne has been a favored author).[24] Although such yes/no lists became a quintessential rhetorical form for the movement, comparable in importance to the mailed questionnaire, popular culture as such was not always on the menu. This was the case even while core members, such as Louis Aragon, were enamored of pulp material. It was also so in spite of the fact that film villains such as Musidora and Fantômas loomed large in the fomenting surrealist imagination long before the movement was officially launched.[25]

In all likelihood, Rosemont's fondness for certain mainstream material, such as the cartoon character Bugs Bunny, was directly impacted by younger members of the Paris surrealist group who were more engaged with a popular culture phantasmagoria than Breton was himself (fig. 5).[26] Notably, while abroad in 1966, the Rosemonts befriended Robert Benayoun, a writer and critic who was devoted to *surrealizing*, if you will, popular culture by locating traces of the marvelous or the ludic hiding amid packaged consumerism and spectacular forms of entertainment, such as comedic cinema.[27] In such books as *Anthologie du nonsense* (1959), *Le dessin animé après Walt Disney* (1961), and *Érotique du surréalisme* (1964), and in his essays for the film journals *L'Âge du cinéma* and *Positif*, Benayoun demonstrated the surrealist method of combing through the reservoir of culture to identify surrealist candidates and appropriate surrealist components for the movement (figs. 6 and 7). In his copious writings, Benayoun celebrated the likes of Tex Avery, Buster Keaton, and the Marx Brothers. His enthusiasm for mischievous cartoon characters like Woody Woodpecker may have been the direct counterpart to Rosemont's adoption of Bugs Bunny as a personal symbol, while Breton's notion of black humor certainly undergirded both Rosemont's and Benayoun's identifications with chaos-loving animated characters.[28]

Other members of the Paris group, such as the artist Toyen, who was a dedicated cinephile, also exerted an influence on the fashioning of the

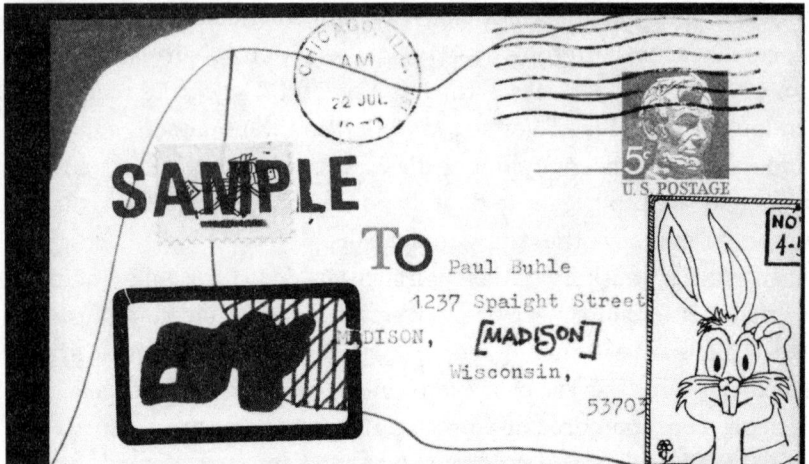

Fig. 5. Franklin Rosemont, decorated envelope for Paul Buhle, 1970. Radical America Records, 1966–75, Wisconsin Historical Society, Madison. Courtesy of Paul Buhle.

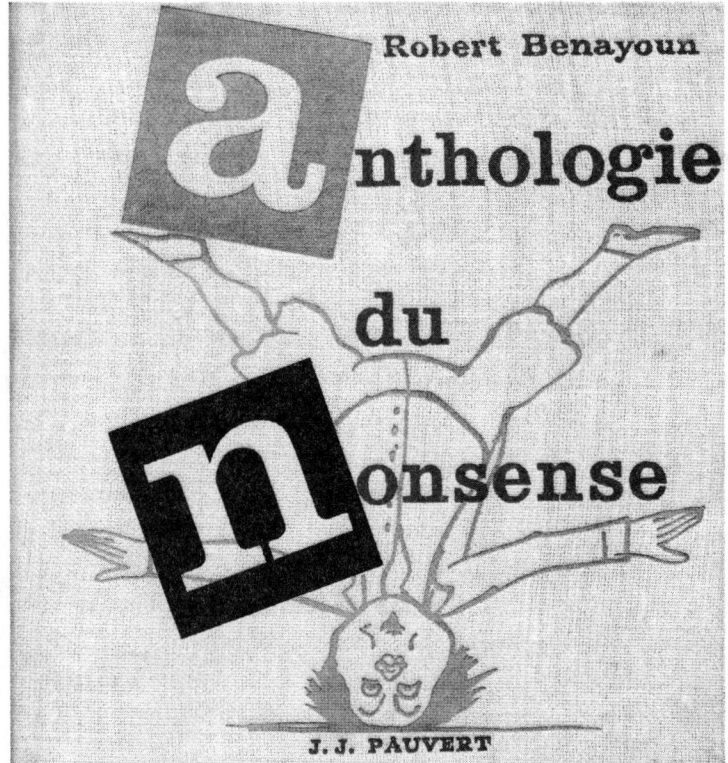

Fig. 6. Robert Benayoun, *Anthologie du nonsense* (Paris: J.J. Pauvert, 1959). Author's collection.

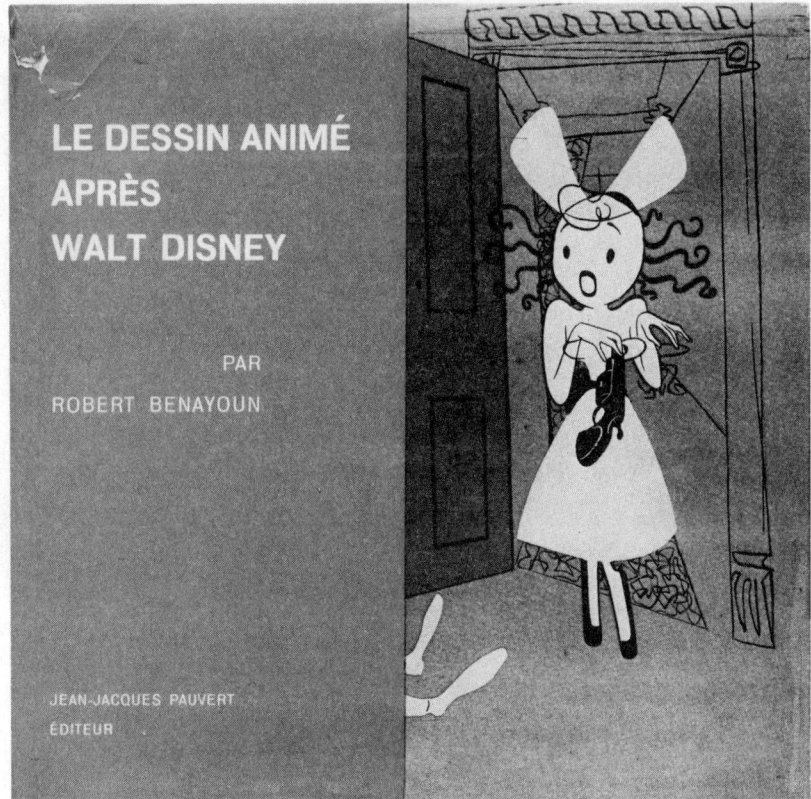

Fig. 7. Robert Benayoun, *Le dessin animé après Walt Disney* (Paris: J.J. Pauvert, 1961). Author's collection.

Rosemonts' surrealist pantheon. Alain Joubert, another Paris surrealist not much older than the Rosemonts, became an acquaintance during the couple's initial trip to Paris.[29] Like Franklin, Joubert was a keen jazz fan and cinema buff with wide-ranging yet exacting tastes. For Joubert, a practice of finding surrealist elements in nonsurrealist phenomena was a paradigm endemic to the movement itself. For instance, in an interview from 2011, Joubert spoke of the "trans-aestheticism" of surrealism, a radically associative state of mind or mode of experience in which self-identified surrealists in turn identify with nonsurrealist material and phenomena.[30] Magpie-like, surrealists are often able to find themselves, Joubert asserted, in the surrounding world of signs through aggressive homologies or inventive processes of imaginative subject-object identification. Like Joubert, Rosemont accomplished a reclamation of kernels of popular culture in part via the surrealist technique of the *dérive*, by which he undertook a drifting, wandering path into the popular sphere. In this vein, Rosemont also cultivated the surrealist state of mind known as *disponibilité*, or openness and availability to what may arrive by chance.

How exactly did Rosemont come to merge his New Left activism with Old Left traditions, all the while hand-selecting aspects of post–World War II American youth culture that might resonate with his adherence to internationalist surrealism? What might seem like a conflicting worldview between old and new amounted to a lifelong combinatory ethos for Rosemont. Arguably, surrealism became the continuous baseline in all these inflections of his thinking; even a glimpse at his copious writings on popular culture reveals that he never stopped seeking accomplices and partners in crime for his surrealist activities and inquiries.

Formed in 1966 after Franklin and Penelope Rosemont returned from Paris and still alive today, the Chicago surrealist group was the earliest and most extensive manifestation of a vast interconnected front of organized activity known as the surrealist movement in the United States, which included centers in New York, Los Angeles, San Francisco, Columbus, Ohio, and elsewhere as well as individual participants dispersed across the country.[31] Marking a central point between the hubs of North American surrealism in urban capitals of the eastern and western United States, the Canadian metropolises of Montreal and Vancouver, and the Caribbean and Mexico City, Chicago has served as a crucial nexus of interchange for the migration, development, and persistence of transnational surrealism in the Western Hemisphere over the last half century.

Even so, Chicago's location as a strategic meeting place and conduit for continental surrealism in North America was always more than a question of geography. Despite its internationalist positioning and extensive interaction with surrealist groups in Amsterdam, Lisbon, Paris, Prague, Stockholm, Tokyo, and elsewhere, Chicago surrealism must be understood from the perspective of its quintessentially vernacular localism. As its members attest, theirs is a "Chicago Idea" surrealism inseparable from the worldwide reputation Chicago gained for its proletarian leftism in the wake of the 1886 Haymarket Affair.[32] Long before Chicago surrealism appeared, this capital of the Midwest became the premier site for leftist organizing in the United States, with the Industrial Workers of the World union headquarters established in 1905, the founding of the Communist Party of America following in 1919, and the national office of the Students for a Democratic Society relocating there from New York City in 1965. The history of Chicago surrealism is inextricably tied with the city's leftist past, since preexisting organizations like the IWW and SDS were instrumental in its development and perseverance.[33]

The Chicago surrealist group's foundation depended on the travel of members in the early to mid-1960s to San Francisco, Mexico City, New York, London, Paris, and beyond, where key interactions occurred with surrealists and radicals, and publications were exchanged, collaborated on, and distributed. Chicago surrealism was also catalyzed as the result of its members' exposure to various communities and informational circuits operating under the auspices of existing political organizations such as the IWW, public institutions such as Roosevelt University, and independent bookstores like City Lights Books in San Francisco, Gotham Book Mart in Manhattan, and Solidarity Bookshop and Barbara's Bookstore in Chicago. The group eventually pioneered its own series of sites, display spaces for artworks and publications, and participatory experiences for anyone interested in the convergence of poetic and political revolution in the form of collectivist dissidence. Central Chicago locations included the Gallery Bugs Bunny in Lincoln Park and Gallery Black Swan in River North. Rosemont's love of the blues was further catalyzed when Paul Garon, a self-taught student of psychoanalysis and one of the foremost blues experts in the United States, became a friend and member of the group, initiating soon thereafter the Surrealist Research and Development Monograph Series (figs. 8 and 9).[34]

Surrealist publications from Paris and Prague, such as *La Brèche: Action surréaliste*, *L'Archibras*, *Bulletin de liaison surréaliste*, and "The Platform of Prague" (1968), saluted the activities of the Chicago group. Likewise, the many publications issued by Chicago surrealism's Black Swan Press/Surrealist Editions starting in 1965, such as its journal *Arsenal/Surrealist Subversion* (nos. 1–4, 1970–89), were acknowledged for their role in a broad network of international countercultural publications, historically marked by the formation of the Underground Press Syndicate in 1966 and including connections to well-known periodicals

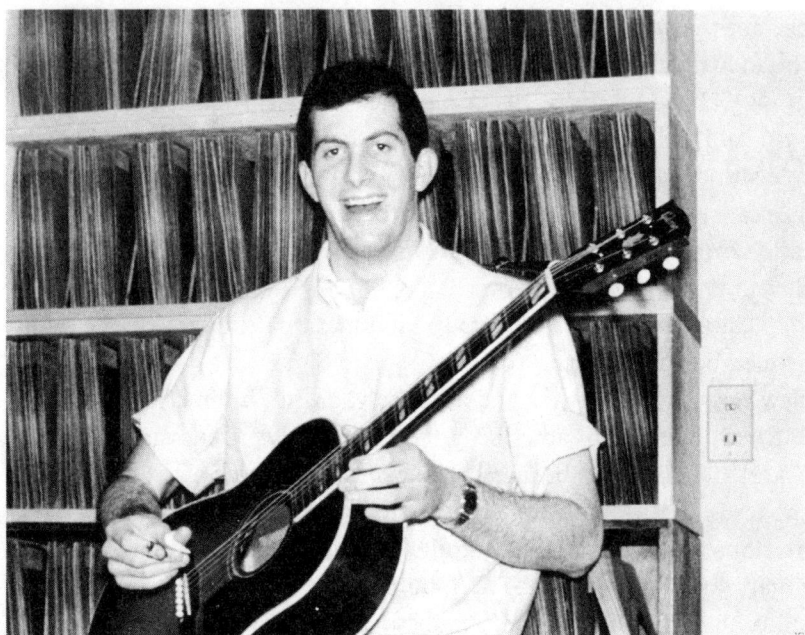

Fig. 8. Paul Garon, c. early to mid-1960s. Photo by Ken Garon. Reproduced with permission of Beth Garon from the personal archives of Paul and Beth Garon.

such as *Fifth Estate, Internationale Situationniste,* and Paul Buhle's afore-mentioned project for the SDS, *Radical America* (with one issue and sections in two other issues edited by Franklin Rosemont).[35]

The Chicago surrealist group's simultaneous commitment to these three orientations—localism in their home city, intensive interaction with developing surrealist networks across the United States, and cease-less participation in the growth of surrealist internationalism—form the foundation for a more intimate understanding of Rosemont's views on popular culture. Even when Rosemont wrote about nonsurrealist vernac-ular material, he nearly always included some reference to surrealism or perhaps a series of citations that ultimately demonstrated the surrealist basis of his thought. Readers might be surprised to find, for instance, in an erudite essay by Rosemont about some aspect of Chicagoana, Americana, or radical history, citations for asides by Paris surrealist André Breton about nineteenth-century French poetry. Readers might also notice a book or article by Robert Benayoun embedded in a works-cited list of labor history references or a photo of a Gerome Kamrowski sculpture illustrating an article on a nineteenth-century utopian novel.

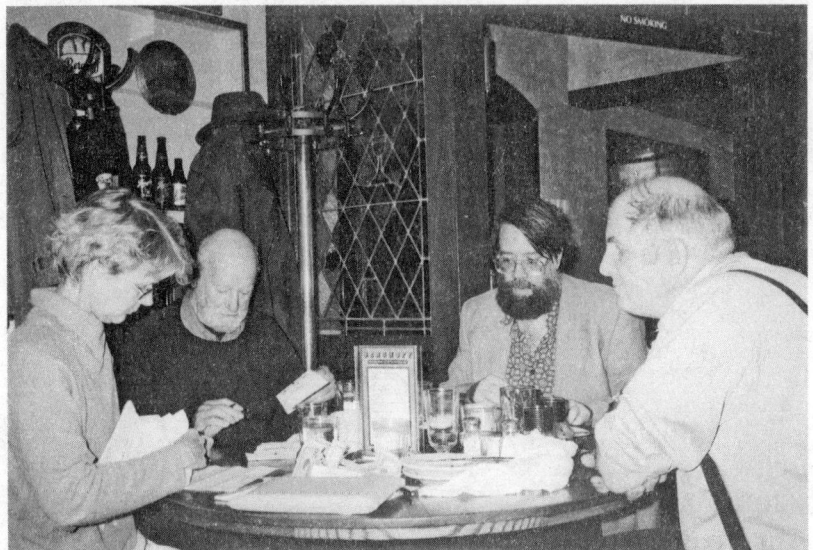

Fig. 9. Beth Garon, Lawrence Ferlinghetti, Franklin Rosemont, and Paul Garon at the Berghoff, Chicago, c. 1992. Courtesy of Penelope Rosemont.

Rosemont's purview was at once focused on his immediate surroundings and the zeitgeist in Chicago during the postwar era and on a prewar realm of surrealist collectivism in search of the means of social and political revolution. As Franklin and Penelope Rosemont exclaimed in a postcard to Paul Buhle sent from Paris in 1970, "Long live Krazy Kat! Long live the Surrealist Revolution!"[36]

Take, for example, Rosemont's important essay on Edward Bellamy, author of the utopian science fiction novel *Looking Backward: 2000–1887*, which was published in the special double issue of *Cultural Correspondence* that he guest-edited in 1979. Titled "Free Play and No Limit: An Introduction to Edward Bellamy's Utopia," Rosemont's essay is primarily concerned with the political and social ricochet effect that Bellamy's novel had on the American populace, especially among progressive reformers of the contemporaneous late nineteenth-century era (fig. 10). Of course, Rosemont was interested in analyzing Bellamy's general intellectual objectives and to some degree the contents of the novel itself. However, he was primarily invested in what might be called the reception history of Bellamy's time-travel text or the character of the intellectual shock waves that the book sent through Bellamy's milieu and beyond, resulting in the formation of more than 150 Bellamy clubs in the United States.[37] This macrocosmic lens on the

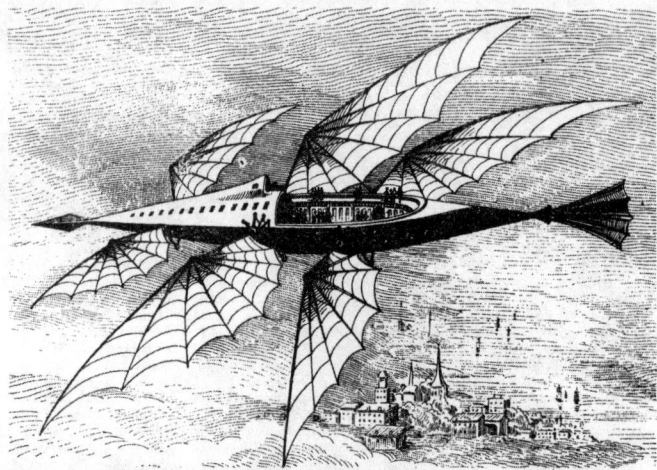

Artist's Conception of Future Aircraft, as Suggested by Thomas A. Edison (1880)

FREE PLAY & NO LIMIT

AN INTRODUCTION TO EDWARD BELLAMY'S UTOPIA

Looking Backward opens in 1887. A wealthy young Bostonian retires to his bedroom in a secret basement vault which he has had specially constructed to shut out street noise. A chronic insomniac, he is put to sleep by a hypnotist. He wakes up in the morning — 113 years later.

Like Rip Van Winkle, Julian West finds the world in which he wakens very different from the world in which he fell asleep. The intervening years have witnessed nothing less than a "complete transformation in the human condition," (1) the result of a thorough-going social revolution that has realized, for the first time, full human equality. In abolishing private ownership of the means of production, society also has done away with social classes, exploitation, poverty, hunger, war, sex slavery, race discrimination, slums, crime, jails, money, rent, banks, charity, corruption, taxes, advertising, housework, politicians, merchants, servants, lawyers, the army, the navy and the State Department.

Government itself scarcely exists, its functions having been reduced to the coordination of industrial production and distribution. There is very little disease, insanity or suicide, and virtually no legislation ("we might be said to live almost in a state of anarchy"). Churches have all

but disappeared. There are no locks or locksmiths, and no safes ("because we have no more thieves"). Coercion is a thing of the past, everything having become "entirely voluntary, the logical outcome of the operation of human nature under rational conditions." Working hours are short. Work itself has been greatly simplified and, as far as possible, rendered attractive. Vacations are ample; emigration is unrestricted. In the new society of the year 2000, "liberty is the first and last word."

All this has in turn fundamentally transformed the human personality. "The conditions of life have changed, and with them the motives of human action." In Bellamy's utopia there is no more selfishness, greed, malice, hypocrisy, apathy; no more "struggle for existence"; no more hunger for power; no more anxiety or fear as to basic human needs. "The highest possible physical, as well as mental, development for everyone" is the aim of the new education. Everyone is happier, healthier, brighter, friendlier; more active, more adventurous, more creative.

"Perhaps the most notable single aspect of the Revolution" was "the elevation and enlargement of woman's sphere in all directions.... Since the

Revolution there has been no difference in the education of the sexes nor in the independence of their economic and social position, in the exercise of responsibility or experience in the practical conduct of affairs. . . . In every pursuit of life [women] join with men on equal terms."

Moreover, "the sentiment of brotherhood, the feeling of solidarity, asserted itself not merely toward men and women, but likewise toward the humbler companions of our life on earth and sharers of its fortunes, the animals. . . . The new conception of our relation to the animals appealed to the heart and captivated the imagination of mankind."

The 113 years also have seen, thanks to the Revolution, an unprecedented flourishing of science, technology and the arts. Bellamy differs from many utopians in his confidence that modern technology can be conquered and put at the service of human desire. His forecast — in *Looking Backward* and its sequel, *Equality* — of such things as automobiles, radio, television, helicopters, air-conditioning and waterbeds, has assured him a permanent place in the history of science fiction. Interspersed through a charming love story and an unremitting attack on capital-

6

Fig. 10. Franklin Rosemont, "Free Play and No Limit: An Introduction to Edward Bellamy's Utopia," in "Surrealism and Its Popular Accomplices," special issue, guest-edited by Franklin Rosemont, *Cultural Correspondence*, nos. 10–11, Fall 1979. Author's collection. Courtesy of Paul Buhle.

public reception of the book is what allowed Rosemont, no less than five times over the course of his essay, to convincingly step even further outside the bounds of his subject matter by attempting to see Bellamy "above all in the light of surrealism."[38] Rosemont's methodology is therefore inherently comparative as well as reception-based. Citing Breton's theory of "souvenirs of the future," in which the present can be ruptured by consciousness of future possibilities, Rosemont argued that it is an "antagonism to memory" that "brings Bellamy to the very threshold of surrealism."[39] Rosemont surmised that Bellamy dabbled in automatic writing, all the while nurturing a countermodernist view of temporality characterized by an experience of the present moment that is crowded with the jagged fragments of "centuries of limping and broken history."[40]

It is not just in the pages of *Cultural Correspondence* that Rosemont applied this surrealist comparative method to the vagaries of mass reception and the ever-shifting winds of a truly populist popular culture. For instance, Rosemont executed some of the same critical moves seen in the Bellamy piece but on a more subtle scale in an important essay about the visual culture of anarchism in late nineteenth- and early twentieth-century American mass media for his coedited volume with David Roediger, *Haymarket Scrapbook*, first published by the Charles H. Kerr Publishing Company in 1986.[41] True, Breton's name arises only briefly in the body of the essay in tandem with Hegel and Buster Keaton in Rosemont's discussion of rebellious qualities of "genuine humor."[42] For Rosemont, it is the liberatory potential of humor that, in the end, actually transforms slanderous stereotypes and characterizations of generalized and known anarchists into productive tropes that can be reclaimed by the Left. But a glimpse at the essay's footnotes reveals citations to Rosemont's 1978 edited volume of André Breton's writings, *What Is Surrealism?*; the 1979 *Cultural Correspondence* special issue "Surrealism and Its Popular Accomplices" (guest-edited by Rosemont); and references to books by French surrealists Ado Kyrou and Robert Benayoun on surrealism's relationship with the cinema and animation. Rosemont only arrived at his conclusion about anarchism's potential for transformation in popular humor through his foothold in surrealism.

Surrealism's embrace of certain streams of popular culture must be sharply distinguished from mass culture's own adoption of surrealism, something that scholars Joanna Pawlik and Sandra Zalman have been careful to indicate in their research.[43] As Pawlik has written, "For Surrealism's American sponsors during the 1930s, emphasizing and exploiting the movement's apparent proximity to slapstick comedy, animation and circus freak-shows was a way of downplaying its Marxist politics, and making it palatable to American audiences."[44] For her, the adoption of popular culture elements by the Rosemonts, Paul Garon, and others in the Chicago group was in fact a pointed manner of correcting the widespread American misunderstandings and *"mistranslations"* of surrealism in the commercial realm.[45] The Chicago surrealist critique of pop art as fetishistic of capitalism also plays a role in this polemic. Rosemont named pop art one of the "commercially contrived and short-lived pseudo avant-gardes concocted by speculators as 'successors' to surrealism," along with abstract expressionism, op art, conceptual art, and minimalism.[46] Pop, as well as these other art trends, "subscribed to a reactionary 'High Culture' elitism" as opposed to surrealism's durational homage to popular culture against the grain of dominant culture itself.[47]

In contrast, in a jointly written essay from 1996 titled "Surrealism: The Chicago Idea," Paul Garon and the Rosemonts defined their approach to the "popular arts"—"an especially vital terrain of contradiction and struggle"—as a "testing-ground" for "new myths galore, including demystifying myths—or *counter-myths*—of poetry and revolt."[48] Referring to the title of Franklin's 1979 guest-edited issue of *Cultural Correspondence*, "Surrealism and Its Popular Accomplices," they returned to the notion of popular culture as an accomplice or comrade in arms in a protest against the dominance of ideology. Based on the common ground of affinity and association, surrealists become allies or affiliates of popular culture in order to reconstitute hegemonic myths by turning myths against themselves. This secondary mythification, which robs myth of its already-stolen powers of language, is what Roland Barthes, in his 1957 book *Mythologies*, called "artificial myth" or the "counter-mythical."[49] Barthes's text is discussing the subject of realism in literature, but his query "Why not rob myth?" (since, as he says, myth is already a manipulation of language) resonates effectively with the Chicago surrealist position on popular culture.[50] For Franklin Rosemont, the operations of the counter-mythical are close to that of industrial sabotage. The means of production become weapons for slowing or ceasing production; the counter-mythical gums up the works of elitist affirmative culture. Popular culture will be subversive or will not be at all.

References

Barthes, Roland. *Mythologies*. Translated by Annette Lavers. New York: Hill and Wang, 1972.

Boustani, Claire, "Entretien avec Alain Joubert." In *Art et mythe*, edited by Fabrice Flahutez and Thierry Dufrên, 149–59. Nanterre, France: Presses universitaires de Paris Nanterre, 2011.

Buhle, Paul. "Introduction: The 1960s Meet the 1980s." In *Popular Culture in America*, ix–xxvii. Minneapolis: University of Minnesota Press, 1987.

Buhle, Paul, and David Wagner. Untitled editorial statement. *Cultural Correspondence*, no. 1 (August 1975): 1.

Cooper, (Nyala) Joan Smith. "Rebel Worker About Change: Person to Nation." *Rise of the Phoenix: Voices from Chicago's Black Struggle, 1960-1975*, edited by Useni Eugene Perkins, 162–73. Chicago: Third World Press Foundation, 2017.

Garon, Paul. *Blues and the Poetic Spirit*. New York: Da Capo Press, 1979.

Khatib, Kate. "Surrealism's America: Notes on a Vernacular Epistemology." PhD diss., Johns Hopkins University, 2013.

Marcuse, Herbert. "The Affirmative Character of Culture." In *Negations: Essays in Critical Theory*, 65–98. London: MayFly Books, 2009.

Pawlik, Joanna. "Cartooning the Marvelous: Word and Image in Chicago Surrealism." In *Mixed Messages: American Correspondences in Visual and Verbal Practices*, edited by Catherine Gander and Sarah Garland, 67–84. Manchester, UK: Manchester University Press, 2016.

———. "The Comic Book Conditions of Chicago Surrealism." In *Surrealism, Science Fiction and Comics*, edited by Gavin Parkinson, 129–54. Liverpool, UK: Liverpool University Press, 2015.

———. *Remade in America: Surrealist Art, Activism, and Politics, 1940-1978*. Berkeley: University of California Press, 2021.

———. "USA." In *The International Encyclopedia of Surrealism*, edited by Michael Richardson et al., 139–48. London: Bloomsbury Press, 2019.

Pierre, José, ed. *Tracts surréalistes et déclarations collectives: 1922-1939*. Paris: Le Terrain Vague, 1980.

Radcliffe, Charles. *Don't Start Me Talking: Subculture, Situationism and the Sixties*. N.p.: Bread & Circuses, 2018.

Rosemont, Franklin. "Free Play and No Limit: An Introduction to Edward Bellamy's Utopia." In "Surrealism and Its Popular Accomplices," edited by Franklin Rosemont, special issue, *Cultural Correspondence*, nos. 10–11 (Fall 1979): 6–16.

———. "Humor: Here Today and Everywhere Tomorrow." *Arsenal/Surrealist Subversion*, no. 4 (1989): 81–84.

———. *Joe Hill: The IWW and the Making of a Revolutionary Workingclass Counterculture*. Chicago: Charles H. Kerr, 2003.

———. "Rats Live on No Evil Star: A Selection of Palindromes." *Free Spirits: Annals of the Insurgent Imagination*, no. 1 (1982): 153–54.

———. "The Seismograph of Subversion: Notes on Some American Precursors." In "Surrealism in the Service of the Revolution," special issue, *Radical America 4*, no. 1 (January 1970): 50–63.

Rosemont, Franklin, and Charles Radcliffe, eds. *Dancin' in the Streets! Anarchists, IWWs, Surrealists, Situationists and Provos in the 1960s as Recorded in the Pages of "The Rebel Worker" and "Heatwave."* Chicago: Charles H. Kerr, 2005.

Rosemont, Franklin, and David R. Roediger. *Haymarket Scrapbook: 125th Anniversary Edition.* Oakland: AK Press; Chicago: Charles H. Kerr, 2012.

Rosemont, Franklin, Penelope Rosemont, and Paul Garon, eds. *The Forecast Is Hot! Tracts and Other Collective Declarations of the Surrealist Movement in the United States, 1966–1976.* Chicago: Black Swan Press, 1997.

Rosemont, Penelope. *Surrealism: Inside the Magnetic Fields.* San Francisco: City Lights, 2019.

Sakolsky, Ron. *Dreams of Anarchy and the Anarchy of Dreams: Adventures at the Intersection of Anarchy and Surrealism.* New York: Autonomedia, 2021.

———, ed. *Surrealist Subversions: Rants, Writings and Images by the Surrealist Movement in the United States.* New York: Autonomedia, 2003.

Susik, Abigail. "Chicago Surrealism, Herbert Marcuse, and the Affirmation of the 'Present and Future Viability of Surrealism.'" *Journal of Surrealism and the Americas* 11, no. 1 (2020): 42–62.

———. "Subcultural Receptions of Surrealism in the 1960s International Underground Press: *Resurgence* and Other Publications." In *Cambridge Critical Concepts: Surrealism,* edited by Natalya Lusty, 380–400. Cambridge: Cambridge University Press, 2021.

———. "Surrealism and Jules Verne: Navigating Context, Intertext and Subtext for a Collage by Max Ernst." In *Surrealism, Science Fiction and Comics,* edited by Gavin Parkinson, 16–39. Liverpool, UK: Liverpool University Press, 2015.

———. *Surrealist Sabotage and the War on Work.* Manchester, UK: Manchester University Press, 2021.

Susik, Abigail, and Elliott H. King. "Surrealism as Radicalism." In *Radical Dreams: Surrealism, Counterculture, Resistance,* edited by Elliott H. King and Abigail Susik, 2–19. State College, PA: Penn State University Press, 2022.

Walz, Robin. *Pulp Surrealism: Insolent Popular Culture in Early Twentieth-Century Paris.* Berkeley: University of California Press, 2000.

Zalman, Sandra R. "The Vernacular as Vanguard: Alfred Barr, Salvador Dalí, and the U.S. Reception of Surrealism in the 1930s." *Journal of Surrealism and the Americas,* no. 1 (2007): 44–67.

PART I

Americana and Chicagoana

The Seismograph of Subversion: Notes on Some American Precursors

Selection from "The Seismograph of Subversion: Notes on Some American Precursors," in "Surrealism in the Service of the Revolution," special issue, *Radical America* 4, no. 1 (January 1970): 50–63.

The following notes—unsystematic, incomplete, and tending to move forward roughly and unpremeditatedly through a series of mountainous and cavernous digressions rather than comfortably across the smooth terrain of a well-defined subject matter—are intended only to provide at least some opening in a road that has been closed for so long, and is so overgrown with the weeds of verifiable despair, that its very existence has been almost effaced not only from view but also from memory. Along this road, which alone among the avenues of American consciousness really interests me, to the point of fascination, and which at present can be traveled only at night, it has fallen to me to witness occasional flashes from the darkness, which provided sufficient illumination to venture a few steps further. The theoretical and practical ramifications and implications of such illumination are problems I willingly leave to the future: like a strip of magnesium held in flame it is the brilliance of the flash itself here that focuses our attention to the exclusion of all other considerations.

It hardly needs to be said that we shall find few indications of the surrealist spirit in the repressive context of colonial puritan righteousness and wrath. If the early colonists built the cradle of what became America, no less did they dig the grave of poetry. Surrealism is, of course, absolutely incompatible with all forms of religion, and Christianity has naturally received the greatest share of its antireligious violence. "Nothing will ever reconcile me with Christian civilization," said André Breton, to whom we also owe the watchword: "God is a swine." With Puritanism one sees the viciousness, inhumanity, rigidity, and swinishness implicit in all religion developed to an extreme frenzy, which was doubly dangerous because it also controlled the machinery of state power. Everyone was to succumb to an individual and social authoritarianism in the cloak of theology, which effected an almost total censorship of mind and body. Everything that surrealism celebrates—mad love, dreams, freedom, humor, desire, the marvelous, the unfettered imagination—was relegated to the province of Satan. But we know today, to the everlasting credit of Freud, that such human tendencies cannot be entirely suppressed; they inevitably return, unexpectedly and unconsciously, for they are integral to the very life of man in all cultures and in all periods.

Thus, in the colonial period, oppressed with Puritanism, glutted with superstition, one perceives signs of the struggle of the imagination to liberate itself. We cannot afford the luxury of dismissing these manifestations because of their religious mantle: it is necessary to see the truly human poetry, fragmented as it is, that lies beneath it struggling for its emancipation. Perhaps no one has described this process better than Moses Coit Tyler, who wrote thus, in his *History of American Literature, 1607-1765*, of the plight of the Puritan and poetry: "Though denied expression in one way, the poetry that was in him forced itself into utterance in another. If his theology drove poetry out of many forms in which it had been used to reside, poetry itself practiced a noble revenge by taking up its abode in his theology."

Throughout this period many of the most popular works were those that enumerated, with painstaking detail and with imagery suitably somber and stark, the endless terrors of Hell, Cotton Mather's *Wonders of the Invisible World*, Jonathan Edwards's sermon *Sinners in the Hands of an Angry God*, and Michael Wigglesworth's poem *The Day of Doom*—the best sellers of colonial America—are all black, diabolical visions in which the light of the marvelous erupts through the starry eloquence of the satanic, the sinful, the eternally damned. One is reminded of Blake's note in *The Marriage of Heaven and Hell*: "The reason Milton wrote in fetters when he wrote of Angels and God, and at liberty when of Devils & Hell, is because he was a true Poet and of the Devil's party without knowing it." A serious argument could be made, I am convinced, for the poetic superiority of Michael Wigglesworth

over (let us say) T.S. Eliot, whose servile, prostrate sentimentality, and his sensibility of a London banker, seem to me thoroughly
anti-poetic, whereas Wigglesworth possesses at least a certain ruthless,
raw magnificence. "His pages," Tyler notes, "are strewn with many
unwrought ingots of poetry." One senses a desperateness in these
simple narrations of devilish rage and writhing agonies of flesh and
flame, a desperate quest for poetry, for true life, beyond the inhuman
borders imposed by their monstrous theology whose praises they sang
with such sinister, volcanic, almost ironic elegance.

It is certain that this period, the least known of American literature, still obscured by contemporary academicians, needs careful
reinterpretation. Perhaps our sensitivity to its real significance could
benefit from a highly experimental attitude. Surely one should be able
to go beyond the cretinous limitations of "historical fiction" to feel
the real content of a vanished period. For my part, some time ago,
poring over some extracts from Wigglesworth's *Day of Doom*, I found
myself suppressing, with a pen, its religious elements, as well as its
starved metrical form, and at the same time making certain automatic
additions and corrections, thus liberating and extending its remarkable poetic potentiality. These "Wigglesworth Corrections," part of a
series of surrealist experiments, will hopefully be made public in the
near future.

With one splendid exception, there was no poetry in America in
the latter half of the eighteenth century other than the act of colonial revolution: the exception consists of four novels written in great
haste in less than a year (between the summer of 1798 and that of
1799) by Charles Brockden Brown, in whom we recognize the first true
American precursor of surrealism. Very popular and highly regarded in
his own time and throughout the first half of the nineteenth century
(his admirers included Shelley, Poe, Hawthorne), Brown suffered a
subsequent decline of interest in his work that is largely attributable to the rise to power of literary realism and other consolidations
of American bourgeois consciousness. Brown wrote in a specifically
American variation of the Gothic genre, a category of literature since
fallen into complete disrepute; indeed, it is often held up to ridicule
as a veritable model of bad literature. But it is worth emphasizing that
surrealists, who generally scorn the novel as an inherently confined
and mediocre literary form, have always shared a passionate regard

for the masterpieces of Gothic romance: Walpole's *Castle of Otranto*, Ann Radcliffe's *Mysteries of Udolpho* and others, Lewis's *Monk*, and Maturin's *Melmoth the Wanderer*. In the first *Manifesto*, Breton excepts from his severe condemnation of novels in general only these Gothic works whose characteristic devices of terror and apparitions situate them unreservedly in the service of desire.

Although Brown wrote mostly about the formally excluded areas of reality —the marvelous—he was nonetheless, like his contemporaries Blake and Sade, an adherent of the fundamental principles of the Age of Reason and, also like them, disdained religious mystifications. Also comparable to the attitude of Blake and Sade is Brown's early intimation of the Age of Reason's immense boastfulness and its consequent failures. For despite his avowed acceptance of the tenets of the Enlightenment, his work constitutes one of the earliest recognitions of their essential deficiencies. The rational solutions concluding his works really solve nothing, for the reader is finally confronted with problems of even greater magnitude than supernatural mysteries. "The voices that drove the fanatic to madness and murder in *Wieland*," writes Harry Levin in his lucid study *The Power of Blackness*, are produced by a ventriloquist whose avowed intent has been to test his victim's credulity. This raises questions more terrifying in their purport than the superstitions they undermine, for Wieland's voices are easily discredited; but Carwin, the malevolent rationalist, is prompted by that "mischievous demon" who will subsequently instigate Dostoyevsky's *Possessed*.

Brown almost systematically breaks one's confidence in the permanence of immediate reality. His severe attack on religious superstition does not in any way support the pillars of comfortable deist optimism. He too perceived obscure voices calling from the darkest corners: his work comprises a remarkable premonition, an admirable, if unsteady, step toward the definitive conquest of the irrational.

The case of Edgar Allan Poe, put through every conceivable sieve of criticism and analysis, yet holds fast to a certain disdainful obscurity, stubbornly refusing to be laid to rest by too hasty evaluations. Hardly a real influence in the last few years, Poe has suffered the brutal castigation and, alternately, complete neglect not only of conservative and liberal academics but also of what has passed itself off as an American avant-garde. Let us note that his reputation even within surrealism has not been constant: cited in the 1924 *Manifesto* as "surrealist in adventure," by the *Second Manifesto* of 1929 he is attacked as the initiator of police fiction ("Let us spit, in passing, on Edgar Poe"); but he is included in Breton's *Anthologie de l'Humeur Noir* (1939), and, in an interview in *New Directions 1940* on "the meaning of surrealism," Nicolas Calas mentions Poe and Melville as American presurrealists. (It should be mentioned too that Antonin Artaud consistently included Poe among the "accursed" poets—along with Villon, Baudelaire, Gerard de Nerval: "men tortured by language, hemorrhaging as they write.") What we find of special interest in the works of Poe are some of his least-cited tales: "The Angel of the Odd," "The Imp of the Perverse," and "A Predicament" ("At twenty-five minutes past five in the afternoon, precisely, the huge minute-hand had proceeded sufficiently far on its terrible revolution to sever the small remainder of my neck")—tales in which the imaginatively liberating element and "the ego's victorious assertion of its own invulnerability" (Freud) attain vertiginous excess.

Poe's reactionary political pretensions, his fanatical racism, and his hopelessly pompous stance as "literary gentleman" are doubtless sufficient to confine him to a relatively minor position. But it is necessary to challenge and overthrow the particular prejudices against him (based on ideological oversimplifications such as "decadence," "neurasthenia," and even "bad taste") enforced by his academic detractors. Poe's greatest influence in this century, it would seem, has been primarily "underground": it is especially discernible in the work of Lovecraft and Clark Ashton Smith. Perhaps it is given to the sympathetic interpreters of these latter authors to provoke a new recognition of the true significance of this curiously isolated figure, whom Apollinaire touchingly hailed as "the drunkard of Baltimore."

With the single exception of Herman Melville—who remains extremely problematical—the only Americans whose work is wholly or largely admirable in our eyes are either academically discredited or completely unknown. As for Melville, it is necessary to insist, before going on, that the work of this author of indisputable genius possesses disturbingly long and complicatedly interwoven threads of ambiguity that no one has been able to unravel with more than slight success, an attribute he shares with Rimbaud, which explains the origins of the abusive posthumous "alliances" that both have suffered. For us

Melville will always be the one who shouted "No!" in thunder, and it is a source of regret that there were no surrealists in the United States to mobilize their rage on his behalf against the abject critical assimilation campaign of the 1920s and '30s, as the surrealists in France did for Rimbaud with their pamphlet *Permettez!* and the demonstration against the unveiling of the statue of Rimbaud at Charleville.

One can say without exaggeration that the ink of scholarship poured over Melville's works has done more to conceal them, to bury them, than the fog of neglect that shrouded his works in earlier generations. Melville holds steadfast, however, to a position of unassailable defiance—a darkly brooding figure, driven, obsessed, flamingly lucid and commanding inspiration. His ruthlessly total grasp of reality situated itself in a mythology that is haunted and haunting but strangely, distressingly compressed; his intuitive dialectical materialism flew, like an albatross, on wings of the wildest lyricism. I would say without hesitation that *Moby Dick* seems to me closer to Hegel's *Phenomenology* than to any novel. Moreover, no criticism of this work, no explication, annotation, or interpretation has seemed to me one-twentieth as significant as a news story I came across some months ago in a magazine from the 1950s, which told of a remarkable incident that occurred, far at sea, during the production of a film version of *Moby Dick*: the specially constructed model of the white whale somehow broke away from its moorings and led the entire ship—directors, cast, and crew—on a long and terrible chase. How vitally, passionately dangerous Melville remains, how clear his voice rings in our ears, like the sea in a conch shell, years after certain morons have celebrated, with cocktails and sermons, his centennial!

So much has been written about Emily Dickinson, one would almost consider her case closed. The salaried official historians of literature and their goon-squad henchmen, the compilers of textbooks, have been largely successful in their efforts to mold her into a prototype of the sort of "Poet"—lifeless, cold, wooden, saccharine, sentimental, cloistered—rightly despised by schoolchildren. Surrealism intends to rescue her from this stupid lie. It is true that a vague religious strain too often intrudes to mar her sense of wonder, and one could reproach her with surrendering to her isolation and retreating into silence rather than advancing toward a more conscious attitude of revolt. But I think we should have done with such retrospective advice, so easy, so idiotic. What matters is that this woman has left us inexhaustible resources of poetic reverie: "Dust is the only secret," "The Spider Holds a Silver Ball," "We Shall find the Cube of the Rainbow."

The "hatred of the marvelous" decried by Breton in the *Surrealist Manifesto* has been refined in this "land of the dollar" (as the United States has been known for years to the working-class movements of other countries) with technological exactitude. The capitalist road of reification has become a four-lane highway, and the "traffic death toll" a suitable symbol of the state of American civilization that decades ago Freud recognized as a "colossal miscarriage." I think it is impossible, in 1969, to exaggerate the precariousness of the human condition. It is clear today that there is something empty, rotten, and wrong about any "politics" that has nothing to say about the near-extinction of polar bears. It is thus exceedingly important—urgent—for us to give increasing attention to all the truly oppositional voices in our past, to those voices of truthful fervor that raised, under many and divergent circumstances, the most terrible questions. And this is necessary not only for the sake of intellectual survival but also to better comprehend what is to be done in the future. In the fragile hands of Emily Dickinson the sidereal grandeur of the dandelion and the shadow of the Carolina parakeet left the signature of their insolent trajectories. We whose specific task it is to put the English language in a state of miraculous effervescence, to liberate language from commodity fetishism and place it in the service of desire and thus to restore it to a high place in the struggle for the revolutionary transformation of the world, do not hesitate in avowing the pleasure we derive from certain magnificent lines by this admirable mistress of the image, who woke "at Midnight … dreaming of the Dawn."

∽

> *Revolt! and still revolt! revolt!*
> ...
> *Revolt! and the bullet for tyrants!*
> —Walt Whitman (1856)

Ambrose Bierce, according to the writer of the introduction to his very incomplete *Collected Writings*, "is not, of course, a great writer"; following which quaint wisdom the same little literary justice of the peace, who calls himself Clifton Fadiman, goes on to bemoan Bierce's "painful faults of vulgarity and cheapness of imagination," lines that reveal, with incredible clarity, the most repulsive and police-like aspects of literary criticism, calculated—in this case—to convict and imprison the works of Ambrose Bierce (and many others!) behind the four walls of positivist formalism. Fortunately, Bierce's own subversive genius naturally reinforces the surrealist arsenal with highly effective weapons that already permit us to forecast the almost inevitable destruction of the cultural bastille in the wake of an authentic poetic jailbreak. Bierce's sublime pessimism, pushed to the point of paroxysm, placed on American civilization's moral grave monstrous and poisonous wreaths of desecration so boundless that he resists all the conventions of literary classification. Those critics who content themselves with writing him off as a "minor precursor" of realistic fiction should contemplate this definition from his *Devil's Dictionary*: "REALISM, n. The art of depicting nature as it is seen by toads." In relentless opposition to all intellectual fashions of his day, Ambrose Bierce casually swung the unsparing razor of his humor into the stifling hypocrisy of America's philosophical midafternoon of one-dimensional humanism. Today more than ever his is the best introduction to the night in which our footsteps continue to move forward. And in this night, during which the American dream continues to revolve on its axle of anxiety and boredom, we turn again and again to our surest guide, the one who hurled the silverplated platter of progress into the Amazon River of his laughter: Ambrose Bierce, this bitterest beacon of black light.

Samuel Greenberg was a Jewish immigrant from Austria who died in New York in 1917 of tuberculosis at the age of twenty-three. To him we owe some of the most astonishingly hermetic poetry in the English language, poetry whose amazing transparence, extraordinary mobility, and captivating images give it the magical charm of a kaleidoscope, as well as a wildly glistening quality, like rare glass in starlight. It is unfortunate that no collection of his manuscripts (he published nothing during his lifetime) is currently available, and even more unfortunate that he remains known almost exclusively to literary specialists, and even to them only as an obscure verbomaniac frequently plagiarized by that celebrated mediocrity Hart Crane, who happened to come across the Greenberg manuscripts. It is clear that at a period in which most people who thought they were poets in the English language—not only

Hart Crane but also Eliot, Pound, Joyce, etc.—were merely dabbling in the ignoblest sort of literary deception and the most grotesque vanity, leaving behind nothing but various blind alleys of mystifications, Samuel Greenberg, on the contrary, was involved, desperately, in a quest of an immeasurably higher order. On his primitive raft of exhilaration and anguish he set sail on a passionate exploration of the poetic marvelous according to the principles of what Rimbaud had referred to as the "alchemy of the word." It is Greenberg's delirious fidelity to the cause of poetry conceived as a revolutionary and emancipatory activity of the mind that makes his whole work belong as much to the living future as the work of Crane-Eliot-Pound-Joyce & company belongs entirely to the dead past.

There are a host of writers, perhaps more plentiful in America than anywhere else, commonly categorized as "cranks": protagonists of bizarre systems, monomaniacs of unaccepted theories, professors of weird sciences, proselytes of new religions. It should hardly be necessary to dwell upon the facts that such phenomena are especially noticeable among the increasingly pauperized petite bourgeoisie, always in search of the most impossibly utopian panaceas; or that the underlying motivations would almost invariably reveal more or less serious psychological disorders; or that a great majority of such cases would doubtless be found to possess, at best, a conservative political attitude. The career of the Nazi "Cosmic Ice Theory" movement (based on pseudoscientific works) should be sufficient to make us wary of greeting such phenomena with enthusiasm, and confusional literature on the subject (such as the particularly stupid book *The Morning of the Magicians* by Pauwels and Bergier) must be vigorously combated. On the other hand, the immense quantity (and in some cases high imaginative quality) of this literature, as well as the great influence it has exerted and continues to exert on a portion of the population that is by no means negligible, alone make it a subject worthy of consideration. The very least one may expect from research in this area would be some additional light on some of the darker regions of the mind. And perhaps from this foggy terrain there may yet emerge one or two genuine bearers of illumination. It serves to recall Lewis Carroll, for example, who was clearly "psychologically disturbed" and politically a conservative Protestant, factors that do not, however, in any way detract from the sublime and subversive splendor of *Alice's Adventures in Wonderland*.

There is, of course, in this brief preliminary reconnaissance no space to do more than cite an example from this vast literature. Of special interest is Alfred Lawson, baseball player, inventor, and pioneer of US aviation, who developed an extraordinary conception of the universe, reducing all worldly and unworldly phenomena to a handful of superbly idiotic laws, elaborating a veritable "system" to which he gave the name Lawsonomy: "the knowledge of Life and everything that pertains thereto," also defined as "the science of that which is, not that which ain't." Lawson's 1904 novel *Born Again*, more or less science fiction, is interesting for its utopian and prophetic aspects (it forecasts radio, among other things), as well as for its overriding paranoid schizophrenic plot. Lawsonomy could be seen as a kind of homegrown, roughcast species of "pataphysics" (Alfred Jarry's "science of imaginary solutions") though Lawson seems to have had none of Jarry's Faustrollian sagacity. But such Lawsonomian conceptions as the "menorgs" and the "disorgs" (microscopic creatures inhabiting the human body and responsible for organizing and disorganizing its activity) and the "law of zig-zag-and-swirl" (illustrated by the example of a germ moving across the surface of a corpuscle that is traveling up the bloodstream of a man who in turn is walking down the aisle of an airliner that is traveling at 100 miles per hour and at an angle of 32 degrees from the earth, etc.) reveal Lawson's unmistakable (even if unconscious) reservoir of humor. And it is impossible to remain indifferent to an author who could write such lines as these: "When my Eyes no longer see objects about me; when my ears no longer record sound messages; when my Nostrils do not attract odors; nor my Taste distinguish flavors; when external Pressure can no longer affect my mentality, nor internal Pressure register the appeal of my voice; when the power of Suction has deserted me and my body is dissolved and the substances of which it is composed have returned to the great ocean of Density from whence they came; my words must still talk and urge you forward in search of the unlimited knowledge to be found in the unexplored regions of PENETRABILITY."

Situated equidistant from what is called "serious" literature and from most all of the aforementioned "crank" literature is the invaluable body of work left to us by Charles Fort. Interest in this remarkable figure (all of whose books are now in paper editions) has risen greatly in recent years; it would appear as if his work has been permanently retrieved from obscurity. It is too early to perceive what this resurgence of interest will bring in the way of clarification and new ideas; one may expect very little, for instance, from such collegiate pastimes as the rejuvenated "Fortean Society" in which the scathing humor and intelligence of the master are reduced to platitudes and stagnation. Fort was the systematizer and experimental cosmologist of "accursed" phenomena: frogs that fell from the sky, visitations from space, astronomical peculiarities, animals that talk, etc. Noting that the disappearance of Ambrose Bierce into revolutionary Mexico coincided in time with the disappearance of an Ambrose Small, a Canadian, Fort asked: "Is somebody collecting Ambroses?" With untiring intellectual fortitude he compiled and speculated upon his compelling data in books whose fluid style has been compared to collage: quotes from scientific journals, luminous analogies, polemical intrusions, disturbing coincidences, violent juxtapositions give these works a specifically irresistible quality of magical evocation. This philosopher of *Absolute Doubt* chronicled the everyday interventions of the conventionally unexpected and wove from these scattered stars a defiant galaxy of the imagination, far from the fashionable neighborhood of novelists and other gossip columnists and even farther from their psychological maneuvering and scarcely concealed commercial ambitions.

Another writer unique in American literature, whom we regard with great admiration, is the IWW poet and theoretician T-Bone Slim. He is best known for his contributions to the famous *Little Red Songbook*: songs characterized by a deeply cutting humor and a reckless spirit of revolt. But it is in the columns that he wrote regularly for the IWW papers—especially in the 1920s when his texts seem to have been published with little or no editing—that his poetic magistery reached its truest articulation. Like the style of Charles Fort, the poetic method of T-Bone Slim bears a resemblance to the technique of collage: headlines, news stories, advertising slogans, and popular songs provide occasions for the intervention of his laughter, with which he mows down the pillars of simplistic rationality, leaping unpredictably from subject to subject. He did not "organize" his pages; he used no outline, no premeditated plan: using every variety of wordplay, certain of his texts seem to possess continuity primarily through the flowing shapes and sounds of the very words themselves, and through the spontaneous images formed as they collide and roll along the page, rather than in their conventional meaning. But it is his profound humor, and his revolutionary sensibility, that distinguishes these experiments with language from the superficial and contrived "revolution of the word" practiced in the 1920s and '30s by Eugene Jolas and many of the collaborators of the literary magazine *transition*.

Let us emphasize that T-Bone Slim was unquestionably a proletarian writer, which makes his destiny and his message so much more moving in our eyes. It is clear, moreover, that his work obviously resists assimilation into the stifling categories of so-called proletarian or socialist (actually Stalinist) realism, which in fact was never anything else than an essentially petit bourgeois, bureaucratic, guilt-ridden parasitical and repressive ideological device, in flagrant contradiction with the teachings of Marx, Engels, and Lenin: it was "the kind of art functionaries understand," as Che Guevara wrote. Functionaries in the service of Stalinist state capitalism could obviously not tolerate T-Bone Slim: the self-activity of the imagination is as terrifying to them as the self-activity of the working class. "It is up to us," wrote Breton in the *Second Manifesto*, "to move, as slowly as necessary, without any sudden fits or starts, towards the worker's way of thinking." Let us meanwhile render homage to T-Bone Slim, a working man conscious of the oneiric weaponry of language, who gave to poetic revolt in English a resonance peculiarly his own, and to whose memory we are pleased to offer at least this minimal act of reparation.

It is not only in the written word that we recognize poetry. The revolutionary defense of the marvelous must be achieved by any means necessary.

Night weaves the brightest of magical flames in the subtlest folds of its darkness, speaking to us sometimes in a voice as criminal as the sea, burning with purity yet as frozen as the tracks of wolves in the snow before dawn. The BLUES comprise an extraordinarily fertile poetic tradition that is only now beginning to emerge in a new light. The inadequacies of the existing critical literature, which even at its best tends to restrict blues to the categories of the social sciences, should become increasingly evident as Paul Garon publishes his researches into the profound and exalted lyricism emanating from the work of such bluesmen as Peetie Wheatstraw or the better known Robert Johnson. Much has been written of blues lyrics as a means of expression; almost nothing regarding them as an activity of the mind.

We have everything to expect of further exploration of this elusive, important domain, which promises to unravel many tangled mysteries of human expression as well as to liberate new and dynamic forces of inspiration.

COMICS and cartooning comprise one of this century's clearest windows on all that is most marvelous in the imaginative life of man. Heir of folklore and fairy tale, as well as many aspects of "artistic" tradition, the best comics articulate delicious dreams of adventure, revenge, and the realization of the mind's potentiality, offering momentary flights of incomparable exhilaration from the prison walls of immediate reality and permitting the human sensibility to arm itself somewhat against the drab military background of everyday life with its cushioned monotony, its ceaseless procession of inhibitions, laws, cops, courts, priests, and the well-known sterility of truly human faculties in the capitalist epoch, a situation that finds its most adequate expression in best-selling novels cranked off an assembly line of enforced stultification. For me, a single *Bugs Bunny* comic book of the early 1950s (such as "The Magic Sneeze" of 1952) will always be worth more—in terms of freedom and human dignity—than all the novels of Proust, Sartre, Faulkner, Hemingway ... Such a judgment, which will probably strike some as excessive, possesses at least the virtue of complete seriousness. Regrettably the spatial limitations of the present article do not permit me to deal more concretely, or even at greater length, with this subject, to which, however, I shall return in the future. Meanwhile it must suffice to signal certain of the comics that, from the surrealist point of view, seem to offer the greatest promise, the brightest revelation: in the first place, the delirious lyricism of *Krazy Kat* by George Herriman, a mad ballet with eternal variations on a single theme, the simplicity of which only emphasizes the poetic heights and depths it attains at every turn. Also close to us are Winsor McCay's *Little Nemo*, a beautifully constructed celebration of the Pleasure Principle; the wild-eyed buffoonery of *Happy Hooligan* by Frederick Burr Opper; the Toonerville Folk of Fontaine Fox; and the concrete irrationality of Rube Goldberg's elaborate inventions, as well as the sublime ridiculousness of his *Foolish Questions*. From a later period, surrealism singles out especially the comic characters of violent humor: these are most always animated cartoon "stars" who are later featured in comic books and sometimes newspaper strips:

particularly Bugs Bunny and Daffy Duck but also Tom and Jerry and the early Woody Woodpecker, characters whose origins and development are linked to a revolt against the bourgeois banality of the Walt Disney Studios. Among animated cartoonists surrealism affirms the amazing dynamite of black humor in the work of Tex Avery; also the masterpieces of the "gag" by Chuck Jones, Robert McKimson, and others; and the sensitive, penetrating delight of several works of Norman McLaren. Of the "superhero" comics, generally a boring genre, marked with semi-fascist ideology, surrealists point out only certain rare exceptions: *Captain Marvel*, whose bungling humor is in such complete contrast to the dreary unemotionalism of *Superman*; the early *Plastic Man* (like the former, not to be confused with its current dull reincarnation); and Will Eisner's fantastic *Spirit*.

We can do no more here than merely mention the names of certain PAINTERS in whom we recognize preoccupations that foretell, enhance, or parallel our own: some of the curious allegorical landscapes of Thomas Cole (1801–48); certain works of John Quidor (1801–81) illustrating themes of Washington Irving and James Fenimore Cooper; the entire work of Albert Pinkham Ryder (1847–1917), Louis Eilshemius (1864–1941), and Edward Hopper; certain "naive" painters, above all Morris Hirshfield; and Joseph Stella's early and specifically New York interpretation of futurism. More attention should be given to American Dadaism: particularly to Man Ray, who went on to become the first American surrealist—aside from toppling the governing conceptions of "artistic" photography, he has contributed a great number of paintings, drawings, and objects that are still far from receiving their full measure of appreciation. Later there were those who adhered to the principles of the surrealist movement in this country: the sculptor and photographer David Hare (who edited the first US surrealist journal, *VVV*), Joseph Cornell, Kay Sage, Dorothea Tanning, the early Alexander Calder (inventor of the mobile), the Armenian immigrant Arshile Gorky, and Marie Wilson. We should also mention some of the more obsessed abstract expressionists, principally Jackson Pollock. Of recent American painting there has been little that meets the fundamental surrealist requirements of revolt and revelation: a few examples by Rauschenberg and Rosenquist are very small oases in a vast desert. Of foreign surrealists living in the United States let us extend our warmest fraternal greetings to the Spaniard E.F. Granell, whose passionate and ceaseless explorations of the internal labyrinth have brought him into close collaboration with the minotaur; and the Indonesian Schlechter Duvall, who has plunged mercilessly into the imagination's deepest sea of flames to rise as the non-Euclidean phoenix. We may expect the growing presence of surrealism here to overthrow completely the existing tendencies in "art," to restore imaginative vitality to painting and to situate it in the service of poetry and human freedom.

If surrealism tends to reject the greater portion of American CINEMA for its commercialism, its racism, and its State Department ideology, if it agrees with Luis Buñuel that "in none of the traditional arts is there so great a disproportion between potential and achievement as in the cinema," it nonetheless calls attention to certain remarkable exceptions: the entire early work of Chaplin, the Mack Sennett comedies, Buster Keaton, W.C. Fields, all the works of the Marx Brothers, and a few exemplary films (*King Kong, The Phantom of the Opera, Peter Ibbetson*) that reveal the explosive possibilities of the miracle of cinema, which André Breton has called "the first great open bridge" uniting day and night.

Excepting only the igloo, the longhouse, the adobe, and the wigwam, we are quite prepared to say that the architecture of this continent bores us to tears. The only other exception might be the oddities of American building: the isolated "castles" of nineteenth-century eccentrics, certain magnificent grain elevators, the Leadville Ice Palace of 1896, the Chicago Water Tower ... Thus it is with particular pleasure that we affirm the absolute splendor of Simon Rodia's towers in Watts, triumph of automatism and collage, and a delirious promise of the surrealist architecture that will be.

2

Notes on the Legacy of Cthulhu

First published in *Arsenal/Surrealist Subversion*, no. 3 (Spring 1976): 107–8.

The principal originality and greatest merit of H.P. Lovecraft was his creation of an open-ended, continually evolving *experimental mythology* elaborated collectively with the active participation of many friends, some of whom he knew only through correspondence.[1] Drawing inspiration and data from scientific and anthropological works, the literature of magic and alchemy, New England lore, eccentric researchers such as Margaret Murray and Charles Fort, and from his own and others' dreams, Lovecraft and his associates confronted, point-blank, the problem of the absence of a social myth in our time.

Doubtless unaware of all the implications of such a step, they nonetheless took for granted the irredeemably moribund state of all prevailing myths and developed their own mythic frame of reference from scratch, rescuing from past literature only a few tantalizing premonitions (notably from Poe, Bierce, Chambers, and Machen). If this playful idea of utilizing for their own purposes incidents and personages from imaginative works of the past—not to mention freely exchanging characters, backgrounds, and other data with one's fellow writers—is wholly foreign to the alienated individualism characteristic of the specialized craft of literature, it is nonetheless comparable to the procedure of authentic poets as varied as the Eskimos and the Elizabethans. Originating in a sort of *game* played by several writers, the Cthulhu Mythos points *beyond literature* to that exalting future collective creation to be developed in accord with an extensive system of elective affinities and passional attraction. The universal proliferation of this poetry made by all prerequires a society that has largely resolved the contradictions between individual and collective, city and countryside, conscious and unconscious—a society elaborated on the basis of the surrealist revolution.

❧

D.A.F. Sade, in his "Reflections on the Novel" (1800), was the first to recognize that the great Gothic romances of his day were "the inevitable fruit of the revolutionary shocks felt by the whole of Europe." The works of the Lovecraft Circle are similarly inseparable from the revolutionary events of our own epoch, of which the Russian Revolution of October 1917 was the decisive commencement. Once again, as in the age of *Melmoth the Wanderer*, we are living in a *transitional epoch*. But today it is no longer a question, as it was in the epoch of ascendant capital, of one class rising to power only to subjugate others in its turn. This time the future of the whole of humanity is at stake. The question is: Are men and women capable of putting an end to a worldwide system of exploitation and alienation, and of definitively inaugurating the realm of human freedom, or must they lapse into a new and perhaps irrevocable barbarism?

The inescapable universality of the present crisis underlies all Cthulhu Mythos tales. Gone are the isolated crumbling castles, ghostly armor, and other paraphernalia suited to the period of declining feudalism. Lovecraft's action is global and even cosmic; his entire work is imbued with what he called "a sense of spectral whirling through liquid gulfs of infinity, of dizzying rides through reeling universes on a comet's tail." This intuitive insistence on the awesome, truly limitless possibilities opened in the epoch of workers' councils gives his and his comrades' works an implicitly revolutionary character forever unattainable by explicitly "socialist" novels. This is because the Lovecraft Circle grasped the essence of the surrealist view, verified by all great examples of the past, that it is impossible to create anything of significance by expressing only the manifest content of an age, that it is necessary to express, on the contrary, its *latent* content.

In "Limits Not Frontiers of Surrealism" (1936) André Breton wrote: "The 'fantastic,' which the application of a watchword such as socialist realism excludes in the most radical manner, and to which surrealism never ceases to appeal, constitutes in our view the supreme key to this latent content, the means of fathoming the secret depths of history which disappear beneath a maze of events. It is only at the approach of the fantastic, at a point where human reason loses its control, that the most profound emotion of the individual has the fullest opportunity to express itself: emotion unsuitable for projection in the framework of the real world and which has no other solution to its urgency than to rely on the eternal solicitation of symbols and myths."

That Lovecraft held a compatible view is indicated in this passage from a letter to Clark Ashton Smith: "The true function of fantasy is to give the imagination a ground for limitless expansion.... I *know* that my most poignant emotional experiences are those which concern the lure of unplumbed space, the terror of the encroaching outer void, and the struggle to transcend the known and established order."

~

Lovecraft's pessimism, directed against nearly all the false "solutions" at hand, necessarily led him close to the center of the problem of Evil. From such a vantage point, this ardent atheist armed with his improvised mythology challenged at one blow the most cherished illusions of all religions as well as the rationalist's myopic evasion of the Unknown.

Situated precisely at the intersection of humor and terror (or rather of umor and error), Lovecraft's cosmological propositions add to our appreciation of what Breton called "The Great Invisibles"—hypothetical animals whose behavior is as alien to us as is ours to the ant or the whale, and who elude our system of sensory references through secret camouflage; creatures who, however, as Breton suggested, "obscurely manifest themselves to us in fear and in the feeling of chance." This new myth, the subject of many surrealist explorations, was foreshadowed (as Breton acknowledged) by hints from many writers from Cyrano de Bergerac to William James.

Regarding this myth Breton wrote further: "Considering perturbations like the cyclone, in the face of which man is powerless to be anything but victim or witness, or like war, on the subject of which notoriously inadequate views have been advanced, it would not be impossible, in the course of a vast work, which would be constantly presided over by the boldest kind of induction, to even succeed in making plausible the complexion and structure of such hypothetical beings."

When this proposed vast work is compiled, should not a chapter be devoted to the data introduced by Lovecraft, Clark Ashton Smith,

Frank Belknap Long, Donald Wandrei, and others who have heard and heeded "the call of Cthulhu"?

∾

Instead of beating "Literature" to a pulp, Lovecraft allowed himself to be beaten by the racket of pulp literature. Throughout his work the hard cold facts of fury are swept under the rug of mere fiction. His dreams, to which he was remarkably attentive, were for him primarily sources of "plots." The surrealist voice, for him and his collaborators, penetrated only faintly through the earmuffs of literary mystification. If surrealism is the imagination reclaiming all its rights by any and all means, Lovecraft represents the imagination dimly aware that its rights have been violated, but still resigned to employing strictly "legal" means of defense.

Significantly, the most disquieting of Lovecraft's writing is to be found not in his tales or poems but in certain epigraphs to letters to Clark Ashton Smith:

> *Many-columned Arcades of Weed-grown Y'ha-nthlei*
> *Hour of the Unseen Howling*
>
> *Concave Cliffs by the Tam of Kyagoph*
> *Hour of the Reddening of the Dark Waters*
>
> *Tower of Narghan in Pnath*
> *Hour when the Dogs bay at the opening of the Topmost Circular*
>   *Window*

Read in succession, these epigraphs (of which I have quoted only a few) compose an astonishing litany reminiscent of the *Black Book of Carmarthen*. Evidently written in haste and without revision, these lines seem to me to be a remarkable *condensation* of Lovecraft's mythology. His most compelling legacy is given in full in these hurried, fragmentary, cryptic notes to which he probably attributed not the slightest importance.

∾

The Cthulhu Mythos is neither a mirror image of the Christian mythos (as August Derleth lamely argued) nor its simple negation. Rather, it is a kind of hysterical conversion in which the literary symptoms of senile mythologies—Christianism among others—were forced to dance to new and terrible tunes. Lovecraft is beginning to be "acknowledged" today because his bad dreams define the bad dreams of a whole epoch. Perhaps there is no better introduction to his work than Victor Tausk's 1919 paper "On the Origin of the 'Influencing Machine' in Schizophrenia."

Too resigned, while he lived, to being the dupe of other men's afterthoughts, Lovecraft regarded himself a failure. Today his work is a great "success," marketed in mass editions to dupe others in turn. But even the abusive circumstances of the "Lovecraft revival" are proof of a real development. The same historical forces that began in the mid-1960s to make surrealism a matter of life and death in the United States also brought about the "rehabilitation" of Lovecraft. Used by mass market publishers for their own confusionist and profitable purposes, this rehabilitation nonetheless demonstrates once more, in a small way, that the dying social order can continue to live only by killing its gravediggers and then robbing their graves.

There is reason to emphasize that it was Lovecraft's very "failure" that was, in an important sense, his greatest virtue. This is something that inevitably escapes those hostile or condescending commentators such as L. Sprague de Camp and Lin Carter who repeatedly reproach him for not devoting himself more assiduously to being a hack novelist like Sprague de Camp and Carter. What saves Lovecraft for us, what gives his work its special charm and real force, is precisely the fact that he was absolutely unable and unwilling to keep in step with the dominant tendencies of his time, or even with his own declared intentions. The notorious anachronisms that enabled him, posthumously, to become the crowning character in his own mythology also made him (doubtless in spite of himself) a magnificent thorn in the side of all the hypocritically "progressive" literature of his day.

Lovecraft's greatest achievement can thus be said to have been the consequence of a marvelous misunderstanding. Floundering for years in the waters of naive musings and delusions that were often nothing else than paltry, eventually he stumbled onto the uncharted isle of his own deepest fears. Like Columbus, he never knew where he was going or where he had landed, but he too deserves credit at least for not turning back too soon. It is his fidelity to the task of exploring his own terror and horror that makes Lovecraft's work a monument to the aspiration signaled by De Quincey, "to reveal something of the grandeur which belongs *potentially* to human dreams."

3

Frank Belknap Long

First published in *Arsenal/Surrealist Subversion*, no. 3 (Spring 1976): 108-9.

In our day, when a ludicrous mediocrity such as Norman Mailer can pass for a "major" writer, and a groveling imbecile such as Allen Ginsberg acts out a well-paying reputation as a "rebel," it is encouraging that a few writers are still honest and unpretentious enough to concentrate on werewolves, vampires, voodoo, monsters from other dimensions, and adventures on Mars, sparing us the poverty of "psychological literature" with all its aesthetic veneer, and—in spite of inevitable concessions— offering the mind at least the ghost of a chance to wander freely on a terrain from which all surprises have not been weeded out in advance.

Of Lovecraft's old friends and collaborators, none has so unequivocally announced the latent content of the Cthulhu Mythos as has Frank Belknap Long in *The Horror from the Hills* (1931): "Some monstrous *unfettering* is about to take place. That which for two thousand years has lain somnolent will stir again and the 'great things' will descend from their frightful lair"—proof that the Lovecraft Circle had for its fundamental presupposition (though probably without knowing it) the motto emblazoned on a cover of *La Révolution surréaliste* in 1925, pronouncing this "the end of the christian era."

Frank Belknap Long has written over a score of fantasy novels, science fiction, gothic romances, and numerous uncollected tales. These were preceded by two books of poems; it is noteworthy that hints of genuine poetic inspiration, and a particular appreciation for Blake and Swinburne, recur throughout his work. The very abundance of his writing and his acceptance of the etiquette of pulp literature have unavoidably taken their toll, but the same factors underline the unmistakable ingenuousness that gives his best work, his tales, a unique magic touch.

Long is not, however, a "naive." He is well-informed, and more inquisitive, more alert, more open-minded at the age of seventy than most people half his age. His unselfconscious preference for a "superior kind of logic" derived from Lewis Carroll and Picasso (see *This Strange Tomorrow*), and his utter indifference to the usual crafty motives of Literature and its critical police, permit him in his best tales to rise above the anachronistic fictional forms in much the same way that some surrealist painters utilize historically superseded pictorial conventions for new and unexpected poetic purposes.

Even a lesser work such as *This Strange Tomorrow* focuses above all on those moments "when space itself seems to conspire with the strange and the startling to enlarge the boundaries of human awareness." In the same book Long presents his basic perspective, that "reality is never as unyielding as the harshness of everyday experience leads us, at times, to assume. There are shimmering mountain peaks beyond the veil, peaks which you scaled many times as a child. They can be scaled again, for they are still there."

In the stories collected in *The Hounds of Tindalos* (Arkham House, 1947; reprinted in two Panther paperbacks, 1975), and more recently in *The Rim of the Unknown* (Arkham House, 1972), the imaginative sparks produce a true poetic ignition. In these, his finest tales, "the imagination becomes like a pair of white-hot tongs, overheated, and capable of flattening reality to a thin edge of blackness on an anvil without substance." It is here that he evidences his appreciation for an experimental beauty, his full sympathy for the prerogatives of childhood, his defense of Eros, his intrinsic poetic solidarity.

The future researcher who wishes to define more precisely the tradition of the Great Exceptions of American popular culture, and Long's position in it, will doubtless find much to ponder in the fact that his father was a dental surgeon whose patients included George Herriman (creator of *Krazy Kat*), Frederick Burr Opper (creator of *Happy Hooligan*), and other famous cartoonists. An anti-realist alert to the temptations of the marvelous, Frank Belknap Long is situated securely in this tradition of *internal outcasts* whose works, scattered here and there in hidden and unexpected corners, are the only oases in an arid plain of commercial conformism.

4

Free Play and No Limit: An Introduction to Edward Bellamy's *Utopia*

Selection from a piece first published in "Surrealism and Its Popular Accomplices," special issue of *Cultural Correspondence*, guest-edited by Franklin Rosemont, nos. 10–11 (Fall 1979): 6–16.

Looking Backward opens in 1887. A wealthy young Bostonian retires to his bedroom in a secret basement vault that he has had specially constructed to shut out street noise. A chronic insomniac, he is put to sleep by a hypnotist. He wakes up in the morning—113 years later.

Like Rip Van Winkle, Julian West finds the world in which he wakens very different from the world in which he fell asleep. The intervening years have witnessed nothing less than a "complete transformation in the human condition," the result of a thoroughgoing social revolution that has realized, for the first time, full human equality.[1] In abolishing private ownership of the means of production, society also has done away with social classes, exploitation, poverty, hunger, war, sex slavery, race discrimination, slums, crime, jails, money, rent, banks, charity, corruption, taxes, advertising, housework, politicians, merchants, servants, lawyers, the army, the navy, and the State Department.

Government itself scarcely exists, its functions having been reduced to the coordination of industrial production and distribution. There is very little disease, insanity, or suicide, and virtually no legislation ("we might be said to live almost in a state of anarchy"). Churches have all but disappeared. There are no locks or locksmiths, and no safes ("because we have no more thieves"). Coercion is a thing of the past, everything having become "entirely voluntary, the logical outcome of the operation of human nature under rational conditions." Working hours are short. Work itself has been greatly simplified and, as far as possible, rendered attractive. Vacations are ample; emigration is unrestricted. In the new society of the year 2000, "liberty is the first and last word."

All this has in turn fundamentally transformed the human personality. "The conditions of life have changed, and with them the motives of human action." In Bellamy's utopia there is no more selfishness, greed, malice, hypocrisy, apathy; no more "struggle for existence"; no more hunger for power; no more anxiety or fear as to basic human needs. "The highest possible physical, as well as mental, development for everyone" is the aim of the new education. Everyone is happier, healthier, brighter, friendlier; more active, more adventurous, more creative.

"Perhaps the most notable single aspect of the Revolution" was "the elevation and enlargement of woman's sphere in all directions.... Since the Revolution there has been no difference in the education of the sexes nor in the independence of their economic and social position, in the exercise of responsibility or experience in the practical conduct of affairs.... In every pursuit of life [women] join with men on equal terms."

Moreover, "the sentiment of brotherhood, the feeling of solidarity, asserted itself not merely toward men and women, but likewise toward the humbler companions of our life on earth and sharers of its fortunes, the animals.... The new conception of our relation to the animals appealed to the heart and captivated the imagination of mankind."

The 113 years also have seen, thanks to the Revolution, an unprecedented flourishing of science, technology, and the arts. Bellamy differs from many utopians in his confidence that modern technology can be conquered and put at the service of human desire. His forecast—in *Looking Backward* and its sequel, *Equality*—of such things as automobiles, radio, television, helicopters, air-conditioning, and waterbeds has assured him a permanent place in the history of science fiction. Interspersed through a charming love story and an unremitting attack on capitalism and its institutions, these inventions doubtless added to the appeal of his utopia.

Its appeal was, in fact, extraordinary. Indeed, it is generally acknowledged that *Looking Backward* was the most widely read and influential book of the late nineteenth century. It provoked vigorous debate in newspapers and magazines, in lecture rooms and living rooms, in union halls and saloons. It fascinated the "man in the street" as it did the "leading intellectual." Because of *Looking Backward*, said Vida D. Scudder, "the fading emotions of the old Abolitionist era flamed again." A broad movement sprang up, for the purpose of realizing the dream set forth in Bellamy's book. More than 150 Bellamy clubs were formed around the country. Eugene V. Debs and Daniel De Leon were among countless thousands who entered social radicalism through the door that Bellamy opened. J.A. Wayland, founder/editor of the *Appeal to Reason*— the largest-circulated socialist periodical in US history—gave *Looking Backward* credit for having "popularized socialism, made it interesting, and started millions to thinking along lines entirely new to them."

A number of American utopian novels had appeared before Bellamy's, but, except for Nathaniel Hawthorne's *Blithedale Romance* (1852), none had made a lasting impression. *Looking Backward* put utopia on the map of the USA. It started a vogue for utopian romances that ran through the '90s and well into the new century. If it is still unclear to what degree it influenced Mark Twain's *Connecticut Yankee* or L. Frank Baum's *Wizard of* Oz, its impact on many other works—including William Dean Howells's *A Traveler from Altruria*, *Caesar's Column* by Ignatius Donnelly, Frederick Upham Adams's *President John Smith*, and Charlotte Perkins Gilman's *Herland*—is firmly established.

Nor was Bellamy's influence limited to his native land. *Looking Backward* was wildly popular throughout the English-speaking world— in Canada, Australia, and New Zealand as well as England; William Morris acknowledged that he wrote *News from Nowhere* as a reply to it. Tolstoy, finding it "exceedingly remarkable," arranged for its translation into Russian; Maxim Gorky once called the United States "the country of Henry George, Bellamy, [and] Jack London." Jean Jaurès, the outstanding figure of pre–World War I French socialism, saluted this "American masterpiece" that did "wonders toward dissipating hostility and ignorance against our ideas." The renowned Marxist theorist Clara Zetkin, leader of the German socialist workingwomen's movement, translated it into German and wrote an introduction to it. And, by way of exemplifying the exceptional range of its appeal, Helena P. Blavatsky—author of *Isis Unveiled* and *The Secret Doctrine*—declared Bellamy's work "magnificent" and in harmony with the perspectives of Theosophy.[2]

෴

The history of the Bellamy movement in the United States remains to be written.[3] As a link of the older radical abolitionists and reconstructionists with the new generation that would form the Socialist Party in 1900 and the IWW five years later, its study could teach us a great deal.

Few social movements, if any, have been so colorful or so heterogeneous. Under the banner of *Looking Backward* were Unitarians, Theosophists, trade unionists, populists, feminists, Christian socialists, spiritualists, homeopathists, vegetarians, prohibitionists, members of the Farmers' Alliance, an appreciable number who thought of themselves as Marxists, and several Union Army generals—including Arthur Devereux, "hero of Gettysburg," and Abner Doubleday, the apocryphal "father of baseball." Among Bellamy's adherents were Edward Everett Hale, William Dean Howells, Charlotte Perkins Gilman, Thomas Wentworth Higginson, Lucy Stone, Hamlin Garland, Julia Ward Howe, Helen Campbell, Frances Willard, Jesse Cox, Lucien Sanial, Florence Kelley, Thomas Lake Harris, Solomon Schindler, Laurence Gronlund, Thomas Davidson, Burnette Haskell, Sylvester Baxter, and Clarence Darrow.

∽

Looking Backward was written fast and furiously in the dazzling light of one of the pivotal American labor battles: the bloody Haymarket Affair and its aftermath in Chicago, 1886, in which a group of innocent labor leaders were framed and hanged at the behest of Big Business.

The book appeared in a period of unprecedentedly rapid and convulsive change in American society. The Civil War and Reconstruction paved the way for extensive industrialization, which in turn exacerbated class stratification beyond anything even dreamed of earlier in the United States. To meet the mounting threat posed by the great trusts, workers thronged into the Knights of Labor. The year 1887, when Bellamy was readying his book for publication, has been called "the year of ten thousand strikes."

Historians have debated the backgrounds of Bellamy's thought. From book reviews and editorials he wrote for the *Springfield Union* in the '70s, we know that he was familiar with the work of such utopians as Robert Owen, Frances Wright, Charles Fourier, Albert Brisbane, Étienne Cabet, John Humphrey Noyes, Josiah Warren, and others. Greater than any of these, however, was the influence exerted on him by the Old Testament prophets and the millennial/heretical tradition in Christianity—the Anabaptists, for example.

Descended from a long line of Baptist ministers, Bellamy sometimes has been called a "Christian socialist," but the tag does not fit well. His early essay "The Religion of Solidarity" is closer to Transcendentalism than to any Christian creed. Till the end, it is true, he hoped that the remnants of radical egalitarianism in the margins of Christendom would add their resources to the revolutionary ferment. Noting that the church's pro-slavery position had dealt "a blow to its prestige in America from which it had not yet recovered," he warned that "its failure to take the right side in this far vaster movement would not leave any church worth mentioning." Of course, this warning went unheeded; indeed, some of the most venomous diatribes against his utopia came from priests and preachers. His last book, *Equality*, includes a scathing indictment of "ecclesiastical capitalism." After his death, his works were a major influence on the short-lived Social Gospel movement; but the fact remains: he himself stood with the infidels.

We may glean something of Bellamy's literary preferences from a passage in *Looking Backward* in which Julian West looks over the bookshelves in his twenty-first-century home and joyfully discovers the works of Shakespeare, Milton, Wordsworth, Shelley, Tennyson, Defoe, Dickens, Thackeray, Hugo, Hawthorne, and Irving. Dickens he admired above all: "He overtops all the writers of his age.... No man of his time did so much as he to turn men's minds to the wrong and wretchedness of the old order of things, and open their eyes to the necessity of the great change that was coming, although he himself did not clearly foresee it."

Living most of his life in the small mill town of Chicopee Falls, Massachusetts, Bellamy's personal acquaintance with contemporary writers was limited. It is interesting to note that Mark Twain—who found *Looking Backward* "fascinating"—once arranged to meet with him. Twain's friend William Dean Howells became an active supporter of Bellamy's ideas and corresponded with him for years.

To some extent he knew the work of Hegel and even Marx; his acquaintance with the latter would increase appreciably after the publication of *Looking Backward* when, devoting himself unreservedly to agitational/propagandist work in the service of the Revolution, he came into contact with representatives of virtually every radical/revolutionary tendency. Bellamy's critique of capitalism, however, was derived less from books than from the things he saw with his penetrating eye and felt with his dreaming heart.

His critique is as unsparing, in its way, as Fourier's or Marx's. Bellamy denounced capitalism as "the source and sum of all villainies," "utterly unjust in all respects," "mutual throat-cutting," "a system which [makes] the interests of every individual antagonistic to those of every other." Zeroing in primarily from the *moral* angle, he recalls Lautréamont's maxim: "Place a goose-quill in the hands of a moralist who is also a first-rate writer. He will be superior to poets."

Bellamy's historical insight was formidable. He perceived elusive connections between seemingly disparate phenomena—the social reality beneath the ideological veneer. It was he who first pointed out that the millionaire and the tramp entered the American scene at the same time. He called the nineteenth century "the century that invented poker"—because of the bluff needed to sustain its political/economic machinations. He railed against the "utter hypocrisy underlying the entire relation of the sexes, the pretended chivalric deference to women on the one hand, coupled with their practical suppression on the other."

That Bellamy independently, and following a very different method, arrived at certain conclusions of Marx surely is not without interest. But what draws us to a writer, a thinker, an artist, is not so much what he shares with others as it is the unique charms of which he alone disposes. Bellamy's real importance lies precisely in those qualities that distinguish him from all others: his particular moral/revolutionary attitude and its underlying psychological and poetic dimensions. It was these qualities that made *Looking Backward* so vitally a part of its time. And it is these same qualities that render so much of his message as acute and vigorous today as the day it was written....

Transcendence of Time

Throughout his life Bellamy dreamed of the conquest of time by passion.

In *Miss Ludington's Sister* we meet a character for whom "the veil between time and eternity was melted by the hot breath of ... passion, and the confines of the natural and the supernatural were confounded." More audaciously, in one of his most extraordinary tales, *With the Eyes*

Shut, the *clock* is seen almost as the *symbol* of all ideological conflicts rooted in the Reality Principle. We are ushered into a display room of clocks that are equipped with phonographic devices, so that on the hour, on the half hour, etc., they recite excerpts from the works of celebrated writers. These timepieces also feature "effigies of the authors whose sentiments they repeated." "There were religious and sectarian clocks, moral clocks, philosophical clocks, freethinking and infidel clocks, literary and poetical clocks, educational clocks, frivolous and bacchanalian clocks.... Modern wisdom was represented by a row of clocks surmounted by the heads of famous maxim-makers, from Rochefoucauld to Josh Billings." Standing near the religious and skeptical clocks at the hour of ten, he says, "the war of opinions that followed was calculated to unsettle the firmest convictions."

As early as "The Religion of Solidarity" (1874), when he protested "the barrier of time" and affirmed our hunger "not for more life, but for all the life there is," Bellamy took his stand for the poets' *eternity*. "Each moment of fullness," he would have agreed with André Breton, "bears in itself the negation of centuries of limping and broken history." Can anyone doubt that the "free play of every instinct" requires the abolition of time? Against the miserabilists' mechanical measurement of misery, Bellamy called for Blake's "Eternal Delight." The passions— especially the passions of solidarity and love—demand the primal timelessness that alone allows us to live, as Bellamy urged, with "calm abandon, a serene and generous recklessness."

The three themes—supersession of memory, overcoming of divisions in the personality, transcendence of time—reoccur in *Looking Backward* with full force in the subplot telling of the narrator's love life.

In the year 2000 Julian West falls in love with a young woman who, as it turns out, is the great-granddaughter of the woman who had been his fiancée in 1887. Unknown to him, however, this girl—Edith Leete— had known since childhood of her great-grandmother's love for him, and had long felt herself to be, in some strange way, the living spirit of her ancestor, "come back to the world to fulfill some work that lay near [her great-grandmother's] heart."

In a dramatic climax, we find Julian West brooding over his weird isolation in this new world, feeling that "there was no place for [him] anywhere," and that he was "neither dead nor properly alive." It is at this moment, as he is on the verge of suicide, that Edith Leete affirms her reciprocal love and thereby retrieves him from the depths of despair.

Erotic passion thus triumphs—symbolically at least—over time and even death. A further implication is that love will flourish at its wildest best after capitalism has been overthrown. "That evening the garden was bathed in moonlight, and till midnight Edith and I wandered to and fro there, trying to grow accustomed to our happiness."

The Need for Wilderness

[Another] theme is Bellamy's sensitiveness to the call of the wild, which in turn emphasizes the "open-endedness" of his thought.

In his unfinished autobiographical novel, *Eliot Carson*, he wrote rapturously of the remotest wilderness: "to chance all awed and silent upon those secret places of the woods, those room-like nooks whose air is warm with the sense of something living there ... to lie beneath the pines and listen to the song of eternity in their branches till he forgot what manner of life his was."[4] A character in his early story "Deserted" says point-blank: "I wouldn't give much for a country where there are no wildernesses left." This is essentially the view set forth by Thoreau in *Walden*, where it is urged on us that "we need the tonic of wildness, to wade sometimes in marshes where the bittern and the meadow-hen lurk.... We need to witness our own limits transgressed, and some life pasturing freely where we never wander."

Contrary to the misperception of nearsighted critics who persist in mistaking Bellamy for an advocate of some sort of technocratic urbanism, this same attitude characterizes his utopia. It is implicit in the vast reforestation that begins immediately after the Revolution; in the ensuing transformation of relations between man and animals; in his vision of "the works of man blending with the face of nature in perfect harmony."

Extending even beyond the apparent barriers of "external nature," Bellamy's solidarity embraces also the wildernesses of human society, the wildernesses of the mind. Throughout his life he admired the sturdy independence of the American villager, whose unique way of life was vanishing before his very eyes under the blows of bourgeois industrialization. Where others saw only quirks and foibles in these plain and simple folk, Bellamy saw real grandeur, which he reflected in many tales. His utopia could be viewed, in part, as an outgrowth of his desire to *protect* these unpretentious people—and with them, the last remnants of their sturdy independence, their quirks and foibles, their grandeur—from the onslaught of the capitalist juggernaut.

A deep sympathy for "outsiders" runs through Bellamy's work. No one could fail to note his affection for the spiritualists, for example, in *Miss Ludington's Sister*. His stories show him to have been drawn toward eccentrics, dreamers, people in some way "touched in the head." The world of *Looking Backward* leaves room—as too few utopias have done—for such "exceptions," such marginal beings who live "outside the system." In *Equality* it is emphasized that "the new order [has] no need or use for unwilling recruits.... If anyone did not wish to enter public service and could live outside of it without stealing or begging, he was quite welcome to."

Of course, Bellamy believed that the attractions of the new society would be so many and so irresistible that eventually everyone would come into "the new social house." But he insisted that "no sort of constraint [would be] brought to bear upon ... anybody." He preferred to rely on such things as "the undreamed of possibilities of human friendship."

It is worth calling attention to the fact that *Looking Backward* was not intended as a "finished" system; it was deliberately expansive. Recognizing, as he did, that "human nature in its essential qualities is good, not bad," Bellamy was convinced that once capitalism is abolished, and replaced by a rational social system, men and women will know well enough what to do with their lives. To paraphrase his own watchwords, there is *no limit* to the splendor that the "free play of every instinct" can create. "The way stretches before us," he wrote of the year 2000, "but the end is lost in light.... With a tear for the dark past, turn we then to the dazzling future and, veiling our eyes, press forward. The long and weary winter of the race is ended. Its summer has begun. Humanity has burst the chrysalis. The heavens are before it."

Relating *Looking Backward* to his earlier tales emphasizes that his utopia is above all a work of the *imagination*. He himself regarded his stories as "the working out of problems, that is to say, attempts to trace the logical consequences of certain assumed conditions."[5] Acknowledging that it was "in this form" that the plan of *Looking Backward* presented itself to his mind, he added that from that moment "the writing of the book was the simplest thing in the world."

The facility with which Bellamy recorded his utopia is a measure of its truly *inspired* character and helps explain why it has proved so inspiring to so many others. William Dean Howells touched on this point when he wrote, regarding the method of Bellamy's tales, that "he does not so much transmute our everyday reality to the substance of romance, as make the airy stuff of dreams one in quality with veritable experience."[6]

In *Looking Backward*, Bellamy's moral/revolutionary enthusiasm was suffused with *just the right touch* of scientific anticipation, the poetic marvelous and erotic promise for it to become *contagious* for a generation that dreamed at night of Darwinian evolution, baseball, bicycles, boxing, the eight-hour day, Barnum's circus, aeronautics, anarchists, *Whistler's Mother*, world's fairs, the cancan, steam locomotives, the Ferris wheel, the Statue of Liberty, Lily Langtry, Loie Fuller, Tennyson, Edison, Jack the Ripper, and *Alice's Adventures in Wonderland*. As the vivid expression of a dream already lurking in the backs of the minds of millions, the book "caught on" and "sold like hotcakes."

If the same cannot be said for the much longer and heavily didactic *Equality*, it has its own brighter moments nonetheless. Who could be indifferent to the account of the "great bonfire" where, in the midst of the Revolution, masses of people *dance* around an immense conflagration—fueled by a mountain of stocks, bonds, money, deeds, and other examples of capitalism's mystical paperwork—on the site of the New York Stock Exchange?

The chief interest of *Equality* lies precisely in the details it supplies to our image of *Looking Backward*. As a tale it is the meagerest shell, but as an extension of the earlier book it is invaluable.

Among its many suggestive and appealing details, we learn in *Equality* that this utopia is symbolized by the *windmill*, replicas of which adorn the roofs of public buildings: "The mill stands for the machinery of administration, the wind that drives it symbolizes the public will, and the rudder that always keeps the vane of the mill before the wind, however suddenly or completely the wind may change, stands for the method by which the administration is kept at all times responsive and obedient to every mandate of the people, though it be but a breath."

That he would select such a symbol, at once so simple and so strange, tells us much of the man who wrote *Looking Backward*. From the weird effigies surmounting his oratorical clocks, to his indignant Martian critic of Earthian psychology; from the haunted and obsessive wanderers through the anticipatory nostalgia of *Miss Ludington's Sister* to the beautiful and freespirited girl of the year 2000, walking arm in arm with her lover—143 years old but still young!—Bellamy's imaginary world runs far and deep. He has been called "the Jules Verne of socialism." But he deserves better. Could it not be—especially in view of the appreciable role of *glory* in his utopia—that he is rather socialism's Raymond Roussel?

The foregoing presentation of Bellamy, as essentially eros-affirmative, libertarian, and richly imbued with the poetic spirit—one whose approach to key questions is analogous to that of the greatest, most revolutionary poets—is admittedly at variance with, even wholly antithetical to, the prevailing view. In attempting to see his work as a whole, relating his early stories and essays to the later utopian works, I have tried to rectify the false and narrow conclusions of critics whose "critiques" too often have been based on nothing more than a hurried and prejudiced *skimming* of *Looking Backward* alone.

The internal evidence of Bellamy's writings, as I have tried to outline it here, seems to me more than enough to warrant *a new hearing*, so to speak, for him and his work. It will also prove illuminating to call on an interesting if little-known supporting witness. Our effort to see Bellamy and his achievements in the light of Blake, Baudelaire, and Rimbaud—above all in the light of surrealism—is enhanced and substantiated by his association (unnoted by his biographers or commentators) with a remarkable poet: a poet of whom André Breton said that he was one of the few of his generation who "commands the high waves," and who also was among the first to translate Baudelaire and Rimbaud into English.[7] I refer to Stuart Merrill (1863–1915). A major figure of the Symbolist movement in France, he happens also to have organized the first Nationalist Club in New York, 1889.[8]

Born on Long Island, Merrill spent most of his childhood and adolescence in France, where his father, an abolitionist who had fought in the Union Army, was employed as legal adviser to the American legation. By the time his family returned to the United States for a few years in the '80s, young Merrill was already a poet as well as a revolutionary.

Prior to taking up Bellamy, he had helped on Henry George's mayoral campaign, defended the Haymarket anarchists, and sold socialist publications in the streets of New York. His whole life was an impassioned crusade for the transformation of the world. He fought for the freedom of the American blacks, the Chinese, the whole working class; he supported every struggle against injustice. When British hypocrisy imprisoned Oscar Wilde, Merrill spoke out in his defense.

On the walls of his New York apartment were paintings by Gauguin and Rops; on his bookshelves, works of the greatest living poets in French and English. Merrill knew, down to the very marrow of his bones, that the revolutionary spirit of the new painting and the new poetry was fundamentally inseparable from the revolution *in the streets.*

The second issue of *The Nationalist* (June 1889) featured his strident "Ballad of the Outcasts":

> *Beware, O Kings whom Mammon sways,*
> *Lest morrows nearer than ye ken*
> *With our red flags of battle blaze!*
> *For we are hated of all men.*

In an article in the same magazine, Merrill defined the Bellamy movement as the "expression of the evolution of society from competition to cooperation" and summarized its perspectives: "Upon the ruins of the competitive state will arise the Co-operative Commonwealth, with its system of equilibrated production and consumption. Then private interest will no more be hostile to public interest, but they will become identified, and as in a huge partnership, the purest altruism will prove the truest egoism."

As a leader of the Nationalist movement he organized meetings, wrote "articles of combat," and—with his friend Clarence McIlvaine—ran a "correspondence society" to promote the diffusion of radical literature.

As militant in poetry as in politics, he was in more ways than one a follower of Blake, Shelley, and Swinburne. "Modern society," he wrote, "is a badly written poem which one must be active in correcting. A poet, in the etymological sense, remains a poet everywhere, and it is his duty to restore some loveliness on the earth."

Merrill's poetry, nearly all of it written in French, has a touch of the Pre-Raphaelites' sunlit melancholy but is always shot through with a sweetly seductive undercurrent of revolt. It is this quality that distinguished him from most of the Symbolists and made him a notable precursor of surrealism.

His close friends included Stéphane Mallarmé and René Ghil. He was well acquainted with all the leading and most of the lesser figures of French and Belgian Symbolism. During his stay in the United States in the '80s he wrote on French poetry—on Gérard de Nerval and others—for the *New York Times* and the *Evening Post*. It was during his active participation in the Bellamy movement that he prepared a volume of translations from the French titled *Pastels in Prose*, prefaced by his friend William Dean Howells and published by Harper in 1890. This book introduced American readers to the work of Aloysius Bertrand, Baudelaire, Mallarmé, Villiers de l'Isle-Adam, and many others. A second volume, to have been called *Poems of the Symbolists*, was readied for publication but unfortunately never reached print. Merrill also translated works by William Morris, Oscar Wilde, James Thomson, Ernest Dowson, Arthur Symons, and William Butler Yeats into French.

Like many of Bellamy's followers, Stuart Merrill evolved into a revolutionary socialist. But we cannot help being struck by the depth and passion of his youthful commitment to the world of *Looking Backward*. If he later advanced beyond its limits, this was a matter of growth, not renunciation; his underlying motives, his basic orientation, remained unchanged. At the same time, the adherence of such an outstanding poet to Bellamy's movement helps us to see that movement in a new light.

"Regret, remorse, love of the past," Merrill wrote, in an admonition that Bellamy could have written, "are forerunners of mental decay and death.... We have eternity before us." Like Bellamy, Merrill dreamed of a new society founded on freedom, equality, solidarity, love, imagination, and poetry. Like Bellamy, he devoted his life to the realization of such a society. Like Bellamy, he kept his inner eye focused on the *revolutionary future*.

5

A Bomb-Toting, Long-Haired, Wild-Eyed Fiend: The Image of the Anarchist in Popular Culture

Reprinted from Franklin Rosemont and David Roediger, eds., *Haymarket Scrapbook*, 125th anniversary ed. (Oakland: AK Press; Chicago: Charles H. Kerr, 2012), 203–12.

It is only by the whole that one can judge the details.
—Antoine Fabre d'Olivet

Historically, actual bombings attributable to anarchists are very few in number. Long before the "roaring twenties" it was clear that most illegal dynamitings were the work of racketeers and extortionists and that in any case politically or labor-motivated dynamiters tended to be not anarchists at all, but rather protagonists of one or another nationalist cause, or conservative AFL trade unionists who were churchgoing Catholics and supporters of the Democratic Party.

In the comics, however, and in the whole field of popular imagery, bombs are to anarchists what the red-white-and-blue top hat and suit are to Uncle Sam: an aspect of their identity so indispensable that without them they would hardly be recognizable. Everyone knows the ridiculous and unsavory image: besides the one or more bombs clutched in his hands or protruding from his pockets, the stereotype anarchist usually is furnished with a variety of other weapons, including daggers and revolvers, and is further identifiable by his evident aversion for barbershops, bathtubs and fine clothes, as well as by his eyes, fixed as they almost always are in a distracted stare that one associates with lunatics.

This cartoon version of The Anarchist is an enduring legacy of Haymarket. It portrays the self-proclaimed enemies of the state exactly as middle-class editors and prosecuting attorneys wanted them portrayed during the first American Red Scare: as poor, ugly, unwashed, animal-like, mentally deranged, and dangerously violent foreigners.

The premier examples, which established the basic image once and for all, appeared in newspapers and magazines the same month that the famous bomb was thrown. The fact that none of the Haymarket anarchists even vaguely resembled the stereotype did not matter in the least. All that mattered was that 1) a bomb had been thrown, and 2) anarchists had been charged with the crime.

The quaint image grew out of an anti-anarchist tradition that is actually much older than anarchism itself. "Anarchy" as a pejorative term has been traced back as far as 1539,[1] but the first person to proclaim himself an anarchist was Pierre-Joseph Proudhon, in 1840, and he seems to have originally adopted the label largely out of his predilection for paradox and scandal. There were earlier anarchists and quasi-anarchists, of course—including people as different from each other as the Englishman William Godwin (1756–1836), the Frenchman D.A.F. de Sade (1740–1814), and the American Josiah Warren (1798–1874)—but they did not use the word.

Long before Haymarket, American readers had had ample opportunity to encounter attacks on anarchy in popular literature. The republic was barely ten years old when, in 1786, a group of "Hartford Wits" brought out *The Anarchiad*, a ponderous rhymed satire with the anarchy-is-chaos theme, aimed at the poor farmers who had just taken part in Shays' Rebellion. This early propaganda was by no means leveled only or even primarily at those who opposed all government; more often than not, "anarchy" was merely a convenient term of abuse used by advocates of one form of government against proponents of other forms. In an early American best seller, Judge Hugh Henry Brackenridge denounced "the horrors of that dreadful state of anarchy, with crop after crop of atrocities"; he was referring to the Jacobin dictatorship during the French Revolution.[2]

Underlying these early expressions of hostility to anarchy is the age-old statist notion that government is all that stands between humankind and the total war of each against all. Ignorant of the non-statist and communal-property forms of many "primitive" societies, ideologists of government the more easily convinced themselves that society without government would automatically and immediately revert to bloody chaos. Such a view implied, in turn, that anyone who dared to question the usefulness of government must necessarily be mad.

That our cartoon anarchist is mad is suggested by his shaggy hair and overall raggedy appearance, though these are also meant to connote poverty and ill-breeding. The cartoon anarchist's eyes, however, leave no doubt that he is a creature utterly bereft of reason.

The "wild-eyed" expression is well known in the history of art. Readily accessible pre-Haymarket versions of it include a curious self-portrait of Gustave Courbet from 1843–44 and Gustave Doré's impression of Coleridge's *Ancient Mariner*. Pictorially it is a variant of the sorcerers' and necromancers' "evil eye," known to us through Renaissance paintings and engravings of witches, demons, devils, and tormented souls in Hell, as well as by later offshoots of this popular iconography, especially the illustrations for the early Gothic romances. The cartoon anarchist is, in fact, a direct albeit proletarianized descendant of the Gothic/Byronic villain. Like the sinister Schedoni in Ann Radcliffe's *The Italian* (1797), and like the somber rogues in Byron's long poems *The Corsair* (1813) and *Lara* (1814), the cartoon anarchist has unforgettable eyes and an unsmiling, malevolent, horror-inspiring demeanor. Like them, too, he is a monster of energy equipped with obsessive single-mindedness, an abiding hatred for society and its conventions, and an endless capacity for evildoing.

If the cartoonist's image of The Anarchist can be traced back to more or less traditional prejudices against "anarchy" and to Gothic and "shilling shocker" villains, its more immediate sources lie in the mainstream press reaction to insurgent labor after the Civil War. Anti-anarchist propaganda in the 1880s, even before Haymarket, emphasized that anarchists almost by definition were foreigners and violence-prone to a terrifying degree. Journalist J.W. Buel, in a book on Russian Nihilism published in St. Louis in 1883, pointed out that "anarchists, like violent maniacs, strike in obedience to a distracted mind, having the one desire to kill, ruin or subvert."[3] Two years later the Christian missionary Josiah Strong, in an influential racist, xenophobic, and imperialist tract, did his best to scare his conservative readers out of their wits by alluding to the radicals' interest in dynamite and arguing, "There never was a time in the history of the world when an enemy of society could work such mighty mischief as today.... We are preparing conditions which make possible a Reign of Terror that would beggar the scenes of the French Revolution."[4]

At around the same time Prof. Richard T. Ely of Johns Hopkins University was issuing panicky warnings of his own: "There are those who, when extensive and riotous strikes occur again, will remember the teachings which are entering into their flesh and blood, yes, into their very soul, and will take their muskets and their dynamite, and 'descend into the streets,' and, thinking the great day has arrived, will cast about right and left, and seek to demolish, to annihilate all the forces and resources of wealth and civilization."[5]

Each of the various components of the stereotype anarchist was thus ready to hand well before May 4, 1886. All that was needed was a sensational pretext—the Haymarket bomb provided it—to fuse them all together, definitively, into a single repulsive image made to order for front-page promotion of police and vigilante terror against militant workers and their organizations.

The Chicago martyrs themselves had virtually nothing in common with the stereotype beyond the facts that some of them wore beards, that they were mostly foreign-born and far from prosperous, and that they had openly supported the right of workers to defend themselves against police violence and hence could easily be portrayed as violent themselves. Not one of them, however, is known ever to have committed a violent deed; on the contrary, examples of their sociability and even gentleness are abundant. There is not the slightest evidence, moreover, that any of them were mentally unbalanced. All were neat and clean in appearance; their speeches and letters were articulate and thoughtful. Throughout the entire ordeal they bore themselves with remarkable dignity and forbearance. Even in the newspaper and police sketches of the prisoners, which attempted to present them at their worst—those in Capt. Schaack's book, for example—it seems hardly possible that anyone not already hopelessly biased could see any trace of a depraved monster. Wealthy young socialite Nina van Zandt wrote, "[I] entered the court, for the first time, expecting to see a fiendish looking wretch in each one of the chairs set for the prisoners, but prejudiced as I was, I could not detect an ill-looking man amongst them; several had noble faces."[6]

It is true that, in the months and especially the weeks preceding Haymarket, there were well-armed gangs of law-breaking thugs roaming the streets of Chicago—trigger-happy hoodlums who were notorious for their wanton use of violence; who regularly and for no apparent reason broke up orderly meetings of peaceable and unarmed citizens; who forced their way into men's homes, stole their property, and abused their wives and children; who beat up innocent people and shot them and killed them without cause. These were not gangs of anarchists, however, but of policemen, and their leaders were the very ones who directed the anti-anarchist hysteria: Bonfield, Ward, and Schaack.

This irony was not lost on the Haymarket prisoners. While the anarchists, who had hurt no one and had broken no law, were being portrayed as bloodthirsty criminal maniacs—as "a newly-discovered species of cannibal," as August Spies put it—the police, who were known to have committed endless acts of brutality and even murder, were feted as heroes of the hour.[7] The stereotype anarchist was thus not a mere caricature but a *complete inversion of the truth*: to the extent that the image was meant to portray mindless and excessive brutality, it fitted the anarchists not at all, but rather their bitterest enemies, the police. "You are an 'anarchist,' as you understand it," defendant Oscar Neebe said to Capt. Schaack in court; and then, addressing the judge and the rest of the prosecution, he added: "You are *all* 'anarchists,' in this sense of the word."[8]

That the guardians of the capitalist state should use, as the symbol of their most feared enemy, an image that embodies the essence of the capitalist state itself, suggests that George Orwell's *1984* "newspeak" is not so new after all, and that it even predates Hitler's "Big Lie" by nearly half a century. This is not the place to examine the interrelationship of capitalism and schizophrenia, but let us note in passing that it is perhaps not *only* a coincidence that the famous tale of *Dr. Jekyll and Mr. Hyde* was published in that fateful year of 1886.

Significantly, when Bonfield, Ward, and Schaack were removed from the police force a few years after Haymarket for trafficking in stolen goods and receiving payoffs from prostitutes, the result was not an admission on the part of newspaper editors that they might have erred in the Haymarket case, but rather a whole new wave of anti-anarchist editorials and cartoons. The firing of the crooked policemen was viewed by many as "Anarchy Triumphant" (fig. 11). When Governor Altgeld pardoned the three surviving Haymarket prisoners in 1893—with a message that fully vindicated all the defendants and excoriated Bonfield as "the man who is really responsible for the death of the

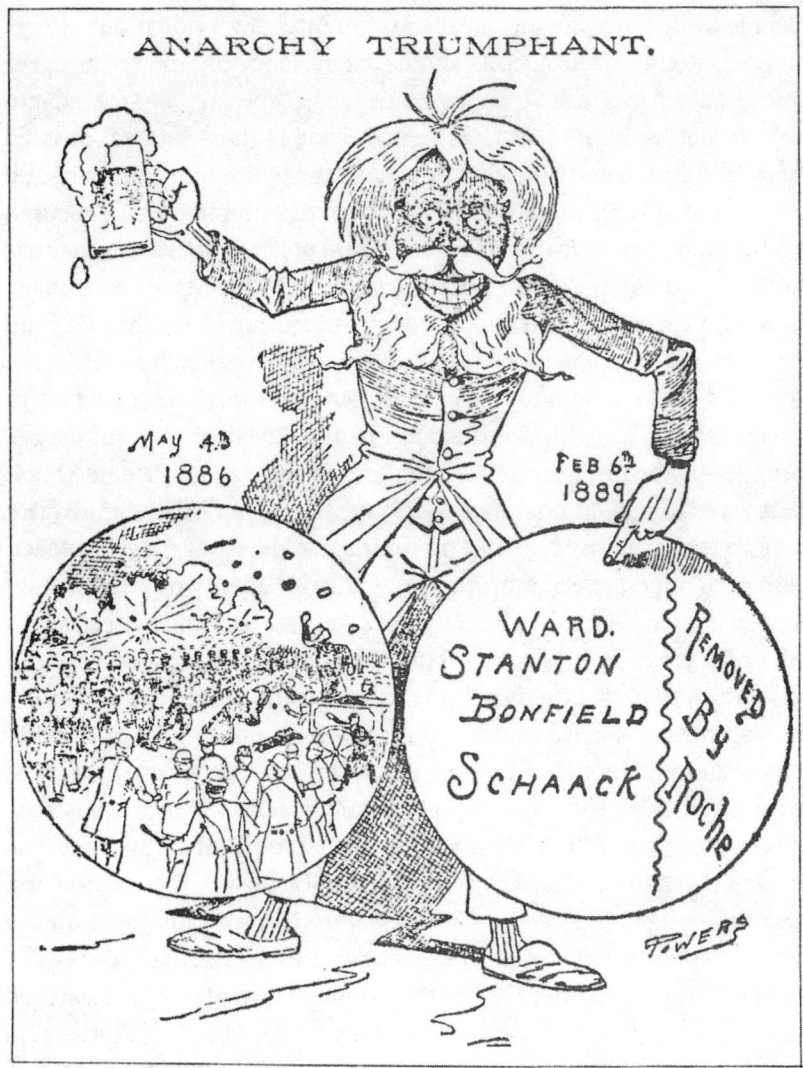

Fig. 11. "The Mayor Playing into the Hands of Officer Degan's Murderers." One newspaper's response to the firing of crooked policemen. *Cook County Herald*, February 8, 1889.

police officers" at Haymarket—editors and cartoonists attacked *him*, the governor of Illinois, as a bomb-toting, wild-eyed anarchist, and they continued to do so almost to the end of his life.[9]

The fact that the Chicago martyrs had next to nothing in common with the stereotype anarchist did not prevent the press and prosecution from pretending otherwise. Had the affair not ended so tragically, people would have laughed at the State's Attorney's ridiculous efforts to portray these courageous and excellent labor organizers as ogres and ghouls in league with Satan. Louis Lingg especially was forced into the stereotype simply because he had made bombs—indeed, boasted of it—and conducted himself throughout the police interrogations and trial with supreme intransigence. Public attention inevitably focused on the twenty-one-year-old firebrand, and police as well as journalistic accounts adjusted their descriptions of him to the readymade image of what an anarchist was supposed to look and act like. When Captain Schaack, in his *Anarchy and Anarchists* (1889), wrote, "Lingg's teeth gnashed with rage, and his eyes fairly bulged from their sockets with savage scorn" and "the arch-Anarchist looked the picture of desperation"—and again, nearly four hundred pages later in the same book, "His face became almost livid with rage, his eyes fairly snapped fire, and he fumed in his cage like an imprisoned beast of prey ... speechless with anger, every motion betray[ing] an energy of passion that was fearful to behold"—he offered not only some exquisite examples of a policeman's purple prose but also precisely the sort of frightful caricature that everybody already expected and recognized.

Of other real-life anarchists who were to one degree or another "incorporated" into the stereotype, Johann Most is not only the most obvious but also the most important and has been identified as such by Paul Avrich.[10] "The most vilified social militant of his time," as Avrich has called him, the renowned agitator was the author of a German-language *Science of Revolutionary Warfare* (a manual on the use of explosives and other weapons for urban guerrillas) and editor of the incendiary paper *Freiheit* (Freedom). The daily papers featured him as a terrifying homicidal zealot—an insane monster of destruction hell-bent on indiscriminate and wholesale arson, bomb-throwing, and bloody murder. Countless German workers who knew and admired the "Rabelais of the Proletariat," and who loved his rousing songs and biting wit, would hardly have recognized the capitalists' caricature of their venerable comrade who had been twice elected to the Reichstag before he came to the United States in 1882.

By a strange and amusing coincidence, an engraved portrait of Most was included in the May 1886 issue of *Frank Leslie's Popular Monthly*, which was already on the stands when the Haymarket bomb was thrown. The picture of Most is sensitive, dignified, and plainly

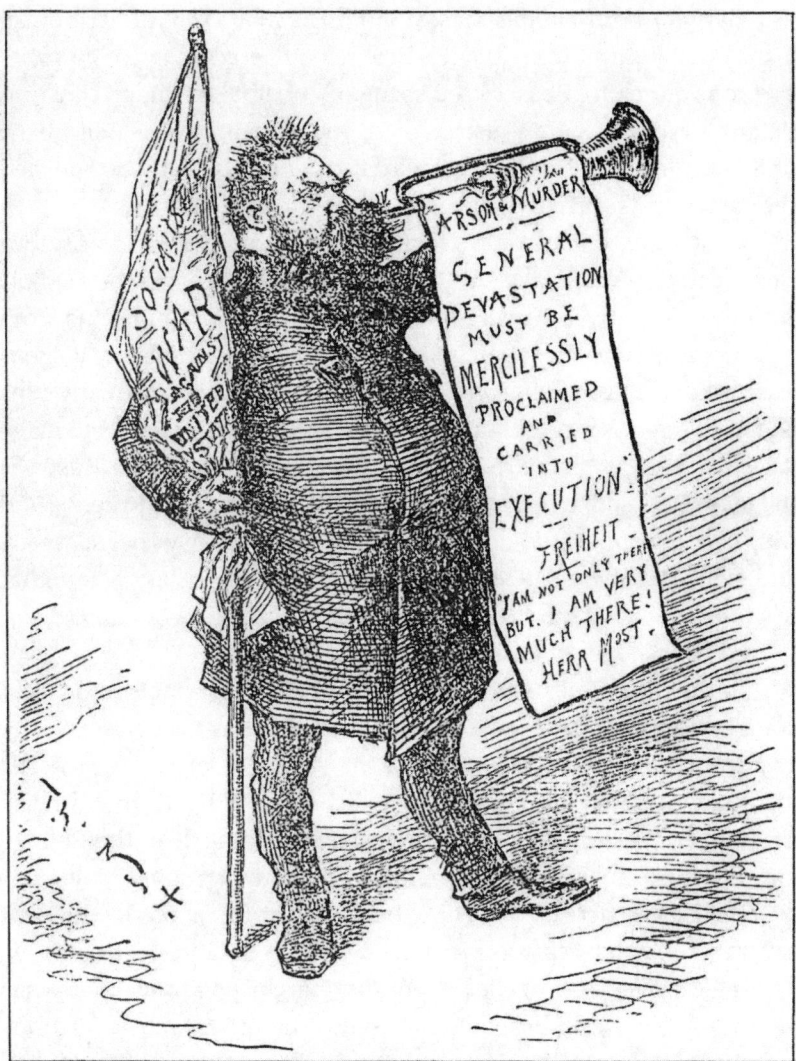

Fig. 12. Anti-Most Cartoon by Thomas Nast, *Harper's Weekly*, May 22, 1886.

captioned: "John Most, Socialist Leader." The accompanying article explained, "There is no risk of Anarchical Socialism ever becoming a serious danger among us." Later the same month, the old German anarchist was being portrayed very differently throughout the land. Thomas Nast, the most famous American cartoonist of the nineteenth century, did a whole series of anti-Most cartoons for *Harper's Weekly*, featuring Most as a disheveled, pistol-waving, bomb-carrying luna-tic—and a coward to boot).

German-born Thomas Nast (1840–1902) was a prolific cartoonist; his work spans over four decades. Best remembered today for his many cartoons attacking Boss Tweed's ring of corrupt Tammany Hall politicians in New York, he is also credited with devising the classic image of Santa Claus. It was Nast, more than anyone else, who established the cartoonist's stereotype anarchist.

Nast's anarchist was a variation of a more general anti-labor cartoon image—often labeled "Knights of Labor" but sometimes simply "Agitator"—that was already familiar when the news bulletins from Chicago suggested the anarchist as a far more serviceable scapegoat. Nast, who had been doing anti-labor cartoons at least since early 1871, had to change his representative Knight/Agitator only slightly to make it serve anti-anarchist purposes. His anarchists, except when Most was the model, tended to be physically much thinner than his Knights, and they had, of course, a wilder look in their eyes. But their overall seedy and malicious character remained intact. It is interesting to note that with the advent of the cartoon anarchist, the Knights of Labor disappeared from stage center in the world of cartoons.

In the four months from mid-May to mid-September 1886 Nast contributed nearly a dozen anti-anarchist cartoons to *Harper's Weekly*. They show that his hatred of anarchism was as obvious and as total as his ignorance of it. His anarchists do little more than trample on the US flag, throw bombs, and carry placards reading "Kill the Police!" and "Burn the Town!" For Nast, anarchists were thoroughly dehumanized devils who deserved nothing but death at the hands of the Law; several of his grisly cartoons feature a gallows equipped with nooses. The inglorious career of the stereotype anarchist was well on its way.

Many hundreds, probably thousands of anti-anarchist cartoons followed. All through the Haymarket trial and all through the ensuing defense, clemency, and amnesty campaigns these monotonous editorial drawings bombarded the American public, demanding death for the Haymarket prisoners, death and/or deportation of other anarchists, and assorted repressive measures against labor radicals in general.

A product of America's first Red Scare, the cartoon anarchist has turned up at every subsequent Red Scare as well as at every major and many a minor labor struggle. Altgeld's pardon provoked a deluge in 1893, and so did the Pullman Strike the following year. Coxey's Army of the unemployed and Bryan's campaign for the presidency in '96

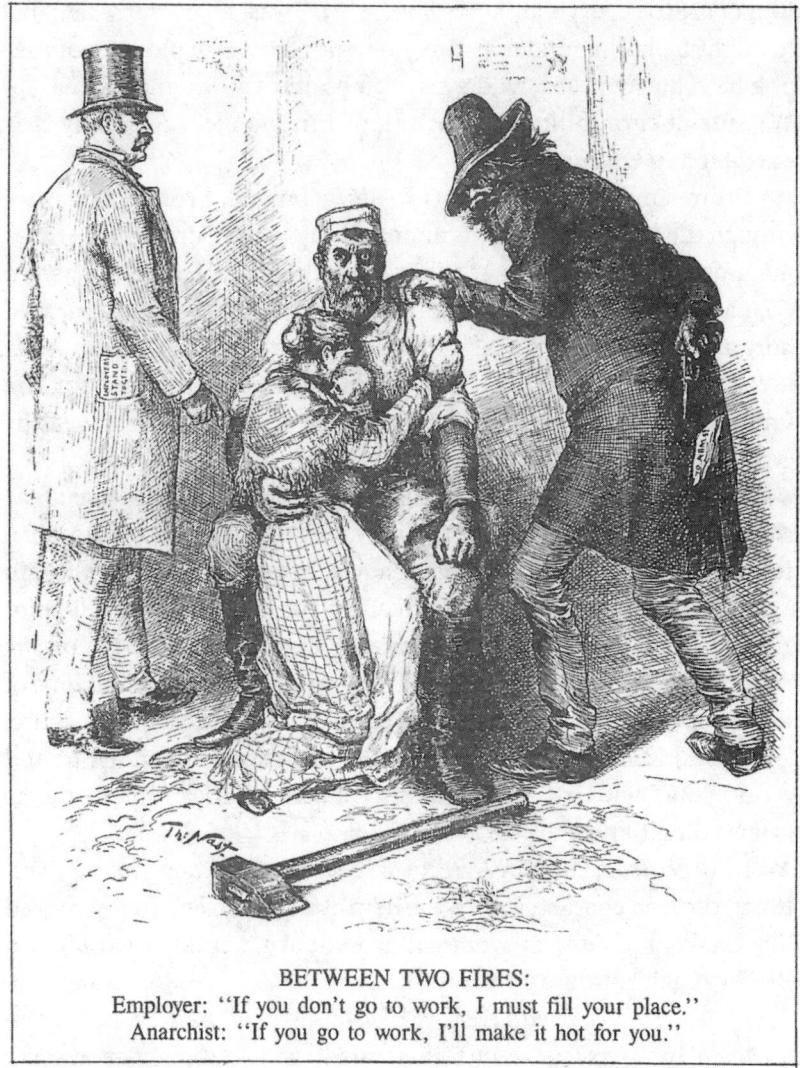

BETWEEN TWO FIRES:
Employer: "If you don't go to work, I must fill your place."
Anarchist: "If you go to work, I'll make it hot for you."

Fig. 13. An early version of the stereotype by Thomas Nast, *Harper's Weekly*, May 22, 1886.

brought forth yet another wave, as did the series of anarchist attentats in France in the 1890s, and Leon Czolgosz's assassination of President McKinley in 1901.

The great labor defense cases—the McNamaras, Mooney and Billings, Sacco and Vanzetti, and others—showed that the bomb-toting cartoon character was always available for active duty in the anti-labor press. He rarely wore a label identifying himself as an anarchist. He didn't *have* to—everybody *knew* who he *really* was, no matter what label he might be hiding under at the moment. The same old stereotype—long hair, bushy beard, wild eyes, bombs and all—often passed as an IWW member or militant trade unionist in the 1910s and early '20s, and later as a Communist.

From time to time his nationality changed. From Haymarket through the early 1900s he was almost always a beer-drinking German, like most of the Haymarket Eight, and like those fearful monsters Most and Altgeld. After 1905, and especially after 1917, he appeared more and more frequently as a Russian. During World War I, however, he went back to being German again, now working hard for the Kaiser and receiving large payments from the suspiciously wealthy I-Won't-Works.

Very early on, the cartoon anarchist branched out into other areas of literary and artistic life. In the very year of the Haymarket police riot he made his debut in the dime novel, to which he returned again and again. Just to make sure that readers got the point, the full-color cover of *The Red Flag, or The Anarchists of Chicago*, number 192 of *The New York Detective Library*, featured two red flags and five bombs, one of them exploding (fig. 14). We are informed that, at an anarchist meeting described in the book, "the men in the audience were unkempt and wild-looking" and that "there was not a native American among them." As if we didn't know!

In *Belle Boyd, the Girl Detective: A Story of Chicago and the West* (1891), the lead character, with the help of a local street urchin named Billy the Waif, triumphs over terrible Red Mag, her dog Death, and a whole gang of ruthless dynamiters.

An issue of *Old Sleuth Weekly* titled *The War of the Reds, or Trailing the Bomb Throwers* (1911), introduces us to a vicious gang of Russian anarchists led by a blackmailing hypnotist, Alceste Valieres. Attractive and wealthy young Honora Gannett was briefly a member, but she assures the Old Sleuth that she had been *forced* to join: "I met [Alceste] at one of the Settlement houses ... where I used to have a girls' class. His socialistic patter first amused me and then interested me and before I knew it, I found that when I was near him, I could have no thoughts of my own." If this sounds merely idiotic and puerile, it should not be forgotten that for many years the Chicago police regarded Jane Addams's Hull House as a hotbed of anarchy.

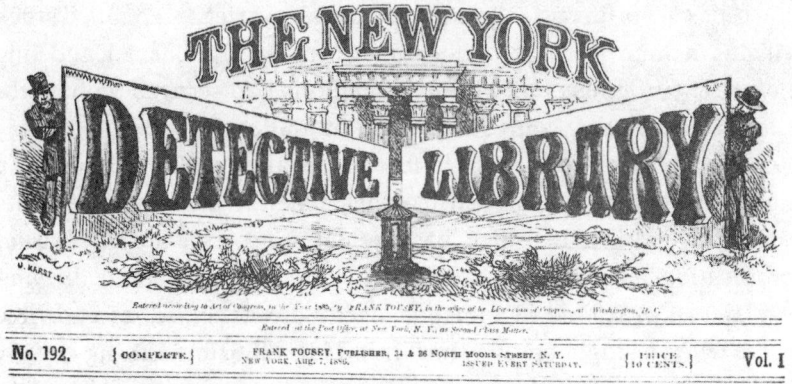

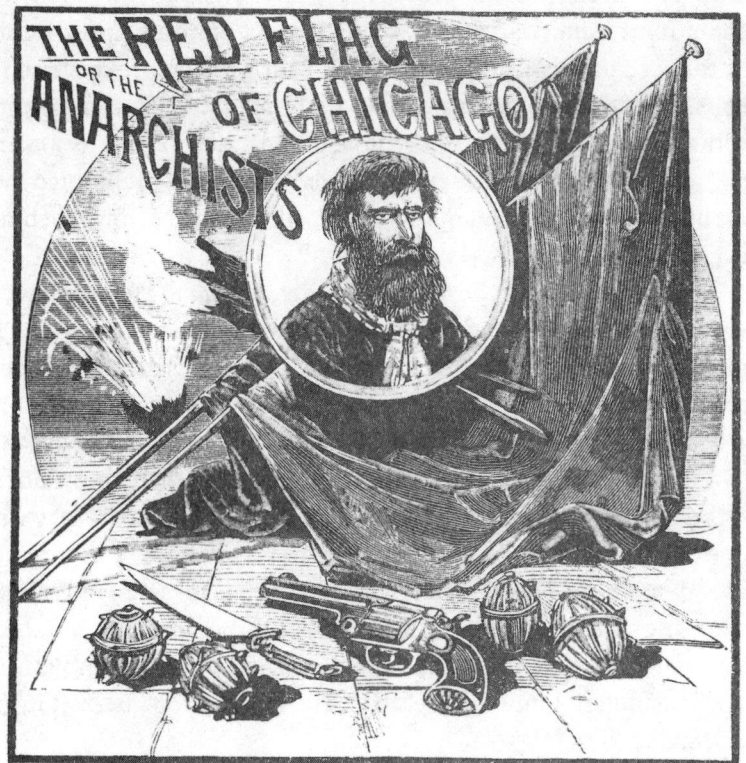

Fig. 14. *The Red Flag, or The Anarchists of Chicago, The New York Detective Library*, vol. 1, no. 192, August 7, 1886, cover.

One of the most prolific dime novelists, the onetime soldier of fortune Prentiss Ingraham—best known for a two-volume tale of the pirate Jean Lafitte that he plagiarized from his own father—devoted several of his Buffalo Bill tales to combating the anarchist menace.

Anarchists, in fact—the editorial cartoon variety—remained stock villains in dime novels as long as dime novels were published, and long before their demise our wild-eyed hellions had secured a niche for themselves in other genres of popular literature.

Retaining all the standard features of the graphic original, the literary version of the cartoon anarchist added an important element—*conspiracy*—which, of course, had been at the core of the Haymarket prosecution, but which had been difficult to convey by means of drawing.

Here is a curious phenomenon: having given themselves a horrible scare when a single bomb went off in May 1886, and having eagerly and gullibly swallowed the prosecution's fiction of a "conspiracy" to account for it, American readers avidly sought more and more fiction that told of hundreds and thousands of infinitely more destructive bombs being hurled by throngs of anarchists involved in gigantic worldwide conspiracies of incredible complexity. In the 1890s and early 1900s there appeared several novels featuring anarchist-led invasions of vast armies of dynamiters equipped with huge flying machines specially designed for total war (fig. 15).[11]

The classic of this type is undoubtedly *Hartmann the Anarchist, or The Doom of the Great City*, by E. Douglas Fawcett (London, 1893). The reader knows right off that Hartmann is an anarchist for he is a "bushy-bearded man with straight piercing glance" and of "cruel hardness." No one could be surprised to learn that he became an anarchist because he wanted to revenge himself on the human race, "which produced and then wearied" him. His followers' faces, of course, are "filthy with grime and brutal to a degree." One comrade affirms: "I live for the roar of dynamite." The plan of Hartmann's aerial invasion of England is thus summarized: "During the tempests of bombs, the anarchists below will fire the streets in all directions, rouse up the public, and let loose pandemonium upon earth." The object? You guessed it: "to wreck civilization."[12]

The Angel of the Revolution: A Tale of Coming Terror by the once-popular English science fiction writer George Griffith (London, 1894) is a Hartmann-like tale but nearly twice as long and painted on a wider canvas. It is of interest chiefly because it builds on the suspicion shared by Bonfield and Schaack, and later taken up by J. Edgar Hoover and the John Birch Society, that the Red Conspiracy is in fact vastly larger and more inclusive than most people have been willing to admit: "That

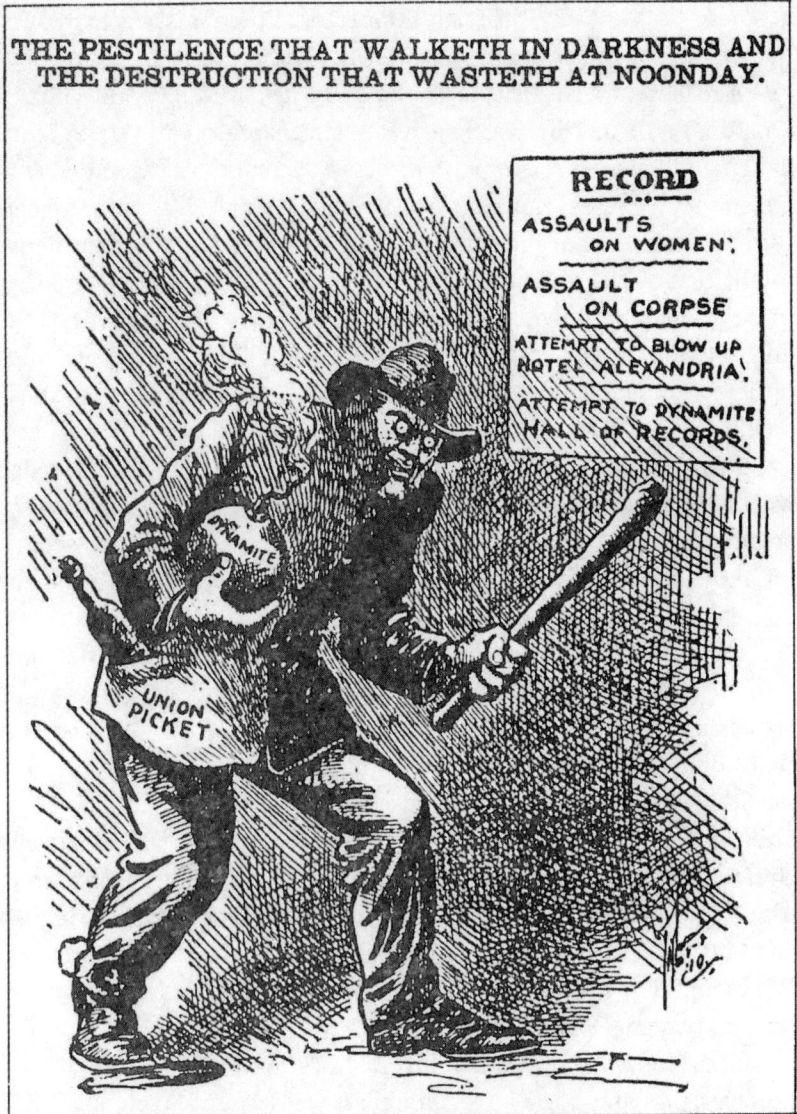

THE PESTILENCE THAT WALKETH IN DARKNESS AND THE DESTRUCTION THAT WASTETH AT NOONDAY.

RECORD

ASSAULTS ON WOMEN.

ASSAULT ON CORPSE

ATTEMPT TO BLOW UP HOTEL ALEXANDRIA.

ATTEMPT TO DYNAMITE HALL OF RECORDS.

DYNAMITE

UNION PICKET

Fig. 15. This cartoon appeared in the labor-hating *Los Angeles Times* in 1910. Soon afterward, a bombing by two pro-union brothers destroyed the *Times* building.

which is known to the outside world as the Terror is an international secret society underlying and directing the operations of the various bodies known as Nihilists, Anarchists, Socialists—in fact, all those organizations which have for their object the reform or destruction, by peaceful or violent means, of Society as it is at present constituted."

Yep—the Women's Christian Temperance Union was never anything but a front for the *Lehr und Wehr Verein*.

A real literary curiosity is *The Electric Thief*, by Neil Wynn Williams (Boston, 1906), in which we meet a Russian anarchist with "dark," "brilliant," and "piercing" eyes who directs a "remarkable, widely-spread conspiracy" to steal—good grief!—*electricity*!—and on a massive scale too, "by means of accumulators." The idea was to gather immense quantities of the stuff and then to begin "selling it below market price in the large towns," using the income for "propagation of the anarchistic cause by emissary and document." With the aid of a huge underground electromagnet and cleverly used microphones, these dastardly fiends bring London to an economic and political standstill by staging sound riots: "As the atmosphere grew more and more loaded with vibrations, scores of human brains proved unable to stand the strain and horror of this strange siege by sound." This does seem a lot like the world we live in today, doesn't it?—except that it is not the anarchists who have the microphones.

Over the years, anarchist villains continued skulking their way into virtually every category of popular literature. They can even be found as bit players in books whose titles offer not the slightest hint that bomb-throwing terrorists are hiding within. *Under the Ocean to the South Pole, or The Strange Cruise of the Submarine "Wonder"* by a ghostwriter under the house name Roy Rockwood (1907), part of The Great Marvel Series of "good books for boys," includes a subplot in which the two lead characters are mistaken for the sons of an English anarchist who had blown up a hotel "in an attempt to assassinate Lord Peckham." The mystery of the "Boy Anarchists" is cleared up only in the last two pages of the book.

Anarchists are not common in boys' and girls' series books, however, probably because the moralists who assumed control of such publications from the start would have regarded anything to do with anarchism as unsuitable for juvenile readers. The dime novel had given us the boy student nihilist in the late nineteenth century, but anyone who proposed a "Boy Anarchist Series" to the syndicate that owns Nancy Drew and the Hardy Boys would have been lucky to get off with a sternly worded rejection slip and a friendly visit or two from the FBI.

The immense field of pulp fiction—direct successor to the dime novel—featured anarchist bad guys aplenty, but they added little to the stereotype and in fact actually diluted it considerably. Pulp anarchists increasingly tended to be interchangeable with any and all other villains, less interested in attacking capitalists and destroying government than in pilfering diamonds and robbing banks. Probably in part because of the formulistic character of so much of this writing, the original anti-radical propaganda motivation for including such characters in fiction was sometimes discernible only in the barest undertones. A pulp writer who dashed off full-length novels at the rate of one or two or even more a month, and whose hero had just vanquished—in one story after another—river pirates, counterfeiters, jewel thieves, opium smugglers, a mad scientist, cattle rustlers, kidnappers, and train robbers, would almost inevitably introduce an anarchist bomb-thrower or two into one of his stories, sooner or later, just for variety, and without necessarily taking the trouble to sermonize, as had so many of the dime novelists, about the divine goodness of government, the eternal nobility of the police, and the hideous evils perpetrated by the demons of "mutual aid."

Satan's Death Blast, by Grant Stockbridge, published in the pulp magazine *The Spider* in June 1934, has many of the trappings of cartoon-anarchist terrorism. It features a gang led by a criminal mastermind known as The Devil who has at his disposal a supply of tiny electronically controlled super bombs, prepared from a substance distilled from electric eels by German chemists working in subterranean laboratories. "Police stations, electric plants, radio and telephone exchanges" were "blown into the dust! ... the city was being looted, house by house, bank by bank.... A mad mob, filled with the mania of destruction, infuriated against all civilized authority." Here is a lurid tale firmly and unmistakably in the tradition of *Hartmann the Anarchist*. However, apart from a single reference to the fact that "absolute anarchy reigned" after one of the bombings, the book contains not even a hint of the ism cherished by all those bearded, long-haired, bedraggled, and wild-eyed characters we have come to know so well.

The fact is that while the stereotype anarchist has endured in the world of cartoons, where traditional symbolic representation is a recognized and even indispensable convention, it proved to be only a transient in literature. Even before the end of World War I, fiction writers who wanted to write about labor violence or revolutionary conspiracies had begun to call their villains Wobblies—as in the case of Zane Grey's vicious tale *The Desert of Wheat* (1919)—and, of course, increasingly as the years went by, Bolsheviki and Communists. The stories had much in common with the old anti-anarchist novels; they were xenophobic, anti-radical, and filled with a lot of superpatriotic rhetoric. But the anarchist, as such, was retired from the role of leading monster in favor of newer-style radicals who were, at least for the time being, better news-makers.

A much later example of anti-anarchist fiction—a sleazy science fiction paperback, *Anarchaos* by Curt Clark (1967)—shows how thoroughly incomprehension and hatred of anarchism can be set forth without recourse to the old stereotype. Set on a planet whose founding colonists relied on Bakunin's writings "as the core of their social philosophy," *Anarchaos* introduces us to an entire population of "anarchists" who, in the absence of Law and Authority, seem to spend most of their time enslaving and murdering each other. The chief interest of the book lies in the naive clarity with which it reveals the absurd horror to which the authoritarian fear of freedom inevitably leads. At the end of the story the anti-anarchist hero actually becomes a mad bomber, no less. He places bombs all over the planet, hoping thereby not only to kill as many anarchists as possible but also to destroy their transportation and communication systems. The fact that countless innocent people were to perish in these bombings fazes our hater of anarchy not at all: "Tourists might be slaughtered, missionaries and merchants might be slaughtered, engineers and prospectors and all honest work men might be slashed and hacked ... but now something was going to happen"—that is, the forces of interplanetary government would have to step in and impose state power on this unpleasant population, or whatever fraction of it managed to survive the anti-anarchist's devastation.[13] The book is a kind of unintentional parable of US foreign policy in the Third World.

In literature the anarchist stereotype held on for about thirty years; his film career was considerably shorter. Around 1907–8 he had the starring role—a typically crazed, slovenly, drunken, wild-eyed, foreign-looking agitator inciting the mob to violence—in a series of anti-labor propaganda shorts produced by open-shop employers: *Lulu's Anarchists, The Riot, Gus the Anarchist, The Dynamiters, The Murderous Anarchist,* and *Dough and Dynamite.*[14] A writer for the *Cleveland Citizen* suspected that "behind this class of pictures if the veil is removed would be the National Association of Manufacturers." The brevity of these films precluded the outrageous plots and incredible adventures that gave at least a semblance of substance to the dime novels. Apart from their significance as ridiculous anti-labor documents, these early examples of the anarchist in cinema are of slight interest.

Some fifteen years later, however, Buster Keaton's classic two-reeler, *Cops* (1922), included a marvelous sequence that must be counted as one of the most memorable episodes involving the anarchist stereotype in any medium: In the course of a police parade, an anarchist hurls a large, round, black bomb at the cops, but it falls short and lands next to Keaton, who, however, fails to notice it. After several suspenseful seconds, Keaton sees the bomb at last, whereupon he nonchalantly lights his cigarette with it. Then, as if it were a burnt match, he tosses the bomb aside—at the police!

This hilarious moment from Keaton's *Cops* highlights a ramification of the anarchist stereotype we have not yet considered: *humor*. The early anti-anarchist cartoons by Nast and others presumably were meant to be funny and may well have provoked an occasional chuckle from railroad magnates, bank presidents, Pinkertons, and others who shared their view of the world. But such graphic effusions, so narrowly didactic and malevolently shrill, really belong—at best—to the domain of wit or sarcasm, for they are utterly devoid of the *elevating, liberating,* and *rebellious* qualities that theorists from Hegel through Freud to Breton invariably have attributed to genuine humor.[15]

Keaton's *Cops* demonstrates an important point: that the humorists' use of the anarchist stereotype differs appreciably and in some cases totally from its editorial/propagandistic use. The anarchist in *Cops* is neither frightening nor otherwise repulsive because the humor of the situation transcends such conformist reactions. Moreover, Keaton, the hero of the film, proceeds (innocently enough) to carry out the stereotype anarchist's deed—and thus in a sense becomes an anarchist stereotype himself, or at least an accomplice thereof: very much so in the eyes of the cops, hundreds of whom spend the rest of the film pursuing him every which way.

Cops is in fact a wildly *anti*-cop film: a glorification of the freedom of the individual against the forces of institutional repression symbolized by the police. And it would not be an exaggeration to affirm that all of Buster Keaton's films—indeed, all the great film comedies—are pervaded

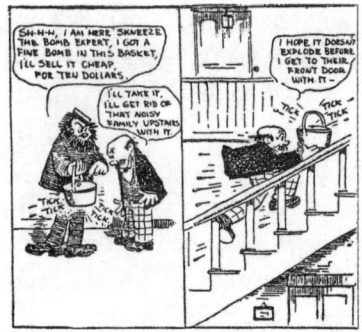 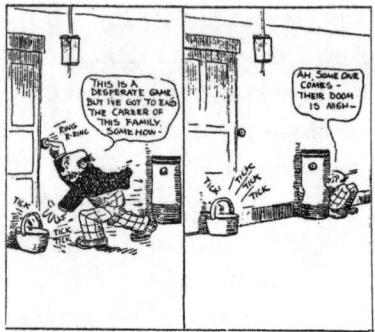

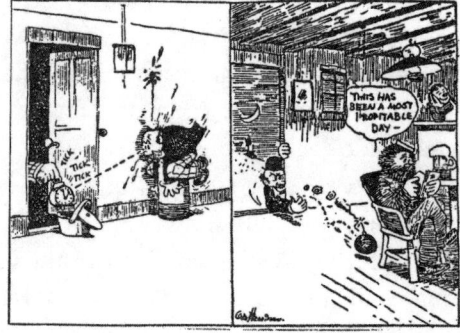

Fig. 16. An episode from George Herriman's strip *The Family Upstairs* (1910).

by much the same spirit. In the films of Charlie Chaplin, Fatty Arbuckle, Ben Turpin, Harry Langdon, Laurel and Hardy, the Marx Brothers, the Three Stooges—and in the early Bugs Bunny and Woody Woodpecker cartoons—cops, bureaucrats, government figures, and military officers seem to exist primarily to be kicked in the pants, knocked down, hit in the face with pies, and in countless other ways heckled, abused, and made fun of. When Antonin Artaud hailed the Marx Brothers' *Monkey Business* as "a hymn to anarchy and wholehearted revolt,"[16] he hit on one of the most striking signs of the times: that, from the days that we now call the "golden age" of film comedy, the silver screen has bristled with elements of an authentically anarchist attitude.[17]

The anarchist intrusion into American humor did not start in films, however, but in the columns of the daily newspapers, where so much of the best—as well as the worst—writing of the late nineteenth century first saw the light of day.

Finley Peter Dunne, in his "Mr. Dooley" column in the *Chicago Evening Post* for September 25, 1897, told of listening to socialist street-corner speakers who advocated the use of "dinnymite." "I'm not afraid,"

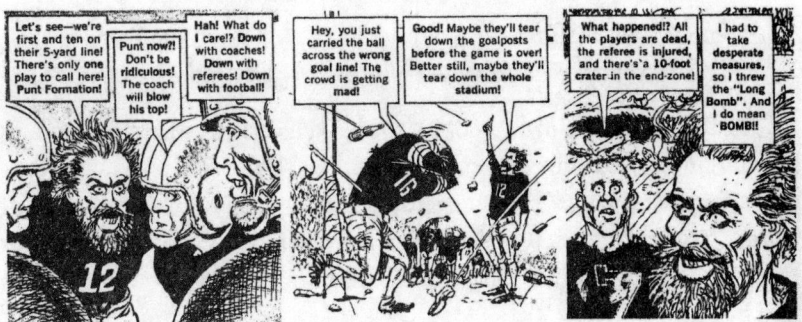

Fig. 17. "The Anarchist Pro-Football Quarterback," in *Mad* magazine, mid-1960s (artist: George Woodbridge; writer: Frank Jacobs).

says Mr. Dooley. "Th' American rivolutionist is th' most peaceful man on earth. He's as law-abidin', as ca'm an' as good-natured as anny livin' man. Did ye iver hear iv wan iv thim torch an' bomb lads swingin' a torch or peggin' a bomb? Not wan. After they're through th' little song an' dance on Sundah afthernoon they go home an' play with th' babies."

In another column from the same period, titled "On Anarchists" and reprinted in *Mr. Dooley in Peace and War* (1899), "Mr. Dooley" concluded a fable with the moral "arnychists is sewer-gas"—that is, anarchists are not the cause but the result of social conditions.[18]

George Wilbur Peck, a union printer who became governor of Wisconsin, introduced anarchists into several of his popular "Peck's Bad Boy" series, which grew out of a column originally run in his own paper, *Peck's Sun*. When the Bad Boy and his pa visit Switzerland in *Peck's Bad Boy Abroad* (1904), they quickly run into the familiar stereotype: "There are more anarchists in Geneva than anything else, and they look hairy and wild-eyed, and they plot to kill kings and drink beer out of two-quart jars." The Bad Boy's pa thinks it would be a "good joke" to pass himself off as a fugitive wanted for attempting to assassinate someone, so the Bad Boy promptly starts a rumor:

[Dad was] wanted for attempting to blow up the president of the United States by selling him baled hay soaked in a solution of dynamite and nitroglycerine.... It wasn't two hours before long-haired people were inviting dad to dinners, and the same night he was taken to a den where a lot of anarchists were reveling, and dad reveled till almost morning. When he came back to the hotel he said his hosts got all the money he had with him, through some game he didn't understand, but he understood it was to go into a fund to support deserving anarchists and dynamiters.

In *Peck's Bad Boy in an Airship* (1908) Pa is again suspected of being an anarchist, "and since the assassination of the king and crown prince of Portugal the police had overhauled his baggage in his room several times." Later the Bad Boy sets off a firecracker. "The police came in to ... find the anarchist who threw the bomb," and a good time was had by all.

Ambrose Bierce's specific references to anarchists and socialists are neither numerous nor humorous, but his sharpest barbs were directed against government, politicians, religion, business, law, the police, the military. In view of his prestige as a master humorist in his later years, it seems certain that his *Devil's Dictionary*, started in 1869 and continued at intervals through the first decade of this century, contributed significantly to the diffusion of generally nonconformist and particularly anti-authoritarian sentiments. Notwithstanding Bierce's peculiar pseudo-aristocratic cynicism, many of his definitions would not have been out of place in *The Alarm* or the *Arbeiter-Zeitung*:

> *Arrest*: Formally to detain one accused of unusualness.
> *Arrested*: Caught criming without the money to satisfy the policeman.
> *Commerce*: A kind of transaction in which A plunders from B the goods of C, and for compensation B picks the pocket of D of money belonging to E.
> *Jury*: A number of persons appointed by a court to assist the attorneys in preventing law from degenerating into justice.
> *Trial*: A formal inquiry designed to prove and put upon the record the blameless character of judges, advocates and jurors.

A later newspaper humorist, Don Marquis, went so far as to have his most famous character, Archy the cockroach, declare himself an anarchist. In one story the six-legged libertarian sets out to foment an insects' revolution. Silly? Of course! But it was a kind of silliness unthinkable in the 1880s.

Marquis's *Archy's Life of Mehitabel* (1933), in which the roach's anarchist agitation plays a role, was illustrated by George Herriman, whose sublime *Krazy Kat* is widely regarded as the greatest comic strip of all time.[19] Comic strip artists quickly followed their humor-columnist colleagues in perceiving the endless possibilities of the stereotype anarchist in "gag" situations. Herriman, Harry Hershfield, and Gus Mager are only a few of the Old Masters of the comic page who appropriated the old editorial cartoon character for new and very different purposes of their own. Even Frederick Burr Opper, who did some cold-blooded anti-anarchist editorial cartoons from the late '80s through the '90s, in later years, as he saw the monopolists strangle what little was left of America's democratic institutions, came to view radicals less maliciously while portraying "plutocracy" with all the savage humor at his disposal.[20]

The humor of "Mr. Dooley," Peck, Bierce—and of Herriman and other comic strip artists—extracted the poison from the established anarchist stereotype. Their anarchists are still long-haired and wild-eyed, and they still carry bombs, but they tend to be funny rather than fiendish. More importantly, by allowing these funny anarchists to encounter funny cops and funny capitalists, humorists and comic strip artists helped to expose the hypocrisy and meanness—and especially the ridiculousness—of so much of the prevailing "constituted authority."

The fact that an anarchist, or at least an anarchic, humor has flourished in the popular media does not mean, of course, that the creators of this humor have been anarchists, or even sympathizers with anarchism. Indeed, a few outstanding comedians have actually avowed reactionary views: W.C. Fields and Jonathan Winters are examples. But what is important is that their consciously retrograde attitudes rarely affect the quality of their humor, as such, which in fact retains the provocatively emancipatory essence of humor at its best. One of the most humorous things about the dialectics of humor is that it proceeds without, and often in spite of, the conscious intentions of the humorist.

That humor—as a broad social phenomenon—should increasingly provide refuge for genuinely anarchist ideas and aspirations is not really surprising when one considers the inevitable instability of repressive ideology in the modern world. Throughout this century in most countries, and especially in the United States, anarchism has not been "taken seriously" as a movement, a body of ideas, a critique of society, a way of life—except by rare individuals and small, widely scattered groups. Precisely because it has not been taken seriously

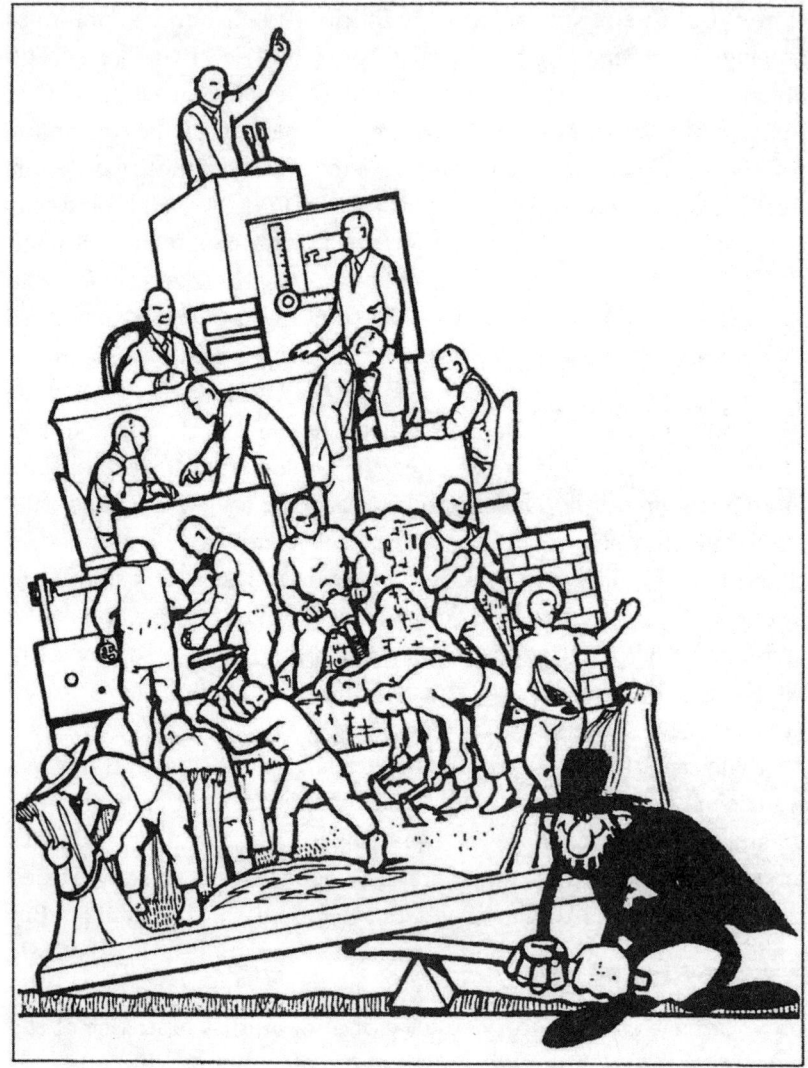

Fig. 18. Anarchik at work: Cartoon by Roberto Ambrosoli, c. mid-1960s.

by the leading authorities on seriousness, it has often found its best transmission belt to a larger public in uproarious humor.

Predictably, the worldwide reawakening of social radicalism that began in the 1960s revived the old anarchist stereotype—directed now against "campus anarchy," "black ghetto anarchy," and a sickeningly ill-defined "terrorism." But this time there was—lo!—something new under the sun. It is no secret that the "new radicalism" in its initial

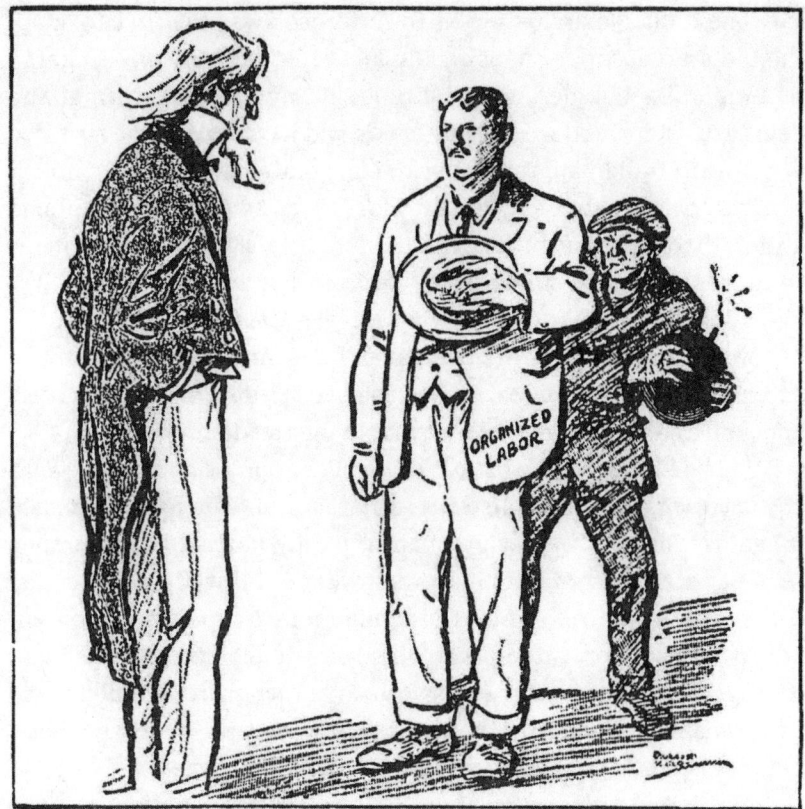

Fig. 19. Uncle Sam: "You are all right, my friend, but who is that behind your back?" Cartoon by Rollin Kirby in the New York *Evening Sun*.

heyday reflected a profoundly radical libertarian tendency; not accidentally, the anarchist movement also enjoyed its greatest resurgence in decades during the same years. It is well known, too, that one of the principal ways in which the New Left differed from the Old was in the degree to which it drew its inspiration from popular culture—and from humor above all. Many "new radicals" owed as much to Tex Avery, Harpo Marx, Ernie Kovacs, and *Little Lulu* as to any social theorist, and not a few found their appreciation of Karl Marx's *Capital* heightened and deepened by Carl Barks's studies of the world's richest duck.[21]

In such conditions, it might have been anticipated that the old editorial cartoonists' anti-anarchist, anti-labor, anti-radical stereotype was destined to change. What actually happened, however, was even funnier and better: the old image was seized by *radicals* and turned against the upholders of Law 'n' Order.

The Italian anarchist Roberto Ambrosoli was the first to adapt the old stereotype for specifically anarchist purposes. His character Anarchik—bearded, long-haired, wild-eyed, bomb-toting, and delightful—appeared in the mid-1960s and has flourished ever since, not only in Italian anarchist periodicals but also in radical publications all over the world.[22] Anarchik's merry adventures in applied anti-authoritarianism have in turn inspired many cartoonists in many countries to develop similar characters of their own (fig. 18).

Today, we might say, following Hegel's *Phenomenology*, that the old stereotype is no longer the slave of another, doomed to stoical submission to a reified reality, but has mastered its onetime masters and surged forth anew as an image of living freedom.

Humor in the service of revolution! The appropriation of the anarchist stereotype by anarchists and other radicals who have unleashed it against the very worldview that originally nurtured it is surely a glimmer of the Haymarket martyrs' revenge at last (fig. 19). Against the *esprit de sérieux* with which the administrative apparatus of contemporary wage slavery attempts to delude itself and everyone else that its reign is safe and sound, Ambrosoli and other anarchist and radical cartoonists have demonstrated once again, in their own way, that a burst of laughter has the unsettling effect of—*dynamite!*

Fig. 20. Roberto Ambrosoli: Anarchik poses the question.

6

Writing on the Telephone

Reprinted from Franklin Rosemont, *An Open Entrance to the Shut Palace of Wrong Numbers* (Chicago: Surrealist Editions, 2003), 15–22.

———

Searching high, low, and in between for clues, hints, suggestions, rumors—*anything* that might shed a ray of light on the mysteries of Wrong Numbers—I inevitably stumbled into numerous dead ends and detours. Once, in a far-from-pleasant mood combining lethargy, boredom, frustration, and a decidedly pessimistic humor, I undertook a side-trip into the obscure domain known as the "literature of the telephone." For several listless and exhausting weeks I read, voluminously albeit haphazardly, everything I was able to find (around the house, at secondhand bookstores, at nearby libraries) pertaining to the subject of telephony. I read histories, biographies, encyclopedia entries, journal articles, and even consulted a few technical works.

Much of this material was unbelievably dull, superficial, and repetitive—and none of it mentioned Wrong Numbers. Here and there, however, I found a book or article of real interest, such as Robert Hopper's charming 1992 sociological study, *Telephone Conversation*, and a few others that at least contained curious bits of telephone lore.

Best of all, however, was a splendid article by the distinguished historian/biographer Frances Winwar, in which she argued (convincingly, in my view) that the true inventor of the telephone was not Alexander Graham Bell, as is still widely believed in the United States, but rather an Italian immigrant, Antonio Meucci (1808–82). According to this well-documented study—published in the September/October 1976 issue of the Chicago-based magazine *La Parola del Popolo*—Bell was a child of two in Edinburgh when "Meucci first heard the sound of the human voice transmitted by electricity in 1849."

Meucci is an altogether fascinating character. Active in the Italian revolutionary cause, he was a close friend of Giuseppe Garibaldi, who in fact lived at Meucci's house in Staten Island during his American years. Among his thirty-odd other inventions was a type of hygrometer that is still in wide use today.

Meucci originally named his telephone the *telegrafo parlante* (speaking telegraph) and later shortened it to the more euphonious *teletrofono*. Written up at length in the New York *Eco d'Italia* in 1850, his invention was also featured in well-attended public demonstrations. For several years, as Winwar tells it, the Meucci Telephone Company provided "highly satisfactory service to some two hundred subscribers in Elizabeth, New Jersey." Between 1850 and 1862 he designed no less than thirty different models of the phone. Too poor to afford a patent, he later—after a series of personal calamities, including a ruinous fire and declining health—sold the prototypes to a telegraph company whose directors in turn gave them to Bell, who then patented Meucci's invention as his own.

Frances Winwar's pioneering defense of Meucci has since been fully vindicated by other historians, most notably Basilio Catania, whose research has drawn extensively on Meucci's diagrams and other rare documents in the National Archives. The evidence for Meucci has proved so strong that the US Congress, on the 15th of June 2002, officially acknowledged him as the true inventor of the telephone.

Thus Alexander Graham Bell, celebrated for six generations as *the* inventor of the phone, has been definitively exposed as an impostor. As has happened so often throughout the history of class society, the *wrong person* got the credit, the fame, and the money that rightly belonged to someone else. We know now that for more than a century, all that we were told about the history of the phone—the "standard literature on the subject"—was based on lies. Much more is involved here than the obvious fact that the history of the telephone needs to be rewritten. The very meaning of "telephony" and the role of the phone in our society are also called into question. The huge contrast between the prosperous, well-connected, boastful Bell and the quiet, unassuming Meucci, an unswerving radical, fluent only in Italian, and destitute in his later years, is quite revealing in this regard, for their conflicting personalities are reflected in their divergent views on the telephone.

For Meucci, the telephone was fundamentally democratic, almost anarchic—an instrument to facilitate communication among friends and family, to bring people together, to expand humankind's spirit of solidarity and cooperation. For Bell, it was above all an instrument of commerce and power—a device that was not only highly profitable but also served to strengthen government, bureaucracy, and in a broader sense, all forms of social obedience and conformity. Bell's authoritarian model prevailed, of course, and what was commonly called the "Telephone Company" soon became the largest and most powerful monopoly in US history.

With Alexander Graham Bell's fall from grace, most of what has passed for "telephone history" can no longer be regarded as nonfiction. Fortunately for the avowed writers of fiction who have introduced the telephone into their work, very few ever bothered to introduce Bell along with it. How the phone insinuated itself into the short story and the novel, first as prop and later as "character," would no doubt make an interesting study. In Mark Twain's *A Connecticut Yankee in King Arthur's Court* (1889), for example, the telephone is basically a gimmick: We are ushered into "the den of a medieval hermit turned into a telephone office," and the cast includes a baby named "Hello-Central"—a greeting that dates from the telephone industry's own infancy. One of the earliest stories in which the phone itself is a central character, playing a vital role, was Elizabeth Stuart Phelps's "The Chief Operator," a turn-of-the-century tale of torrential rain, a broken dam, and a devastating flood, featuring as heroine a switchboard operator, a young widow who sacrifices her life that others might live.

Telephones and telephone talk figure significantly in the work of writers as different as Villiers de l'Isle-Adam, James Joyce, Franz Kafka, Upton Sinclair, Ring Lardner, Claude McKay, Dashiell Hammett, Dorothy Parker, Harry Stephen Keeler, Nelson Algren, Chester Himes, Craig Rice, David Goodis, Lionel White, Jack Kerouac, Barbara Neely, and thousands of others, but it is a topic too remote from Wrong Numbers to consider here. The same is true of the telephone in poetry. Jones Very, Guillaume Apollinaire, Carl Sandburg, Robert Frost, Benjamin Péret, Langston Hughes, Kenneth Fearing, Diane di Prima, Joyce Mansour, Jayne Cortez, and Paul Garon are just a few of the poets who have brought phones into one or more of their poems. Rarely, however, have any of them raised, even elliptically, the burning question of Wrong Numbers. Nancy Cunard, by way of exception, in a little-known poem titled "Between Time and Etc.," seems to me to have captured something of the fugitive irrationality and desperate hope that certain solitary states of mind share with the Wrong Numbers of the world:

> *One hand on the telephone …*
> *Everywhere the*
> *Ephemeridae of nights, alone and not alone.*
> *…*
> *Are we the real?*

Telephones are also conspicuous in popular poetry, most radiantly in blues and jazz songs. Elmore James's "Talk to Me, Baby" is a blues classic:

> *I talked to my baby*
> *on the telephone.*
> *She say, "Stop what you're doin'*
> *and come on home."*

Tin Pan Alley also had plenty of telephone tunes; Irving Berlin's "All Alone by the Telephone" was one of the key clichés of the Roaring Twenties. A study of songs about phones and other electrical and electronic devices, from the late nineteenth century through R&B and rock to reggae and hip-hop, could tell us a lot about the society we live in. Even the barest sketch of such a project, however, would take us too far from the present object of our inquiry.

Popular literature abounds in phones and has also proved to be a fertile field for Wrong Numbers. Some of the most illuminating writings on the "telephone experience" are the hilarious skits from the old *Bob and Ray* show on radio—such as "Lucky Phone Call" (in the book *Write If You Get Work*) and "Speaking Out" and "Phone Call to Anywhere" (in *The New! Improved! Bob and Ray Book*). Apart from a couple of *Daffy Duck* comics from the 1950s and '60s, nothing else in the literature equals the raw power of Bob and Ray's revelation of the telephone as an instrument for the communication of explosive poetic humor, conversational zaniness, and all-out pandemonium. Although not specifically concerned with misdialed numbers, these inspired classics of anti-rational dialogue, spotlighting the endless possibilities of telephonic funny stuff, have a lot in common with Wrong Numbers.

The mystery thriller appears to be the literary genre in which telephones—and Wrong Numbers—figure most prominently and often, sometimes as a major theme or recurring sub-theme. Dan Marlowe's *Doom Service*, a 1960 "paperback original" centered on corruption in the "fight game," oddly ignores the Wrong Number but includes no less than forty-six mentions of telephones in its 160 pages—about one every third page—not counting references to "picking up the receiver" or "putting in a call." In this as in many other mysteries, the phone is no mere decorative prop but a disturbing "object" or brooding presence.

The story that made the Wrong Number famous, or rather infamous, was Lucille Fletcher's 1948 radio drama *Sorry, Wrong Number*—the suspenseful tale of a woman who, by chance, as the result of a faulty phone connection, overhears what turns out to be a plot to murder her. An instant hit, it was replayed again and again on radio, expanded (with the collaboration of Allan Ullman) into a best-selling novel, and made into a major feature film (starring Barbara Stanwyck), which in turn has been shown repeatedly on TV. It has also been released as an LP recording and in audio and videocassette. Largely under its influence, the Wrong Number became a staple of *noir* films, and fiction as well, although for the most part it was simply a momentary device to add a touch of eeriness or to intrude, suddenly but more or less irrelevantly, on a prolonged silence. In Thomas B. Dewey's *Don't Cry for Long* (1964), the narrator anxiously awaits a call from a young woman he met the night before:

> I looked at my watch....
> She promised to call, I kept telling myself....
> She will call....
> Maybe.
> I finished the coffee and ate a couple of dry rolls. [She] still hadn't called....
> The thing rang at eleven-thirty and I grabbed it the way you grab a plate as it falls off the table.
> A wrong number.

Here, as usual in films and fiction, the Wrong Number is reduced to its traditional role as irritation and hope deferred.

Alfred Bester's "Out of This World" (in *The Dark Side of the Earth*, 1964), is an interesting exception. In this science fiction tale, what *seems* to be a Wrong Number is actually something much more complicated. As one of the callers explains to the other toward the end: "We're on different time-tracks.... We're in alternative worlds.... The telephone lines between our alternate worlds have gotten crossed." When the crossed lines are repaired, a budding romantic dalliance ends abruptly.

A handful of oddities aside, the "literature of the telephone" was practically of no use in my exploration. The great bulk of this literature completely ignores Wrong Numbers, and the mentions of them in fiction tend to be condescending, negative, even hostile. Symptomatic of the "official" attitude on the matter is the fact that "Wrong Number" is not even a referenced subject in the Dewey Decimal or Library of Congress cataloging systems.

My disappointing peregrination through this literature was long over when I chanced upon a felicitous little book titled *Hello ... Wrong Number* by Marilyn Sachs. Penelope found this ninety-seven-page novel in August 2001, on one of our long walks; it was near the top of the "Free Box" outside a secondhand bookstore in Evanston. "Here's a book for you," she said, and handed me what I soon realized was a true marvel of marvels: a book unequivocally sympathetic to Wrong Numbers.

A winsome love story told entirely in telephone conversations, *Hello ... Wrong Number* is a veritable refutation and negation of *Sorry, Wrong Number.* Unlike the latter, Sachs's book is uninterruptedly playful, eros-affirmative, free of "stranger/danger" paranoia, and openly receptive to the wonders of chance. As a front cover blurb says, the Wrong Number that starts the story "turned out to be the best mistake she ever made!" Fittingly, too, for a book that calmly breaks so many conventions, *Hello ... Wrong Number* is a book for children (ages 9–13). And like so many books for children, it contains a strong message for us all.

If the literature on the subject of telephony proved of little help to me in my expedition to the Land of Wrong Numbers, I did find a wealth of material in literature *off* the subject. Indeed, the further away from the subject a book turned out to be, the more likely it was to contain precious information. The most helpful books of all—the ones that provided the deepest insights, contributed the boldest perspectives, and did most to expand my awareness of the depth and scope of the many questions involved—included several that were published years or even centuries before the birth of Antonio Meucci, and, among more recent works, many that contained not so much as a single reference to phones.

What this book owes to the many poets and thinkers who, without ever having heard of such a thing as a Wrong Number, have nonetheless illuminated its place and role in and beyond our history and culture will become obvious as the story unfolds.

7

The Rise and Fall of the Dil Pickle

Reprinted from Franklin Rosemont, ed., *The Rise and Fall of the Dil Pickle: Jazz-Age Chicago's Wildest & Most Outrageously Creative Hobohemian Nightspot* (Chicago: Charles H. Kerr, 2003), 7–13, 24–26.

DilPicklemania, or Disorderly Conduct as One of the Fine Arts

More famous people in all lines of creative work have passed through the Dil Pickle than through any fifty universities in the world.

—Jack Jones

There is simply no getting around the fact that the Dil Pickle was a very special place, but it was also a lot more than a "place." An intersection of nonconformist ideas and the unfettered imagination, an uprising of new sensibilities, a playground for the experimental life, it gave Chicago a vibrant example of freedom, creativity, wonder, and humor that the city had not known before and needs more than ever today.

Chicago, in the hundred and seventy years since twelve of its residents somewhat presumptuously voted to declare themselves a town in 1833, has had thousands of popular and memorable hangouts—spaces cherished by a loyal clientele in their own time and fondly retained in the public memory. Countless are the bars, hotels, eating places, cafés, nightclubs, jazz joints, bookstores, art galleries, theaters (big and little), gyms, union halls, meeting halls, pool halls, and back rooms that have helped make people's lives a little better and brighter. Among them all, the Dil Pickle stands apart and stands supreme, for it was far and away the best-loved, most notorious, most stimulating, and most influential little gathering place in the city's history.

In its day, the Pickle—as most of its habitués called it—was regularly packed to full capacity. A rare outpost of free speech, intellectual funhouse, and joyful rendezvous of hobos, poets, artists, revolutionists, and various unclassifiable oddballs, its poetic and carnivalesque reputation has not only survived but also prospered over the years. Early on it became a legend, and Pickle legends (including legends about particular Picklers) have never stopped multiplying. While it lasted, no other place in town was so frequently mentioned in the daily press. Year after year, as an oft-repeated remark put it, the Pickle's Sunday evenings made Monday morning news stories.

Even in its decline in the late 1920s, when several dozen well-advertised competitors operated within a mile of the original, only the Pickle really drew the crowds and made headlines—and with good reason, for no other place came even close to attracting even one-eighteenth as many celebrated and/or fascinating writers, poets, artists, radicals, cranks, and "characters." So numerous, varied, and contradictory were the tales of what happened at the Pickle—what so-and-so said there, saw there, did there—that the spirit of the place continued to enjoy a long and productive afterlife. Well into the 1960s—that is, some thirty years after the club was shut down—journalists were still recalling the Pickle's good old days in their columns.

The club's place in the history of US bohemianism, its broader cultural/political influence, and above all its seemingly endless shenanigans have been invoked in dozens of books: memoirs, mysteries, tourist guides, biographies, sociological studies, and histories of literature.

Oddly, despite its enduring renown, no one has ever taken the trouble to write a full-length history of the Dil Pickle, or even to make it the centerpiece of a novel or movie. Those who were best qualified to chronicle its life and times—the club's founders, members, and habitués—are no longer with us, and historians attempting to approach Pickle history from "outside" have inevitably run into daunting obstacles. Picklers were noted for their wide-ranging achievements but not for their archivist inclinations. The club's surviving records are woefully incomplete, confusing, and scattered; indeed, most appear to be irretrievably lost. The Newberry Library houses an impressive Jack Jones/Dil Pickle Club Collection that is full of important documents and charming memorabilia, but its gaps are immense and frustrating. The Ben Reitman Papers at the University of Illinois Circle Campus

Library also contain a wealth of manuscripts and printed ephemera, but they are maddeningly fragmentary and largely unsorted.

The present book [*The Rise and Fall of the Dil Pickle*] is not offered as a comprehensive history but rather as a collection of raw materials that should help prepare the way for more detailed studies. Gathered here are eyewitness accounts of the Dil Pickle by a broad range of individuals who actually ventured through its orange door, savored the peculiar magic of the place, and in most cases made the acquaintance of at least a few dyed-in-the-wool Picklers.

This book, in short, is a collective portrait of the Pickle by those who experienced it first-hand.

Anarchists at Work and Play

Only in an anarchist society will humankind be happy, for everybody will have the opportunity and the environment and encourage-ment to develop him or her self—to develop in the anarchist spirit of respect for the freedom and individuality of others, in a spirit of justice and equality for the well-being of all.

—Maximiliano Olay

What *was* the Dil Pickle? In twenty-five words or less, it was a night-spot that served food, coffee, tea, and soft drinks and provided entertainment along with intellectual stimulation, education, and the opportunity to speak out freely. The club's principal founder and janitor, Jack Jones, liked to think of it as "the world's greatest univer-sity, where all isms, theories, phantasies and other stuff can have their hearing."[1] Ben Reitman, one of the Pickle's central figures, summed up the character of the place when he called it "a radical, literary, bohe-mian discussion center" and "a popular forum for the oppressed and downtrodden."[2]

As the reminiscences in this book show, no one remembers the club for its cuisine (never more than light snacks) or its drinks (non-alcoholic until mobster bootleggers muscled in during the mid-1920s). Nor was the Pickle solely a place of "entertainment." Its roster included singers, actors, musicians, dancers, and an incredible assortment of oddball performers worthy of vaudeville, but, like the food and drinks, they tended to be secondary. What the Dil Pickle was famous for in its own time, and is still remembered for today, was *talk*: unmuzzled self-expression, passionate debate, lively and open discussion, the uninhibited exchange of ideas, poetry, theory, polemic—free speech at its freest. Controversy was its raison d'être—and the more controversial, the better.

Simply by combining an open forum with a café and entertainment—and by accentuating the controversial—the Dil Pickle came up with an exciting new blend. Its antecedents extend way back. Sophia Fagin, in her University of Chicago master's thesis, "Open Forums in Chicago" (1939), traced the forum as a social institution back two thousand years to ancient Rome. Evidence may be hard to find, but I suspect that group discussion and debate were already ancient in the days of the cave people. Closer to home, the Pickle could count among its inspirations and forerunners a long and illustrious line of individual thinkers and agitators, as well as social movements, right here in the United States—from William Ellery Channing, whose 1833 lecture started many on the path of do-it-yourself non-academic education, to the numerous forums promoted by land reformers, abolitionists, Bellamyists, Marxists, suffragists, single taxers, Knights of Labor, and religious dissidents. In Chicago, shortly after the turn of the century, a former Presbyterian minister named M.M. Mangasarian of the Independent Religious Society regularly attracted audiences of six thousand to his Sunday morning lectures at Orchestra Hall.

Chicago, truth to tell, was then—and long remained—the forum capital of the country.[3] No other city had so many well-attended forums going on simultaneously under so many different auspices. Chicago was also the recognized center of the labor movement in the United States, and no one emphasized forums more than the labor radicals: socialists, anarchists, and later the Industrial Workers of the World (IWW). The Haymarket anarchists of the 1880s and their successors all through the 1920s were assiduous forum-goers. Several prominent figures from Haymarket days were later active in the Pickle—among others, Lucy Parsons, Nina Spies, J.H. "Doc" Greer, and their single-tax friend George Schilling. And that was no accident, for the Pickle's prime movers—former Wobbly and self-styled "industrial anarchist" Jack Jones, and (a little later) Emma Goldman's long-time lover and press agent Ben Reitman—had known those old-timers for years.[4]

According to Sophie Fagin, who interviewed many veteran Picklers in the 1930s, the Pickle may well have been inspired by the

Open Forum, run by the "Philosophical Anarchist," fortune-teller, and feminist Huldah Potter-Lewis. A more immediate model, Fagin urges, was a weekly radical discussion group at the home of a couple of other Philosophical Anarchists, Howard and Lillian Udell, who, with the backing of their friend, socialist publisher Charles H. Kerr, also ran the Radical Bookshop on North Clark Street. As it happens, one of the participants in the Udells' Sunday speak-outs was Jack Jones.

A decisive influence on the origins of the Dil Pickle, anarchism—and particularly "Chicago Idea" anarchism, with its cultural component—remained one of the club's constants over the years. An authentically anarchist atmosphere pervaded the place from the start, and anarchists of very different persuasions—individualists, anarchist-communists, anarcho-pacifists, and anarcho-syndicalists—clearly felt at home there and regarded themselves as Picklers in good standing.

The sheer anarchy of the place no doubt also accounts for the extreme aversion to the Pickle on the part of Stalinists, fascists, hoodlums, the police department, and other authoritarians.

Here Come the Wobblies: Welcome to Bughouse Square!

Bughouse Square was one place where the unexpected was commonplace.

—Jack Sheridan

The IWW influence on the Pickle, though rarely noted by commentators, was even greater than that of the anarchists. Wobblies, as IWW members began to be called around 1913, were among the most vociferous forum-hounds of their time. Several nights a week, speakers held forth at IWW halls throughout the city, and they were also highly audible at the forums of other groups. The Wob specialty, however, was not platform oratory or formal debate or panel discussions but rather soapboxing: on streetcorners, in parks, at factory gates, on Skid Road (West Madison Street in Chicago), wherever working people gathered.

Chicago's most celebrated soapboxing site, from the mid-1910s through the early 1960s, was known as Bughouse Square, officially Washington Square. A onetime cow pasture, it was the city's second-oldest park, located at Clark and Walton Streets, just across from the Newberry Library. In its heyday during the 1910s, '20s, and '30s, Bughouse Square was the best-known outdoor free-speech center not only in Chicago but also in the entire nation. It was not the biggest (that distinction belonged to its South Side counterpart, Washington Park), but it was the most renowned and notorious. At Bughouse Square you were sure to hear the best speakers on the most outrageous topics, and—as a bonus—the fiercest hecklers. Especially on weekends, weather permitting, crowds numbering as high as five or ten thousand would turn out to hear two or three dozen "ozone orators" air their views.

Old-time vaudevillians had a saying: "If you haven't played the Palace [a then-famous New York theater], you haven't arrived." On the transcontinental soapbox circuit, a speaker didn't amount to much if he or she hadn't held forth at Chicago's Bughouse Square. In the 1910s and '20s, Wobblies held power in Bughouse Square. Non-Wob speakers were welcome—variety was the spice of soapboxing—but the "hegemonic influence," as contemporary Marxists might put it, was exercised by the IWW.

When the Dil Pickle emerged circa 1914–16, the IWW itself was still a youngster. Founded in Chicago in 1905, the IWW maintained its international headquarters in the city until the late 1980s. An explicitly revolutionary organization, it was determined to organize the working class into "One Big Union" in order to abolish the wage system (capitalism) and to create a free society. In contrast to the American Federation of Labor, the railroad brotherhoods, and even the Socialist Party, the IWW was not only a labor organization but also a far-ranging intellectual and cultural movement. For Wobblies, working-class education was a high priority. Its periodical press and its pamphlet literature were as outstanding as its public speakers. The IWW gave the US labor movement its finest songs, most memorable slogans, and funniest cartoons. Wob soapboxers were widely recognized as the top stand-up comedians of their time.[5]

Humor, indeed, remains one of the IWW's greatest legacies to all subsequent labor and radical movements, and the Dil Pickle Club was among the first to adapt it to its own needs. The fact that a Wobbly spirit—and above all Wobbly humor—permeated the Pickle has not been generally acknowledged. To most of the club's contemporaries, however, the strong IWW connection, especially in the early years, must have been as obvious as Charlie Chaplin's moustache. After all, the club was founded by Bughouse Square soapboxers: Wobs, ex-Wobs, and close friends of Wobs. And despite occasional changes of personnel, Wobs, ex-Wobs, and their friends continued to provide the Dil Pickle's hard core for a decade or more. As Slim Brundage put it, "It seems like all of us were Wobs at one time or another."[6]

Those in the know often called the Pickle "the Indoor Bughouse Square."

Apart from Jack Jones and Jim Larkin, the names of the founding Picklers cannot be verified, but the likeliest suspects include John Loughman, Edward P. "Triphammer" Johnson, Bill Shatoff, Eddie Guilbert, Jimmy Rohn, Bertram L. Weber, and G.G. Florine. The last two were primarily poets and playwrights, but the rest were heavyweight champion soapboxers—agitators known from coast to coast. Most of them had written for *Solidarity* and other IWW publications. These fellow workers were in effect the Dil Pickle regulars: on hand not only in case a featured speaker failed to show up but also to lead the heckling and, more generally, to keep the discussion lively.

A list of other Wobs and former Wobs who had some association with the Pickle could easily fill a page or two. Let us note only a few of those who had already distinguished themselves in the union before taking up the cause of Dil Pickledom. Roscoe T. Sims was the IWW's first African American organizer. Rudolf von Liebich, the IWW's leading composer-musician (among other things, he played the piano at Joe Hill's funeral in 1915), became the Pickle's musical director. Charles Ashleigh and Jim Seymour were prominent Wob poets. Lionel Moise, another Wob poet, is better remembered as the hard-boiled news reporter who taught a young Ernest Hemingway how to write.

T-Bone Slim (Matt Valentine Huhta), the IWW's greatest man of letters, does not appear to have joined the Picklers; indeed, he spent very little time in Chicago. During a fall 1923 visit, however, he did allude to the Pickle in his *Industrial Solidarity* column. Other Wobs recall running into T-Bone in Chicago from time to time, but nothing further is known of his possible Pickle connections.

Several postwar IWW members were also active Picklers, including Myron "Slim" Brundage, Jack Sheridan, Robert Hardoen, Sam Dolgoff, Paul Mattick, and Kenneth Rexroth. Many newspaper reporters, and more than a few artists and poets, carried red cards in those years. Few of them were active members, but they paid their dues now and then as a sign of solidarity. Even that pretentious aesthete Sam

Putnam was a "fellow worker" for a little while. His reminiscences of the Pickle and its milieu are among the sourest in this book, but the record shows that he was up to his ears in Pickle activities for many a long year.

Wobblies and Picklers were among the first in the United States to attempt a Marx-Freud synthesis. (As Eddie Guilbert put it in a 1919 poem, Picklers could "babble of Freud till their senses were cloyed.") Where else but the Pickle could Wobs have met Lionel Blitzsten, Chicago's first psychoanalyst (and indeed, the first west of New York)? A few years later Franz Alexander, cofounder of the Chicago Institute of Psychoanalysis, became a frequent Pickle lecturer. The scant literature referring to the Pickle's founding fathers rarely acknowledges any founding mothers. In the reminiscences collected here, Mary "Mother" Jones (no relation to Jack) and Elizabeth Gurley Flynn are mentioned as cofounders or early members, but there seems no evidence of their involvement, which in truth appears doubtful. One or both, of course, may well have visited the club now and then. Most of the women "regulars" at the Pickle were, like their male counterparts, highly skilled soapboxers. Among the best known were "Red Martha" Biegler, Lucy Parsons, Nina Spies, and Elizabeth "Lizzie" Davis—all Bughouse Square stars with close ties to the Wobblies.

Who Packed the Pickle? Notes on a Highly Atypical Bunch

No one means more to me than my friends from my Chicago adolescence. I remember them all and feel the closest sort of bond with them.

—Kenneth Rexroth

Anarchists, Wobblies, former Wobs, ex-SLNA [Syndicalist League of North America] members, and the "Kerr group" were guiding forces in the Dil Pickle, but they never made up more than a tiny fraction of the crowds that gathered there. The throngs who stepped high and stooped low through the orange door into the heart of Pickledom seem to have been as diverse as the topics discussed there. The Pickle crowd was multiracial and multicultural long before those terms found their way into the dictionary. No sociologist appears to have drawn up a profile of a typical Pickler, probably for the very good reason that no such thing as a typical Pickler ever existed.

By definition atypical, Picklers were of all ages and nationalities and social classes. Those who were close to the core group were mostly, like that group, of working-class background, decidedly internationalist, and unequivocally on the side of the workers of the world in the struggle against capital. Demonstrating that this was no ordinary, middle-of-the-road forum, even the minority of well-to-do Picklers such as real estate investor Edward Chichester Wentworth tended to be vigorous supporters of workers' struggles ("traitors to their class," in the parlance of the day). The club's spirited Haymarket commemorations, as well as its fund-raising drives for the defense of Sacco and Vanzetti, Tom Mooney, the "Scottsboro Boys," and other class-war prisoners, leave no doubt in this regard.

Beyond this rather vague Far Left and pro-working-class sensibility, divergences among the Picklers were many and immense. Indeed, Burton Rascoe was not too far off the mark when he wrote, in the *New York Tribune*, that the Pickle was "equally attended by North Shore society leaders, pickpockets, morons, soapbox theists, University of Chicago professors, and derelicts of all kinds." Rascoe's quip, which Jack Jones liked so well that he used it in Pickle publicity, does hint at an important point: that this notorious hotbed of radicals refused on principle to restrict itself to debates about radicalism. Its appeal was not to the like-minded but to the other-minded. Preaching to the converted was simply not the way of the Pickle. Whatever their faults, Jones, Reitman, and their co-conspirators had a real genius for the heterogeneous.

As in politics and social issues, so too in matters of religion. A hotbed of atheists and bitter enemies of organized religion, the Pickle included on its roster of speakers many ministers, priests, bishops, rabbis, and other spiritual advisers. Some, no doubt—evangelist Aimee Semple McPherson, for example, as well as Bishop Francis of the Old Catholic Church (a nineteenth-century breakaway from the Church of Rome), and the Spiritualists—were there mostly for laughs: bait, so to speak, for the likes of Harry "Kill Christ" Wilson, Frank Midney, Martha Biegler, and other soapboxers and 'boes who specialized in exposing "Jesus screamers" and other "sky pilots." Other speakers, however—notably the historian of religion Shirley Jackson Case and the many who lectured on Buddhism, Hinduism, and other religions of the Far East—provoked serious debate.

Who were the people who packed the Pickle? To Rascoe's short list we should add, for starters: poets, labor editors, artists, doctors, dancers, authors, strike leaders, lawyers, cartoonists, architects, paleontologists, explorers, news hounds, booksellers, biologists, physicists, several Chicago aldermen, literary critics, an occasional cop, a ballplayer for the White Sox, anthropologists, printers, actors, psychiatrists, wrestlers, second-story men, phrenologists, strippers, world travelers, hangers-on of the arts, malcontents of all kinds, curiosity seekers, tourists, and even a few self-confessed right-wingers. As for the professors, in addition to the many from the University of Chicago, as noted by Rascoe, there were also an impressive number from Northwestern, the University of Illinois, DePaul, and at least a couple of dozen other institutions of higher learning from all over the Midwest and as far away as Paris and Bombay. Some profs were forum-bugs themselves. Robert Morss Lovett, for example, frequently attended the Hobo College and IWW meetings as well as the Pickle, and he sometimes brought his classes along.

The Pickle's more academic lectures—Walter Starkie, of the University of Dublin, on Gypsy lore; Northwestern University physicist Lester Irving Bockstahler on "Trends of Modern Physics and Their Influence on Intellectual Development"; the University of Chicago's A.C. Lunn on "Einstein's Theory of Relativity"; and Henri Peyre, of Yale, on contemporary French literature (quite possibly the first public discussion of surrealism in Chicago)—attracted sizeable and appreciative audiences. Interestingly, they seem to have been especially popular among the hoboes. However, their purely informative and therefore non-polemical character tended to inhibit the vehement exchanges of opinion for which the Pickle was so justly renowned. On the Pickle calendar, such presentations were wisely balanced by more topical and controversial talks. "Causes"—political, poetic, philosophical, spiritual, sexual, and other deeply felt causes—were always the Pickle's specialty of the house.

Every known ism had advocates in Tooker Alley, and a number of new isms were born there. Because it was an open forum, and also because humor was a recognized part of the goings-on, the opponents in a debate—no matter how extreme their differences—generally got along with each other, even when the yelling was loudest and the crowd on the verge of riot. Yes, the peace of the Pickle was sometimes disturbed by unseemly shouting matches or a sudden bout of fisticuffs, and in the course of its nineteen years as Chicago's most innovative and energetic counter-institutional institution, the place did experience a few all-out brawls, such as the one described by comic strip artist Boody Rogers. Such incidents, however, were far from common.

PART II

Comics, Animation, and Self-Taught Artists

8

Introduction to the Life and Times of the Incredible Hulk

Reprinted from Franklin Rosemont and Charles Radcliffe, eds., *Dancin' in the Streets! Anarchists, IWWs, Surrealists, Situationists and Provos in the 1960s as Recorded in the Pages of "The Rebel Worker" and "Heatwave"* (Chicago: Charles H. Kerr, 2005), 319–20.

"When the air is cooler than the earth," G.P. Quackenbos assures us, in his *Natural Philosophy* (revised edition, 1873), "the moisture imparted to it ... is partially condensed and thus rendered visible, forming either *fog* or *clouds*. The only difference between the two is in their height. When the condensation takes place near the earth's surface, fog is the result; when in the upper regions of the atmosphere, clouds."

So, too, criticism, when confined to surfaces, gives us only fog; but when allowed to rise into the upper regions of the intellectual atmosphere, provokes the appearance of marvelous clouds, in whose formation we can perceive elements of a new mythology. In the fog we see only dim lights and perhaps hands signaling vaguely before our eyes. In the clouds we may witness the unfolding of a universe, the revelation of *desire*.

In the history of comics, the most *amazing* characters, from our point of view, are those who seem to be *least finished* from the cartoonist's point of view—characters whose personalities are only very lightly sketched: that is to say, incomplete, leaving wide margins for the unexpected. Hastily conceived, such characters seem to have been pushed into the comic field of action before their authors could draw up the full scale of their capacities and limitations. Unlike such predictable, straitjacketed characters as Prince Valiant or Superman (to cite only two particularly boring examples), the "unfinished" characters tend to be ambiguous, amorphous, experimental, stubbornly indefinable, and somehow strangely *free*.

Most important of all, the less a character is defined, the more that character is capable of expressing defiance, the poetic marvelous, and other subversive thought. "Funny Animal" comics abound in such beings (Krazy Kat, Bugs Bunny, Daffy Duck, Woody Woodpecker); superhero equivalents are much rarer. Jack Cole's Plastic Man is surely the brightest example from the so-called Golden Age. And now we have Jack Kirby's the Incredible Hulk—a kind of raging street-kid version of Frankenstein's monster, with strong touches of Jekyll-Hyde, King Ubu, and the Wolf Man. This far-from-jolly green giant—a bitter, vengeful product of the "Atomic Age"—enjoys wrecking US missile bases and miscellaneous military installations, along with countless other outposts and dwelling-places of power and authority.

Listen to the Incredible Hulk, the complete nihilist, in his own words:

"Human? Why should I want to be human?"

"The Hulk *has* no friends!"

"You dare attack the Hulk?"

"Hate you? Why *shouldn't* I hate you?"

"I can't spend the rest of my life running and hiding! It's time for everyone else to run from *me*!"

"The Hulk waits for nobody!"

"Everyone runs from the Hulk! Everyone!"

"I owe the human race nothing!"

"The Hulk takes orders from no one!"

"Nothing'll stop the Hulk!"

"Every man on Earth is my enemy!"

"The Hulk is *free*! Free—to do what?"

"Nothing can hurt me! Nothing can stop me! I'm the Hulk! I'm the strongest there is!"

Bugs Bunny and Dialectics

First published in *Marvelous Freedom, Vigilance of Desire: Catalog of the World Surrealist Exhibition* (Chicago: Gallery Black Swan, 1976), 13.

It is no accident that all that is revolutionary and scandalous in the work of Georg Wilhelm Friedrich Hegel came to be symbolized, in a uniquely *umorous* way on the eve of the second world imperialist slaughter, by a little gray rabbit whose very name embodies a dialectical resolution of contradictions: Bugs (nickname of a notorious gangster) Bunny (almost a synonym for gentleness).

A more or less urbanized descendant of Br'er Rabbit, Bugs Bunny (whose ancestors include also Lewis Carroll's eccentric White Rabbit and the psychotic March Hare) is categorically opposed to wage slavery in all its forms. Content with a modest subsistence on the edge of the forest, his residence is marked only by a mailbox bearing the name Bugs Bunny, Esq. Aside from wondrous adventures that only rigorously applied laziness can lead to, his major vocation is pilfering carrots from the garden of a certain Elmer Fudd and, more generally, heckling this same Fudd in ever new ways.

It is impossible to appreciate the genius of the world's greatest rabbit without understanding Fudd: this bald-headed, slow-witted, hot-tempered, timid, petit bourgeois dwarf with a speech defect, whose principal activity is the defense of his private property. Fudd is the perfect characterization of a specifically modern type: the petty bureaucrat, the authoritarian mediocrity, nephew or grandson of Pa Ubu. If the Ubus (Mussolini, Hitler, Stalin) dominated the period between the two wars, for the last thirty years it has been the Fudds who have directed our misery: Fudds and more Fudds in the White

House, Fudds on the Central Committees of the so-called Communist parties; all the popes have been Fudds; the best-selling novelists are all Fudds; Louis Aragon and Salvador Dalí, beginning as anti-Fudds, degenerated into two of the worst of all possible Fudds. Almost alone against them all, Bugs Bunny stands as a veritable symbol of irreducible recalcitrance.

If the Bunny-Fudd choreography reflects a particular historic moment in the class struggle—a period of class "symmetry" in which the workers here and there win a few of their demands, only to be chased back into their holes in the ground—nonetheless the mythic content of this drama exceeds its original formal limitations. The very appearance on the stage of history of a character such as Bugs Bunny is proof that someday the Fudds will be vanquished—that someday all the carrots in the world will be ours.

Until then, one can scarcely imagine a better model to offer our children than this bold creature who, with his four rabbit's feet, is the good luck charm of total revolt. Confronted by any and all apologists for the status quo, Bugs Bunny always has the last word: "Don't think it hasn't been lovely, because it hasn't."

Homage to Henry Darger

Reprinted from *Revolution in the Service of the Marvelous* (Chicago: Charles H. Kerr, 2004), 111–12.

NOTE: The Chicago Surrealist Group show Surrealism in 1977, *at the Gary Art Center in Gary, Indiana, was the first exhibition anywhere to feature works by Henry Darger, now recognized as one of the greatest of all outsider artists. The following statement, prominently posted at the 1977 exhibition, appears to be the first text ever written on Darger and his work.*

Henry Darger (c. 1893–1973), examples of whose works are shown here for the first time anywhere, was a self-taught artist single-mindedly devoted throughout his life to recording his deepest obsessions, which he elaborated into a personal mythology of monumental scope.[1]

Born in Brazil, Darger lived most of his life in a small apartment on the North Side of Chicago, where he was employed as an orderly at a nearby hospital. Nearly all of his free time was given to his unique project, titled *Realms of the Unreal*, a wild chronicle of cataclysms of all sorts: hurricanes, earthquakes, world wars. The story unfolded in incredible detail in many thousands of typed and handwritten pages, and in scores of 3′ × 8′ tableaux done with pencil, ink, crayon, felt-tip pen, and water-color, freely utilizing the technique of collage with traced and cut-out figures from children's coloring books, comics, and advertisements.

For his epic Darger invented thousands of characters and even dozens of nations (for which he designed flags). He supplemented the large tableaux with many smaller works, such as the sketches of "monsters" shown here [in the Gary show], as well as portraits of the most important personages of his tale.

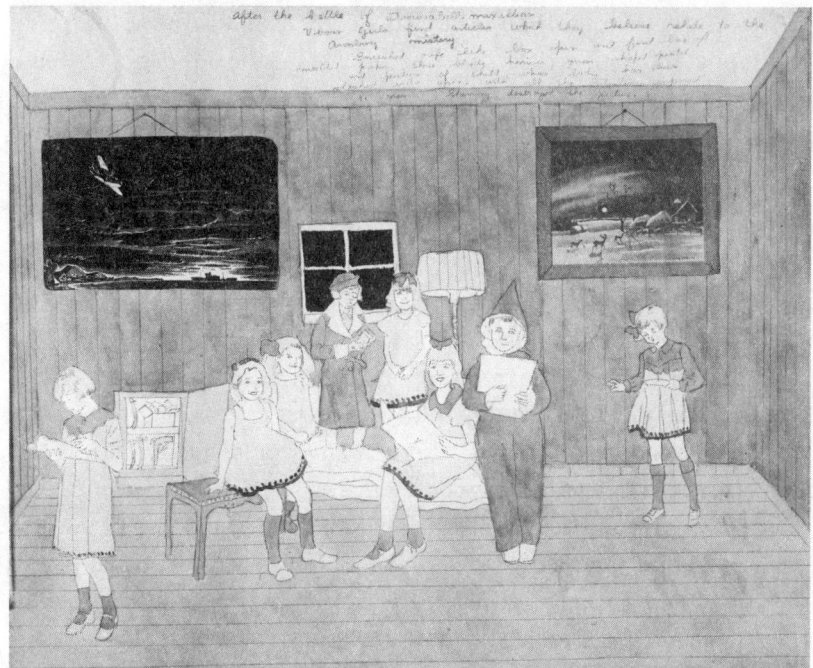

Fig. 21. Henry Darger, *After the Battle of Drowsabella*. Image courtesy of the Art Institute of Chicago.

The central theme of Darger's work is the "eternal war between Good and Evil." But, as is also true of the experimental mythology devised contemporaneously by H.P. Lovecraft and his circle, Darger's "realms of the unreal" exceed the boundaries of conventional mythical frameworks, in favor of an intensely personal vision that is dazzlingly vivid and fresh. Working wholly independent of traditional aesthetic preoccupations, Darger all the more willingly and easily made himself a "modest recording instrument" of his passions and dreams.

The distance separating his personal vision from all prevalent myths—unmistakable throughout his work—is perhaps most discernible in the special role played in his work by little girls, hundreds of Alices in Wonderland: above all the enchanting and heroic "Vivien Girls," who embody all that made up Henry Darger's conception of "the Good, the Beautiful and the True." By all the despicable standards of the existing social order, based on repression and profit, Henry Darger was merely "psychotic," "feeble-minded," "insane." With such meaningless categorizations as these, the guardians of Things As They Are try to shield themselves from the invasions of the imaginary. It suffices, in this regard, to recall the declaration of André Breton in his important 1948 article, "The Art of the Insane: Freedom to Roam Abroad":

> I have no hesitation in putting forward the idea, which is paradoxical only at first sight, that the art of those who are classified as mentally ill constitutes a reservoir of mental health. This is precisely because it is wholly unaffected by all those considerations which tend to falsify the evidence which we others are preparing, considerations such as external influences, conscious calculations, success or disappointments encountered on the social level, etc. The mechanisms of artistic creation are here freed of all such shackles. Through an astonishing dialectical effect, the factors of close confinement and the renunciation of all worldly vanities, despite their pathetic aspect in terms of the individual, together provide the guarantees of a total authenticity which is sadly lacking everywhere else, and the absence of which affects us more and more gravely day by day.

It is for these reasons that the surrealists today are pleased to grant the place of honor to Henry Darger in the exhibition *Surrealism in 1977.*

Homage to Henry Darger, fervent herald of the Vivien Girls!

11

Basil Wolverton (*Powerhouse Pepper*)

First published in "Surrealism and Its Popular Accomplices," special issue of *Cultural Correspondence*, guest-edited by Franklin Rosemont, nos. 10–11 (Fall 1979): 71.

The post–World War II war on comics—which led to the infamous Comics Code—was not, as is commonly believed, an exclusively right-wing campaign. Of course it was McCarthyist in essence and championed by fascists and churchmen. But it also was supported by liberals, freethinkers, Communists, and leftists of all kinds. That is just the sort of thing that happens in counter-revolutionary periods.

Leaf through some comic books of those days and you will see just what it was that the guardians of the "American way of life" were so eager to suppress. Horror comics with foaming-at-the-mouth ghouls, half-rotted corpses, ax-murderers and necrophiles on the rampage; crime comics showing honest citizens getting their heads blown off by joy-riding, machine-gunning gangsters and their heroin-using teenage girlfriends; adventure comics featuring voluptuous, scantily clad, high-heeled heroines in the clutches of an endless series of sadists. Middle-class parents simply didn't want to look at such things—above all didn't want their children to look. For these comics contained a stark, brutal, unmistakable message: the war for "democracy" may have been won, but barbarism flourished everywhere.

The anti-comics crusade was not aimed primarily at the publishers, who easily adjusted themselves to the changed conditions and put out a new "safe" line. The war on comics was aimed at—and hit—the most vulnerable sector of the proletariat: schoolkids. Some artists, of course, and countless kids, fought back with all they had. Harvey Kurtzman's

Mad served as a rallying point for a whole generation of recalcitrant American youth. Eventually it too was domesticated, but not before unloosing some of the most vigorous satire of the 1950s. And at least one of the *Mad* stars never gave up: the heroic Basil Wolverton, a one-man war against everything the Comics Code stands for.

Wolverton is a truly *scandalous* artist: insolent, uncompromising, ruthless. His work ranges from the white-hot to the unbelievably cold. He has created an immense number of comic characters and has worked in nearly every genre, including humor, westerns, horror, and science fiction. His haunting *Spacehawk*, featuring the "lone wolf of the void," is superior in all respects to better-known outer-space strips, such as *Flash Gordon*. *Powerhouse Pepper*, probably Wolverton's best work, is a hard proletarian sock at the corny bourgeois Joe Palooka, drenched in the blackest humor. In "Disk-Eyes the Detective" a cast of cold-blooded, hard-boiled maniacs play a goofy cops-and-robbers. "Flap Flipflop, the Flying Flash" featured a tiny pilot of a tiny plane; unable to concentrate on flying, he prefers to read or sleep. In his first appearance he crashes through an army depot control tower but is too engrossed by Einstein's *Theory of Relativity* to notice: "This book I brought hasn't got such a hot plot for a tot," he remarks, "but it's not a lot of rot."

In all his work, Wolverton defies the law and spits in the face of authority. Incessantly excessive, he always has refused to "know when to stop." Yet even at his most outrageous, he is always *princely*: elegance runs through his uproariousness. Much of his work might be in the worst possible taste, but still: it's the highest-quality bad taste in the world.

12

Bill Holman (*Smokey Stover*)

First published in "Surrealism and Its Popular Accomplices," special issue of *Cultural Correspondence*, guest-edited by Franklin Rosemont, nos. 10–11 (Fall 1979): 66–67.

———

In 1928, in *La Révolution surréaliste* no. 11, Louis Aragon and André Breton published a manifesto hailing "The Fiftieth Anniversary of Hysteria."[1] Deeply inspired by some photographs of hysterical women patients—taken a half century earlier but just discovered in the archives of the Saltpètriere Hospital where Charcot pursued his research into this most elusive of "mental ailments"—the surrealists affirmed that, for them, hysteria was "the greatest poetic discovery of the end of the 19th century," and a "supreme means of expression." Their manifesto not only indicates the gulf separating surrealism from traditional aesthetic categories but also suggests to what extent the surrealist practice of poetry had superseded all merely "clinical" frameworks in understanding the "real functioning of thought."

Elsewhere I have had occasion to remark that "independently of the surrealist movement, but wholly in the surrealist spirit, qualified defenders of the poetic spirit staged, right in the midst of American popular culture, nothing less than their own celebration of hysteria."[2] In the forefront of this celebration was Bill Holman, who was already actively cartooning in 1928 but whose magnum opus was not to begin for seven years. March 10, 1935—a red-letter day for black humor—*Smokey Stover* was unloosed on the world.

All that the word *hysteria* implies gushes from this fast-paced strip in unheard-of quantities, every which way and all at once.

The setting is a firehouse where Smokey Stover and the Chief, with an unending supporting cast, pursue their nonstop rapid-fire misadventures. These frantic firefighting clowns—who, incidentally, start more fires than they put out—seem to live by a single principle: extravagant disorder at all times and at all costs.

In his own way Holman does exactly what the surrealist painter does: *concretize the irrational.* Throughout *Smokey Stover* we see the craziest furniture (an easy chair, for example, rests not on legs but on the letters E and Z); incomprehensible household gadgets ("windshield viper," "scrambled ax"); and vast ultra-elaborate contraptions that prove Holman a worthy disciple of Rube Goldberg. Ever-changing portraits adorn the walls. The figures in these portraits lead adventures of their own, often wholly unrelated to the rest of the story. These portraits smoke real cigars; wear hats or beards that protrude beyond their frames; leap entirely outside these frames; recline in hammocks slung between one frame and another; or shoot peas through a peashooter at figures in other pictures or even at the main characters.

And everywhere—on the walls, doors, windows, floors, furniture, and even on the characters themselves—are *words.* The world's zaniest graffiti grow wild, simply wild, all over *Smokey Stover.* Words and images freely collide in a frenzied Brownian movement, to the tune of Universal Analogy. In Holman's hysterical hieroglyphic, a never-ending array of labels, tags, and captions indicate the never-ending possibilities of relationships between signs and things signified.

As a master of punch lines, Holman has few peers. But no one in comics comes even close to his prowess as a wizard of wordplay; unquestionably, per square inch, he packs in more puns—visual as well as verbal—than any artist before or since. He shows us green P's, blue J's, brown I's. The picture of a little boy with the seat of his pants on fire is labeled "Flaming Youth." A government official's writing implement is a "state pen." A small globe in which two hatchets are imbedded becomes "The Earth and Its Axes." Puttering around in the kitchen, Smokey holds a whip in his hands—a "prune whip." A man standing amid a cluster of taxicabs sings "Deep in the Heart of Taxies." And so it goes, pun after pun after pun—sometimes over a dozen in a single strip. "Of chorus," as Smokey says, "it could be verse."

All this mad "handwriting on the wall," all these goofy pictures within pictures, all these irrational objects whose sole function is symbolic—all these elements of a background in constant metamorphosis—form a kind of oneiric counterpoint that serves above all to emphasize the pervasive, total, definitive delirium that characterizes the whole strip. Nothing is stable or static in Holman's world. His images refuse to stay put; his words are out looking for trouble; his objects are eager to make known their *objections*.

Smokey Stover could be regarded as the last holdout of vaudeville and burlesque slapstick. But it is something more. For in order to enable his slapstick to survive at all, Holman had to raise it to the third—or fourth or fifth—power. Quantity inevitably passed into quality, and lo! a new and unhoped-for marvel was added to our lives.

When every one of these strips is collected and published in book form, it will be one of a very few books of which we can say that it is *surrealist from cover to cover*.

I have said it before and I'll say it again: Everlasting glory to Smokey Stover!

13

Carl Barks (*Uncle Scrooge*)

First published in "Surrealism and Its Popular Accomplices," special issue of *Cultural Correspondence*, guest-edited by Franklin Rosemont, nos. 10–11 (Fall 1979): 71–72.

If the Comics Code made few waves in the world of Walt Disney, it was because "Citizen Walt, the Last Tycoon" had long before enforced a repressive, parochial code of his own on his employees. Disney's ambition seems to have been to impose bourgeois respectability on the raucous nihilism of the early comics and animated cartoons—to *tame* these savage genres: for a fee, of course. His success is only too well known.

It so happens, however, by one of those "twists of fate" that make life always more interesting than philosophy, that the Disney Studios harbored for decades an artist who can be regarded as truly and wonderfully *subversive*, in the best sense of the word.

Carl Barks never explicitly quarreled with the Disney Code. Quietly taking the formulas as handed to him, he nonchalantly transformed them from top to bottom. Out of readymade material he elaborated a universe precisely as he wanted it, gradually adding to it until soon there was far more in it of his own than of Disney's. He is the creator of *Uncle Scrooge* and author of most of *Walt Disney's Comics and Stories.* His comics were so immensely popular that his departures from orthodox Disneyism were allowed to pass; Barks enjoyed an autonomy that no other Disney artist ever approached. And it is our good fortune that he consistently made the most of it.

The greatest of all comic *storytellers*, Barks is at his best in the narration of marvelous *quests*. He takes us to the Seven Cities of Cibola, King

Solomon's Lost Mines, ghost towns of the Old West, the Everglades, Atlantis, the Yukon, and even to the center of the earth, which, we learn, is inhabited by tribes of rolling ball-like people known as Terries and Fermies (their favorite sport is making earthquakes). With Barks, the oldest myths spring to life and lead to heroic adventures. We follow his dauntless ducks eagerly as they search for the Golden Fleece, the lost crown of Genghis Khan, the Flying Dutchman, the Fountain of Youth, the Philosopher's Stone.

We encounter outstanding adversaries, most notably the "terrible Beagle Boys," a gang of cutthroats who wear their masks all the time, even when locked up, and wear their prison numbers even when outside. In or out of jail, they spend most of their time contriving schemes to plunder Scrooge McDuck's untold fantasticatillions. There is also the "spitfire sorceress" Magica De Spell, who lives on the slope of Vesuvius, and who, seeking to devise a powerful talisman, will stop at nothing to get Scrooge's first dime.

The heroes of most of Barks's tales are not the world's richest duck or his scatterbrained nephew Donald, but Donald's trio of nephews: Huey, Dewey, and Louie, members of the Junior Woodchucks of the World. Armed with their *Junior Woodchucks' Guidebook*, that incomparable fount of universal wisdom, the brilliant duckling brothers find answers to questions that leave their elders paralyzed and helpless. It is Huey, Dewey, and Louie who, for example, in ancient Colchis, literally pull the wool over the eyes of the sleepless dragon.

What I have called Barks's subversive quality is manifest particularly in the delightful irony that permeates his work. Beneath a naive and taciturn exterior, he is clearly a man of great passion and deep integrity. Subtly and serenely, he kicks the ground out from under numerous retrograde cultural assumptions. He has the highest regard for primordial innocence and distrusts the enemies of that innocence. The story of Scrooge's sojourn in the faraway valley of Tra-la-la is a devastating attack on money. In the tale of the "Seven Cities," the hidden splendor is destroyed through greed. "The Land of the Pygmy Indians" (featuring a lost tribe who speak in metered verse, like Hiawatha) is a poignant denunciation of capitalist rapacity. Steeped in history and mythic lore, and scorning empty didacticism, Barks inspires a thirst for *knowledge* in keeping with Hegel's principle: "The hand that inflicts the wound is also the hand that heals it."

Because of his obsession with voyages of *seekers*, his preference for symbolic discourse, and his ambiguous irony, Barks could be regarded as the Herman Melville of comics. Unquestionably, as the art of graphic storytelling develops, he will be recognized as one of those who did most to advance it. He has given the comic strip power to express things considered inexpressible before him. Perhaps the time is not far off when people will speak of Melville as the Carl Barks of literature.

For those of us who grew up in the 1950s, Barks's work was a life-saving oasis. It was his work that first made us aware of the extent to which comics could express our *deepest aspirations*.

This much is sure: without comics, surrealism would be very different from what it is in the United States today. Those who wish to know the *specifically American sources* of surrealism here and now could hardly do better than to study the comics—especially of the '40s and '50s—and above all the works of the tireless chronicler of the doings in Duckburg.

14

Chester Gould (*Dick Tracy*)

First published in "Surrealism and Its Popular Accomplices," special issue of *Cultural Correspondence*, guest-edited by Franklin Rosemont, nos. 10–11 (Fall 1979): 67–68.

———

It is the same with comics as with movies or paintings or poems: out of a hundred, one or two may hit the mark. The dominant ideas of an epoch, as the ABC of Marxism demonstrated so irrefutably so long ago, are the ideas of the ruling class; and when the ruling class is the bourgeoisie—intrinsically hostile to art and poetry, as Marx observed—the things expressed in the great bulk of what passes for art, including popular art, inevitably are saturated with bourgeois values.

And thus for every Krazy Kat or Little Nemo or Smokey Stover—sparkling with all the colors of freedom and love—there are dozens, scores, *hundreds* of Steve Canyons, Mary Worths, Brenda Starrs, Rex Morgans, Captain Americas, Little Orphan Annies, and Star Wars: four-color props for a dying social order, fundamentally prosaic and hopelessly subservient to the ideological needs of the whole repressive apparatus, from the State Department all the way down the chain of churches, Boy Scouts, and Ku Klux Klan to the stool pigeons for the CIA.

In the comics, as everywhere else, the struggle between the marvelous and the miserable is waged unrelentingly. We want comics that dream and inspire dreams; comics that challenge musty traditions and overturn mental habits; comics that give a chance to the "impossible" (the mask behind which the *desirable* is so frequently forced to hide). Is it necessary to add that virtually nothing that matters to us—nothing inspiring, subversive, emancipatory, poetic—will be found in the plethora of comics devoted to family life, soap operas, spies, military exploits, sports, pets, or the shenanigans of "bobby soxers"? That there are, here and there, a few rare exceptions serves only as usual to prove the rule.

Still less should we expect to find subversive/poetic qualities in those comics that consciously aim at the glorification of detectives and cops. And yet, though the great majority of these comics are irredeemably dreary, the exceptions are both sufficiently numerous and of such indisputably high quality that we are confronted with what might seem to be an anomalous circumstance. The problem, however, is easily solved: the extreme intensity of conflict in these comics, their fevered acceptance of the omnipresence of crime and malevolence, their dark obsessiveness and constantly recurring violence are such that the artists often are carried away by their creations. On such emotionally charged terrain, conscious intentions count for little: it is the *latent* content that commands our notice. What do these comics show us? A mercilessly steady stream of snapshots: brutally altered primal scenes, traumatic memories, Oedipal rages, savage impulses, fits of ferocity, lust, and vengeance. The seven deadly sins multiplied a thousandfold cavort and grovel in these stark panoramas of unconscious mental processes. In Will Eisner's compelling *Spirit*, in *The Shadow* (drawn by several hands), in Jack Cole's admirable *Plastic Man* we are presented with shattering, nightmarish dramas—as gory and disfigured, perhaps, as Grunewald's *Crucifixion* or Goya's *Disasters of War* but also just as authentic in their passionate portrayal of the *return of the repressed*.

Pride of place among the comics' detectives belongs to Chester Gould's pioneering Dick Tracy. Starting on the 4th of October, 1931, this laconic, angular, trench-coated knight has ventured boldly through the streets of Chicago to do battle with an astonishing cast of villains. In the very nerve center of America's criminal underworld, Depression/ Prohibition Chicago—the Chicago of Al Capone and Bugs Moran, whose rival gangs of bootleggers were machine-gunning each other all over town—Tracy was the first in comics to begin, in Chester Gould's words, "fighting it out face to face with crooks via the hot lead route." Gould has expressly denied being influenced by Dashiell Hammett or other "hard-boiled" mystery writers. But there is no doubt that the work of such writers, which enjoyed such wide popularity from the mid-1920s through the '40s, helped prepare an audience for Tracy. And Tracy, in turn, has influenced the crime/mystery genre, not only in comics but also in literature, radio, movies. Ellery Queen has credited him with being "the world's first procedural detective of fiction."[1]

The real interest of *Dick Tracy*, however, lies elsewhere. Tracy himself is of decidedly minor interest, always peripheral to the strip that bears his name. The central figures of the strip, its prime attractions and the reasons for its success, invariably have been the "bad guys." The real theme of *Dick Tracy* is: *the fascination of Evil*.

Look at its unparalleled roster of grotesque rogues: Little Face, B-B Eyes, Mole, Flattop, Pruneface, Mrs. Pruneface, Mumbles, The Brow, The Blank, Shaky, and a host of others. It is these incarnations of Satan—these insatiably cruel, deformed, horrible abominations—who hold the spotlight as they move from outrage to outrage, gun or dagger in hand, through an immemorial darkness spattered with moonlight and blood. We are in the old Gothic wilderness; it has been industrialized and urbanized, of course, and the moldering castles replaced by skyscrapers, but the atmosphere remains essentially the same. A cold metallic solitude rings through the Tracy epic in its early years. Wet streets glisten with greed and fear as we follow crazed killers in their gloomy sedans, roaring through the shadows to an inexorable doom.

It is beyond question that Gould consciously—with all his heart—is on the side of the cops. He is an inveterate champion of law 'n' order, a hater of crooks who likes to spend his free time visiting police stations to see how the boys are doing in their war on crime. But at night, when he shuts his eyes, he can't help dreaming; and sometimes dreams enjoy the sweetest revenge. "I don't outline the whole story when I start," Gould has admitted. "I feel if I don't know how it is going to come out, then the reader can't, and if you keep enough punch and enough interest, the intervening ground seems to be covered automatically."

Even such a casual concession to automatism has serious consequences. In spite of Gould's precautions, poetry wreaks its own havoc and achieves its own infallible justice. To cite but one example: When one of the *Dick Tracy* villains, the psychopathic killer Flattop, died,

> Gould received half a dozen telegrams from people who offered to claim the body.... The day of the funeral, several floral offerings and a stack of sympathy cards arrived at the office of the syndicate which distributes the strip. That night a crowd of

bereaved citizens gathered … and held a wake, complete with a coffin and candles, for Flattop. Many people have since written Gould touching letters, expressing their deep sense of personal loss.… A woman living on the West Coast asked the ageless question, "Why did he have to die?" and added sadly, "All America loved Flattop."[2]

We read *Dick Tracy* the way we read Cotton Mather's *Wonders of the Invisible World*. Both are works of apoplectic puritanism, bursting at the seams with an uncontrollable and "righteous" fury. But we are as little interested in Gould's respect for the law as we are in the fine points of the old witch-hunter's theology. What interests us is the insuperable violence of the dramatic collisions and the dazzling profusion of obsessive detail.

Let us conclude by paraphrasing Blake: the reason Chester Gould writes in fetters when he portrays Law-Abiding Citizens and Cops, and at liberty when he portrays Evildoers and Criminals, is that he is—unconsciously at least, and in spite of himself—"a true Poet and of the Devil's party without knowing it."

15

George Herriman (*Krazy Kat*)

First published in "Surrealism and Its Popular Accomplices," special issue of *Cultural Correspondence*, guest-edited by Franklin Rosemont, nos. 10–11 (Fall 1979): 58–64.

———

Next to "What is Truth?" the question "Who is Krazy Kat?" is the most perplexing in the annals of philosophy.

Rather than even attempt a definition, let us begin on more modest terrain with a simple *description* of George Herriman's magnificent creature and the drama that unfolds around it.

Nominally a cat (or at least a kat)—albeit with few typically feline characteristics—and of indeterminate gender, Krazy is a gentle, wistful, poetic, eccentric, innocent, impractical, exuberant, inspired, idealistic, and amorously passionate dreamer wildly in love with a mouse named Ignatz. If Krazy is not like other cats, Ignatz is not at all like other mice. Inordinately strong, Ignatz is not easily frightened. He regards himself as coldly logical, realistic, rational, materialistic, practical, and unsentimental; he is also hot-tempered, short-sighted, and malicious. He is by no means scrupulously honest; he is sometimes hypocritical and is always thoroughly cynical and pugnacious. In contrast to Krazy's unabashedly lowbrow tastes, Ignatz prefers Mozart, Beethoven, the classics. Perhaps the mouse's most endearing quality is his wholehearted disrespect for the law; indeed, we can forgive him much (and even grow fond of the little demon) because he is such an incorrigible sinner.

Far from returning the kat's affection, the mouse insists that he despises his krazy admirer and, to demonstrate his scorn, hits the kat again and again—many thousands of times over the years—with a brick.

Krazy, however, does not interpret Ignatz's overt aggression as hostile. For the kat, the brick is the proof, a veritable symbol, of the mouse's deep devotion. Time and again Krazy is anxiety-stricken that no brick has hit his head that day; time and again, following such moments of despair, the kat is duly clobbered in the end and sings, "Now I'm a heppy, heppy ket."

At this stage in the drama we meet the third and last of its central figures: a sort of bulldog, Coconino County's official representative of "law 'n' order," who happens to be in love with Krazy, and who is ever vigilant in protecting his love from the violence of the mouse. As often as Ignatz tosses a brick, Officer Pupp tosses Ignatz into jail.

Officer Pupp, also known as Kop, may be more or less doglike, but he is hardly coplike. Aside from his touching fondness for the kat, his incessant philosophical soliloquies—delivered with old-time oratorical grandiloquence and accompanied by exaggerated theatrical mannerisms—makes him, as a law enforcer, odd indeed. And if he does, several times a week as a rule, apprehend Ignatz and lock him in a cell, nonetheless the mouse—repeated offender though he is—always is back on the street next day: rather a poor showing, by police standards.

There are many other characters in the story: among the regulars are Mrs. Kwakk Wakk, the gossipy duck; Kolin Kelly, the brickmaker; Y. Zowl, an owl with an MD; and Joe Stork (sometimes referred to by his Spanish name, Jose Cigueno), "purveyor of progeny to prince and proletarian." But the aforementioned trio—kat, mouse, and kop—hold an indisputable centrality in the strip: they are the driving forces in Herriman's irreducible dialectic.

It is necessary to emphasize the peculiar *symbiosis* of these three characters. They are engaged in a complex contest in which there is no question of our "taking sides." They are all in it together. In one strip Officer Pupp has lost his memory ("lost about a quart of memory where but a pint existed before"). Leaving the doctor's, he runs into Ignatz but fails to recognize him. Upon questioning, he admits that he does not know the name Krazy Kat. Gleeful at this turn of events, Ignatz rushes off, brick in hand: "At last I'm free to toss this 'brick' at that 'kat' without that kop's interference." But by the time he finds the kat he has forgot what he intended to do; indeed, he has forgot who he is and, face to face with Krazy, recognizes him not. Whereupon an alarmed kat runs off shouting, "Oh-h doctor!" But when Krazy finds the doctor, he too has a memory failure—can't remember what he wished to say. The final panel shows all three—mouse, kat, kop—together in the amnesia ward of Dr. Ambrose Phleeze's sanitarium, each ignorant of the identity of the others.

In *Krazy Kat* the old cat-and-mouse game is remorselessly inverted, subdivided, stirred up, hopelessly confounded, and, ultimately, *superseded* in a unique "eternal triangle" adjusted to non-Euclidean specifications. The action takes place as far as possible from Reason (probably in that very domain where, once upon a time and long, long ago, Reason was invented—as a plaything). Everyone and everything appears here with a staggering freshness. All stereotypes have been forced through the sieve of schizophrenic derealization. The world is not only topsy-turvy but also shifted into unexpected and ever-changing dimensions. Here is a universe governed exclusively by its own laws, which essentially are the laws of free association, passional attraction, Jacques Vaché's immortal umor, spontaneous play, and the physics of poetry.

Through it all, year in and year out, we are treated to a laugh a minute—or oftener. Fortunately for us, we know now that laughter—like everything truly desirable—must lead *somewhere*.

Herriman's magisterial strip has elicited numerous paeans of praise, a few detailed commentaries, several widely conflicting interpretations, and, most plentifully, polite confessions of despair to the effect that, tantalizing as the strip is, it doesn't have a bit of meaning. Although it is "universally acclaimed as the greatest comic strip of all time," as Bill Blackbeard says in *The World Encyclopedia of Comics*, surprisingly little light has been shed on Herriman's motives, methods, or achievements.

Traditional critical approaches will always shrivel to nothing before this unpretentious yet sublime work. The arduous search for "sources," with which philologists like to commence their exegeses, has turned up little more than the faintest clues. It is unquestionable, for example, that Herriman was influenced by Cervantes. This is plain from any number of internal details (there is even a character in *Krazy Kat* named Don Kiyote), as well as from abundant affinities of atmosphere and theme. Krazy is very much like Don Quixote: a romantic knight-errant who faces impossible odds in a madcap effort to revive the Golden Age. And the perils that Krazy confronts, like those of Don Quixote, are all the greater, all the more hilarious, in that the kat does not see them the way we do. All that Krazy Kat does, moreover, surely qualifies as *quixotic*. Society, for Herriman as for Cervantes, is a welter of meretricious schemes and devious designs, all working at cross-purposes—over which a solitary dreamer may somehow, almost "accidentally," triumph, doubtless thanks to his perseverance in his solitude and to the integrity of his dreams.

If Krazy Kat is a passable Don Quixote, Ignatz is rather a poor Sancho Panza. And Officer Pupp is wholly unsatisfactory as Rocinante. Some critics have attempted to compensate for these shortcomings by compounding the confusion. It has been suggested, for example, that Krazy is not only Don Quixote but also Parsifal; and Gilbert Seldes proposed, no doubt jocularly, that Ignatz is not only Sancho Panza but also Lucifer. We could add that Krazy is both Romeo and Juliet, and probably also Hamlet and Ariel; the kat has much in common with Immalee in Maturin's *Melmoth the Wanderer* and embodies the principal qualities of Queequeg, Tashtego, and Daggoo in *Moby Dick*. This sort of thing, of course, can go on forever—but does it help us understand anything?

If the Don Quixote analogy collapses in a heap after a few faltering steps, e.e. cummings's effort to see in the strip an allegory about Democracy versus all extremism—in which Krazy represents Democracy struggling against the Individual (Ignatz) and Society (Officer Pupp)—never even gets to its feet: Herriman's mighty epic just does not conform to such shallow and lukewarm prejudices.[1] Just as little are we aided by a more recent attempt to read the strip through the double lens of Kierkegaard and Sartre.[2] Hard as it may be for the partisans of simple solutions to accept, *Krazy Kat* simply is not reducible to any simple formula: literary, philosophical, political, psychological, aesthetic, or otherwise.

There are indeed very real difficulties posed by Herriman's many-sided message. The strip developed, day in and day out, for more than thirty years; and if its thousands of incidents retain an unmistakable coherence—and form what can be regarded as a unified whole—still there were countless digressions, sidelong glances, and a multiplicity of subtle ramifications. The very magnitude of the work and its incontestable complexity—together with the mediocre attempts made thus far at critical interpretation—have led some critics to conclude that it is not in fact interpretable at all, that it is "meaningless." The most assertive proponent of this view, Robert Warshow, bluntly stated: "We do best, I think, to leave Krazy Kat alone."[3] For Warshow, and for others who have followed his lead, Herriman's strip is without significance except perhaps as a symptom of the "extremity of ... alienation" in "*Lumpen* culture." Behind this abstentionism we cannot miss the ill-concealed sneer of the snob. He recognized the power of the strip, and even begrudged it "a certain purity and freshness," but only by way of condemning it all the more for being outside the purview of High Culture. Warshow typifies the unhappy bourgeois intellectual who would choose at all costs to remain unhappy rather than cease to be bourgeois. He perceived that once it was admitted that the "mass image" deserved the same consideration as any other "work of art," then traditional aesthetic values (and beyond those, traditional *social* values) would stand exposed as laurel wreaths whose leaves have long since withered to dust.

As if to illustrate the extreme backwardness of American critics as far as the "popular arts" are concerned, Warshow's bitter polemic has sometimes been mistaken for an "appreciation" of Herriman. That there is more than a little hypocrisy in the voluble acclaim of *Krazy Kat* is further indicated by the fact that seventy years after the kat's initial appearance, and thirty-five years after Herriman's death, only a minute portion of his complete works ever has been printed in book form. Surely the prerequisite for serious evaluation of any artist's or writer's contributions is that the work under consideration be accessible. To read Herriman, however, one has to pore over musty and crumbling newspapers or scan mile after mile of microfilm.

The many and disparate attempts at analysis to which *Krazy Kat* has been subjected have at least the virtue of demonstrating the extraordinary and lasting power of fascination that this comic strip has exerted on minds very different from each other. If one recalls, first, that it was a highly *popular* strip, perhaps less widely read than *Blondie* or the later *Peanuts* but nonetheless appearing daily for decades in dozens of papers, and second, that although its publisher was William Randolph Hearst (the most demagogic and reactionary figure in the US news media of his day) it aroused the sympathetic interest and even devotion of many who were generally antipathetic to everything Hearst stood for, then it becomes clear that with *Krazy Kat* we are in the presence of an extraordinary phenomenon. Such coincidence of taste between "advanced intellectuals" and "the masses" testifies to Herriman's rare prescience, which reveals in turn a deeper truth: that *Krazy Kat* expressed, in a uniquely captivating way, the latent content of the historical drama that convulsed the first half of the American twentieth century.

∾

The following notes are offered as jottings from a "log," so to speak, of repeated journeys through the kat's enchanted domain. I never have been able to view Herriman's work as primarily a problem to be solved. It is rather a gift to be enjoyed. It seems to me to be neither a chess game nor an allegory nor a riddle, but rather a series of radiant glimpses into a unique world of the imaginary: a window—a kaleidoscope of windows—opening on the Marvelous, through which it is our privilege and our pleasure to look and see. And how could one expect to see anything there if one does not seek, first and above all, *emotions?* Confronted with such splendor, our affective responses, provided that we allow them the fullest freedom to roam far and wide, could hardly fail to throw light not only on the work under consideration but also on our whole destiny—our destiny as individuals as well as the collective destiny of humankind.

To avoid misunderstandings, it is necessary to begin with some first principles—a trayful of kategorical aperitifs:

1) *Krazy Kat* is not only a work of "fantasy"—it is, much more importantly, a work of *nonsense:* indeed, one of the masterpieces of nonsense. This does not mean, of course, that it therefore lacks "significance"; on the contrary, there is more significance and worth in the best nonsense than there is in the great bulk of what passes for sense. It so happens that the significance of nonsense lies outside of formal logic, but this in no way diminishes its interest, for logic itself is almost negligible as a factor in human affairs.

The strip's dialogues often have the flavor of Zen koans or the surrealist "one-in-the-other" game, or—at times—the excruciating ambiguity of certain mystical paradoxes, such as St. Teresa's "I die because I cannot die." A riot of rhyme and "reasons beyond Reason," and therefore situated outside of any traditional discipline, *Krazy Kat* drinks from sources deeper and more far-ranging than philosophy or religion. "The world as it is, my dear K," Ignatz explains, "is not like it was, when it used to be." To which Krazy responds: "An' wen it gets to be wot it is, will it?"

2) *Krazy Kat* is before all else a *poetic* work, and George Herriman is one of the greatest American poets. If he kept his distance from the abject literary cabals that writhed and bribed their way through the English language of his day, it is all the more to his credit. *Krazy Kat* is definitive proof of our oft-reiterated contention that American poetry in this century has lived primarily *outside the poem*.

It is astonishing that no one has yet taken the trouble to approach Herriman's work from the linguistic angle. Such an exploration could not help yielding important discoveries. Herriman's language was drawn more or less equally from lush Victorian prose and the Yiddishized street lingo of New York's Lower East Side: something like a synthesis of Emily Brontë and Groucho Marx. This gives his dialogues a very special rhythm, a *baroque pulsation*, found nowhere else.

Herriman's wordplay is invariably loose and lively. The kat would never say "Of course I wouldn't," but rather "If coarse I wooden." Richard Wagner becomes "Rigid Vogna"; "solar eclipse" is "solo eeklip." In strip after strip we find enticing queries ("Do the moom always come ova the mountin? Dunt the mountin evva come ova the moom?") and grand assertions: "You turn off the light and turn on the dark. You turn off the dark and turn on the light. Positivilly marvillis!" and "I like my kit fits in riddim—I do."

3) *Krazy Kat* was not "conceived," not "born"—it "jes grew."[4] Herriman was as surprised as his readers by the doings of his kat, whose "marvelous secrets," moreover, were as elusive to him as to us.

Consider these words by Herriman himself, which I think may be taken as a kind of testament: "You have written truth, you friends of the 'shadows,' yet be not harsh with 'Krazy'—he is but a shadow himself, caught in the web of this mortal skein. We call him 'cat'; we call him 'crazy': Yet he is neither. At some time he will ride away to you, People of the Twilight. His password will be the echoes of a vesper bell; his coach, a zephyr from the west. Forgive him, for you will understand him no better than we who linger on this side of the pale."[5]

Wonderfully nonsensical, defiantly poetic, and proceeding unconsciously—or rather *sur*consciously, *as if by magic*—*Krazy Kat* is one of the triumphs of pure psychic automatism. It is its essentially *surrealist* character—recognized by nearly all commentators—that not only makes it resistant to every variety of "specialized" criticism but also renders it endlessly appealing. With this in mind, let us look more closely—a telescope to one eye, a microscope to the other—at just what's happening in Coconino County.

∽

The origins of the strip—how it "jes grew"—are revelatory. Born in New Orleans in 1880, Herriman sold cartoons and other drawings to leading magazines while still in his teens. It is striking that his early work included illustrations for short stories by Charles Fort, that important precursor of surrealism, whose later works—starting with *The Book of the Damned* (1919)—elaborated a worldview as unpredictably and humorously surrational as Herriman's.

After several more or less short-lived strips—most notably the deliriously zany *Major Ozone's Fresh Air Crusade*, which gave more than a hint of the grandeur to come—Herriman in June 1910 started *The Dingbat Family*, soon retitled *The Family Upstairs*. This remarkable strip featured the constant struggle of E. Pluribus Dingbat and his wife, Minnie, to drive away the noisy and otherwise extremely irksome family that lived in the flat above. The Dingbats never see their tormentors; do not even know their name. They try everything—a raging bull, a cannon, sneeze powder, a quartet of boxers (Jack Johnson, Sam Langford, Young Peter Jackson, and Joe Walcott), a bomb, a jujitsu champion, wild bees, a ventriloquist, a cobra, the Pied Piper and three man-eating rats, an elephant, a hypnotist, bagpipe players, a trio of suffragettes, Desperate Desmond (a villain borrowed from another comic strip), a scorpion, a tarantula, a Gila monster. They even try patience, kindness, generosity—to no avail. All their efforts fail; the Dingbats always get the worst of it. The more the Dingbats suffer, the more the Family Upstairs flourishes.

In view of Herriman's zeal for suggestive ambiguities, puns, and innuendoes, it seems reasonable to see in this strip a critique not only of apartment living and obnoxious neighbors but also of all "higher authority"—including the highest: the Holy Family Which Art Upstairs in Heaven, credited by believers with being almost as omnipotent as the Dingbats' persecutors, and surely just as unseen. Significantly, in this regard, Herriman's Family Upstairs is intimately allied with the whole gamut of power; their visitors and friends include Teddy

Roosevelt, William Howard Taft, Buffalo Bill, the Czar, the Ku Klux Klan, Ty Cobb, and many, many more.

The Dingbats' travail ends—as the struggle against religion and all oppression must end—with the toppling of the entire structure. The last strip of *The Family Upstairs* shows a wrecking crew demolishing the whole apartment building—to the great joy, let it be said, of Mr. and Mrs. Dingbat.

Meanwhile, momentous developments had taken place literally "between the lines." In the Dingbats' apartment, almost wholly independent of the story, we meet a cat, soon to be called Kat; and we meet also a mouse who, very early in the series, hits the cat with a brick. These unobtrusive and appealing cat-and-mouse adventures are soon set off in a small strip directly below the Dingbats' story. From these modest subterranean beginnings emerged, a few years later—in October 1913—the separate strip known as *Krazy Kat*.

∾

"Come, let us dedicate the Great American Desert to Terpsichore!" This curious exhortation from one of Edward Bellamy's early stories is realized in Herriman's saga. The choreography of *Krazy Kat* is set precisely in the wide open spaces of Arizona, a brick's throw from the Grand Canyon and the Petrified Forest.

Choreography is the word. I am convinced that the strip's special appeal owes much to its graphic interpretation of the primordial urge to *dance*: the sense of standing on pins and needles, jumping for joy, falling head over heels in love; the sense of dizziness, swooning, of being swept off one's feet. It is no accident that so many commentators on *Krazy Kat* should call it a *ballet*.[6] Attentiveness to dance imagery permeates its every panel. (It is worth noting that the period when the strip began was the most dance-conscious in US history.)

Even in the earliest strips, when it still supplemented *The Family Upstairs*, we meet Krazy in the guises of "Katlova, the Russian dancer" and "Little Egypt"; once Ignatz mistakes the kat for the popular nightclub singer/dancer Eva Tanguay. Moreover, from ballet to ballroom, from vaudeville to voodoo, from jig to jitterbug, Krazy Kat is always dancing up a storm.

Indeed, *Krazy Kat* offers us a unique example of a "danced drama" within the limits of a printed page. Everything contributes to this effect: the bold play of chiaroscuro; the constantly changing background; the exceedingly resilient *line*. Few artists have a line so sinuous and yet so strong as Herriman's. René Crevel wrote of Paul Klee that "he takes a walk with a line"; for his part, Herriman takes a line out for a mad fandango. In portraying his characters he was deeply aware of centers of gravity, of nuances in poise and differences in gait; each movement, each gesture, each glance, conveys depths of meaning. With the slightest agitation of a pen, he brought to life an imagery vibrant with rhythms unknown before him.

When we read a text or look at a picture—or do both at once, as in a comic strip—we too easily forget that it is our *whole bodies* that read. Beyond the eye that exists in its "savage state," invoked by Breton, the *kinesthetic sense* is ready to avenge itself on the immobile. Krazy Kat, too restless to stay confined in the world of two dimensions, leaps out into a third, a fourth, and a fifth, thereby appealing powerfully to this too-little-understood "sixth sense."

In his classic *Code of Terpsichore* (1828) Carlo Blasis wrote that love—"of all passions the finest and most powerful"—was "the principal spring of action in a ballet." It is the spring of action too in *Krazy Kat*: "Love," as the kat says, "will fine away."

In *Krazy Kat* dance does not appear as an alienated spectacle but as the simultaneous emancipation of body and mind, which are, moreover, no longer perceived as contradictory. Krazy's dances are the untrammeled expression of a free and imaginatively exalted life.

Without dance, how could we account for the most overwhelming quality of the whole strip: its *supreme grace*?

Krazy Kat is not only the "danciest" comic strip but also the most *musical*. Herriman's knowledge of music was considerable. He was even something of a musician himself: in the '90s he wooed his girlfriend with songs, accompanying himself on mandolin. The mandolin is also Krazy's favorite instrument, but the kat, "imbillivibly" versatile, also plays piano, bass viol, several kinds of horn, harp, drums. And he bursts into song at every opportunity—even when it isn't opportune at all.

I do not know what music accompanied, or was meant to accompany, the *Krazy Kat* animated cartoons made (under Herriman's supervision) by Vitaphone in 1916–17. But I know what music fits the strip to a T—the music that shares the same freewheeling insouciant magic: it is the music of the early, crazier black swing bands. When I read *Krazy Kat* I can hardly help hearing Jimmie Lunceford's "I'm Nuts About Screwy Music" or Cab Calloway's "Kickin' the Gong Around."

Is it purely by accident that the first recorded blues vocal (by Mamie Smith, 1920) was called *Crazy Blues*? When jazz musicians, some years later, began talking about "crazy cats"—meaning *inspired men*—were they not heralding the proliferation, rather, of Krazy Kats: that is, a new generation of footloose dreamers, rebellious and innovative outsiders, whose sensibilities had been shaped to an appreciable degree by events in Coconino County? Weren't the "hep cats," who later evolved into hipsters, following in the footsteps of a certain "heppy, heppy ket"?

Let it be borne in mind that jazz and the comic strip—universally acknowledged as this country's most important contributions to the arts—were equally subject to derision by the guardians of bourgeois High Culture. These two *despised media* were thus well situated to express the deep and secret longings of the most despised sectors of the population: the most exploited of the proletariat, immigrants, blacks, slum-dwellers, hoboes, drug victims, prostitutes, lunatics, and jazz musicians.[7]

16

Homage to Tex Avery

Selection from "Surrealism and Its Popular Accomplices," special issue of *Cultural Correspondence*, guest-edited by Franklin Rosemont, nos. 10–11 (Fall 1979): 53–55.

———

Tex Avery is not merely the greatest of all animated cartoonists; he is one of the freest spirits of our age or any age. He has given the imaginary a force of propulsion that for generations will carry passionate dreamers on voyages beyond their most extravagant hopes.

Tex is a direct descendant, on his mother's side, of Judge Roy Bean, a genuine old Wild West hero of folkloric dimensions. Avery shares his illustrious forebear's taste for freewheeling violence and a rollicking good time, but there is a sharp distinction between them: Judge Bean introduced "law 'n' order west of the Pecos," whereas Tex has fomented lawlessness and disorder on both sides, as well as all points north, south, up, down, and inside-out.

It has often been remarked that film animation provides freedom unparalleled in other media. It makes the impossible easy and places the inconceivable within reach. Such freedom exists, of course, precisely so that surrealist use can be made of it. And indeed, from the early days of Winsor McCay and Émile Cohl, through Pat Sullivan's Felix the Cat and Max Fleischer's Koko the Clown, no medium has brought forth such an abundance of surrealist moments as the animated cartoon. And no animationist has been so consistently and relentlessly surrealist as Tex Avery.

In *Slaphappy Lion* a kangaroo vanishes into its own pocket. In *Billy Boy* a goat is rocketed to the moon, eats it, and then proceeds to eat the movie screen as well. In *Dragalong Droopy* gunfighters firing at each other from behind boulders "just happen" to shoot away bits of rock so as to form perfect replicas of the Venus de Milo and Rodin's *Thinker*. In all of Avery's work, the marvelous "just happens." The adage "wonders never cease" loses its lame irony and assumes a breathtaking actuality. The unexpected occurs with such rapidity and force that it becomes as natural as breathing—and as intoxicating as breathing nitrous oxide.

If he had done no more than create Bugs Bunny (*A Wild Hare*, 1940), Avery's immortality would be assured. But if bringing into being the world's greatest rabbit can be regarded as his crowning achievement, it must not diminish our appreciation of Avery's other achievements, which are both numerous and impressive. He has given us, among others, Daffy Duck, Porky Pig, Chilly Willy Penguin, Droopy Dog, and Screwy Squirrel.

This last, although he starred in five cartoons (1943–46) remains too little known. It is he, perhaps more than any other of Avery's characters, who best exemplifies the vast gulf separating Avery from Disney. Screwy is a ferocious, psychotic "wise guy" opposed *absolutely* to everything that Disney stood for. He is Avery's exterminating angel out on a mission to mop up every trace of the sickeningly sweet sentimental cute little fuzzy-wuzzy claptrap. Screwy Squirrel is so hopelessly unendearing that he finally becomes admirable. The cartoons in which he is featured are generally regarded, even by many Avery enthusiasts, as a bit *excessive*. But shouldn't we be grateful that Avery always has had the courage to *go too far*? The disarming nonchalance with which he annihilates common sense, elementary decency, and good taste is the surest proof that his poetic reflexes are attuned to the infinite.

In addition to his creation of characters—many of whom, of course, have gone on to enjoy long and fruitful careers under other directors—Avery has made several one-shot features of such rare poetic quality that to call them nothing more than masterpieces would be to demean them.

Who Killed Who? (1943) is an uproarious distillation of all whodunits and ghost stories, set in a huge old mansion. An elderly gentleman is seated in an armchair nervously reading a book titled *Who Killed Who?—From the Cartoon of the Same Name*. His chair is furnished with a sign telling us that he is "The Victim." A skeleton in the cuckoo clock announces that "at the sound of the gun, the time will be exactly twelve o'clock." The gunshot is followed by an incredible whirl of gangsters, malevolent butlers, and ambulatory corpses pursued by a dopey, heavy-set, cigar-chewing detective. There are numerous mad chases up and down long winding marble staircases and along ominous and gloomy corridors. Searching for clues, the detective comes to a closet labeled "Do not open until Christmas." Opening the door, he finds himself face-to-face with an indignant Santa Claus who immediately reshuts the door—and is not heard from again. In the end it is the chief lawman—arguably J. Edgar Hoover—who turns out to be the culprit.

In *King-Size Canary* (1947) we meet a hungry cat who wants a canary for lunch, except that the canary is pitifully small. Discovering a bottle of Jumbo-Gro plant food, the cat tries it out on the canary, who grows indeed: in seconds he is larger than the cat. So the cat too drinks some Jumbo-Gro and is soon even larger than the giant canary. But before the cat can get his hands on him, the bird takes another drink. And so it goes. A mouse and a bulldog also get into the act. Soon we see them on the boulevards, looming larger than the skyscrapers. Each of the four keeps taking drinks to get larger than the others until, in the end, only two immense and forlorn figures are left standing atop a seemingly very small planet Earth, holding each other for dear life as a close-up shows the now-empty bottle of Jumbo-Gro.

Bad Luck Blackie (1949) shows us a defenseless kitten tormented by a vicious bulldog. Along comes Blackie, a black cat whose calling card announces that he specializes in bringing bad luck wherever it is needed. Immediately he goes about afflicting the bulldog with a spate of misfortunes such as no one has ever seen. Each of Blackie's avenging intrusions is accompanied by a few bars of "Comin' Through the Rye." It is our privilege to see, falling from the sky onto the bulldog—as if out of one of the cantos of *Maldoror*—a flowerpot, and then another, a trunk, a piano, a cash register, a locomotive, a horse, a fire engine, a brick and then a whole brick wall, an anvil, a tree, a kitchen sink, a bathtub, a steamroller, a passenger plane, a Greyhound bus, and a battleship.

Because they are unpretentiously and extremely funny—and also because everyone presumes (wrongly) that they are intended only for children—Avery's cartoons have rarely been "taken seriously," as the expression goes. Hard as it may be to believe, some full-length studies of animation have relegated them to a disparaging paragraph or two, or even a footnote. However plain it is that hokum is never *only* hokum, and that Avery's is always—or almost always—sublime, those who manipulate Critical Opinion in this country have largely succeeded in excluding his cartoons (and cartoons generally, for that matter, except Disney's) from the field of Serious Consideration.

A number of critics, without actually deigning to discuss Avery's work, have been nonetheless eager to go on record against his "violence." A veritable hue and cry has been raised over the wonderfully insatiable mayhem in cartoons of the Avery "school." A special study should be made sometime of the particularly disgusting variety of hypocrite who, having no objection to nuclear weapons or to imperialist oppression, reserves his self-righteous wrath for cartoonists and others whose imaginary violence never hurt anyone but is supposed to be such a "bad influence" on children. Doesn't this show all the signs of being a rather shabby *defense mechanism*? Do not these protestations against cartoon violence conceal a deep-seated fear of primary process thinking, a contempt for the child's modes of apprehension, a horror of unrestrained sexuality? Themselves repressed, these custodians of bourgeois Virtue seek to repress others. They are against violence only when it is liberating, revolutionary, amorous, poetic. They hate Avery's work not because it is violent, but because its violence is in the service of freedom and the marvelous.

In its essence, Avery's violence—comprising the qualities of exaggeration, distortion, spontaneity, and aggression that are the principal characteristics of his work—is the violence of Jonathan Swift and of Isidore Ducasse, Comte de Lautréamont. And it is precisely in such company that Avery's work must be situated, not merely on account of formal or stylistic similarities but because of all-pervasive affinities of *content*.

17

Mel Blanc, Wizard of Audio

First published in "Surrealism and Its Popular Accomplices," special issue of *Cultural Correspondence*, guest-edited by Franklin Rosemont, nos. 10–11 (Fall 1979): 32.

———

It is not by his image alone that everyone knows Bugs Bunny; it is also by his *voice*. That tough, nasal, Brooklyn/Bronx twang is as distinctive as any of the rabbit's other features. His voice—as well as the voices of Daffy Duck, Sylvester Q. Pussycat, Porky Pig, Woody Woodpecker, Screwy Squirrel, Pepe Le Pew, Elmer Fudd, Tweety Pie, Yosemite Sam, and countless others—are all the work of one man, "The Man of a Thousand Voices": Mel Blanc.

Even as a child Mel Blanc invented voices and performed at grammar school assemblies. "The teachers would laugh," he recalls, "then give me lousy marks."

When an intended musical career didn't seem to be getting anywhere, he applied at Leon Schlesinger's animated cartoon studio. "I kept coming in looking for a job, and this fellow kept saying, 'Sorry, we have all the voices we need.' Eventually he died, so I tried again." That was 1937; forty-two years later Blanc still remembers the first voice he did for a cartoon. "They said, 'Can you do a drunken bull?,' and I said, 'Sure,' and did it."

Leon Schlesinger Productions eventually became the Warner Brothers cartoon studio. Over the years Blanc did voices for virtually the entire cast of some three thousand cartoons by Tex Avery, Chuck Jones, Robert McKimson, Friz Freleng, and others.

In his introduction to *The Looney Tunes Poster Book* (New York: Harmony Books, 1979) Blanc describes his modus operandi: "In creating all my character voices I followed the same pattern. First I would be shown a storyboard and would be given a brief summary of the situation and moods in which the character would be placed…. All of the Looney Tunes were done in full animation. The process followed for every cartoon was always the same. After I recorded all the voice lines, the animators would then draw the characters to fit these voice tracks. Precise mouth movements were thus created to match each word being said by the character."

During much of his long stay at Warner Brothers, Blanc was also on radio. For a while there was even *The Mel Blanc Show* (also known as *The Fix-It Shop* and *Mel Blanc's Fix-It Shop*). For years he was a regular on the Jack Benny show (on radio and later on TV); at first he did only the growling of Carmichael, the polar bear who stood guard over Benny's subterranean vault, but later he did the voices of the train announcer, the sarcastic parrot Cheapskate, and others. One day, when a radio technician neglected to plug in the recording of Benny's sputtering Maxwell, Blanc managed to provide the "voice" of a struggling antique automobile.

Voices by Mel Blanc were also heard on the Abbott and Costello program, the Burns and Allen show, *The Cisco Kid*, and the *Major Hoople* comedy show (based on Gene Ahern's daily newspaper comic panel, *Our Boarding House*).

It is a long way from Daffy Duck's raucous "woo-woo" to the gravelly snarl of Yosemite Sam; and when we recall that he has made a romantically inclined skunk sound exactly like Charles Boyer and that he can make a horse whinny with an English accent, we are inclined to agree with those who insist that there is no sound that Mel Blanc cannot make. He says he once started to count the number of voice characterizations that he had devised but fell asleep after four hundred.

Warner Brothers shut down its cartoon studio in the late '50s, but Blanc has not been idle. Among his many activities in recent years, he taped all the voices for a two-hour revue, "The Bugs Bunny Follies," performed by live actors and dancers; and he did Bugs Bunny's voice on a CBS-TV special, "A Connecticut Rabbit in King Arthur's Court." He also does radio and TV commercials, speaks at college campuses, and dreamed up the Bugs Bunny Birthday Call Kit: for only five dollars and a postcard, you can arrange for a birthday telephone greeting from Bugs Bunny himself.

Some of Blanc's best work has long been available on record. *Bugs Bunny and the Tortoise, Bugs Bunny and His Friends,* and *Bugs Bunny in Storyland* recently have been reissued by Capitol.

Now in his seventies, Blanc refuses to slow down. "My wife talks to me a lot about retiring. I say to her, 'What the hell for?' I never want to stop."

Something of the poetic power and the secret glory of Mel Blanc's voices is suggested by a poignant anecdote. In 1961 he was injured in an automobile accident, so severely that it seems he was actually listed in the obituary columns of some papers. For three weeks he lay in a coma in his hospital bed. "They say that while I was unconscious, the doctor would come into my room and ask me how I was, and—nothing: I wouldn't answer him. So one day he comes into my room, he gets an idea, and he says, 'Hey, Bugs Bunny! How are you?' And they say I answered back in Bugs's voice, 'Ehh, just fine, Doc, how are you?' Then he said, 'And Porky Pig! How you feeling?' and I said, 'J-j-j-just fine, th-th-th-thanks.' So you see, I actually live these characters."

And if these characters in turn continue to live and to contribute their magic to our lives, it is only fair that a good share of the credit should go to the grand audial wizard behind the scenes. It is touching to read that Mel Blanc considers Bugs Bunny one of his "closest friends." We can add, for our part, that any friend of Bugs Bunny is a friend of ours.

18

Dream-Conscious Times:
Surrealism and Early Cinema

Reprinted from Franklin Rosemont, *Jacques Vaché and the Roots of Surrealism: Including Vaché's War Letters and Other Writings* (Chicago: Charles H. Kerr, 2008), 241–49.

We are not yet accustomed of thinking of ourselves as primarily spontaneous beings.

—Angus C. Graham

The period 1900–1933 may have been the most dream-conscious third of a century on record. Heralded by Jarry's *Days and Nights* (1897) and Freud's *Interpretation of Dreams* two years later, books and essays on dreams just kept on multiplying. L. Frank Baum's *The Wizard of Oz* (1900), F.W.H. Myers's *Human Personality and Its Survival of Bodily Death* (1903), Winsor McCay's *Little Nemo in Slumberland* (1905), Karl Abraham's *Traum und Mythus* (1909), Apollinaire's "Oneirocriticism" (1908), William Hope Hodgson's *The Night Land* (1912), J. Sadger's *Sleep Walking and Moon Walking* (1914), Jack London's *The Star Rover* (1915), H.P. Lovecraft's *The Dream-Quest of Unknown Kadath* (1926), Breton's *Surrealist Manifesto* and Aragon's *A Wave of Dreams* (1924), J.W. Dunne's *An Experiment with Time* (1927), Giorgio di Chirico's *Hebdomeros* (1929), Max Ernst's *A Little Girl Dreams of Taking the Veil* (1930), Tristan Tzara's *Grains et issues* (1935), and Breton's *Communicating Vessels* (1932) are only a few of the most world-renowned dream-related works published in those vertiginous years in which awareness of humankind's oneiric life reached heights previously undreamed of, so to speak.

Is it an accident that this massive worldwide explosion of interest in dreams occurred precisely during the heyday of the silent film? Luis

Buñuel's definition of cinema as "a machine for dreaming" suggests otherwise, as does the oft-remarked oneiric quality of the great majority of early films. Georges Méliès, Émile Cohl, Mack Sennett, and other cinema pioneers offered veritable riots of images that seemed to have no counterparts in waking life. Indeed, dream-life was a significant object of inquiry in film, as in Buster Keaton's splendid *Sherlock Jr.*, made the very year that surrealism made itself known as an organized movement.

It is well known nowadays that the surrealists were deeply interested in film and even that they made films themselves. What is still too little known is that motion pictures, as they were called in the "silent" days, were instrumental in bringing surrealism into being. Important too in this thrilling, action-packed episode of surrealism's prehistory is the fact that Jacques Vaché played a leading role.

In his autobiographical *Life Among the Surrealists*, the American tourist Matthew Josephson recalls that, in the early 1920s, "Breton attended the silliest old American films, hoping to discover what Jacques Vaché had seen in them: the surprising, the unexpected, the incongruous in the action of a cowboy, the galloping of western ponies, the huge toothsome smile of Pearl White that (for Soupault) announced the beginning of a new order."[1]

Soupault himself adds: "Those darkened halls ... became the living theater of our laughter, our anger, our pride. In those miraculous crimes and farewells our eyes read the poetry of our age. We were living with passion through a most beautiful period of which the U.S. cinema was the brightest ornament."[2]

It would be nice if we had a list of the films that the inventor of Umour actually saw, along with his detailed commentaries. Such conveniences, however, are denied students of the slipperiest of human eels. What information we have is so little that it fully warrants the old-fashioned adjective *precious*. That we have managed to secure even the faintest glimmer of what Vaché beheld on the silver screen is thanks to a very few passing references in his letters and in Breton's writings. The only film we can say with near certainty was seen both by Vaché *and* Breton—and probably seen together—is *Les Vampires*, a ten-part serial made by Louis Feuillade in 1915. Increasingly recognized as one of the all-time greatest films, *Les Vampires* recounts the bizarre exploits of a Parisian gang of criminal geniuses known as the Vampires, one of whose leaders, Irma Vep (an anagram of *vampire*), is played by the captivatingly adorable actress Jeanne Roques (1897–1957), better known by her screen name, Musidora.

Adventure, humor, eroticism, danger, cataclysms, mad chases, breathless escapes, and surprises galore—all the intoxicating entice-ments of the silent film—are here in massive doses.

The most marvelous scenes show us the Vampires at work and play. Notwithstanding the atrociousness of their crimes, Feuillade has his audience unhesitatingly rooting for the "bad guys" all the way. In their black tights and hoods, these silhouettes of fun-loving evil keep appearing out of nowhere: climbing up buildings, tiptoeing on roof-tops, wandering trancelike through endless doors, hallways, passages, and alleys and down dark and winding brick roads in huge, glorious motorcars, all the while eluding the police, terrorizing the bourgeoisie, and having a grand time.

Aside from the fact that *Les Vampires* was one of the most popular and scandalous films of the day—which movie addicts like Vaché and Breton could hardly have missed—a number of indications persuade us that this wonderful film was an experience they shared together. "It is in *Les Vampires*," Breton wrote, "that one must look for the great reality of this century," a comment revealing the profound impression it made on him. At least once, moreover, he mentions it in connection with Vaché.

In his 1919 preface to the *War Letters*, he recalls "The fine playbill: *They are back—Who?—The Vampires*, and in the dark auditorium, those red letters for *That Very Night.*"

Strong as this allusion is, it is not quite conclusive. Further evidence, however, is contained in the *War Letters* themselves, where Vaché twice uses the word *vampire*. Of course, he probably had read vampire stories or seen vampires in other films. But the fact that *Les Vampires* is *not* a vampire film, and that there is nothing even remotely Dracula-like about Vaché's vampire references, leads us to conclude that his use of the term applies not to the vampires of literature and legend but rather to the criminals portrayed in Feuillade's film.

When, for example, in regard to his famous dream of joining a purposeless Chinese secret society in Australia, Vaché remarks "there may be some vampire in all this," it seems obvious that he is not refer-ring to any nocturnal blood-drinker from Transylvania or elsewhere but rather to the incredibly convoluted and exotic plots characteristic of Irma Vep's gang.

Vaché's invocation of a "vampire dance" is even more directly related to the film, for the concluding episode, "The Bloody Wedding," features a hilarious, dizzyingly wild "Apache" dance at the Vampires' orgy celebrating Irma Vep's marriage to "The Poison Man."

It is also characteristic of Vaché and Breton that the films they saw entered their personal (and interactive) mythology in such allusive ways.

Probably they saw Feuillade's other sensationally popular and even more controversial serial, *Fantômas*, which appeared on the eve of the war. Like *Les Vampires*, *Fantômas* provoked vehement protests from the press and clergy as a "bad example" for French youth, and it was banned in many theaters. For Vaché and Breton, as for countless other young people in France, such condemnation by the "powers that be" added a little extra spice to the pleasure of watching the film.

The film was based on the popular *Fantômas* series of popular novels by Pierre Souvestre and Marcel Allain, which began in 1911 and ran to thirty-two volumes. English translations of eighteen of them appeared in the 1920s as "The Fantômas Detective Series," but they are not really a "detective" series at all. They chronicle the continuously victorious exploits of the supercriminal Fantômas who, in volume after volume, outwits the police and other authorities of all countries as he and his army of lawbreakers gleefully perpetrate their "atrocious pleasantries."

Shadowlike, a master of disguise, "everywhere and nowhere at once," Fantômas is the Lord of Terror, the Genius of Evil, the very personification of crime. Supremely calm, self-assured, always in control, dressed (whenever it pleases him) in the finest clothes, equally at home in the lowest dens of iniquity and the poshest palaces of the ruling elite, he also exemplifies dandyism at its zaniest and blackest. For Fantômas and his gang, the most fantastic improbabilities are the order of the day. "Nothing is impossible for Fantômas!"

Dictated at high speed, with Souvestre and Allain taking turns doing alternating chapters, each Fantômas novel, which averaged around three hundred pages per volume, took five days to write. Their collective creation, and the speed with which they proceeded from conception to completion, facilitated the constant eruptions of the Marvelous that are the very hallmark of the series. As Philippe Soupault wrote in *La Révolution surréaliste*: "I challenge any author anywhere in the world to write, or even more to dictate, fourteen hours a day, day after day, without finding himself under the total control of an absolute automatism."

Fantômas was indeed a lively presence in the surrealist movement's first decade. Copies of the novels, with their lurid color covers, were an important part of the decor of the group's storefront Bureau of Surrealist Research, affixed to the walls with forks. René Magritte did several Fantômas paintings, and Robert Desnos wrote a beautiful "Complainte de Fantômas," which he read over French radio in the 1930s, and for which Kurt Weill wrote the music. References to the Genius of Evil abound in the writings of other surrealist poets and painters, including the Romanian Gherasim Luca, who featured a *Fantômas* cover in his book *Le Vampire Passif.*

For Breton and his comrades, the image of Fantômas tended to superimpose itself on the image of Jacques Vaché, and vice versa. Elusive, improbable, unpredictable, audacious, elegant, and *outrageously* humorous, the Genius of Umour had more than a little in common with the Genius of Evil. Passages from the novel read like descriptions of projects hinted at in the *War Letters*: "There was nobody like Fantômas for staging," we are told in *Juve in the Dock*, "comedies that were at once a defiance of all humankind and a retaliation on society at large." As the Three Musketeers burned their bridges behind them, using the journal *Littérature* more and more for the purpose of having done with Literature, the masked mime from Nantes lived on as a symbolic Master of Terror—master, in any case, of the *poetic* Terror, deeply rooted in the new humor—that Breton, Aragon, Soupault, and a few others were dreaming about.

In such reveries, images of Fantômas/Vaché were doubtless conflated with other images as well: How could it have been otherwise in the case of two masters of disguise? In his last letter-collage to Vaché, Breton included a comic sketch of a character named "Double Face" from a contemporary novel, to which Breton added a caption: "It's *you*, Jacques!"

Commentators have not failed to recognize in Fantômas the imaginary realization of the proletariat's latent desire for revenge against its oppressors. Seeing Fantômas's crimes portrayed on the big screen, working-class audiences saw their dreams fulfilled, just as their employers saw their worst nightmares.

In popular consciousness, Fantômas was comparable to the anarchist Bonnot Gang, whose "mythical" role as symbolic avengers was also widely acknowledged. Far from being the neurotic fantasies of an alienated intellectual, therefore, Vaché's speculations on "amusing eccentricities" were drawn straight out of the most truly popular culture of the day.

It was not only the silent adventure thriller that fueled the fires of Umour and nascent surrealism but also the silent comedy, particularly the American comedy—the films of Chaplin, Keaton, Langdon, Arbuckle, and Semon—in which the passion for freedom and the revolt against boredom reached a fever pitch that refused to cool off.

Chaplin especially won the surrealists' hearts and minds, and Vaché's first of all. In the film he dreamed of making, the inventor of Umour reserved an honored place for "Charlot," as he was known in France. Chaplin is, in fact, the only film personage Vaché mentions.

The Three Musketeers venerated the "little tramp." Aragon wrote about him in his early article "On Décor," in the pioneering French cinema journal *Film*; he also titled a poem "Charlot mystique" in his collection of poems, *Feu de joie* (1919), and later authored the surrealists' militant tract in Chaplin's defense, "Hands Off Love!" In the 1920s Soupault, too, wrote enthusiastic reviews of Chaplin's films and a book about him. Breton refers to Chaplin several times, always with high esteem. "The most glorious artist of our time," as Michel Leiris called him years later, is mentioned often in the writings of other surrealists as well.[3]

In the silent film language of gestures, action, and expressive movement at its most intense and delirious, Vaché found the fulfilment of many aspirations he had cherished as an ardent young mime. Where else but on the silver screen did "the grandeur of silence" develop with such astonishing results? But he also found a point of departure for some new experiments in Umour.

In his letters as in his life, his strategy always avoided the obvious. Just as Vaché was much more than a writer of letters, he was also much more than a *watcher* of films. Constitutionally incapable of reducing himself to the requisite immobility of the thoroughly domesticated spectator, the "joyful terrorist" was an active participant in the films that he saw and initiated Breton into this radically participatory cinema. Breton's accounts of their modus operandi spotlight the rule-smashing praxis of Umour. In *Nadja* he fondly recalled, "With Jacques Vaché, we would settle down to dinner in the orchestra of the former Théâtre des Folies-Dramatiques, opening cans, slicing bread, uncorking bottles, and talking in ordinary tones, as if around a table, to the great amazement of the spectators, who dared not say a word."[4] Some years later, he wrote:

> When I was at the "cinema age" (it should be recognized that this age exists in life, and that it passes) I never began by consulting the amusement pages to find out what film might chance to be the best, nor did I find out the time the film was to begin.
>
> I agreed wholeheartedly with Jacques Vaché in appreciating nothing so much as dropping into the cinema when whatever was playing was playing, at any point in the show, and leaving at the first hint of boredom—of surfeit—to rush off to another cinema where we behaved in the same way, and so on (obviously this practice would be too much of a luxury today).
>
> I have never known anything more magnetizing: It goes without saying that more often than not we left our seats without even knowing the title of a film, which was of no importance to us anyway.
>
> On a Sunday several hours sufficed to exhaust all that Nantes could offer us: the important thing is that we came out "charged" for a few days, as there had been nothing deliberate about our actions, qualitative judgments were forbidden.[5]

No doubt some moviegoers would have classified such behavior as irresponsible mischief—if not outright vandalism. Film critic Linda Williams, however, in a 1981 study, identified the Vaché-Breton approach to movies as nothing less than an innovative strategy "to defeat the passivity inherent in the filmgoing experience."[6]

Willing and eager to take part in other people's dreams, Vaché insisted on doing so on his own terms. Aware that his autonomy was at least equal to that of the filmmaker's and of those who resigned themselves to being simply "the audience," it was obviously his pleasure to *interact* freely with the filmed events before his eyes. Far from being mere rudeness, this procedure not only reflected his distrust of what he called "the lamentable *trompe l'oeil* of universal simili-symbols," but also was wholly in keeping with his effort to avoid getting caught in "the hidden and sneaky life" of things. Disdainful of everything static, reified, and formalized, Vaché regarded films not as "works" in themselves, much less as "Works of Art," but rather as passports to ecstasy, provocations to adventure, guides to the unknown, stimulants for action.

His procedure, moreover—seeing part of a film, leaving at the first appearance of boredom and then seeing part of a second film, and then part of a third—can also be considered a cinematic prefiguration of the surrealist game known as The Exquisite Corpse.

Not surprisingly, our uninvited intervener in the films of others also dreamed of making films of his own: "What a film I would make—with crazy motorcars, you know, crumbling bridges, and enormous hands crawling all over the screen toward some document! ... With colloquies so tragic, in formal attire, behind the listening palm-trees! Charlot, of course ... his eyes peaceful. The policeman is forgotten in the trunk!" (December 19, 1918).

Vaché, alas, never found his place in the director's chair. Months after outlining the film he dreamed of making, he himself came to an end, not in a fire but in the haze of opium.

Cinema, however, lies at the very heart of the outlook and action of the inventor of Umour. He was, as Aragon argued, the first to adopt humor as a central and distinguishing "point of view."[7] Everything leads us to believe that the elaboration of this new and radical humor owed a lot to the fact that its inventor spent countless hours—what his parents must have considered an inordinate amount of time—rushing from one motion-picture palace to another.

To grasp what is truly original in Umour it is necessary to realize that Vaché had learned to think and act cinematically. The monsters of Umour become visible in close-ups from new angles, in enlargements of unnoticed details, and in sudden, unexpected juxtapositions—a basically cinematic way of focusing attention and discovering the unknown.

The mysterious "octopus-typewriter" and other creatures from his modern menagerie—the Ubuesque "tank/pachyderm," for example—suggest new episodes for *Les Vampires* or *The Perils of Pauline*.

His *War Letters* too exemplify the writing style of an inveterate moviegoer. Vaché's slapstick vocabulary, rapid shifts of scenes from one paragraph to the next, sudden zooms and fade-outs all reflect the rhythm and mood of the silent film short. Some of his interjections, in capital letters—"WHEN ONE KNOWS"—pop up in the middle of his flickering sentences like title cards in an action serial. With Vaché, writing itself supersedes literature by becoming "a night at the movies."

19

A Short Treatise on Wobbly Cartoons (1988)

Reprinted from Joyce L. Kornbluh et al., eds., *Rebel Voices: An IWW Anthology* (Oakland: PM Press, 2011), 425–43.

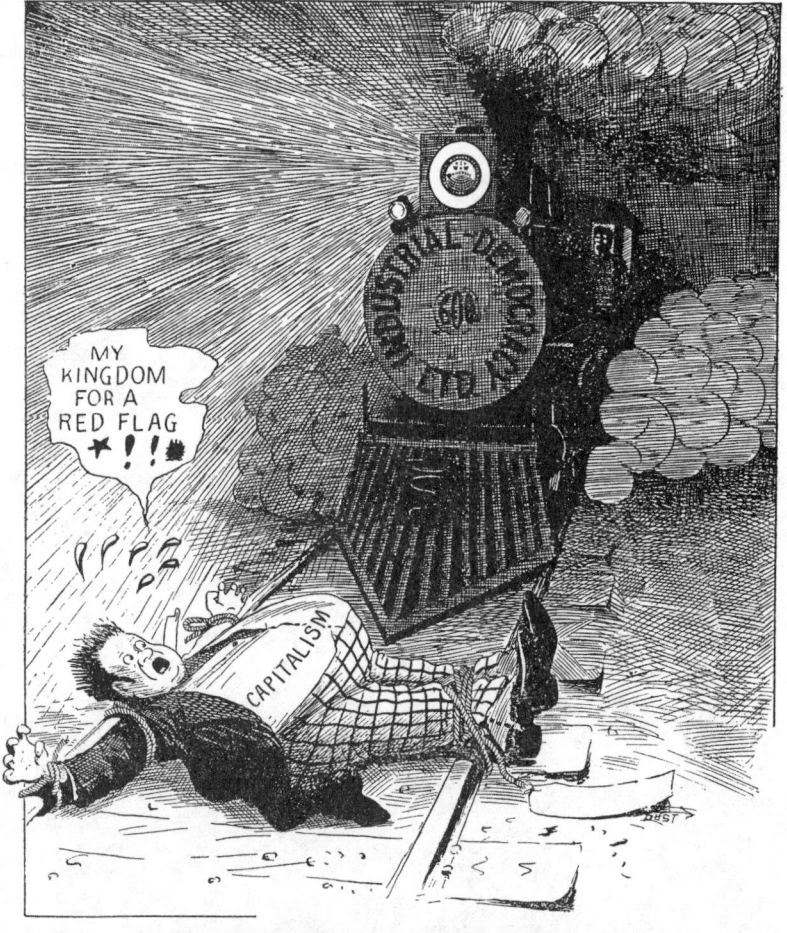

THE DREAM THAT CAME TRUE

Fig. 22. "Dust" Wallin, *One Big Union Monthly*, May 1920.

That the Industrial Workers of the World always was "more than a union"—that its social/economic revolutionary perspectives were broadened and deepened by a no less revolutionary cultural dimension—was plain truth to Wobblies themselves as well as to lucid outsiders in the union's heyday and has been recognized to one degree or another by most later historians. Even before Joyce Kornbluh's *Rebel Voices* appeared in 1964, an extensive critical literature had accrued, for example, on IWW songs.[1] One of the many virtues of Kornbluh's anthology is that it has immeasurably expanded our awareness of the depth and scope of IWW culture. The sheer quantity and quality of this book's four-hundred-plus pages of Wobbly evidence brings home to all the point that the IWW made history not only on the job and in the jungles, but also in poetry, fiction, theater, and the graphic arts.

It is not really surprising that this last remains perhaps the least-studied realm of Wobbly culture. Serious scholarship on mainstream comic art scarcely existed before the 1960s and is still in its beginnings.[2] Even today adequate biographies of such outstanding figures as Frederick Burr Opper (*Happy Hooligan*), George Herriman (*Krazy Kat*), and Elzie C. Segar (creator of Popeye)—universally regarded as three of the greatest cartoonists of all time—are still to be written. As for the non-mainstream comic art that appeared in labor publications, trade journals, small-town weeklies, and the American foreign-language press, it has hardly been studied at all. Few historians of cartooning have been interested in labor, and even fewer labor historians seem to be interested in cartooning. What little has been written on labor cartoons has focused on those artists (Art Young and others) who contributed freely to the labor and radical press while "making a living" by selling very different cartoons to large-circulation commercial magazines and newspapers.[3]

Readers of *Rebel Voices* will have noted that each text reprinted in this book is preceded by a short introduction telling something of the biography of the author. Just how little was known about Wobbly cartoonists in 1964 is suggested by the fact that their artwork is reprinted here with only a line indicating the source and date of publication. Nonetheless, by bringing together what is still, nearly a quarter of a century later, the largest collection of Wobbly cartoons ever united in one volume, *Rebel Voices* laid the foundation for the serious study of this sadly neglected field and inspired some of us to keep digging in the hope of turning up some valuable information on the elusive creators of these images of humor and rebellion.

Labor cartooning had virtually no traditions behind it when the IWW was founded in 1905, and the Wobblies deserve a large share of the credit for developing the new art. Early on, Wob organizers and editors were aware of the propagandistic power of the cartoonist's art, and many times over the years they actively solicited cartoons from the artists in their ranks. Under the heading "Worker Needs Cartoons," the *Industrial Worker* for March 30, 1918, noted that the paper desired "cartoons on industrial union or revolutionary subjects" and that "cartoons in line with the IWW principles and program" were "acceptable at all times." "These should be drawn on heavy white paper in India ink where possible [but] black crayon work reproduces well where the lines are heavy and clear."

The technical difficulty of reproducing much of the work submitted by inexperienced artists was evidently a constant editorial aggravation, for in a similar notice ("To Aspiring Cartoonists") in the same paper for March 25, 1922, precise drawing instructions were again emphasized. Complaining that the paper had recently received "two very good drawings" that could not be reproduced because they were "done with lead pencil on orange-colored cardboard," the editor urged that "it would be a good idea for fellow workers with an aptitude for drawing to look up a book on 'commercial art' or 'cartooning' in a library."

Judging from the great number of first-rate cartoons published in the IWW press, many fellow workers must have heeded this advice. A few may even have taken one of the several inexpensive correspondence courses in cartooning that even then were advertised in mass media and "pulp" publications. The resemblance of some IWW cartoons to the work of such then-popular artists as Opper, Rube Goldberg, T.A. Dorgan ("Tad"), Harry Hershfield (*Desperate Desmond*), and George McManus (*Bringing Up Father*) suggests too that Wob cartoonists were careful students of the comics pages of the big dailies.

What is certain is that Wobbly papers made plenty of room for cartoons—far more than the publications of other unions or of most socialist or other radical groups. The final count is not in, but it seems reasonable to estimate that several thousand cartoons have appeared in the IWW press. Surely it is no exaggeration to say that cartoons have played as large a role as songs in spreading the Wobbly message of working-class education, organization, and emancipation.

We know more today than we did in 1964 about many of these cartoonists, but the gaps in the picture are still enormous, and it is more than likely that some of these gaps will never be filled. Of many Wobbly cartoonists we know nothing beyond their cartoons and their names. Of others we know even less: many signatures are illegible, many artists signed only their IWW numbers, and some failed to sign their work at all. With a few notable exceptions, the union's cartoonists were self-taught amateurs—eager to help build the new society in the shell of the old but utterly indifferent to any prospects of a "career" in cartooning (the IWW press has never paid for contributed material). We must keep in mind, too, that not a few of these cartoonists were hoboes and that anonymity is a built-in feature of hobo life.[4]

Obscure as most IWW cartoonists have remained, a few of them happen to be well known—as Wobblies, if not as cartoonists. One of the union's principal founders, Thomas J. Hagerty—designer of the "wheel of fortune" [a diagram of trade unions comprising the IWW] and chief author of the preamble [to the IWW constitution]—did some humorously captioned caricatures for socialist cultural journal *The Comrade* in 1902.[5] In view of the enormous role of humor in the course of its development, the fact that one of the IWW's cofounders had tried his hand at cartooning seems not only fitting but actually prophetic.

How many people are aware that the most renowned Wobbly of them all, Joe Hill (1879–1915), penned cartoons as well as songs? Although less than a dozen of his cartoons have survived, they are all the more precious to us inasmuch as they picture the same raucous class war humor of such lyrics as "The Preacher and the Slave" and "Casey Jones, the Union Scab." We know that Hill's interest in pictorial expression began early—one of his youthful paintings is on exhibit at the Joe Hill Museum in his hometown of Gävle, Sweden—and remained with him throughout his life.[6] While awaiting his judicial murder, America's most celebrated labor martyr declared, "I have lived like an artist and I shall die like an artist."[7]

Ralph Chaplin (1887–1961), best remembered today as the author of the IWW song "Solidarity Forever," which long since has become the anthem of the entire American labor movement, was also a cartoonist—indeed, one of the union's finest and most prolific.[8] One of the few Wobblies to enjoy the benefits of art school, he worked for many years in the field of commercial art. As staff artist for Charles H. Kerr's socialist publishing house in Chicago he illustrated and designed covers for many books and pamphlets, including Edward Bellamy's *Parable of the Water Tank* and that early radical ecological classic *Germs of Mind in Plants*, by Austrian botanist Raoul Francé. Chaplin contributed lettering and numerous drawings to the Kerr Company's *International Socialist Review*, edited by that colorful libertarian socialist (and later Wobbly) agitator Mary E. Marcy. He also illustrated Marcy's novel *Out of the Dump* and collaborated with her on a deck of socialist playing cards featuring his drawings and her satirical verses.

At his imaginative best when portraying gleeful "sab-cats" menacing blustering bosses as malignant as they are rotund, Chaplin also did many serious editorial cartoons of great power; his salute to Wobbly martyr Frank Little is a prime example. Remarkably versatile, Chaplin also conceived and designed many of the IWW's famous "silent agitators" or "stickerettes" and served as the union's principal letterer-calligrapher in the 1910s (his front-page design for the tenth anniversary issue of *Solidarity* and his program cover for the Joe Hill Memorial are good examples of his work in this area). Chaplin the cartoonist produced an impressive and many-sided body of work, for which he deserves greater recognition.

Though less celebrated than Hill or Chaplin, Ernest Riebe enjoys considerable prestige among Wobblies as the creator of the union's best-loved and most enduring comic strip, *Mr. Block*, which chronicled the misadventures of a blockheaded worker who, in spite of everything, believes the boss is always right.[9] The strip debuted in the Spokane *Industrial Worker* on November 7, 1912, and continued, albeit less frequently in later years, through the early 1920s.

Little is known of Riebe's life beyond the facts that he was born in Germany and lived in Minneapolis during his IWW years. He seems never to have held union office and was not a public speaker. His comic art was his decisive contribution to the cause. The union's earlier cartoons had been mostly of the serious editorial type. What came to be known as characteristically Wobbly humor was largely a creation of the 1910s, and few contributed more to its elaboration than Riebe. It is now established, for example, that Riebe's strip inspired Joe Hill's "Mr. Block" song. Hill's lyrics, which summarize some of the early strips, appeared in the *Industrial Worker* in January 1913. Later that year a *Mr. Block* comic book was published, containing twenty-four strips and an introduction by *Industrial Worker* editor Walker C. Smith. Evidently the first use of the comic book form as a vehicle of revolutionary propaganda, it was reprinted by Charles H. Kerr in 1984. In 1919 two other Riebe comic booklets appeared in pocket-size format: *Mr. Block and the Profiteers* and the ironically titled *Crimes of the Bolsheviki*, which, like all IWW literature of that period, was emphatically pro-Bolshevik in content. Riebe also supplied the IWW press with a poem and a play involving Mr. Block, and some of the early strips were reissued as IWW postcards. Other early Wob cartoonists, including "Dust" Wallin and Ern Hanson, introduced the Mr. Block character into their own cartoons, and the strip has several times been revived in various IWW publications, even in recent years.[10]

Riebe also drew many single-panel cartoons, including a striking antipatriotic series, "Under the Stars and Stripes," that was featured on page one of the *Industrial Worker* from May through June 1913. Later he did several covers for the *One Big Union Monthly*. But *Mr. Block* was his major achievement. Vigorously drawn in a breezy style well-suited to its slapstick content, *Mr. Block* was the Wobblies' greatest comic in the golden age of *Happy Hooligan* and the *Katzenjammer Kids*.

Described by the *International Socialist Review* as "one of Chicago's best known revolutionary artists," L. Stanford Chumley may have been a member of the Socialist Party as well as of the IWW; he also had a hand in organizing the union's General Defense Committee, formed to provide legal and other assistance to the many Wobblies jailed during the World War I anti-radical hysteria. A cover artist for the *Review*, Chumley also produced some notable charcoal portraits of prominent Wobblies and Socialists, including Joe Hill, William D. Haywood, Eugene V. Debs, and Mother Jones. After the war he edited the New York IWW paper, the *Rebel Worker*, and wrote the pamphlet *Hotel, Restaurant, and Domestic Workers: How They Live and How They Work*, published in 1920.[11]

Another artist who drew covers for the *International Socialist Review*, Arthur Machia, designed the sheet music for Joe Hill's song "The Rebel Girl."[12]

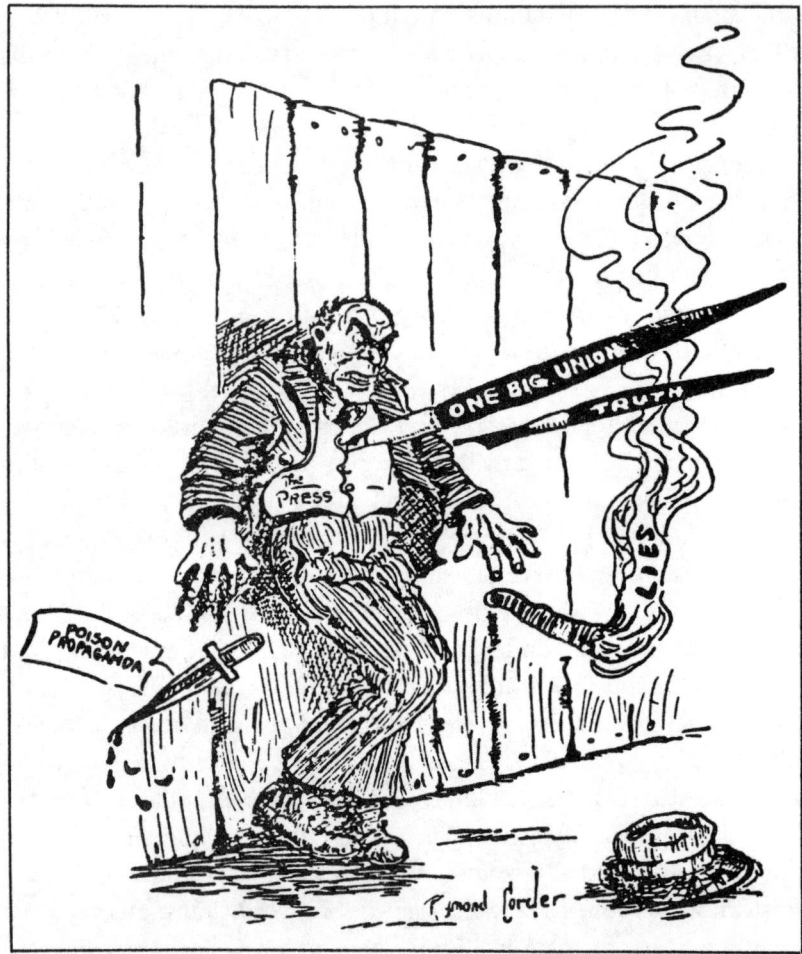

Fig. 23. Raymond Corder, *One Big Union Monthly*, April 1920.

Raymond Corder (1890–1968) was better known for his poems than for his handful of cartoons.[13] One of scores of Wobblies imprisoned for obstructing America's war effort in 1918, he did much of his writing and drawing in jail. His cartoon from *The Can-Opener*, the IWW prisoners' handmade in-house organ while they awaited trial in Cook County Jail, is not truly representative of his work; most of his published cartoons are exceptionally well drawn. Indeed, notwithstanding his evidently small output, Corder ranks as one of the union's more accomplished artists (fig. 23).

Apart from the inferences that he was of Scandinavian origin, lived in the Northwest, and probably worked as a logger, all we know about I. Swenson is his abundant work as a cartoonist. He contributed numerous excellent single-panel cartoons to the *Industrial Worker* in the early 1920s, many of them published on page one. Later he drew some splendid though short-lived strips, most notably the hilarious logging-related *Mackinaw Mike*.

IWW historian Fred Thompson thought that "Dust" Wallin and possibly James Lynch may have been professional cartoonists who sold work to capitalist papers under other names while donating their services to the One Big Union. If so—and the high caliber as well as the great number of their cartoons lends weight to the possibility—their non-Wobbly work has not yet been identified. The Gustave Doré of the IWW, "Dust" drew in the elaborate, minutely detailed style of the old-time engravers, and much of his best work featured classical or "Gothic" imagery. In addition to his many cartoons for IWW newspapers and magazines, he illustrated and designed covers for several pamphlets; one especially elegant example is Abner E. Woodruff's *Evolution of American Agriculture*, published around 1919. Several of his cartoons also appeared as "silent agitators," and during the IWW revival in the late 1960s one was issued as a poster. James Lynch drew several Mutt-and-Jeff-type strips and many single panels as well as caricatures of well-known labor and political personalities. His fine sense of gags was strengthened by a crisp, smooth line and occasional dramatic use of heavy black-white contrast. A steady contributor of articles as well as cartoons to IWW publications through the 1920s, he is also known to have submitted at least one cartoon to the Proletarian Party press.

Whether Wallin and/or Lynch were indeed professionals further research should reveal. No doubt exists, however, regarding the professional cartoonist who contributed most to the IWW press: unquestionably it was Art Young (1866–1943). Born in Orangeville, Illinois, and raised in rural Wisconsin, Young was inspired to become an artist when he saw Gustave Doré's illustrations to Dante's *Inferno* as a child; later he studied under the reactionary academic painter Bouguereau in Paris.[14] One of the best-known cartoonists of his time, he sold cartoons regularly to the leading comic weeklies—*Life*, *Puck*, and *Judge*—as well as to such mainstream periodicals as the *Saturday Evening Post* and even the Hearst papers. Although he had sketched the Haymarket anarchists in Cook County Jail for the *Chicago Daily News* in 1887, his own radicalism did not emerge until the new century was well on its way. One of the driving forces that made *The Masses* the liveliest socialist magazine in US history during the 1910s, Young developed an appealing, exuberant style distinctively his own, both in watercolors and in India ink. A Socialist most of his adult life, he aimed his best cartoons at a broad working-class audience. Since the great majority of his cartoons were free of sectarianism—simply pro-labor and anti-capitalist—they appeared not only in organs of the Socialist Party and the IWW but also in anarchist, Communist, and AFL trade union publications.

Scores, maybe hundreds of Art Young cartoons were published in the *Industrial Worker* and other IWW papers. One on the theme of new machinery creating unemployment, "A Cartoon with a Thought," was drawn especially for the union.[15] During 1921–23 they appeared almost weekly, sometimes more than one per issue. No doubt many readers, Wobs included, thought Young carried a red card himself. No one has portrayed the devastation, wastefulness, and stupidity of capitalism more convincingly than he. His "Poor Fish," spouting good bourgeois conventional wisdom ("The Poor Fish says that he knows labor produces all the wealth but that the capitalists produce even more"), was one of Mr. Block's cousins. His cartoon rallying calls for workers' solidarity and united action were such effective propaganda they were reprinted again and again. Part of the enduring strength of Young's work lies in the fact that he never took himself too seriously. His ruthless attack on the iniquities of class society was balanced by a playful anticipation of the pleasures of socialism. What he wrote of the early English comic artist Thomas Rowlandson could also be said of Young himself: "He kept his banners for the free life flying: to him the free life was the good life."[16] In most of his finest cartoons, a bright humor sparkles with an always youthful, glad defiance.

Very different was Fred Ellis (1886–1941), in whose work humor played almost no role at all. A deadly serious editorial cartoonist, Ellis focused his grease pencil on the tragedy and gloom of class society; the cover of a General Defense Committee pamphlet is typical of his work. Even his occasional "upbeat" cartoons tend to be cold and somber. Never really a part of the Wobbly milieu the way Young was, Ellis was the featured cartoonist of John Fitzpatrick's radical Chicago Federation of Labor paper, the *New Majority*, in the early 1920s when the CFL played a leading role in the nationwide movement for a Labor Party.

For a time he was associated with the packinghouse workers' union. Later he became staff artist for the Communist *Daily Worker* and even spent six months in Moscow in the mid-1930s, cartooning for *Pravda*.[17]

In the late teens and early '20s many other professional cartoonists with Left sympathies either offered their services to the IWW or allowed Wobbly editors to reprint cartoons that had originally appeared elsewhere. Many of the leading cartoonists of the day, including Ryan Walker (1870–1932), Maurice Becker (1889–1975), Boardman Robinson (1876–1952), Robert Minor (1884–1952), and William Gropper (1897–1977), had work published in IWW newspapers or magazines. All of them worked for the big commercial press: Robinson for the *New York Tribune*, for example, and Minor for the *St. Louis Post-Dispatch*. But their most important cartoons, the ones for which they are remembered today, appeared in Socialist or IWW publications.[18]

Sometimes Wobbly papers reprinted particular cartoons by famous artists not known to have had any Left leanings. In addition to his inimitable *Little Nemo* and other imaginative strips, the renowned Winsor McCay also did editorial cartoons, and at least one of them, showing a coal-miner's dream of a better life, was deemed worthy of repeated reprinting in the IWW press.

Much stranger is the case of A.D. Condo. Never really well-known in his own day, he was almost completely forgotten until his collection of two-panel strips, *The Outbursts of Everett True*, was reprinted in 1983 (it was originally published around 1907).[19] The exploits of a heavyset and violent-tempered old man who, often at the slightest provocation, inflicts corporal punishment on just about everyone he meets, *Everett True* would seem to be the work of a misanthrope wholly unsympathetic to socialism. However, another of Condo's strips, *Osgar und Adolf*, ran in the *Chicago Daily Socialist* in the early 1910s. Curiously, in one of Ernest Riebe's *Mr. Block* strips, *Osgar und Adolf* was singled out for special denunciation because, like many strips in the capitalist press at that time, it made fun of foreigners.[20] Even more curiously, in July 1919 a Condo cartoon was published in the *One Big Union Monthly*. The cartoon shows the hand of an unseen person offering assorted weapons to an astonished capitalist portrayed in classic Wobbly style: enormously fat, with top hat, diamond stickpin, and cigar, and with dollar-signs all over his suit. A balloon has the unseen person saying: "Here, if you're so keen for intervention in Mexico, take these tools yourself and go to it!!!" One wonders: Did Riebe's strip help radicalize the cartoonist of *Everett True*?

In the late 1930s the *Industrial Worker* ran a single-panel series titled "The Upper Crust." Although they were signed "A. Redfield" they were really the work of well-known *New Yorker* cartoonist Syd Hoff.

From time to time over the years IWW publications ran cartoons by John Baer, onetime North Dakota congressman—he is said to have been the only cartoonist ever to have held a seat in the House of Representatives—and longtime cartoonist for the Nonpartisan League, and later for the railroad brotherhoods' paper, *Labor*.[21]

In the 1940s Fred Zinn, for many years a contributor to the AFL Lumber and Sawmill Workers' *Union Register* and eventually its staff cartoonist, also carried a red card for a while and drew cartoons for the *Industrial Worker*. He even designed a new masthead for the paper; introduced in the December 14, 1946, issue, it was used for many years and then revived in 1969 for several more years.[22]

Now and then the Wobbly press reprinted cartoons from the radical and labor press of other countries. The original *One Big Union Monthly* used some from the French syndicalist organ *La Vie Ouvrière*, and in May 1924 the *Industrial Pioneer* reproduced an example of the work of an imprisoned Spanish anarcho-syndicalist cartoonist, Juan Bautista Acher, known as Shum. During and after World War II the *Industrial Worker* ran several extraordinary antiwar drawings by German-born John Olday (1905–77), one of the greatest radical cartoonists.[23] A lifelong anarchist who took part in the anti-Nazi underground, he escaped the Gestapo in 1938 and fled to London, where he collaborated on the anarchist paper *War Commentary* and its successor, *Freedom*, as well as on the surrealist journal *Free Unions*. In 1943 Freedom Press published a collection of his bitter, haunting cartoons, *The March to Death*. Toward the end of his life Olday joined the IWW's General Defense Committee and contributed cartoons to its *Industrial Defense Bulletin*.

For every cartoon IWW papers borrowed from abroad, the radical labor press of other lands borrowed dozens from the Wobblies. "From all parts of the world," *Industrial Pioneer* editor John A. Gahan noted in 1926, "we are daily receiving labor press exchanges containing reprints of the cartoons and drawings first run in our own IWW press."[24]

☙

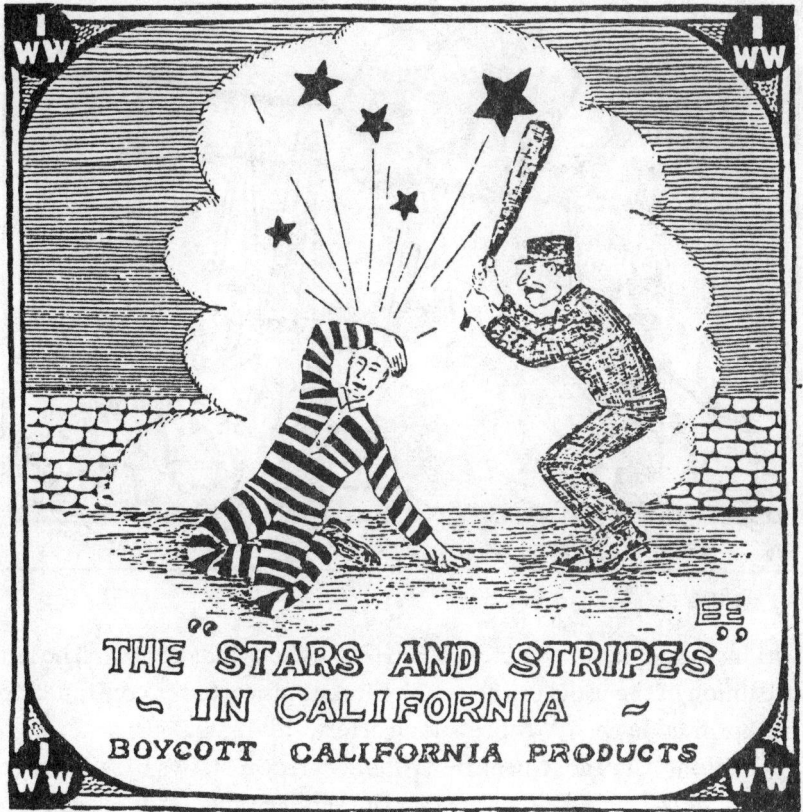

Fig. 24. Ern Hanson, *Tie Vapauteen*, March 1925.

Of the early IWW cartoonists not represented in the original edition
of *Rebel Voices*, Ernest Henry Hanson (1889–1981?) is probably the
most important.[25] Born in Iowa, raised on the Pacific Coast, and radicalized in Arizona in his early twenties, he joined the IWW in 1914 on
his way to the North Dakota harvest and became a "traveling delegate"
three years later. Hobo, logger, trapper, and trail cook, he lived most
of his adult life in the Northwest, especially Montana and Idaho. One
of the wildest Wobbly cartoonists, Ern Hanson unleashed a hysterical
and hard-hitting hobo humor that in many ways was a kind of visual
equivalent of the peppery poetry and prose of his great contemporary,
T-Bone Slim. (Interestingly, of two known sketches of T-Bone, one is
by Hanson.) His sublimely hideous portrayal of Scissor Bill, based on
Joe Hill's song about that abysmal character, is his greatest creation
and appeared in many of his cartoons. Hanson signed his work with

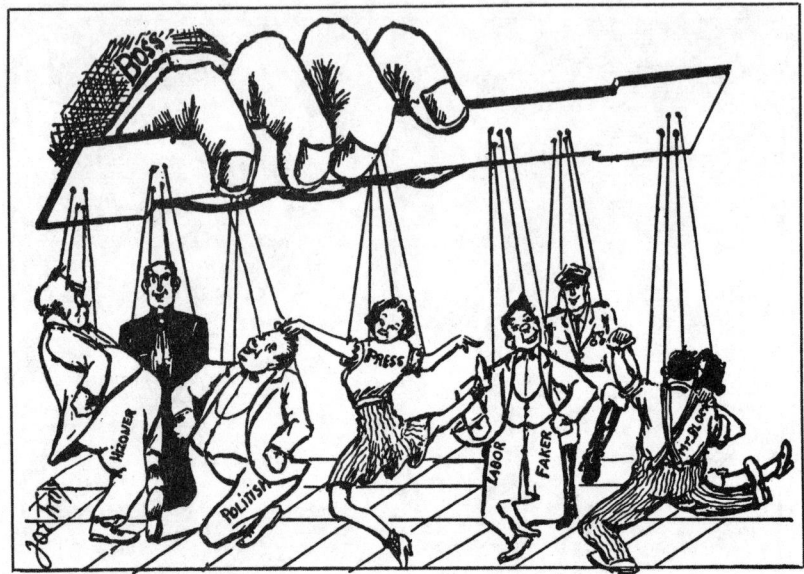

Fig. 25. Joe Troy, c. 1930s–1940s.

various monograms, sometimes EHH. Like thousands of others, he left the union in the wake of the 1924 split, but his cartoons continued to be reprinted in the IWW press long afterward (fig. 24).

Among the most prolific Wobbly cartoonists was Joe Troy (c. 1873–c. 1953), an artist actively in the service of working-class revolution for nearly seventy years. According to Carlos Cortez, Troy (born Treu) contributed drawings to the Chicago anarchists' *Arbeiterzeitung* before Haymarket, when he was only thirteen.[26] Little is known about him otherwise except that he was a lifelong itinerant worker. Fred Thompson recalled meeting him in one of the hobo jungles out west in the late 1920s. More than twenty years later, in the early 1950s, Troy was still sending cartoons to the *Industrial Worker*. Unlike most of his fellow Wob cartoonists, who preferred a loose, "cartoony" style, he favored a strong, naturalistic, yet unpretentious realism; this did not, however, inhibit his boisterous and often bizarre imagination. A large number of Troy's original cartoons and drawings have survived, and in 1986 Carlos Cortez organized an exhibition of his work, in Chicago, to commemorate the hundredth anniversary of the Haymarket Tragedy.

Like several other Wobs, Eugene Barnett did most of his cartooning behind bars.[27] Born in North Carolina, he went to work in the coal mines at the age of eight. A member of the United Mine Workers as well

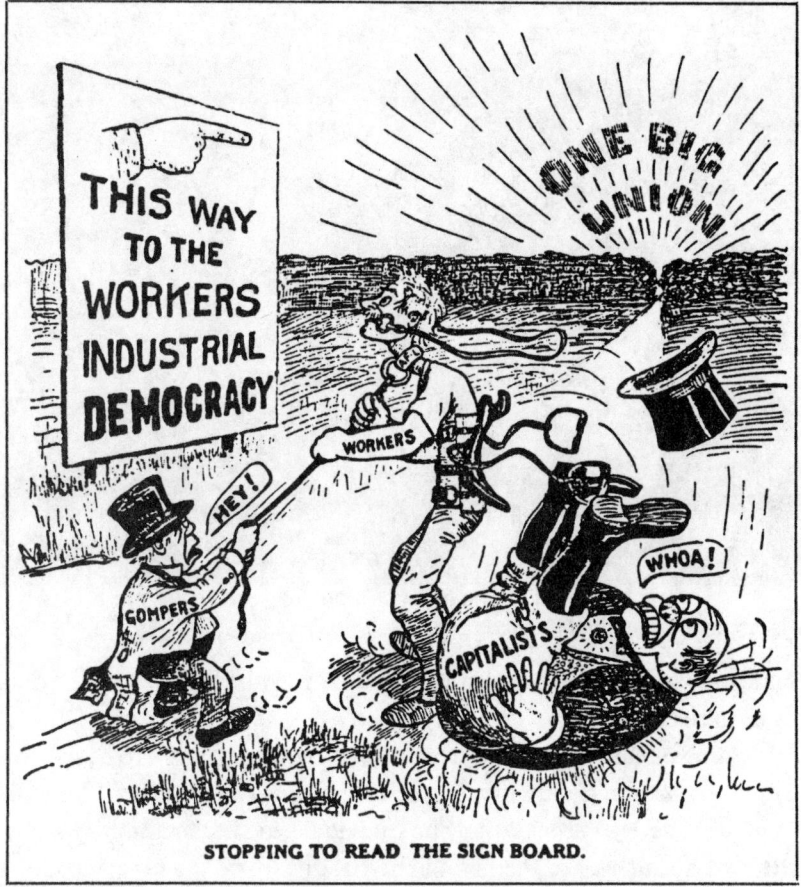

Fig. 26. Eugene Barnett, *One Big Union Monthly*, April 1920.

as of the IWW, he was one of seven Wobblies framed and convicted in the notorious Centralia Conspiracy of November 1919, when the IWW hall in Centralia, Washington, was attacked by armed American Legion thugs in the pay of the lumber barons (it was during this attack that the businessmen's mob murdered Wesley Everest). Paroled in 1931 following a long agitation by the IWW's General Defense Committee, Barnett took up ranching in Idaho, became an organizer for the CIO's International Woodworkers Union, and supported the short-lived Progressive Party in 1948; he died in 1973. Like the work of Swenson and Hanson, his action-packed cartoons showing obese and bug-eyed bosses calamitously beleaguered by Wobs on the job admirably convey the freewheeling insolence of the revolutionary-minded hoboes who

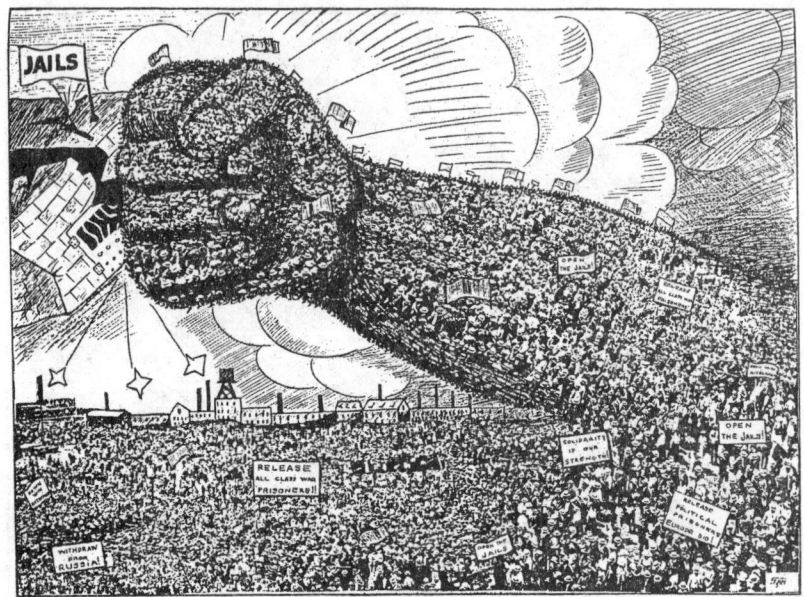

THE GENERAL STRIKE

Fig. 27. Sam, *One Big Union Monthly*, July 1919.

made up such a large percentage of IWW membership in the union's most active days.

Some of the most interesting IWW cartoons happen to have been drawn by artists about whom nothing seems to be known. Most of them were active in that largely unstudied period in the union's history, the 1920s. In the late teens and the first years of the new decade, a Wob who signed himself Sam drew many cartoons—all unusual, many of them technically or otherwise innovative, and in an astonishing variety of styles (fig. 27).

One of the Union's most imaginative artists was Fred Jerger (whose cartoons are variously signed Jerger, FJ, Eff Jay, and Jay). His "Labor and the Up-to-Date Pest Dispenser" (*One Big Union Monthly*, December 1920) is markedly similar to a series of "Quick, Henry, the Flit!" cartoons done by Theodore Geisel, better known as Dr. Seuss, for a pesticide company, but Jerger's predates the latter by three-fourths of a decade.

In a category all by himself is William Ekman, whose chief contribution to Wobbly art consists of a handful of stick-figure cartoons. Were it not for the fact that his work is provocative and humorous he could easily pass for a precursor of the mordant

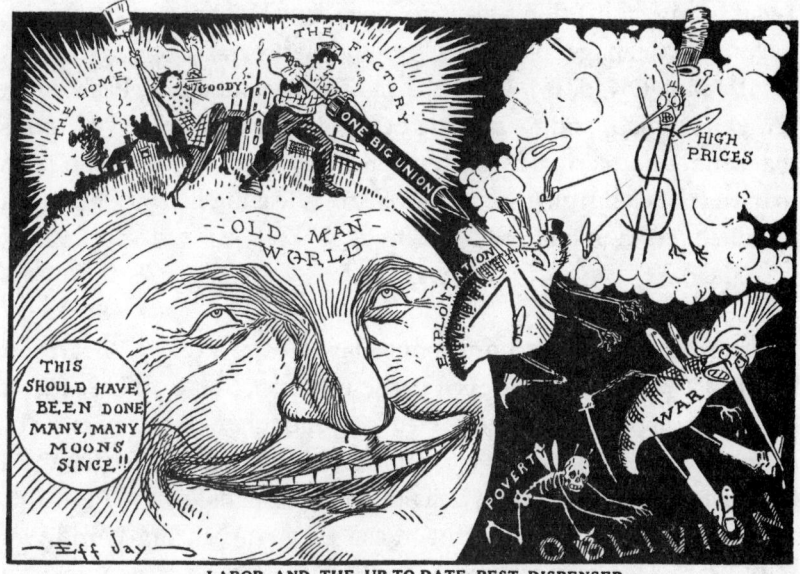

Fig. 28. Fred Jerger, *One Big Union Monthly*, December 1920.

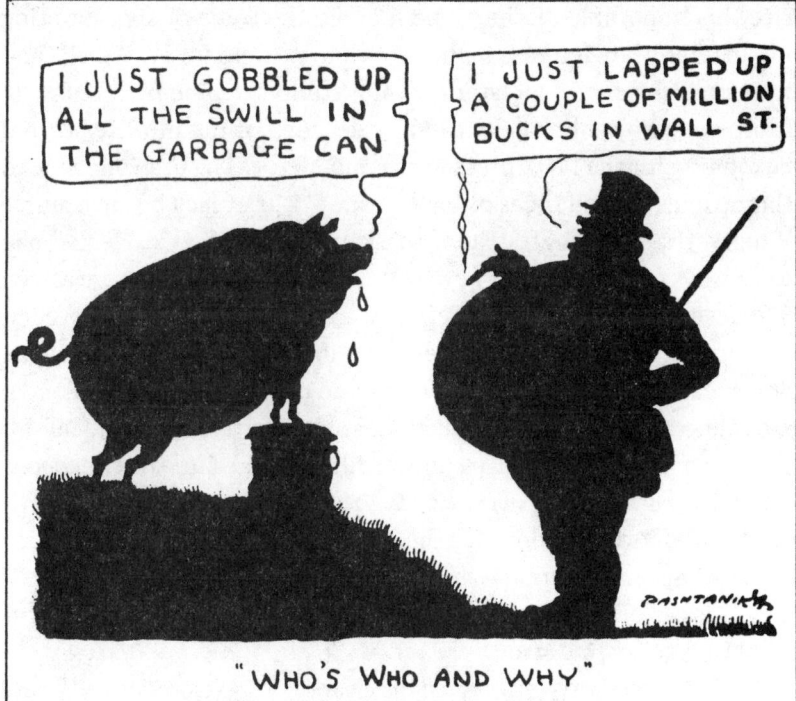

Fig. 29. Pashtanika, *Industrial Pioneer*, November 1921.

"I-can't-draw-and-I-don't-want-to-learn-how" school that dominates the uninspired pages of today's "trendy" Left press.

De Moi, OK (or is it CK?—the signature is not clear), Pashtanika, J.A. Van Dilman, and F. Vose are other worthy authors of "cartoons that cannot be excelled for making proletarians think," but who seem to have vanished from the stage of history, leaving no trace beyond a tantalizing trail of humorous drawings.[28]

◌◌

We know considerably more about many of the later IWW cartoonists, those whose work dates from the 1930s on. Some of these fellow workers are still living; others lived long enough to be interviewed by younger Wobs; still others left some autobiographical record; and a few have been rescued from oblivion by old friends.

A machine-gun instructor in the US Army during World War I, William Henkelman (1894–1986) was among the American Expeditionary Forces who mutinied when sent to Russia at the close of the war in the US government's attempt to crush the Revolution.[29] After his honorable discharge he took up the trade of sign-painting and in later years lettered many signs and posters for IWW halls and meetings, as he did still later for the Veterans' Home in Yountsville, California, where he spent the last decades of his life. He started cartooning for the IWW press in the mid-1920s. The drawing on Fred Thompson's "Bread Lines or Picket Lines" leaflet may be an example of his work. A fine draftsman with a rousing comic style, Henkelman was always on the alert for new ways to get the IWW message across. His cleverest efforts in this regard are his humorous Wobbly adaptations of mass media advertisements, in which famous commercial slogans are made to serve IWW aims. He prepared an IWW calendar to commemorate the union's fortieth anniversary in 1945, and he also did the cover for the twenty-eighth edition of the *Little Red Songbook*. For many years starting in the late 1930s he drew, with a stylus, directly on stencils, cover cartoons for the IWW's mimeographed Convention Proceedings and internal *General Organization Bulletin*. A substantial file of his cartoons is housed at the Archives of Urban Affairs at Wayne State University in Detroit.

C.E. Setzer (1905–70) signed his cartoons X13 (from his IWW card number: X13068) or sometimes CES.[30] He joined the IWW's Lumber

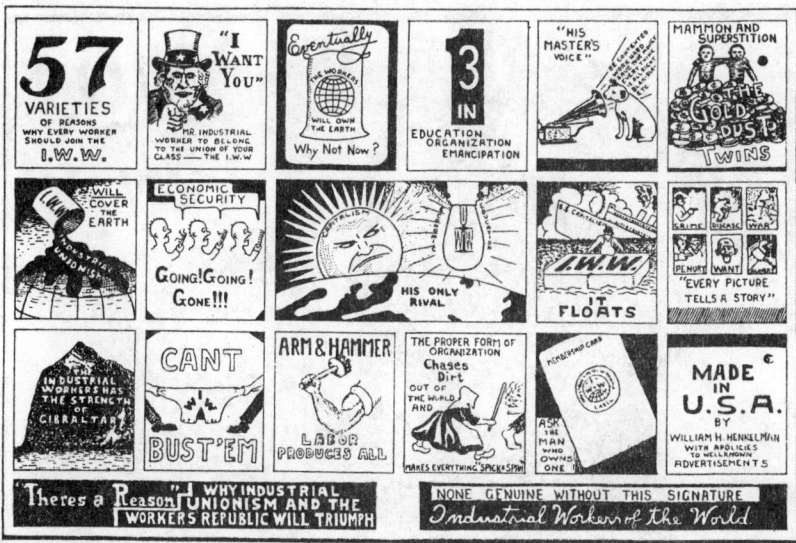

Fig. 30. William Henkelman, *Industrial Worker*, May 18, 1946.

Workers Industrial Union 120 on June 10, 1922, and in later years worked as a harvest hand, in general construction, and finally as a machinist. He served the union as branch secretary, as organizer on the Boulder Dam project in the early 1930s and later on the Los Angeles aqueduct, as a member of the General Executive Board, and as delegate to the twenty-third convention in 1938. His cartoons, however, are his greatest legacy. Although he occasionally drew with pen and ink, his best work was done in linoleum block, a medium he chose simply to save the *Industrial Worker* the high cost of photoengraving. It was a happy choice. From the start he hit on a thick-lined, often grotesque, completely original style, strangely reminiscent of certain chapbook illustrations from much earlier years of the printers' art but unlike anything else in the world of twentieth-century cartooning. Inevitably, some of his work has dated: his use of the theme of species extinction is—and so much the better for all of us—no longer funny in our ecology-conscious age. But much the larger part of his appreciable output of linoleum-block cartoons remains as implacable and as ferocious as a cornered badger. With the blackest sarcasm and a sadistic clowning worthy of the Three Stooges, X13 fought the good fight against the horrors and hypocrisies of his age and ours.

Taisto Luoma was an American-born Finn who studied at the IWW's Work People's College in Duluth, Minnesota, in the early 1930s.[31]

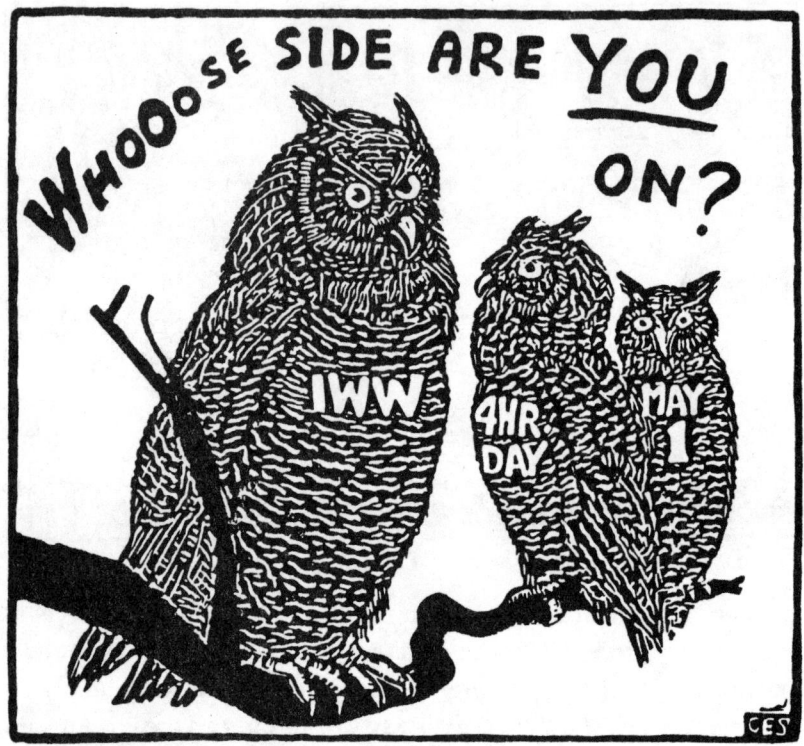

Fig. 31. C.E. Setzer, "Whooose Side Are You On?"

An active member of Marine Transport Workers Industrial Union 510, he started contributing cartoons to the Wobbly press in the 1930s; some were reproduced on covers of the new series of the *One Big Union Monthly*. In 1938 he was a delegate to the union's twenty-third convention. Old-timers recall that Luoma's life was a tragic one, afflicted by an unhappy marriage and prolonged illness—perhaps tuberculosis; he evidently died in the 1950s. His personal suffering seems to have affected his work as an artist, for although he did produce a few cartoons on the lighter side, most were done in a sullen, grim style, full of dark foreboding.

During World War II the pages of the *Industrial Worker* were enlivened by contributions from several young opponents of militarism who, for the duration, were unwilling guests of one or another federal penitentiary. One of those who saw no good reason why the workers of one country should go off and kill the workers of another was Theo "Whitey" Matysik, who spent the war years locked up in Danbury,

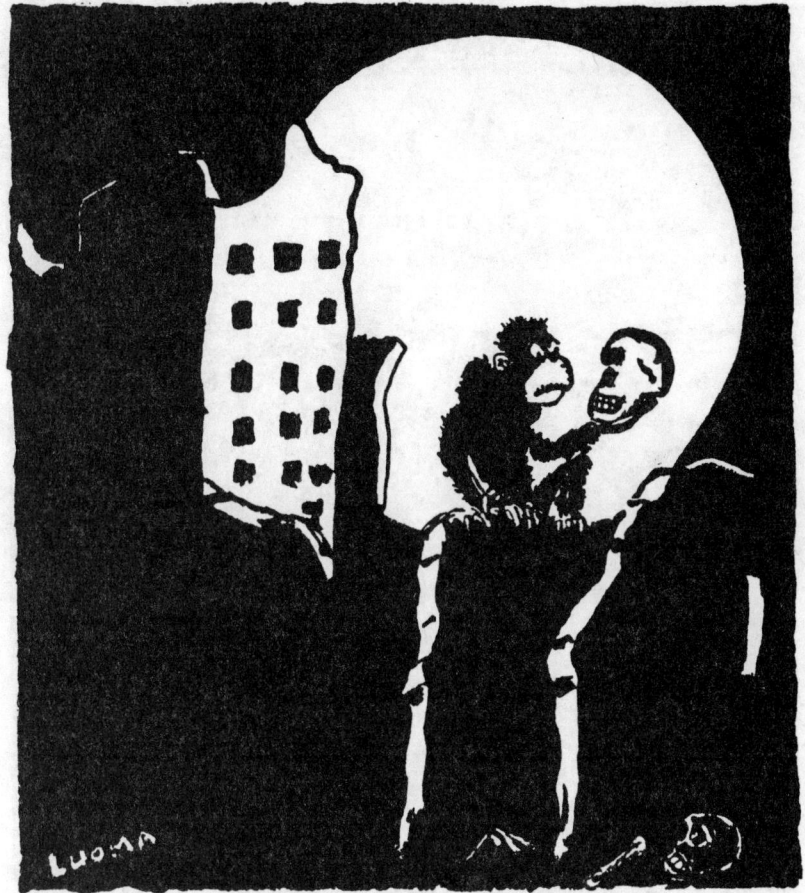

Survival of the Fittest?

Fig. 32. Taisto Luoma, *Industrial Worker*, January 10, 1948.

Connecticut, drawing cartoons.[32] Whitey—as he signed his work—was
clearly influenced by such popular cartoonists as Gene Ahern, Clare
Briggs, H.T. Webster, and Gaar Williams, whose syndicated single
panels concentrated on the foibles and vicissitudes of everyday life.
In 1945 Whitey did the cover illustration for the fourth revised edition
of the IWW's basic programmatic pamphlet, *One Big Union*.

Another young rebel cartoonist who had no use for capitalism's
war machine, and got thrown in the slammer for his opinion, was
Clif Bennett. A sensitive and articulate critic of authoritarian social
relations, he contributed penetrating commentary on prison life to
the most creative American anarchist journal of the period, Holley

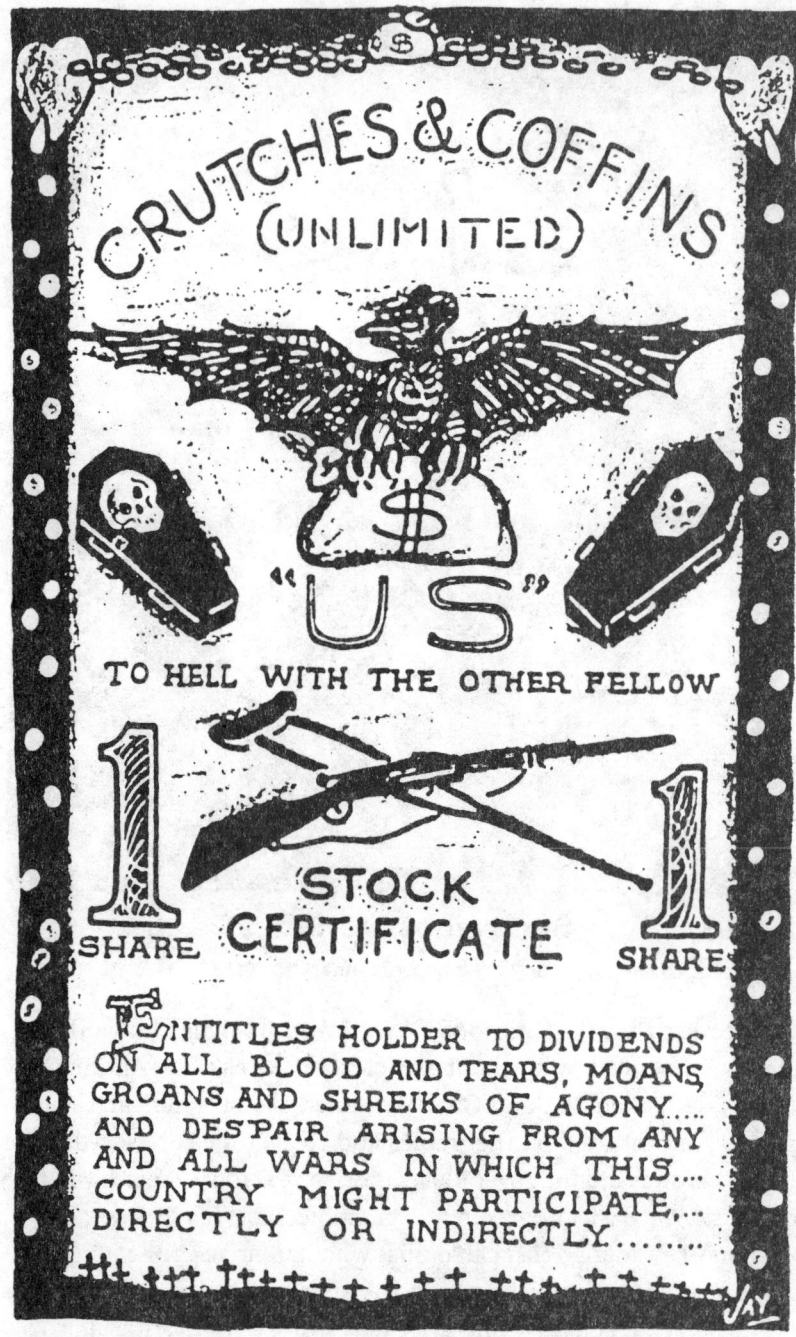

Fig. 33. Fred Jerger, *Industrial Pioneer*, July 1925.

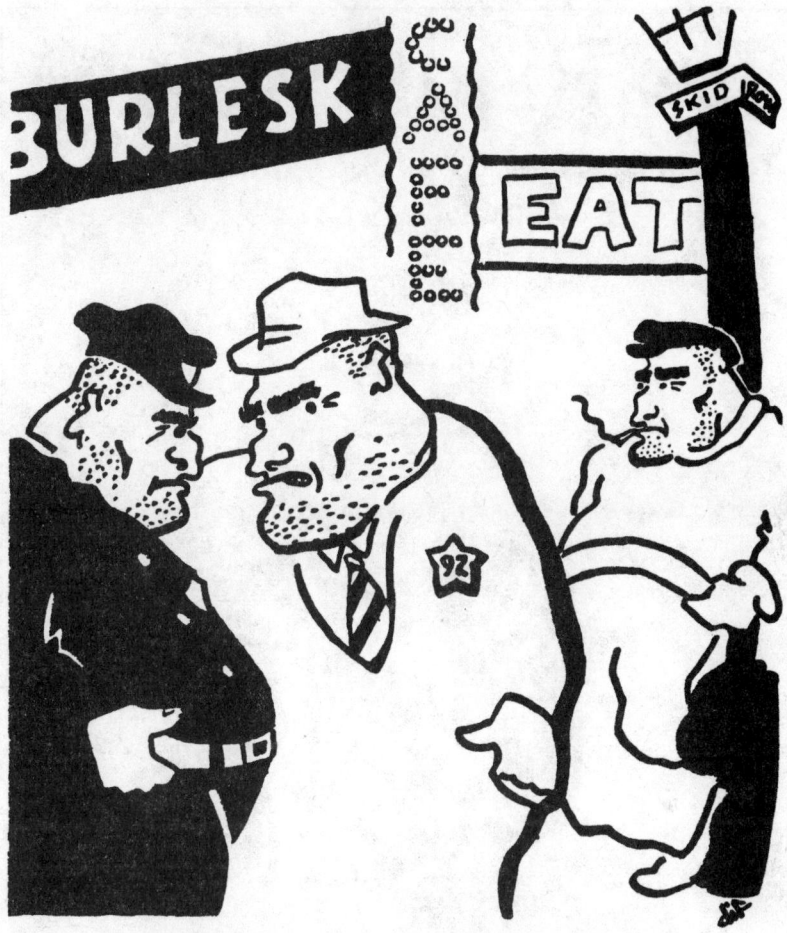

Looks like a criminal type, eh?

Fig. 34. Clif Bennett, *Industrial Worker*, August 3, 1946.

Cantine's *Retort*. His cartoons for the *Industrial Worker*, drawn on prison
stationery, exude a wry, iconoclastic humor, enhanced by a nervous
semi-expressionistic style probably inspired by some of the more mani-
acal animated films of those years. "As many of his cartoons displayed
little respect for the minions of law and order," Carlos Cortez recalls,
Bennett "was usually in hot water with the prison authorities."[33]

Cortez (born 1923), himself a war objector and a two-year resi-
dent of the federal pen at Sandstone, Minnesota, during World War
II, became the union's foremost cartoonist in the postwar years and is
probably the only IWW artist whose work has been exhibited in New

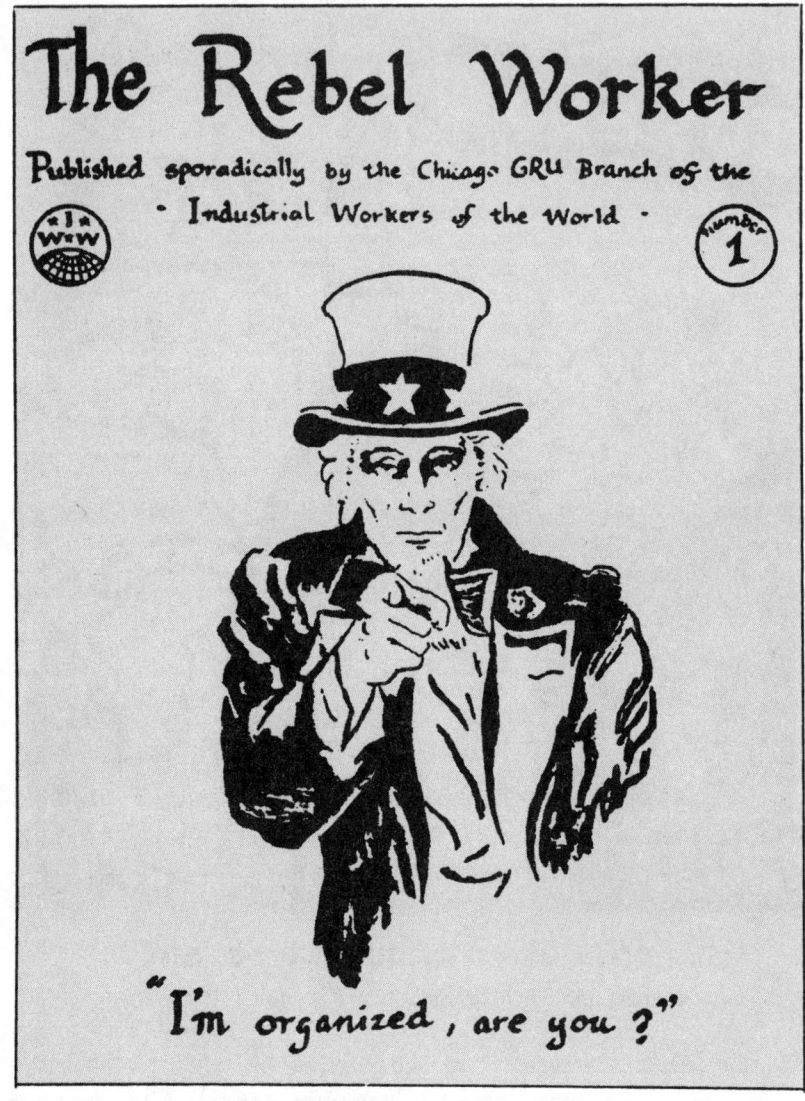

Fig. 35. Tor Faegre, cover for the first issue of the *Rebel Worker*, journal of the Chicago branch of the IWW, May 1964.

York's Museum of Modern Art.[34] X13's able successor in the linocut medium, Cortez acknowledges the inspiration he found as a youngster in the work of the celebrated printmaker of the Mexican Revolution, José Guadalupe Posada, and the early German expressionist Käthe Kollwitz—international influences reflecting his own heritage as the son of a Mexican Wobbly father and a German socialist-pacifist mother.

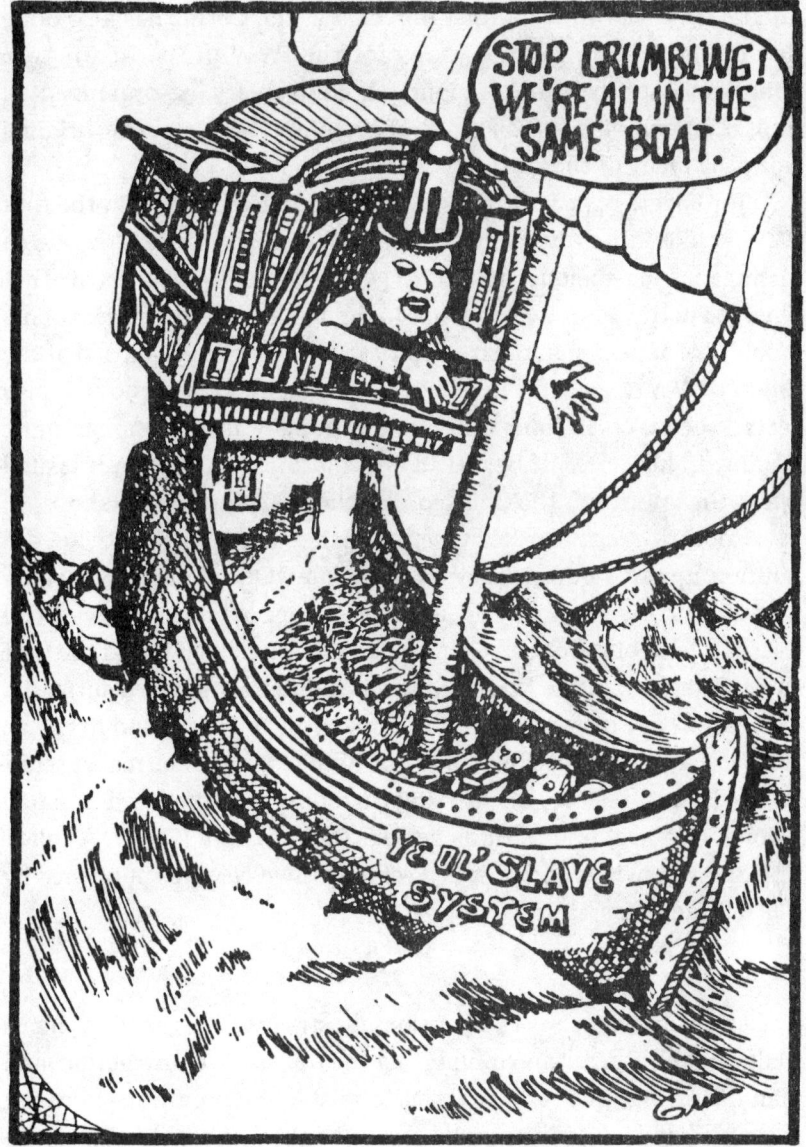

Fig. 36. Robert Green, *Industrial Worker*, January 1986.

When the *Industrial Worker* converted to offset in the 1960s he continued to use the lino technique in the production of large IWW posters,
including an outstanding series of portraits of Joe Hill, Ricardo Flores
Magón, Lucy Parsons, and Ben Fletcher. Poet, songwriter, General
Executive Board member, sometimes editor of the *Industrial Worker*,

and its best-known columnist in recent years, Cortez has also done numerous pen-and-ink cartoons for the IWW press. In 1985, to commemorate the union's eightieth anniversary, he organized an important exhibition, *Wobbly: 80 Years of Rebel Art*, featuring original works by many of the cartoonists discussed here.

Tor Faegre, a peace activist who played a leading role in the first IWW strike in nearly twenty years—a blueberry-pickers' strike in Michigan, 1964—belongs to a third generation of Wobbly artists that emerged in the union's resurgence in the 1960s and '70s.[35] Most of his Wobbly art appeared in the free-spirited mimeographed journal of the Chicago IWW branch, the *Rebel Worker*, between 1964 and 1967. He also served the union as sign painter and especially as calligrapher, most notably in his series of beautiful "Revolutionary Calendars" issued under the imprint of the Chicago Wobblies' Solidarity Bookshop.

Robert Green, another veteran of the '64 blueberry strike, did not take up cartooning till several years later. One of many '60s Wobs with links to the so-called Beat Generation (one of his friends was Neal Cassady, hero of Kerouac's *On the Road*), Green helped found the first surrealist group in the United States in 1966, co-organized surrealist exhibitions at Chicago's legendary Gallery Bugs Bunny, and in recent years has won wide recognition as one of the foremost surrealist sculptors.[36] His aggressive, disquieting cartoons have appeared in many labor and radical publications besides the *Industrial Worker*. A collection of his drawings and poems, *Seditious Mandibles*, was published by Black Swan Press in 1981.

We have seen that nearly every major industry in which the IWW organized—lumber, agriculture, mining, marine transport, construction, and manufacturing—had its Wobbly cartoonists. The conditions in which they lived and worked were the same conditions in which their non-cartoonist fellow workers lived and worked; it is unlikely that any of the union's early cartoonists (the commercial artist Chaplin excepted) ever had anything that could be called a studio. We have every reason to believe that many of these cartoons were drawn at cheap diners during lunch breaks; some, undoubtedly, around the fire in the hobo jungles; others—many others—in the cold grayness of prison. (Has any other social movement in US history created so much behind bars?)

It seems to me virtually certain, however—although there is no way to prove it—that the great majority of IWW cartoons were produced in those havens of revolutionary working-class culture: the IWW halls. Among other enticements, every hall would have been able to provide the sine qua non of the cartoonist's art: plenty of good black ink and clean white paper.

To what extent Wobbly artists were acquainted with one another, compared notes, or influenced each other we do not know. But acquainted or not, these rebel worker cartoonists made up a remarkable art movement—beyond question the greatest and most influential in the history of American labor. Stylistically as heterogeneous as the so-called Ashcan School of painters (most of whom were also cartoonists, incidentally) that emerged around the same time as the IWW, the Wobbly cartoonists developed a vital art of their own, rooted in struggle at the point of production and aimed at hastening the self-emancipation of the working class. Without sacrificing their individuality of expression, these artists emphasized the revolutionary values they all shared.

It would be interesting to know something more about the work that influenced these artists, but in this area we can do no more than speculate. The influence of mainstream comic strips and editorial cartoons is clearly paramount, but other influences—especially the work of such popular nineteenth-century illustrators and caricaturists as F.O.C. Darley, A.B. Frost, and Dan Beard, who were, in fact, formative influences on the pioneer daily comic strip artists—are not unlikely. Every IWW hall had a library that might well have included old editions of Dickens illustrated by Darley, or editions of Mark Twain illustrated by Beard. Upton Sinclair's anthology, *The Cry for Justice* (1915), a volume no IWW branch secretary would have failed to order for the local hall, featured full-page illustrations by many artists of "social protest," including William Balfour Ker, Théophile Steinlen, Käthe Kollwitz, Gustave Doré, Walter Crane, and Will Dyson.

Some notable affinities between the work of IWW cartoonists and the various currents of modern art afford an even wider field of conjecture. Historically, the radical literary/artistic milieu has provided an important meeting-ground for rebellious and creative characters of the most diverse class and cultural backgrounds. Wobblies made no secret of the fact that they wanted "more of the good things of life" for

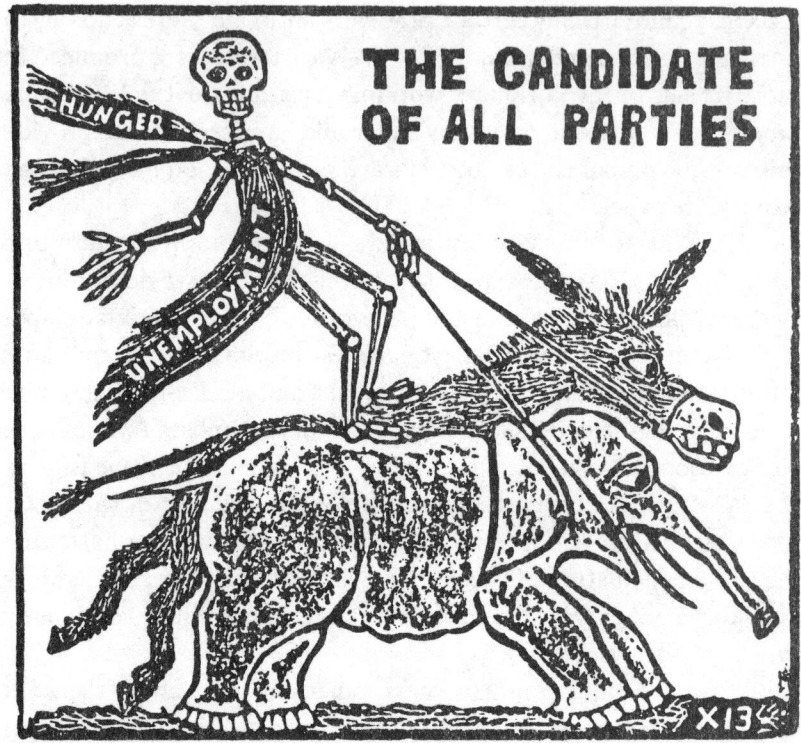

Fig. 37. C.E. Setzer, "The Candidate of All Parties."

the workers of the world, and that among these "good things" were the fine arts that the bourgeoisie had appropriated for its own exclusive enjoyment. "In addition to searching for the job," IWW songwriter and onetime General Executive Board member Richard Brazier pointed out, "we were looking for something to satisfy our emotional desire for grandeur and beauty."[37] Many of the several dozen old-time Wobblies I have known have been authentic working-class intellectuals—self-taught, independent-minded men and women of considerable culture, frequenters of libraries and art museums, with extensive knowledge of poetry, philosophy, and painting. Unfortunately, none of the IWW's early cartoonists has left us so much as a scrap of testimony on these matters. I, for one, would give a lot to know what Joe Troy thought of Courbet or whether C.E. Setzer ever dreamed of Van Gogh.

The celebrated 1913 Armory Show in New York (and later in Chicago [and Boston]), which introduced the American public to the work of Europe's impressionist, post-impressionist, fauvist, and cubist painters, attracted widespread attention in the daily papers and popular magazines, not least of all on the part of cartoonists: F.B. Opper and others spoofed the exhibition, and the new art generally, in countless comics that, in their own way, helped familiarize millions with some essential characteristics of these avant-garde currents. Was it purely by accident that comic artist Gelett Burgess, best known as the author of "The Purple Cow," happened to write the first important article in the US on those then-shocking convulsionaries of color, the fauvists?[38] In any case, more than a few Wobblies were active participants in America's far-flung left-wing bohemia in the days of the Armory Show. Would they have missed this epoch-making event in US cultural life?

Or again: We know from the memoirs of Ralph Chaplin, Big Bill Haywood, and others that one of the favorite Wobbly hangouts in Chicago in the 1910s and '20s was the Radical Bookshop on North Clark Street. According to Kenneth Rexroth, a modernist poet and painter who himself carried a red card in those years, this bookshop imported "the avant-garde poetry of the Twenties from France and Germany and Russia."[39] Were Wobblies reading Francis Picabia, Tristan Tzara, Hans Arp, and Vladimir Mayakovsky?

Although direct influence is impossible to specify, it does not seem implausible to suggest that the antiacademic orientation of these modern movements, their tendency to exalt the artist's expressiveness over technique, and their overall emphasis on revolt and originality may have been regarded sympathetically by at least some Wobblies, and may even have had a liberating effect on those among them whose urge to draw had perhaps been inhibited by traditional aesthetic prejudices.

Far more significant, however, than these vague points of contact, as uncertain as they are tantalizing, are the very real, unmistakable parallels between the methods and achievements of some of the more adventurous IWW cartoonists and those of artists associated with the most extreme modernist currents. At the very moment that the German Dadaists—Hannah Höch, George Grosz, John Heartfield, Raoul Hausmann, and others—unleashed their powerful photomontages against the bourgeoisie and its image of the world, an IWW cartoonist known to us only as Sam made effective use of the same medium in the One Big Union Monthly (July 1919). His full-page cartoon captioned "The General Strike" shows an immense arm and fist shattering the walls of

America's jails; the arm and fist are cut out from an aerial photograph of a massive demonstration of workers carrying banners demanding "Down with Autocracy" and "Open the Jails."

The free use of preexisting images, mostly newspaper clippings and parts of magazine advertisements, is characteristic of the work of many cubist, futurist, Dadaist, and surrealist painters and has also had many different IWW applications. The *One Big Union Monthly* for June 1920, for example, published two slightly different versions of the same cartoon. The first, titled "How the *Chicago Evening Post* Sees the IWW," is an unretouched reprint of an anti-IWW cartoon from that paper showing a tall, handsome man (representing the solid citizenry of the United States) removing his coat to give a sound thrashing to an ugly, knife-wielding killer, labeled "IWW," who stands menacingly over a bloody corpse. Beneath this cartoon is an altered version captioned "How the IWW sees the *Chicago Evening Post* and all the rest of the capitalist press." The man in the foreground is now labeled "IWW" and the murderous plug-ugly about to be knocked around is labeled "*Chicago Evening Post.*" Here we have a specifically Wobbly variety of what Marcel Duchamp designated a *readymade*—slightly "assisted" in this case, and one that, moreover, humorously exposes the platitudinous monotony and superficiality of anti-labor cartoons.

Similarly, one of Ralph Chaplin's best-known cartoons is a close copy of a World War I Liberty Bond poster by the famous Hearst cartoonist Winsor McCay.[40] The original shows a husky central figure labeled "America," standing with sword upraised behind a Liberty Bond shield, warding off a gang of attackers labeled "Devastation," "Starvation," "War," "Pestilence," and "Death." In Chaplin's version the central figure represents the working class, the shield is emblazoned with the IWW emblem and the words "One Big Union," the upraised sword has been changed to a club labeled "Organization," and the attackers are relabeled "Labor Hatred," "Hunger," "Slavery," "Slander," and "Frame-Ups." In McCay's original the figure of War had been a black man raising a sword; in Chaplin's, significantly, he is white, labeled "Slavery," and wielding a bullwhip.

Deceptively simple, such transformations only superficially resemble the common, commercially motivated practice of copying a competitor's efforts (a standard procedure in the art departments of daily newspapers and advertising agencies). There is much more here than mere plagiarism. It is a question, rather, of a process of ideological demystification, in which workers seize control of oppressive images, undermine their specifically oppressive content, and turn them against their class enemies. Analogous if more complex procedures were developed by Dadaists in the late 1910s and by surrealists starting in the '20s; decades later, the "subversion of images" remains an integral part of the surrealist project and has proved itself capable of almost infinite elaboration, as evidenced by such recent contributions as J. Karl Bogartte's *photomorphs*, the *coated collages* of Anne Ethuin, and the *gommages* of Abdul Kader El Janabi.[41] A supremely effective means of irritating the mind's critical faculties, such *playful rearrangements* seem to be discovered by each revolutionary generation as if for the first time. When a small group of French radical intellectuals who called themselves Situationists took up the technique and dubbed it "détournement" in the 1960s, a legion of critics predictably hailed it as the latest innovation of the avant-garde.

An interesting variant of the same process of radical demystification, Henkelman's altered advertisements, which he began drawing around 1926, prefigured the recent art of billboard revision, a medium of expression so far outside the academy that it is covered by the penal code.[42] A billboard advising youngsters to "join the Navy and meet interesting people in faraway places" has been dramatically revised simply by adding the words "*and kill them.*" The propaganda effect of thus revealing (and ridiculing) the repressive latent content of modern advertising can hardly be denied and surely explains the steep fines and jail sentences awarded any practitioners of this art careless enough to be caught at it. I have no doubt that Fellow Worker Henkelman would be proud to be recognized as a forerunner of this new creative method of calling the bosses' bluff.

The fact that obscure Wobblies coinvented the radical new art form of photomontage, and anticipated other techniques of pictorial subversion still daring enough in our own time to be hailed as something new under the sun, challenges the musty conventions of art history and helps us situate the art of the IWW in the broad panorama of working-class culture. In its hobo disdain for traditional values, its appeal to the irrational, the bizarre, the fantastic, its frequently excessive and violent humor, and its overriding "bad taste," the best and most characteristic Wobbly art differs sharply from what became known as "proletarian" art, and especially from the dull, regressive works codified under the unhappy label of "socialist realism." The delicious irony that flourishes in the cartoons of Riebe, Hanson, Setzer, and Henkelman has nothing in common with the shameless glorification of workers *as workers* so typical of the essentially bourgeois art that usurped the adjectives "proletarian" and "socialist" for purposes of ideological/bureaucratic obfuscation. Mr. Block and Scissor Bill have no equivalent in the art concocted according to the sentimental aesthetics of "proletcult" or, for that matter, in the humdrum productions of mainstream business-union cartoonists. Often transcending the didactic limits of their work, the great Wobbly artists reflect the spirit of poetic revolt and utopian revery that underlies the finest art through the ages. Few IWW cartoons are as unarguably surrealist as the wildly inspired writings of T-Bone Slim, but the free-for-all imagination, untamable, reckless, perhaps a little bit "crazy," holds its own in the best of them.

Far from being servitors of a domesticated realism, Wobbly artists identified themselves with the shadowy, half-hidden, but inexhaustible tradition of the popular imagination—a tradition, or complex of traditions, as old as (and even older than) the working class itself.[43] Earlier exemplars of this subterranean current, always so "embarrassing" to the straitlaced wardens of High Culture, include a veritable legion of anonymous balladeers, chroniclers of "tall tales," itinerant Punch-and-Judy men, authors of "shilling shockers," architects of ice palaces and carousels, cabaret singers, and strolling silhouettists on the carnival midway. Among its ancestors it could claim the best of Chaucer and Shakespeare and the whole of Bosch and Blake. Among its central figures in modern times we could cite Henri Rousseau, an obscure collector of tolls at the gates of Paris before he dramatically altered the course of twentieth-century art by taking up painting at the age of sixty; Ferdinand Cheval, who, over a period of thirty years, built his "Ideal Palace" with stones and shells he collected on his daily route as a mailman; the Italian-born anarchist construction worker Simon Rodia, creator of those marvelous towers in Watts, California; blues singers such as Memphis Minnie and Peetie Wheatstraw, the "Devil's Son-in-Law"; silent-film comedians, pulp-writers, radio-scripters, and comic strip artists galore.

In the early decades of this century, when this great popular heritage was increasingly jeopardized by rapid technological change, commercialized and smothered by monopolization of the media, and completely denied or reduced to footnotes by the official critics, Wobblies developed their own fearless, adventurous, iconoclastic art, poetry, and song and recognized them for what they were: inseparable components of a new, revolutionary way of life. Preserving age-old traditions of working-class culture while class-consciously striving to transform this culture into a coherent and organized negation of the bourgeois order, the IWW dreamed of a universal, truly human culture, free at last of the crippling, stifling influence of an exploitative social system. It is worth emphasizing that, in the movement's brightest days, artists were never "outsiders" in the One Big Union. Indeed, Wobblies held out the promise that, in the new society, all would be artists. As old-time Wob Sophie Cohen recently put it, the IWW was itself, for its members, an incomparable "means of expression."[44]

Revolutionary internationalism—global working-class solidarity—is implicit in the very name Industrial Workers of the World. In addition to its long and epoch-making history in the United States, the union has also flourished, at one time or another, in Australia, Canada, Chile, Mexico, South Africa, and many other countries. Scholarly research into IWW activity abroad is still in its early stages, and the study of Wobbly cartoonists around the world remains a task for the future.[45] Judging from what little we have seen of Australian IWW cartoons—the wonderful and elaborate contributions to *Direct Action* by Syd Nicholls, who went on to become one of Australia's most famous comic artists, and Joe Ryan's strip, *The Amazing Adventures of Mr. Simple* (rather like Riebe's *Mr. Block*), in the same paper—some pleasant surprises are in store for diggers in this little-known terrain.[46]

Future research into the international dimension of Wobbly culture should also reveal important data on the origins and diffusion of characteristic IWW imagery. It is well known that the Wobblies' wooden shoe (sabot) as a symbol of sabotage derives from the syndicalist movement in France. Nineteenth-century American cartoonists, notably Thomas Nast, provided the fat capitalist (no "friend of labor" was Nast, however, for he also cooked up that notorious comic product of the Haymarket Tragedy, the bomb-toting, long-haired, wild-eyed anarchist, a stock villain even today in the capitalist press), but such

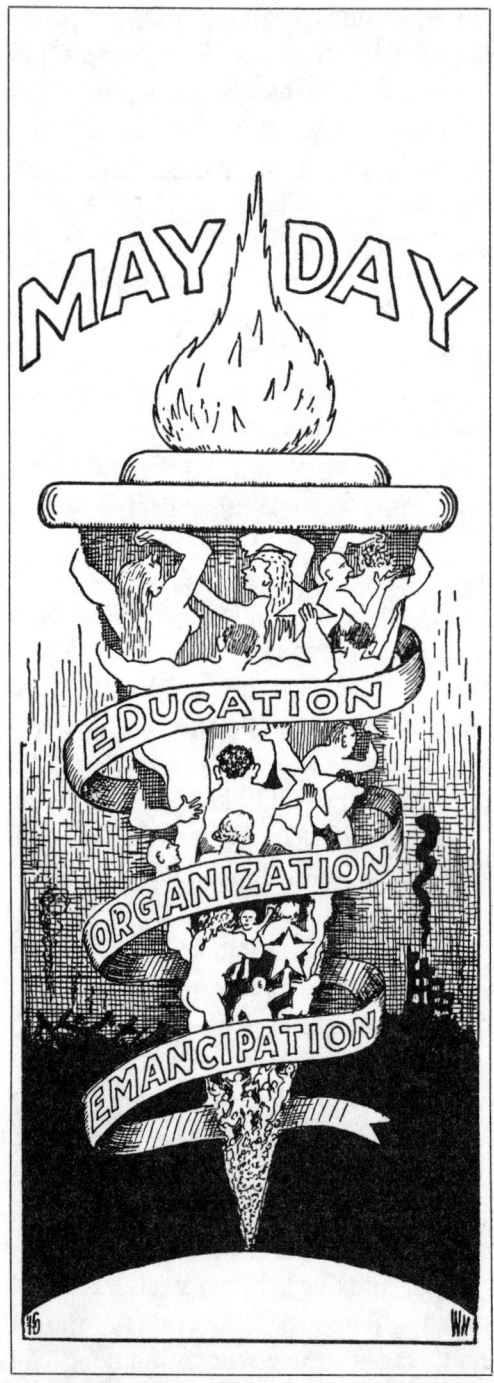

Fig. 38. William Henkelman, *Industrial Worker*, April 27, 1946.

stereotypes had numerous antecedents in popular European art and literature.[47] To what extent other images are the products of individual invention or of now-forgotten tradition is far from clear. Big Bill Haywood's oft-vocalized and sometimes-cartooned simile comparing craft-union divisiveness to the separated and therefore weak fingers of a hand, while the One Big Union unites all the fingers into a powerful fist, goes back at least as far as the Sioux chief Sitting Bull and probably has folkloric equivalents in other cultures as well.

An interesting example of an American IWW image that originated on the other side of the globe is Ralph Chaplin's drawing for the General Defense Committee, captioned "Fellow Workers, Remember! We are in here for you; you are out there for us." This forceful sketch has been reproduced countless times in IWW newspapers, magazines, and pamphlets as well as on posters, buttons, and "silent agitators." Note, however, that beneath Chaplin's nom de plume of "Bingo" is the name "Dino," signifying that Chaplin was only providing the artwork for an idea suggested by another fellow worker. (This was a common practice among Wob cartoonists; another noteworthy example is one of Riebe's *Mr. Block* strips, in the last panel of which we find that it was "suggested by J. Hill.") "Dino" turns out to have been an Australian IWW artist who, early in 1917, did a crude poster of a Wob behind bars for use in defense agitation "down under."[48] Months later Chaplin, a far better draftsman, turned Dino's basic idea into a dramatic image that quickly became one of the most famous pieces of IWW art.

Another aspect of IWW history that is just starting to attract serious attention is the impact of the union's foreign-language branches, and other minorities, within the United States.[49] Full equality regardless of sex, race, or national origin was an IWW principle from day one, and women as well as racial and ethnic minorities have played a large role in the union throughout its history. An extensive IWW literature exists in Finnish, Russian, Hungarian, Czech, Italian, Spanish, Swedish, Bulgarian, Polish, Romanian, Lithuanian, Croatian, Yiddish, French, and German; there are even a few things in Chinese and Japanese. None of the existing histories of the union have drawn more than peripherally on these sources. Most of these foreign-language groups had their own Wobbly songs, and many had their own cartoonists. Frequently their publications also reprinted cartoons from the English-language IWW press, with translated captions. In the 1940s, for example, the

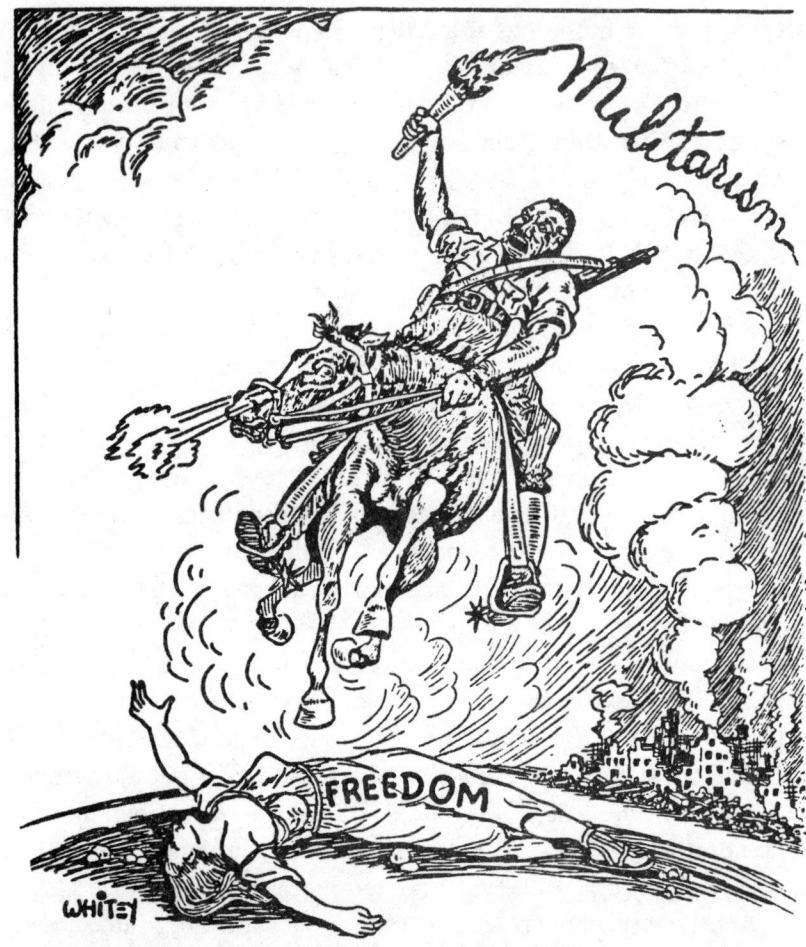

Fig. 39. Theo Matysik, *Industrial Worker*, 1943.

lavish Hungarian *Bermunkas* almanacs reprinted many works by C.E. Setzer.

Many thousands of black workers have been active in the IWW, especially from the mid-1910s through the big split of '24. Among those who attained national renown as organizers and orators were Roscoe T. Sims, Alonzo Richards, and especially Ben Fletcher, one of the leading Marine Transport Workers Industrial Union 510 organizers, in Philadelphia and later in Baltimore, and one of the Wobblies sent to Leavenworth for "obstructing" World War I.[50] If there were black IWW cartoonists they have thus far eluded our attention. It cannot be emphasized too strongly, however, that the history of IWW cartooning, like IWW history generally, is a field in which the unknown vastly outweighs the known, and in which new discoveries are constantly being brought to light. Only recently San Francisco Bay Area IWW organizer Dick Ellington made available a letter from the late Guy B. Askew (an old-time Wob also known as Skidroad Slim) that includes a detailed recollection of a heretofore unknown black Wobbly songwriter and vocalist from the Pacific Northwest, Paul Walker, complete with the lyrics of one of his songs.[51]

We would also like to know more about the experience of women in the IWW, though here the record is somewhat clearer. We do know that two of the most prominent figures at the founding convention were Mother Jones and Lucy Parsons and that many of the union's best organizers and poets have been women, as one may easily verify by reviewing the texts by and about Matilda Robbins, Elizabeth Gurley Flynn, Vera Moller, and others. But did any Wobbly women of yester-year draw cartoons? We do not know.

In the late 1950s and early '60s at least one notable woman cartoonist was part of the larger IWW community, if not a dues-paying member. One of the finest cartoon stylists of our time, Trina Robbins is well known as an important forerunner and exemplar of "underground" comics. In 1970 she put together the first all-woman comic book, *It Ain't Me, Babe*. By the mid-'80s she had produced an impressive quantity of highly original work, including the *Misty* miniseries for Marvel, *The Legend of Wonder Woman* for DC, and *California Girls* for Eclipse; she also found time to coauthor, with Cat Yronwode, an invaluable reference, *Women and the Comics*. In her teens she was active in a milieu of radical science fiction enthusiasts who were mostly IWWs. "I always hung around with Wobblies," she recalls of her life in the San Francisco Bay Area in those years, "but somehow I never actually joined." Interestingly, her first published cartoons appeared in *The Bosses' Songbook*, a compilation of satirical lyrics edited by Wobblies Dick Ellington and Dave Van Ronk in 1958. Her later work includes several labor-related comics, among them a powerful narrative of the Triangle Shirtwaist Fire.[52] Robbins is still active in the Left today [1988], especially in the women's movement.

The feminist agitation of the early '70s brought women into activist politics in unprecedented numbers, and many, inspired by the Wobbly heritage, took out red cards. In 1976 Kathleen Taylor was elected general secretary-treasurer—the first woman to hold the union's highest office. Gloria T. Nelson, from Iowa—to the best of our knowledge the IWW's first woman cartoonist—made her appearance in the pages of the *Industrial Worker* early in the same decade. Unfortunately, her membership in the union seems to have been brief, and her cartoons are few in number. Shortly after her arrival on the scene, however, Leslie Fish started drawing for the paper.[53]

Like most of the new IWW cartoonists of the '70s, Leslie Fish reflected the influence of the "undergrounds" and the "counterculture" of which these anti-establishment comics were a part. The Wobblies portrayed in these cartoons are rarely the traditional, well-muscled, male proletarian giants of so much older IWW art but rather young men and women with long hair and colorful clothes: in a word, *hippies* who in fact made up a large portion of the union's membership in those years. While other "Old Left" groups tended to echo the mass media fear and hatred of the new youth revolt, the IWW alone welcomed this revolt and even embraced it—or rather absorbed it into its own incredibly persistent counterculture.[54] Fish's many well-crafted strips and single panels (some signed with her nom de guerre, Pat Kovalik, and others with a tiny drawing of a fish) are perhaps the best illustrations of this little-known phase of IWW history. Several of her cartoons also focus on specifically women's issues, a topic touched on—but hardly more than touched on—by a few earlier Wob cartoonists such as Ernest Riebe, "Dust" Wallin, and Joe Troy.[55] A songwriter/musician as well as a cartoonist, for years Fish has played guitar and sung in an IWW band, The Dehorn Crew, whose albums include the Star Trek–based *Wobblies in Space* and a 1987 cassette release, *It's Sister Jenny's Turn to Throw the Bomb.*

Underground comics had a lasting impact on the course of cartooning. Paradoxical as it might seem, one of their most important contributions was their defiant anti-professionalism. Thanks to these sometimes crudely drawn but most always energetic and provocative effusions, many thousands of young recalcitrants were encouraged to try cartooning themselves ("Geez, I could draw as good as that!"), just as years earlier many wage earners had been inspired to take up the art by seeing cartoons drawn by their fellow workers in the IWW press. Significantly, more cartoons appeared in the *Industrial Worker* during the early 1970s than at any period in IWW history. This may

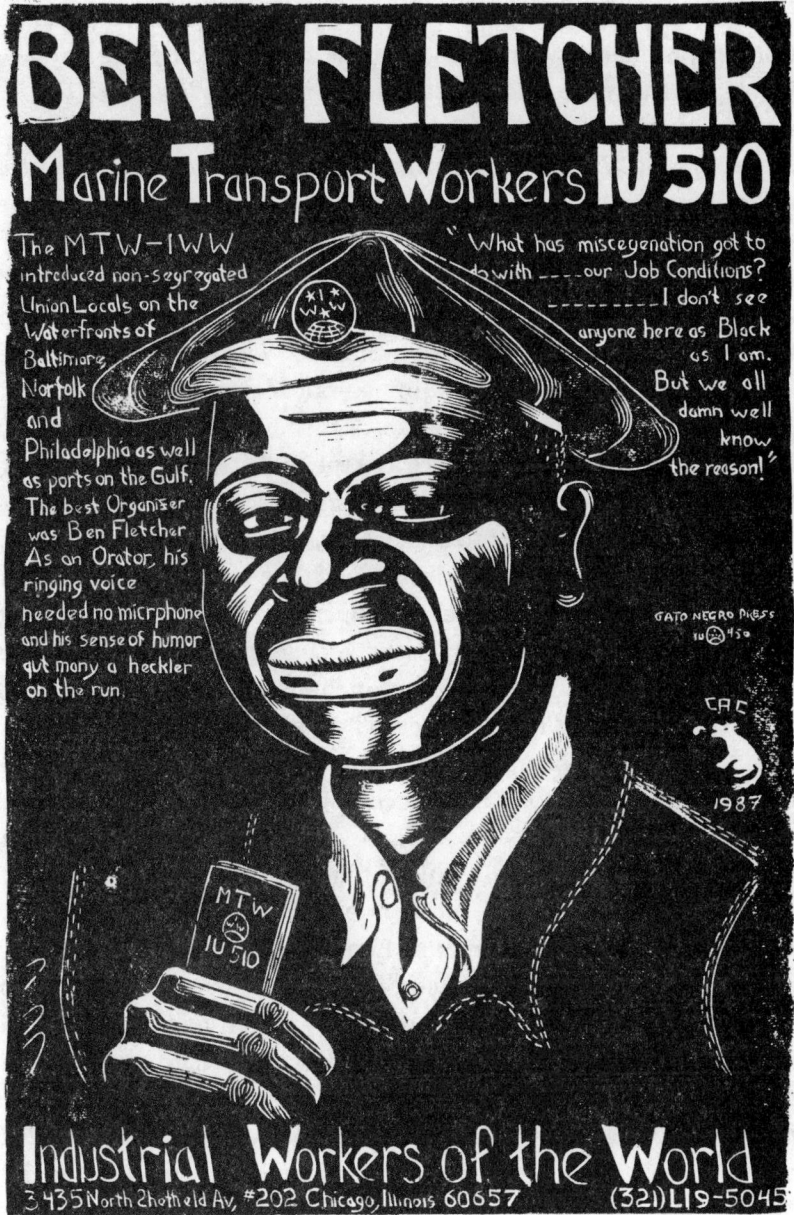

Fig. 40. Carlos Cortez, linoleum-block poster of Ben Fletcher, 1987.

be partly explained by the fact that the editor in those years, Carlos Cortez, was himself a cartoonist, but the sudden proliferation of new Wobbly artists was a crucial factor.

A few well-known "underground" personalities took out red cards, including Skip Williamson (*Conspiracy Capers, Bijou Funnies*), who drew one cartoon for the July 1970 *Industrial Worker* before he retired into the pages of *Playboy*. Bill Crawford was another Wobbly-for-a-couple-of-months-or-so, during which the IWW official organ published several of his *Rufus the Radical Reptile* strips. Influenced by the underground ferment but more enduringly committed to Wobbly ideals were Mike Zaharakis of Oregon and T.J. Simpson of Maine—two of the most prolific IWW cartoonists of the 1970s. Affirming the historical affinity between the underground comics and their illustrious IWW ancestor, both contributed to the ongoing saga of *Mr. Block*.

The underground cartoonists' association with labor radicalism reached its peak early in the decade with the formation of a union, largely thanks to the initiative of Manuel "Spain" Rodriguez. One of the relatively few new comic artists who clearly identified with the revolutionary Left, Rodriguez had included a Wobbly sequence in one of his early *Trashman* comics. The United Cartoon Workers of America (based in the underground comics capital of San Francisco, though it also had informal locals in Chicago, Milwaukee, and other cities) attracted the best-known figures in the field—Gilbert Shelton, R. Crumb, Trina Robbins, Denis Kitchen, Bill Griffith, Jay Kinney, and others—and succeeded, albeit briefly, in raising cartoonists' pay rates and effecting other benefits. Loosely structured, with irregular meetings, no officers, and no dues, the UCWA reached a membership of somewhere between thirty and seventy-five. It had its own union button—featuring the New Left's raised fist clutching artists' pens and brushes—and for a few years its union label appeared on the covers of many comic books. Affiliation with the IWW was seriously considered, and at least once an organizer from the San Francisco IWW General Membership Branch was invited to a UCWA meeting to discuss the possibility. Regrettably, however, affiliation was never decided on, and by 1973 the first and last underground cartoonists' union had passed into oblivion.[56]

∽

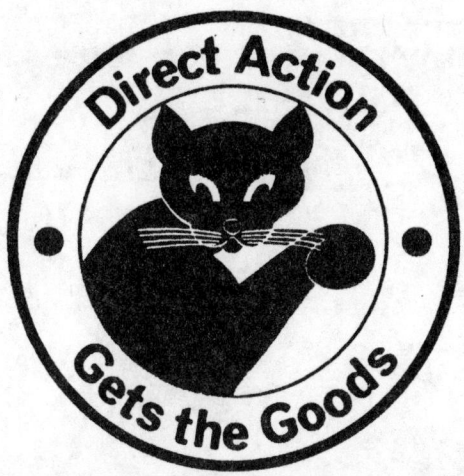

Fig. 41. Nancy Kellerman, "Silent Agitator," c. 1980s.

Now over eighty years old [in 1988], the IWW continues to attract rebellious young artists eager to lend a hand, along with their pens and drawing boards, to the struggle against wage slavery and the struggle against the destruction of the earth that wage slavery inevitably entails. Denny Mealy of Austin, Minnesota; Ben Trant of Shreveport; Hal Rammel, Debra Taub, and Joel Williams of Chicago; Nancy Kellerman of Boston; and Mike Donovan of New York are only a few of the newer artists with red cards in their pockets. Issue for issue, in proportion to its size, the *Industrial Worker* in recent years [mid-1980s] has probably published more cartoons than any other labor paper in the United States or Canada.

Many recent IWW cartoons, visual parables on the evils of capitalism and the virtues of working-class solidarity, are basically updated versions of the union's earliest art—which is hardly surprising, for the social conditions that brought the IWW into being still exist. The aim of the IWW ("abolition of the wage system") remains the same, but as the methods and forms of struggle have changed over time, each generation of Wobbly artists has added something of its own. In the '30s they had to come to grips with fascism, Stalinism, the New Deal, sitdowns, the CIO, and revolution in Spain. Truman's atomic bomb and the Taft-Hartley "slave labor law" posed staggering new problems in the next decade. The '50s brought the first workers' revolution in a modern industrialized country (Hungary) and the movement for civil

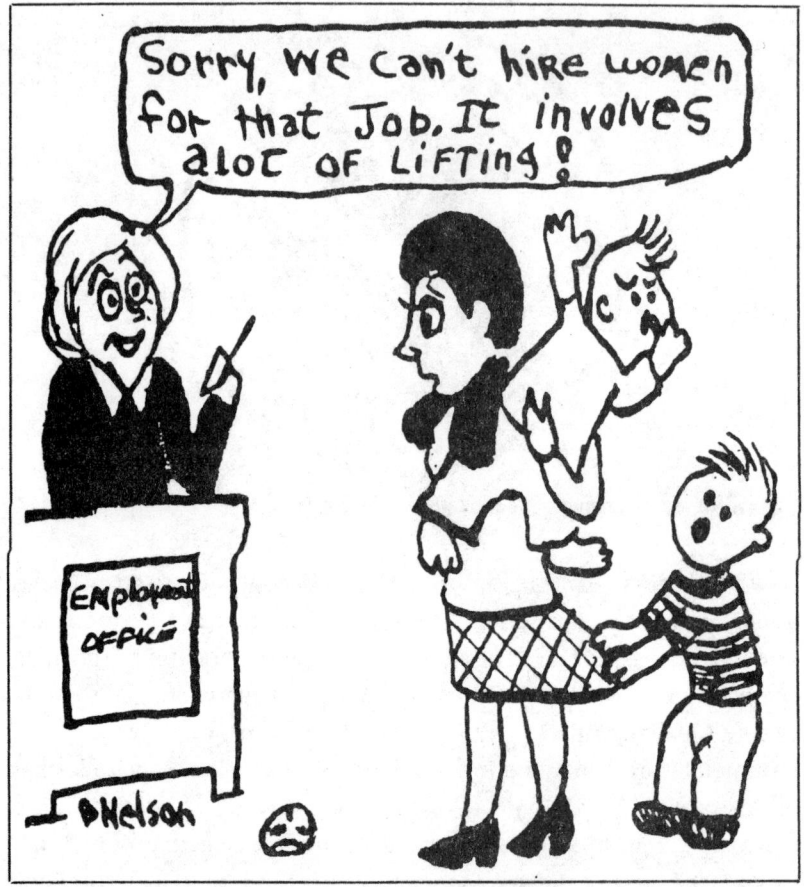

Fig. 42. Gloria Nelson, *Industrial Worker*, December 1970.

rights in the United States. The '60s witnessed a worldwide revolt of students and youth, anti-imperialist struggle throughout the Third World, coast-to-coast insurrections in America's black ghettoes, and the May '68 general strike in France. In the '70s and '80s, questions of women's emancipation and the relation of human society to the natural environment came to the fore. Each of these developments has affected IWW theory and practice, and each has been interpreted in the union's cartoons.

Wob cartoonists today tend to be sensitive to the complex manysidedness of the struggle for radical social transformation in the modern world, and many of their cartoons seem to be intended as *bridges* between the too-often-separated phases of this struggle. Today as yesterday Wobs are active in the workplace, striving to build a labor movement worthy of the name. But just as in the old days the IWW played a leading role in crusades for free speech and women's reproductive rights, so the Wobblies of today are likely to be active also in direct-action movements such as Earth First! and Greenpeace, as well as in struggles against nuclear power, apartheid, sex discrimination, the draft, and other abominations. Long before ecology became a household word, Fred Thompson, the most influential IWW theorist of the last fifty years, advanced a new Wobbly slogan for the modern epoch: "Let's make this planet a good place to live." The many and varied movements in this direction have received the IWW's warm support, and their wide-ranging concerns have been echoed and/or expanded in Wobbly cartoons. As has so often happened in the past, labor's cartoonists are pointing the way forward for the movement as a whole.

Of course, not all the cartoons in the *Industrial Worker* today are drawn by card-carrying, dues-paying members of the IWW. Just as the union published Art Young, Ryan Walker, and John Olday in earlier years, so in the 1960s–70s IWW publications ran work by the genial Fred Wright of the United Electrical Workers, and by many others, including artists as different as Lichty, Wolinski, and Topor. Following the same nonsectarian policy in the 1980s, the *Industrial Worker* has featured such outstanding contemporary cartoonists as Gary Huck, Mike Konopacki, Peg Averill, Bulbul, the team of Estelle Carol and Bob Simpson, and (from Britain) Phil Evans, Arthur Moyse, and Donald Rooum. It is well known, at least in labor circles, that the IWW today includes many of the finest labor songsters and musicians of our time. Bruce "Utah" Phillips, Charlie King, Harry and Sharon Muir, J.B. Freeman, Faith Petrie, Mark Ross, "Haywire Brack," Bob Bovee, Mark Soderstrom, Jeff Cahill, Jay Peterson, Larry Penn, Maureen McElderry, Leslie Fish, and many other members of IWW Industrial Union 630 have demonstrated that the "singing Wobblies" are not a thing of the past but rather a living, fighting, creative tradition. It is no less true that the IWW press today serves as a forum for the finest and most daring labor and radical cartoonists.

"Wherever you find injustice," T-Bone Slim once wrote, "the proper form of politeness is attack." More than ever in our increasingly bureaucratized, militarized, ecocidal, miserabilist society, humor is the secret weapon in the struggle for freedom and real life. In the IWW's cartoons, as in its songs and its dreams of a better world, Wobbly humor breaks the rules, exceeds limits, and *goes all the way*. In a society of byzantine complexity and cowardly complacency, the defiant simplicity and all-or-nothing extremism of these cartoons are not small virtues. In the face of the most massive campaign of ideological mystification in world history these cartoons proclaim that the emperor isn't wearing any clothes after all.

These footloose IWW artists who never made a nickel from their cartoons have left us all a rich legacy. Here as elsewhere, the Wobblies have kept alive that noble ideal: *Nothing but the best for the working class*.

Acknowledgments

In preparing this essay I have drawn on correspondence and discussions with Minnie F. Corder, Carlos Cortez, Sam and Esther Dolgoff, Richard Ellington, Paul Garon, Archie Green, Robert Green, Denis Kitchen, Mike Konopacki, Joyce Kornbluh, Brian W. Myers, Art Nurse, Lisa Oppenheim, Penny Pixler, Hal Ranunel, Trina Robbins, Manuel "Spain" Rodriguez, Dave Roediger, Sal Salerno, Erling Sannes, Nicolaas Steelink, Kathleen Taylor, Michael Vandelaar, Jenny Velsek, and the late Fred Thompson.

PART III

Music, Cinema, and Dance

20

Mods, Rockers, and the Revolution

First published in the *Rebel Worker*, no. 3 (March 1965): 127–31.

Wobblies and other true revolutionaries are much less interested in the vague longings of college professors and Nobel prize-winners for a "better world" than in the day-to-day struggles of our fellow workers—not only the direct struggles against exploitation by the bosses but also the struggle to live some sort of decent life against all the obstacles presented by a society divided into classes. Thus it is essential that we concern ourselves not only with the job situation and economic questions but also with more "superstructural" anthropological factors: working-class culture. In this connection, the significance of rock 'n' roll, and popular adolescent culture in general, has for too long been ignored. That rock 'n' roll is one of the most important working-class preoccupations (among the young, at least) is clearly evident. That it has been ignored by the "left" press is additional testimony to the isolation of the "socialist" intellectuals from the class in whose name they so often enjoy speaking.

Certain unfortunate souls, including many of traditional "left" orientation, have attempted to deny that rock 'n' roll is really a working-class phenomenon, even suggesting that it is imposed(!) on working-class adolescents by Madison Avenue, etc., as a form of exploitation through cheap talent, record sales, and juke-boxes. To them rock 'n' roll is a sign only of the "decadence" of contemporary capitalist society. They can neither take it seriously as a form of music nor see in it anything other than a possible "reliever of tensions" that they feel might better be expressed in more constructive activity. Thus Marshall Stearns, in *The Story of Jazz*, thoroughly puts down rock 'n' roll as a form of music but claims that, by offering "release" to anxious kids, it actually contributes to the decrease of juvenile delinquency. This uneasy, patronizing anti–rock 'n' roll "theory" is, amusingly enough, shared by Stalinists, liberals, Presbyterians, conservatives, and bourgeois sociologists.

We must have done, once and for all, with this kind of evasive excuse-mongering and look at the situation as it really exists. Rock 'n' roll must be recognized not only as a form of music (which, for its players and its listeners, is clearly as "serious" as any other) but also as an important expression of adolescent preoccupations.

As music, rock 'n' roll is certainly "primitive," but this must not be assumed to mean that it is therefore inferior. No one is less able than musicologists and other prisoners of academic limitations to situate this problem in its proper context. For the importance of rock 'n' roll lies not only in the music itself but even more in the milieu that has grown up with it, characterized above all by delirious enthusiasm, a frenzy which is no stranger to tenderness, and which undoubtedly appears scandalous to the easily outraged watchdogs of bourgeois morality. Much could be said for the influence of rock 'n' roll on the emergence of a new sensibility (intellectual as well as erotic and emotional).

Much could be said too of its *unconscious* quality, which, with its roots in speedup and automation (and thus in the class struggle), lends to its "subversive" aspect. For rock 'n' roll is, more than anything else, a *latent cultural expression* of the age of automation. Indeed, a study of the psychoanalytical and anthropological implications of automation might well make rock 'n' roll its point of departure. Witness the fact that almost all of the most popular rock 'n' roll groups are from the most intensely industrialized and highly automated cities: in the United States, Chicago and Detroit; in England, Liverpool, where one out of every fifteen Liverpudlians between the ages of fifteen and twenty-four now belongs to a rock 'n' roll group.

The best of the new groups—Martha and the Vandellas, Marvin Gaye, the Jewels, the Velvelettes, the Supremes, and Mary Wells (all from Detroit), and the Kinks, the Zombies, Manfred Mann, and, of course, the Beatles (all from England)—have brought to popular music a vitality, exuberance, and rebelliousness that it has never seen before.

The Beatles are the most successful group in entertainment history. Their flippant replies to interviewers; their wild, raucous behavior; their riotous and insulting sense of humor remove them far beyond the pale of "respectable entertainers." Their first movie, *A Hard Day's Night*, will remain one of the greatest cinematic delights of 1964, a lone cry of uninhibited freedom and irrationality in a cold desert of "seriousness" and pretentiousness.

The legendary quality, which can almost be called *mythical necessity*, of the Beatles, has not failed to attract the critical attention of some perceptive commentators. Consider this judgment from the pen of Jean Shepherd, who interviewed the Beatles for *Playboy* magazine (February 1965):

> In two years they had become a phenomenon that had somehow transcended stardom or even showbiz. They were mythical beings, inspiring a fanaticism bordering on religious ecstasy among millions all over the world. I began to have the uncomfortable feeling that all this fervor had nothing whatever to do with entertainment, or with talent, or even with The Beatles themselves. I began to feel that they were the catalyst of a sudden world madness that would have burst upon us whether they had come on the scene or not. If The Beatles had never existed, we would have had to invent them. They are not prodigious talents by any yardstick, but like hula-hoops and yo-yos, they are at the right place at the right time, and whatever it is that triggers the mass hysteria of fads has made them walking myths. Everywhere we went, people stared in openmouthed astonishment that there were actually flesh-and-blood human beings who looked just like the Beatle dolls they had at home. It was as though Santa Claus had suddenly shown up at a Christmas Party.

Another British group, the Rolling Stones, has risen to popularity more recently, bringing with them a more disquieting, more sinister, more violent attitude into the rock 'n' roll arena.

It is in England where the adolescent revolt (of which rock 'n' roll is only one constituent element) seems to have assumed its largest proportions. In England the kids are categorized into two "tendencies": Mods, fashionably (often bizarrely) dressed, and who are associated with motor scooters; and the Rockers, who prefer black leather jackets, blue jeans, and motorcycles. In both cases the boys wear their hair long, considerably longer than in America, and (according to a *New York*

Times writer from Britain) "the word in London and Liverpool is that male hair is going to get longer and longer." The girls' hair is usually straight and worn down to the middle of the back.

The hair itself deserves comment, particularly since hair is growing longer in the United States as well as in England and elsewhere in Europe. The social implications of hair fashion have been inadequately studied, if studied at all. Some psychologists and sociologists have confined themselves to brief, unexplained remarks on "sexual confusion," "identity problems," and the like, which help very little. Others, it is true, have gotten a *little* closer to the heart of the matter. Thus the *New York Times* writer referred to above mentions that "sociologists, always a pessimistic lot, look on our jungled tresses and prophesy a future filled with indulgence and rebellion." For it is an undeniable fact that *short* male hair has always been a characteristic of submission to authority. The police, prisons, army, schools, and employers are all in agreement in insisting on short hair and regular haircuts. Also, crew cuts are the symbol, almost, of Goldwater conservatism. Before making unfounded judgments on the "identity problems" of today's kids, one might consider the problems of a culture so obsessed with keeping male hair short.

The riots and brawls of the Mods and the Rockers have also called attention to another aspect of the youth revolt: that rock 'n' roll represents the only *mass protest music* today—another reason why it deserves the sympathetic appreciation of revolutionaries. The most popular jazz has entered the colleges and become respectable. The most important developments in jazz during the last few years (Ornette Coleman, Eric Dolphy, Charles Mingus, Roland Kirk, et al.) are hardly known outside a small audience of connoisseurs. It is useless to point out that jazz is, *musically*, ten thousand times better than rock 'n' roll; that's not the point. The audience for contemporary "classical" music is even more limited.

As for "folk" music and its derivatives (country-and-western, bluegrass, etc.), these have become the official expressions of today's college fraternities. (Real folk music is primarily of historical interest.) Those unhappy souls of the traditional "left" who try to pretend that the "folk revival" has some sort of revolutionary content reflect only their sentimentality and intellectual superficiality. I do not mean to imply that there's not much that is beautiful and important in the folk tradition, and certainly it deserves serious study. But it can no longer be assumed to have anything to do with the working class. At any rate, working-class kids are bored by it. Like it or not, what today's working-class kids are listening to is rock 'n' roll.

The rise of the Mods and Rockers indicates to some degree a rise of young rebellion everywhere: the "new youth" of Tokyo, Berlin, Moscow, etc. Inevitably, this has provoked innumerable journalistic scare stories about "new parent-teen crises" in Sunday supplements throughout the world. Such articles contribute nothing of importance to the understanding of the contemporary adolescent, though they do shed a little light on the problems and preoccupations of adults. Repressed adults, attempting to understand younger people, often merely project their own problems onto the kids.

Many parents, for instance, afraid of participating in uninhibited dancing, approach the question with the presuppositions that there is something wrong with this kind of dancing, and that it must be rooted in some deep emotional anxiety. I do not mean to say that rock 'n' roll dances are expressions of "freedom" (the lack of physical contact between dancing partners is especially problematical). But we cannot advance one step in our understanding of these problems if we begin by saying that the kids are *wrong*.

There can be no doubt that the present development of rock 'n' roll, and the milieu of young workers in which it thrives, is more consciously rebellious than it has ever been before. To be *revolutionary*, of course, is to be more than rebellious, for a revolutionary viewpoint necessarily includes some sort of *alternative*. And popular adolescent culture is pregnant with revolutionary implications precisely because it proposes alternatives—however crude and undeveloped they may be—to the ignoble conditions now prevailing.

Songs like "Dancing in the Street" by Martha and the Vandellas and "Opportunity" by the Jewels show that the feeling for freedom and the refusal to submit to routinized, bureaucratic pressures are not confined to small, isolated bands of conscious, politically "sophisticated" revolutionaries. Rather, they are the almost *instinctive* attitudes of most of our fellow workers. Presently these feelings are to a great extent repressed, and sublimated in bourgeois politics, television, baseball, and other diversions. It is our function as disrupters of the capitalist system, and as union organizers, to heighten consciousness of these feelings, to encourage rebellion, to do all we can to liberate the intrinsically revolutionary character of the working class. Rock 'n' roll, which has already contributed to a freer attitude toward sex relations, can contribute to this liberation.

There is no use being overly romantic about all this. I do not, for example, think that adolescent hangouts and record hops will provide fruitful recruiting grounds for the One Big Union; at least, not right away. And for my part, I vastly prefer the more raucous rhythm 'n' blues—songs sung by ghetto Negro groups—to the lukewarm, diluted sounds promoted in teen-celebrity magazines and on *American Bandstand*.

But what revolutionaries must consider is that many younger workers—rock 'n' rollers—are discontented with existing society and are seeking and developing solutions of their own. If traditional revolutionary politics hasn't appealed to them, it's probably because these politics haven't been as "revolutionary" as their protagonists like to pretend.

We in the IWW are not tied to narrow theoretical traditions and immovable dogmas. We are rising today because we are free to seek new solutions and develop new tactics to meet new situations. If we are going to keep growing, we will have to turn more to the problems of younger workers. It might be noted that jobs most common to kids (stock work, filling station work, store clerking, etc.) are almost completely unorganized and offer us a splendid opportunity to channel the "youth revolt" into a consciously revolutionary movement.

In any case, we cannot go on assuming that the rock 'n' rollers are a helpless, ignorant, reactionary mass; that their problems are not our problems; that they are somehow "irrelevant." We must recognize that the rock 'n' rollers too, despite the hesitations of "socialist" politicians, are our friends and fellow workers.

21

The Jimi Hendrix Experience

Reprinted from Franklin Rosemont and Charles Radcliffe, eds., *Dancin' in the Streets! Anarchists, IWWs, Surrealists, Situationists and Provos in the 1960s as Recorded in the Pages of "The Rebel Worker" and "Heatwave"* (Chicago: Charles H. Kerr, 2005). Excerpted from a piece first published in *Chicago Seed*, November 3–24, 1967.

The "official" function of music in this society is to deceive the purity of the human imagination. From the deceived eye to the confused ear, man is reduced to an idiocy as impotent as it is unforgivable. I am interested in the maximum of consciousness, in liberating the senses from the fetters of concretized ideology in the hideous reality around us. The point is to resolve the arbitrary conflict between the eye and the ear by a truly definitive transformation of reality.

"It is time to realize," wrote the Belgian surrealist Paul Nougé, that we are capable also of inventing feelings—perhaps fundamental feelings—of a power comparable to those of love and hatred. Our point of departure is Rimbaud's "systematic derangement of the senses," an experiment that must be continually renewed. It should be possible to juxtapose auditory, visual, olfactory, tactile, and gustatory capacities, for sheer pleasure. Psychedelic experience validates the ear that sees and the eye that listens.

Several years ago I was listening to an old recording of a medieval chorale by Josquin des Prez, when the ending was submerged by the roaring of jets across the sky. This charming vengeance of a non-Euclidean futurism had the distinct advantage of opening more doors in my mind than it closed. Who can demand more from music than exaltation? Needless to add that such an assumption is vastly removed from most European conceptions of music. So-called primitive people understand music best—its *physical* qualities, or rather its psycho-physical dynamism that absolutizes frenzy in the dance. "Primitive" music provokes a mythology of gesture born of spontaneous ritual.

The Jimi Hendrix Experience (Hendrix, vocals and guitar; Mitch Mitchell, drums; Noel Redding, bass) has recently emerged into the eldritch light that bathes the quotidian splendors of this universe and all others. They play regularly before standing-room-only crowds in Paris, Stockholm, Copenhagen, London. Eight days after the Beach Boys broke the house record at the Tivoli in Stockholm, playing for 7,000 fans at two shows, Hendrix appeared and, to say the least, broke their record—playing for some 14,500 fans at two shows.

The Experience stage show possesses a demonizing convulsive-ness—Hendrix has been known to play his guitar with his teeth and even to burn it on stage—in which the most cherished philosophi-cal prejudices are dismembered on a monstrous scale, during a long midnight, luminous and black. Hendrix has acknowledged the inspi-ration he has found for lyrics in fairy tales and science fantasy. Certain of his songs seem to hover like enchanted owls over the Garden of Earthly Delights, subtly moving from paradise to hell. With profound lyricism, a sense of creative destruction, and black humor, he weaves the tapestry of his violent, delirious myths across a sky that darkens as he approaches.

Nothing is premeditated: everything belongs to the purely auto-matic revelation. With striking simplicity, he improvises a chaos of defiantly realizable beauty. All of Hendrix's commentators have spoken of this remarkable spontaneity. When asked to play certain songs from his first album, *Are You Experienced?*, he admitted that he had forgotten them—that he had invented them during the recording session and never played them since.

Hendrix has united the extraordinary poetic vitality of the blues with the more recent rock scene, which itself originally derived from blues but which, with psychedelic, East Indian, baroque, and other influences, has achieved a musical independence. Certainly he has brought a new tremor into the intellectual atmosphere, introducing us to marvels from cultures as seemingly disparate as those of the Kwakiutl, the natives of New Ireland, the Tarahumaras of Mexico, as well as the Bushmen, Yoruba, and other cultures of Africa.

"Paint It Black," in any case, is a watchword not to be taken lightly. Harlem '64, Watts '65, Newark, and Detroit '67 are moments in the realization of a splendidly magical dream, correctly known as the cause of freedom. Music that does not participate in this dream, music that does not express the passion for liberation that is bubbling through the consciousness of millions—music, that is, that does not *revolt*—is only the auditory reflection of repressive ideology, like the sterile sounds played in department stores as "background," to "'relax" customers into an imbecile stupor in order to increase their consumption of worthless commodities.

I want music that is the opposite of this pathetic servant of commodities. I want a delirious and luxurious music that drinks the space around it and colors it with the vibrations of liberating human impulses; music that concretizes the rhythm of blood and breath— music that burns the exploitative past and assists in the unveiling of the future: the creation of the harmony of passions.

True revolt goes as far beyond politics as politics itself, in its best expression (*revolutionary* politics), goes beyond apathy and false consciousness. Revolt is only very partially "political." It must also be poetic and sexual, putting everything at stake—all or nothing. What is called for today is a total revolution of everyday life, which leaves traditional politics groveling in the obscure categories of the past. Jimi Hendrix, who refers to himself as "apolitical," ruthlessly attacks not only imperialism but also the entire foundation of oppressive Western civilization.

Music as it is known today will be replaced by the free play of human desires, the invention of life itself, the sound of imagination. Images of arson—a magical incendiarism—live in the very heart of all varieties of the new music: Archie Shepp's "Fire Music," the Doors' "Light My Fire," Jimi Hendrix's "Fire." Burn, baby, burn!

Soon there will be no more music, in the specialized and alienated sense, for *everything* will be music. Meanwhile, no one can afford to ignore the sensitive testimony of a man like Hendrix, who sings and plays to share his dreams.

In Jimi Hendrix, the music of revolt has found its poet.

22

A Revolutionary Poetic Tradition

First published in *Living Blues*, no. 25, special supplement titled "Surrealism and Blues," January–February 1976.

———

From the stock market crash of '29 to the outbreak of World War II, what became of the Marvelous in "the land of the dollar"? Where did human freedom situate its boldest promise, its brightest flame?

Those who called themselves poets and artists, with few exceptions, were on the wrong track, in many cases hopelessly derailed. Nearly all who are hailed today by Professors of Literature as the Great Poets of those times, in English, were not truly poets at all, but falsifiers of poetry—false poets hired to depress poetry. The situation had its counterpart in politics: the party that most volubly styled itself revolutionary, the Communist Party, had already consolidated its role as "Left" stabilizer of capitalism, thanks to the "reasonable" Stalin whom the *Wall Street Journal* so much preferred to the "fanatics" Lenin and Trotsky.

Faced by this bewildering spectacle of "poets" who were the enemies of poetry and "communists" who were the enemies of communism, clearly poetry and revolution—two distinct facets of a single cause—had to go underground, gather their forces, to reemerge in new and unexpected forms.

And so they did. The great strike wave that swept the country in the mid-1930s remains to this day the greatest independent mobilization of the American workers. Bypassing outmoded forms of struggle, and increasingly drawing previously unorganized sectors into the struggle, these strikes—beginning with the Minneapolis Teamsters and the Toledo Auto-Lite strikes of 1934 and reaching a climax in the sitdowns of 1937–38—were the American workers' finest contribution to the creation of a free society. Is it necessary to point out that this upheaval caught the "official" Left off guard? As always, mass initiative sufficed to expose the incompetence and treachery of the cliques that want only to ride to power on the workers' backs. The high point in the struggle for freedom in the United States in those years was attained by the working class with little help from its best-known political "friends."

Similarly, the Marvelous, shunned by the collegiate crew whom the "Public" mistook for the sole practitioners of poetry, nonetheless found able defenders, albeit far away from Harvard or Greenwich Village. In the rural depths of the South, and in the black ghettoes of the North, an extensive poetic movement developed, many of whose representatives could not even read or write but whose works even now retain their full imaginative power. Who were the true great poets of the American 1930s? Charley Patton, Robert Johnson, Peetie Wheatstraw, Memphis Minnie, Victoria Spivey, Bessie Smith ...

The surrealists are practically alone among current revolutionary and/ or intellectual tendencies in recognizing blues as a majestic and fertile river of poetic truth, and in referring their own activity to its example. This is not as surprising as it might seem at first glance. After all, who else could do it? The whole comportment of the aforementioned false poets (and of their colleagues, the professors and critics) is a pitiable antithesis to everything blues stands for. Not much can be expected from that quarter. As for the poor fools who delude themselves that they alone represent the one true proletarian faith, and who pretend that the only revolutionary thought is that which passes through their own sectarian funnels (I am referring to the strange birds who continue to build their nests in Karl Marx's beard), they are so isolated from the real life of the working class, so withdrawn into trite fantasies woven from platitudes, that most of them would not recognize a revolutionary or a poetic truth it if bit them on the nose.

If it is left to the surrealists, then, to take up blues as a militant cause—well, then, the pleasure is all ours. We will go so far as to insist that the defense and celebration of blues, and of black music generally, is a necessary component of principled poetic action in the English language today. For us it is no small matter that, during the very period in which T.S. Eliot and Jean Cocteau (and how many other "leading intellectuals"!) were bending their knees in the degrading rituals of christian corpse-worship, the bluesman Kansas Joe McCoy was singing his "Preachers Blues," a lyric effervescing with the pride of a man courageous enough to follow through his destiny without the intercession of "divine" frauds.

It cannot be repeated too often: at a time when the "official" poetry in English was saturated with servility, puritanism, guilt, remorse, and decay, its stale rhythms marked by the clicking heels of fascist law and order, the blues singers sang—and sang splendidly—of freedom, revolt, desire, and love.

Society is a racket; culture is a racket. And all those responsible for these massively organized insults to human dignity—from the politicians, cops, and priests down to the advertising agents, literary critics, and false poets—are no better than any other racketeers. He who would oppose all this, he who would hold out for the golden age, seems at times to face impossible odds. Lautréamont truly said: "Poetry's mission is difficult." It is not an accident that so many poets (and blues singers among them) have lived short and tragic lives ending in horrible and violent deaths. Yet the poetic struggle continues—and will continue until it is victorious across the planet. This is because poetry is virtually synonymous with the noblest human aspirations, and because the need for the Marvelous is as basic as the need for oxygen.

Opposed to all traditions that weigh on the mind like stones of Sisyphus, poetry itself has a tradition: a tradition against traditions, a tradition whose phases are marked by the beats of freedom's heart of hearts. The unity and coherence of this poetic tradition, made up of many tributaries, is proof that there are not different "types" of poetry—there is only Poetry. If in different times and places, under different conditions, it assumes different forms, poetry like freedom and thought remains one and indivisible.

The outstanding characteristics of blues lyrics—materialism, eroticism, humor, atheism, a passion for freedom, a sense of adventure, an alertness to the Marvelous—are the outstanding characteristics of the works of the great Elizabethan poets, of the great Romantics, of all poets worth their salt. In this century, in English (as noted above), the "poetry" that has prevailed, the poetry designed to flatter the age of imperialism, has been a sustained reaction against these character-istics: that is, a reaction against poetry itself.

Of course the Elizabethans and Romantics today receive every official sanction. Their statues are everywhere; their portraits gaze on us from postage stamps and cigar boxes; schools and streets bear their names; and children are taught that they are Great Men like Herbert Hoover and Henry Ford. These mountains of glib praise heaped on the memory of dead poets are intended above all to crush the living ones. The aspirations, the *messages* of such figures as Marlowe and Shelley, are conveniently ignored, discussed only by specialists in "high places"—that is, in the colleges, which are but factories for the produc-tion of bourgeois ideology. There the poets of the past are presented as safely embalmed specimens, to be poked at with instruments of aesthetic dissection.

Only those few who by one means or another have begun to put poetry into practice, and who are therefore engaged in individual insur-rections against all ruling ideas and institutions, are truly aware that these "specimens" are still alive, that their images still breathe, that their breath is fire, and that this fire is capable of burning down the walls separating humanity from true life.

To insist on linking blues to Marlowe and Shakespeare, to Byron and Shelley, will be dismissed by most as the merest impudence. Taught from childhood to look on these hallowed names with awe, as on some-thing very close to gods, we tend to forget that they were men. Most people sooner or later give up the ghost to recoil into cynicism or into fear masked as indifference. They don't think about Shakespeare.

Everything is done to keep poetry at a distance, out of reach—I mean *psychologically* out of reach. Scholars, critics, professors, without even knowing what they are doing, invest these authors with a deadly mystique, concealing their poetic fire beneath shrouds of academic ice. Workers, especially workers who listen to blues, do not know Marlowe or Shakespeare, or Byron or Shelley. If they do know these names, they resign themselves too readily to the mistaken notion, enforced by all common assumptions, that such authors are "over their heads." Yet the throngs who crowded the theaters in Shakespeare's day were the same kind of people, by and large, who today crowd the blues clubs.

Or consider this: most of what is known about Christopher Marlowe is derived from police records and accounts by informers. Repeatedly in trouble, he got into street fights, toyed with the idea of counterfeiting, blasphemed against religion (he held that "all the New Testament is filthily written"), was arrested several times (once accused of murder), and was stabbed to death at the age of twenty-nine in a barroom brawl. Many a blues singer's life could be written with these same words.

The links between the great Elizabethans, the great Romantics, the surrealists, and the blues singers can be stated precisely: all are anti-bourgeois and all are anti-religious and more specifically anti-christian, at least implicitly (explicitly in the case of many Romantics, most blues singers, and all surrealists).

These remarkable affinities are best viewed from the historical perspective. The early English bourgeoisie, when commercialism was just beginning to supplant feudalism, fought its ideological battles under the banner of Puritanism. Without denying this movement its moments of grandeur—especially evident, for example, in the Cromwellian warriors—it should be recognized that the Puritan Revolution, like all bourgeois revolutions, represented only the narrow interests of a small exploiting class, and consequently was led to the systematization of repression to a degree theretofore unknown. Capitalism's sole historic justification (development of the productive forces) was brought to realization only by trampling everything in the human sensibility that longed for the Marvelous and for the freedom that only the unfettering of the Marvelous can assure.

The Puritans hated poetry; Milton was the exception that proves the rule. They regarded poetry as a sinful, dirty, irresponsible, pagan, and even atheistic glorification of laziness, lust, and crime. (Four centuries later the newly formed and small black bourgeoisie in America had only to echo these epithets and direct them against the blues singers.)

For a time, in the seventeenth century, as they were consolidating power, the English bourgeoisie succeeded in shutting down the theaters and in outlawing or restricting other forms of public revelry, which were presumed by the Puritans to be directly inspired by Satan. In the American colonies, the Puritans and Pilgrims carried out the same repressive program with even greater severity. Even the traditional subdued merriment of Christmas was condemned by these pious servants of God, who were not however averse to cheating Indians out of furs, massacring them if they protested, and, more generally, torturing, exiling, or murdering all whose opinions differed from their own.

The Elizabethan poets, though not aristocrats themselves (on the contrary, most of them were poor, hardworking men with families to support), were nonetheless allied to the aristocracy by extensive ties, most notably the system of patronage. Their attack on the Puritans thus naturally assumed an aristocratic content and tone. This alliance, with all its implications, sealed the fate of poetry throughout the bourgeois epoch, which is only now drawing to a close. The rising bourgeoisie banished poetry at the same time that it ousted the aristocracy, sacrificing everything to what they considered the "supreme good": the accumulation of capital. Poetry, which glorifies so many things associated with aristocratic privileges (love, beauty, luxury, leisure, adventure, pleasure), is by definition opposed to work, which is the very cornerstone of the Protestant ethic, the pivot of bourgeois morality.

Marx observed that capitalist production is intrinsically hostile to poetry. With each succeeding efflorescence of authentic poetry—from individual pre-Romantics such as Otway and Chatterton; through Romanticism and its Transcendentalist, Pre-Raphaelite, and Decadent offshoots; all the way to surrealism—the anti-bourgeois sentiment is expressed with mounting vigor. Moreover, poets increasingly assume an extra-literary attitude. William Blake is said to have worn the Liberty Cap in support of the French Revolution of 1789 and was arrested for insulting the British king. The young Wordsworth and Coleridge also supported the Revolution in France, and Wordsworth dedicated a beautiful sonnet to Toussaint L'Ouverture. Byron and Shelley fought for Greek independence and, like nearly all the English Romantics, were ardent abolitionists; eventually they came to oppose not only chattel slavery but wage slavery as well. In the United States Philip Freneau, whose "House of the Night" and "The Jamaican Funeral" were the first glimmers of an indigenous Romanticism, fully merited his reputation as the "Poet of the Revolution." Charles Brockden Brown attacked religion as well as rationalism and took up the defense of women's rights. Emerson and Thoreau were among the most active supporters of John Brown's raid on Harpers Ferry.

This growing revolutionary tendency did not mean that poets renounced their "aristocratic" demeanor. On the contrary, very few failed to affect some sort of aristocratic pose. Byron, after all, was *Lord* Byron. The Dandies and Pre-Raphaelites devised an overtly aristocratic style of living, even in some cases in the midst of their very real poverty. When, in the mid-nineteenth century, the center of gravity of European poetry shifted to France (more specifically to Paris), the same tendency was already well-established. Isidore Ducasse, the single greatest influence on surrealism, styled himself the Count of Lautréamont. Saint-Pol-Roux, often seen in his full-length red cloak, called himself "The Magnificent" and cultivated numerous aristocratic eccentricities. Alfred Jarry, whose play *Ubu Roi* desecrated every civilized value, affected the royal "we." And in the first *Surrealist Manifesto* (1924), André Breton introduces the surrealists assembled in a *castle*.

With the advent of surrealism, however, this entire evolution reaches its climax. Breton remarked that surrealism could be regarded as the tail of Romanticism, but a very *prehensile* tail. World-historically, surrealism is the culmination and supersession of anterior poetic development; it is therefore not a "school," much less a "style," but a new *epoch* in the revolutionary development of human expression. Concretizing and extending the lessons of Lautréamont and Rimbaud, the surrealists have restored to poetry its fundamental reasons for being—restored it to its true revolutionary destiny. The anti-bourgeois, anti-christian tendency of all authentic poetry attains in surrealism its full theoretical coherence. The practice of poetry is divested of its specifically aristocratic limitations without the slightest concessions to bourgeois ideology and its notorious "good taste." This is because surrealism, as Marx wrote of the proletarian revolution, "draws its poetry from the future." Unlike the traditional aristocracy, which was and is a reactionary class seeking to restore its past privileges to a very few, the surrealists, allying their struggle with the revolutionary proletariat, aim at the establishment of a new "universal aristocracy"—that is, at the extension of aristocratic privileges to *all*.

Here too blues corresponds closely in essentials to the course of general poetic development. The indisputably proletarian character of black music did not prevent blues singers and early jazz people from freely borrowing aristocratic titles: we have had King Oliver, Count Basie, Duke Ellington; Bessie Smith was the Empress and Mamie

Smith the Queen. This reflects, in a small way, the blues singers' radical distance from middle-class reformists whose most "daring" schemes call for a slight reduction in the work-week and better public housing. The true proletarian aspiration, as evidenced in so many blues songs, is not merely for a "good" life but for the *best* life.

When asked "What do you want?" IWW organizers used to reply: "Everything." Why should the workers, who produce everything, settle for any less? "All life owes me is some richness now," says Johnny Shines. And that's the truth.

We have seen that the blues singers' entire activity confirms and reinforces the surrealist critique of the poetic situation. It remains only to examine more closely, beyond those elements it has in common with all authentic poetry, its specific and unique contributions to the poetic struggle of our time.

1) Most important, blues is *black*, the autonomous creation of the descendants of slaves stolen from Africa—men and women especially qualified to speak of human freedom. The "prime matter" of blues, the blue note, was drawn from the red-hot forge of a brutal dialectic: it was the unanticipated product of an impossible effort to play African music on European instruments. What a revelation this must have been for those who discovered it! They found in their hands a secret weapon that, in opposition to the Europeanization of the blacks, enabled them to wage the inestimably more honorable struggle to Africanize the whites.

2) Contrary to the general development of poetry, which has been driven by the bourgeoisie into ever narrower circles, blues is a *popular* movement. The fact that sharecroppers, agricultural workers, and hoboes were able to create, almost from scratch, a mass poetic current having affinities with the greatest poetry of the past and present proves only that the need for the Marvelous is universal, and that repressive civilization is only a temporary aberration.

3) Blues is poetry intended not as reading matter but as *song*. Here it rejoins the very origins of poetry, before the dawn of history, when poetry, song, and language were one and the same. The powerful current of Elizabethan poetry was preceded by a long period in which wandering troubadours sang their verses, accompanying themselves on lutes and other instruments. Today's blues, in rejoining this tradition while still holding fast to its African sources, looks ahead to the time when poetry, song, and language will once again be one and the same.

4) Blues is essentially a *collective* creation, antithetical to the anemic individualism of the false poets. Johnny Shines is right to insist that the blues singer has always been an "outsider"; this has been the fate of all poets since the bourgeoisie took power. But the American blacks, passing from chattel slavery to wage slavery, maintained numerous and powerful links, in the deepest recesses of their sensibilities, with the magnificent precapitalist tribal societies from which their ancestors were forcibly removed. In these societies, free of the affliction of private property, the "artists" were not outsiders. They were integral members of society, respected for their distinctive contributions, but not forced into any alienated caste. Important traces of this attitude remain in blues—in the attitude toward lyrics, for example: singers freely borrow one another's lyrics, modifying them as they please (a common practice among the Elizabethans, by the way).

The surrealists always have emphasized the urgency of collective creation. They have invented many experiments and games to stimulate this pursuit of poetic knowledge that exceeds the boundaries imposed on isolated individuals. The social circumstances of the blues singers, of course, enable them only occasionally (as in the "dirty dozens") to attain that *irrational glory* evidenced in surrealist games. But their emphasis on collective improvisation, their splendidly playful attitude toward lyrics, situate them firmly in line with that communism of the Marvelous that the surrealist revolution announces and prepares.

5) An important aspect of blues poetry, which I have not found seriously discussed in any of the literature, is its *muscular* character— muscular more or less in the sense that Gaston Bachelard detected in the poetry of Lautréamont. Its direct, aggressive, energetic, and *physical* presentation distinguishes blues from all other English poetry, written or sung. This seems to reflect something of its remotest African origins and a particular aspect of the legacy of slavery. Deprived of the full utilization of language—first by slavery and later by the system of discrimination—blues is, in fact, *a desperate search for language*: not for the language stolen from their ancestors, or for the language to which they are still not allowed full access, but for a new, exalted, and secret language that takes shape dreamily in primordial gestures and cries. This gives the blues its wild "theatrical" quality, its savage glow in the darkest darkness, its blazing touch of black light that is, as Antonin Artaud wrote of the theater, "a sense of life in which man fearlessly

makes himself master of what does not yet exist, and brings it into being." The *bodily* character of blues, the extent to which its rhythms touch the very pulse of life, is a stimulus to that *total poetry* whose greatest modern annunciator has been Lautréamont: a poetry made by all and by the whole being of each one of this "all"—a poetry that comes into existence with the definitive supersession of christian-bourgeois civilization.

Most commentators on blues seem to recognize only the painfully obvious and the ideologically acceptable. They forget that the blues singers have things to say, and that they say them very well. I have tried to present some of the evidence for a different approach, one that allows the blues singers' latent message to resound with all its magnetic and fiery brilliance.

J.B. Hutto, Johnny Shines, Big Joe Williams, Lightnin' Hopkins, Koko Taylor, Clifton Chenier, Yank Rachell, Louisiana Red, Big Mama Thornton, John Wrencher, Roosevelt Sykes, and so many others: these too are "alchemists of the word" directing their incantations against the shabby confines of a detestable "reality." Their magic, and that of their forerunners, kept alive a spirit of popular poetic revolt during a harsh winter that was decades long. For all this, and for so much more, they deserve our deepest gratitude.

In the deep blue ritual of smoke and shadows, the inner flame burns through the mirror of time and space, opening at last a means of access to the undreamed across the void.

23

Black Music, by Any Means Necessary

First published in *Living Blues*, no. 25, special supplement titled "Surrealism and Blues," January–February 1976.

> *The root of rhythm is its central unit of change.... Rhythm is life the space of time danced thru.*
>
> —Cecil Taylor

Commenting on the diversity of paths leading to an interest in blues, and clearly intending to sound a humorous note, a writer remarked that he knew at least one who came to blues via Ornette Coleman. But is this truly so paradoxical? Is the distance between blues and the newer currents of black music really as unbridgeable as some enthusiasts of one or the other pretend?

Those who thrive on the rigid definitions of chauvinistic prejudice are on shaky ground from the start, for it is universally agreed that blues and jazz derive from the same social sources. We have it from no less an authority than Charlie Parker that "blues is the basis of jazz." And it is significant that many of those who have contributed most to the revolutionary development of black music in recent years began, in fact, as bluesmen: Ornette Coleman, Joseph Jarman, and Pharoah Sanders, among others. Moreover, their subsequent activity has involved no "renunciation" of blues, for their later music has remained passionately imbued with the blues spirit.

Jazz always has been the *continuation of blues by other means*. What is at stake is not merely music or an "artistic" attitude but a revolutionary poetic conception of the world, defined above all by an assertion of the primacy of imaginative modes of apprehension over any restrictive "rationalism" or "realism." Black music helps us recognize the deeper meaning of John Brown's warning that the question of slavery, in all its ramifications, "is still to be settled." How far have we come since 1859? What is certain is that black music is the bold articulation of the dream of freedom—it is the voice of dreamers who awaken only to realize their dreams, "by any means necessary," as Malcolm X put it. At this moment, as the US government and the Gulf Oil Company do everything to strangle the hopes of the Angolan people, and as Robert F. Williams (the first prominent black leader in the United States in recent years to promote the cause of armed self-defense) is again hounded by the racist courts, we perceive only too plainly that the oppressive conditions at the origin of blues and jazz are still with us today.

In this context, those who hypocritically bemoan the "death" of blues and jazz advertise only their own fatal ignorance and play into the hands of the ruling ideologists who pretend that the so-called Civil Rights Bill was more than a waste of paper. Just as bad are those who erect an iron curtain between blues and the music of Cecil Taylor and of the Association for the Advancement of Creative Musicians (AACM) in Chicago. Designed to isolate creative figures from each other and from their community, this divisive tactic is wholly counterrevolutionary. Blues enthusiasts who find jazz too "complicated," and jazz enthusiasts who look down on blues as "obsolete," consciously or unconsciously are victims of an extensive self-deception that has only reactionary consequences.

The truth is that the constellation of black music has many stars, but its dazzling light is one. What the great black musicians of all tendencies share is not only a critique of misery but also a certain *vision* of a new world and a new life. If, as André Breton suggested, the great poets have been *auditories*, then we can add that the great black musicians have been *visionaries*.

The very words associated with black music—words such as *blues*, *jazz*, *swing*, *bebop*, and *reggae*—have a magical, talismanic quality. This vocabulary was improvised to correspond to something still in the process of *becoming*, some unprecedented wonder being born in the deepest rhythms of desire's desire. At the same time, these words retain a full measure of African glory: looking ahead to a non-repressive civilization, they also hark back to Yoruba trickster tales, to the secret lore of slaves, to the underground railroad, to the loa of Haitian voodoo. The grandeur of the course of black music lies in part in its defiant unity. From Tuareg chants through Blind Lemon Jefferson and Elmore James and Koko Taylor to the Art Ensemble of Chicago, the continuity of all "devil music" is affirmed with legitimate luciferian pride.

In black music as in surrealism, no contradiction exists between the wisdom of the ancients and the absolutely modern. When Sun Ra sets foot on Jupiter, rest assured that Papa Legba will be there to greet him.

24

Black Music and the Surrealist Revolution

Selection from "Black Music and the Surrealist Revolution," *Arsenal/ Surrealist Subversion*, no. 3 (Spring 1976): 20–27.

Scattered through Breton's works are many passing metaphorical references to music that assume a special resonance today. In *Soluble Fish* he tells us, "The lure of dreams stimulates the music of my head." In his *Introduction to the Discourse on the Paucity of Reality* he even invokes "the mysterious wind of jazz." It is plain now that, entirely aside from anyone's intentions, the two currents (surrealism and jazz) could not have remained completely apart. I think it is even permissible to speak of a subtle influence of jazz on surrealism from the very beginning. Are we really to believe, for example, that of thirty-two signatories to the 1927 surrealist tract *Hands Off Love!* there was not one whose awareness of the subject of that very document had been touched by the astonishing solos of King Oliver on his Creole Jazz Band recordings of 1923? All authentic jazz, including its earliest forms—no matter how burdened it may have been by absurd residues of the European musical tradition, with all its melodic sentimentality and stale harmonic pretensions—represents an opposition to the "paucity of reality" denounced by Breton.

It appears not at all accidental, in any case, that the entire evolution of jazz from the 1920s to the present reads like a line-by-line response to the challenge advanced by another surrealist, Paul Nougé, in his 1929 lecture published in English under the title *Music Is Dangerous*. Nougé insists, for example, that the prosperity of music and musicians depends on "a deliberate will to act upon the world." One of the most outstanding characteristics of jazz, especially since bebop, has been its elaboration of protest, its unrelenting revolutionary will. Joseph Jarman urges:

construct transformation construct REVOLT
DO NOT INCITE TO RIOT—
INCITE TO REVOLUTION

"Here," Nougé continues, "we rediscover, transfigured, the moving aspiration of magician, healer and thaumaturge," which is also the moving aspiration of the surrealist poet and painter, as of the jazz musician—an aspiration (citing Jarman again) "to offer revelation to revolution," or, in other words, to realize the magic of poetry in everyday life.

Summing up, Nougé declares categorically: "Our desire is to place ourselves altogether in the service of the *possibilities of spirit.*" And in his concluding remarks he adds: "Whether we deal with music or with some other human event, spirit is at our mercy, and we are, in reality, accountable for it."

In the realm of "spirit," of course, many would-be revolutionists lose their footing and retreat lamely to a dismal positivism entirely out of keeping with their presumed intention to lead the struggle for human emancipation. In his best days Archie Shepp replied very well to all varieties of pseudo-radical philistinism, denouncing the Stalinists' "chauvinistic attitude to jazz" and specifying further, in the vein of Nougé's prospectus, that this attitude "seemed to contradict the whole thing, everything I'd ever read of Marx, the whole dialectical process.... Jazz is a symbol of the triumph of the human spirit, not of its degradation. It is a lily in spite of the swamp."

In "Surrealist Situation of the Object" (1935), Breton succinctly traced the modern evolution of poetry and the plastic arts in the light of Hegel's *Philosophy of Fine Art.* Although he refers to music only in passing, the theoretical context and line of argument are sufficient to indicate not only the gap that thus remained in the surrealist conquest but also the direction to be taken to close this gap.

"I cannot repeat too often," Breton says, "that Hegel ... attacked all the problems that on the plane of poetry and art may today be considered to be the most difficult, and that with unparalleled lucidity he solved them for the most part." Hegel ranked music below the "universal art" of poetry, but above the plastic arts. Observing that painting was the first of the arts to come under the sway of poetic imperatives, and that it did so by passing beyond external representation in favor of the *interior model*, Breton points to the influence of photography in precipitating this development. (Movies, he adds, were to effect a similar revolution in sculpture.) He does not add—though his framework implies it and events have established it—that the invention of phonographic recording had comparable consequences for music: the "pure" composer was pushed off his throne by the creative musician; traditional compositional values gave way to improvisation. This technological development undoubtedly hastened the consolidation of jazz, which emerged as the perfect musical expression of the new sensibility.

It is true that this revolution developed more slowly in music than in poetry, painting, or sculpture, and that it developed for the most part in the United States rather than in Europe. These facts help explain Breton's failure to recognize it. Interestingly enough, however, his important article "Silence Is Golden," written while he was an exile in New York during the Second World War and originally published in English in the magazine *Modern Music* (March–April 1944), takes up the problem of music at once more sympathetically, more concretely, and in much greater detail. This article is especially compelling not only because it is the sole text in which Breton considers music at length but also because in it he approaches, albeit tentatively, the possibilities of a new music analogous to surrealist achievements on the poetic and plastic planes. (Not surprisingly, this text is rarely mentioned by critics.)

In the first paragraph Breton admits that his own ignorance of music belongs to the category of *prejudices*, specifying that he had not, however, "renounced all objective judgment" concerning it. Referring again to Hegel's *Philosophy of Fine Art*, Breton continued: "Above all I am convinced that the antagonism which exists between poetry and music (affecting, apparently, poets much more than it does musicians), and which for some ears seems to have reached its height today, should not be fruitlessly deplored but, on the contrary, should be interpreted as an indication of the *necessity for a recasting* of certain principles of the two arts."

Breton argues further: "On the auditive plane, I believe that music and poetry have everything to lose by not recognizing a common origin and a common end in *song*, by letting the mouth of Orpheus get farther every day from the lyre of Thrace. Poet and musician will degenerate if they persist in acting as though these two forces were never to be brought together again." Rejecting "reformist" solutions, such as "poems set to music," Breton insists that "now only the most radical methods could hope for success." He affirms, "ambitious though it may be, that we must determine to *unify, reunify hearing* to the same degree that we must determine to *unify, reunify sight.*"

Moreover, he writes, "It is evident that the fusion of the two elements—music and poetry—could only be accomplished at a very high emotional temperature. And it seems to me that it is in the expression of the passion of love that both music and poetry are most likely to reach this supreme point of incandescence."

The concluding section of the essay is devoted to some reflections touching on the "phonetic cabala," though he does not refer to it as such. "Never to the same extent as in surrealist writing," he says, "have poets so relied on the *tonal* value of words. The negativist attitudes aroused by instrumental music seem to have found compensation here." Approaching the problem of the most hidden recesses of language, he continues: "The 'inner word' that surrealist poetry has chosen to make manifest, and that it has succeeded, whether we like it or not, in establishing as a recognizable means of communication between certain people, is absolutely inseparable from 'inner music' by which it very probably is cradled and conditioned.... Above all, being independent of the social and moral obligations that limit spoken and written language, inner thinking is free to tune itself to the 'inner music' *which never leaves it.*"

Finally, Breton restates his contention, already argued in his essay "The Automatic Message" (1933), that "great poets have been 'auditives,' not visionaries. At least, with them, vision, 'illumination,' is the effect and not the cause"—great poetic images are "seen only after they have been heard."

⌒

"Even as I write," said Lautréamont in *Les Chants de Maldoror*, "new shivers are traversing the intellectual atmosphere. One needs only the courage to face them." Even as Breton was writing "Silence Is Golden," the new shivers of bop were traversing the intellectual atmosphere, confirming, strengthening, expanding the most audacious proposals of surrealism, and unmistakably heading toward the reunification of hearing that Breton called for.

Breton's essay indicates that certain poets, at least, had gone a long way toward opening new lines of communication with musicians. The road they were thus clearing, he insisted, was "the only road that, in times such as these, is great and sure: that of a return to principles." It was also by a return to principles that certain jazz musicians, during the same years, began to find their way to the practice of poetry.

The passage of time has not in the least diminished the radiant glory of bop, which on the contrary extends each day. The luminous integrity of this music—and therefore of the musicians who produced it—stands in striking contrast to various murky, commercial rational-izations and debasements that came after, like so many hyenas, not to mention the shady maneuvers of the critics, eager to cash in on any and all misunderstandings. Many of those who presided over the birth of the "new vice" of bop are no longer with us; most of those who remain tend to act as though they were sworn to secrecy. It is almost impossible for us to reconstruct—even rudimentarily—the climate of those electri-fying months during which Minton's Playhouse served as a Bureau of Bop Research; impossible to reenter, as it were, the "process" by which the original revelations of Charlie Parker and his collaborators were set loose on the world. But one thing at least is beyond dispute: the boppers effected a remarkably explosive, lyrical crystallization of revolutionary sentiments shared to a great degree by the black proletariat as a whole.

Thus, for example, black soldiers during the Second World War organized the "Double V" movement, signifying not only V for victory abroad against the axis powers but Double V for victory at home against racial discrimination as well. The assertive, aggressive, defi-ant, merciless character of bop situates it solidly in this context. Aside from abundant internal evidence on this point, it is also noteworthy that Charlie Parker's celebrated "Now's the Time," according to many of those closest to him, was originally to have been titled, precisely, "Double V."

The new shiver of bop was exemplified by the legato agitation of the cymbal by which the bop drummers, not without a certain arro-gance, conceded to indicate the beat. To be sure, bop also sent chills down the spine of innumerable Western traditions and values. For bop was above all else a revolt against music as a soporific evasion. It was a slap in the face of all the assumptions of the Mickey Mouse world. Nourished on the revolutionary political aspirations implicit in Double V, bop reached out too toward the revolutionary poetic spirit of Triple V, or *VVV* as the surrealists in exile titled their journal in those years. In the lean years of war and counterrevolution, surrealism and bop were rallying points of human freedom, affirmations of the necessity for total revolution. Inevitably they were attacked by all forces of reaction. Hounded, in some cases starved, driven to the wall, persecuted in a thousand large and small ways, neither surrealists nor bop musicians—with very few and partial exceptions—were allowed to prosper. The magnitude and magnificence of their achievements appear all the greater in view of the impossible odds against them.

The bombing of Hiroshima and Nagasaki served as an unspeakably brutal reminder that the old order still held the stage. The bop revolution had little chance to extend itself into new domains. Even in the "music world"—*especially* in the "music world"—its gains were resisted and fought, not only by club owners and critics but also by several older jazzmen from whom one might have hoped for a more fraternal attitude. For Louis Armstrong bop was "that modern malice." It was not truly malice at all, of course, but a genuine pride and self-confidence, a bold exuberance that doubtless seemed to be malice to those for whom jazz was part of "show biz"— those whose whole experience had been so horrible that they wanted to *please their oppressors* at all costs. The boppers were not out to please but to explore and discover. And when necessary—there is no denying it—they were also prepared to destroy, to annihilate obstacles placed in their way.

Another older jazzman, Cab Calloway, himself an eccentric figure and flagrant violator of American bourgeois "good taste," dismissed bop as "Chinese music." Absurd as this charge is, it retains a grain of truth in that bop did represent a purging from jazz of extraneous European debris, simultaneously expanding its receptiveness to non-European influences. In bop one hears the influence of revolutionary waves resounding throughout the nonwhite world. Related to this, filtered through incredible mystification, was the curious Muslim fad that flourished for more than a decade in the black ghettoes, and especially on the jazz scene, beginning in the late 1940s. In essence this had nothing in common with the moribund theology of the decadent slaveholding societies of the Middle East. It was rather a difficult first step toward *dechristianization* and even a rejection of the entire "American way of life." The dialectic of consciousness in this epoch is riddled with such seeming paradoxes of uneven and combined development. Whoever merely ridicules such phenomena only makes himself ridiculous. Out of the Muslim movement emerged a popular revolutionary leader as genuine as Malcolm X, one of the titanic figures of our age.

The tragic destiny of Malcolm X, the heroic sweep of his rise from the most demoralizing lowlife to the threshold of proletarian internationalism, sheds light on the whole question of "black nationalism." It is no accident that the specter of Marcus Garvey returned as the bop revolution reached its apogee. But with all the hypocritical hue and cry about "racism in reverse," and the equally foolish rhetoric of numerous white sycophants who have functioned only as cheerleaders of underdevelopment, few have even tried to discern the sense of the nationalist current as it applied to jazz.

For the jazz musician, black nationalism signified a head-on challenge to the white petit bourgeois monopolists of the sordid night-club circuit and the recording industry; a defiant assertion of the will of the creators of jazz to become independent of its exploiters; a proud conviction in the legitimacy and even superiority of African modes of apprehension over the stagnant fragmentation of men and women characteristic of capitalist/christian Europe. The revolutionary tendency implicit in bop increasingly became explicit in the declarations of younger musicians, beginning in the late 1950s. The adepts of jazz, freed during the bop era of the etiquette of "entertainment," began to emerge as a consciously revolutionary factor in the modern world.

For most jazz musicians, nationalism has been a beginning rather than an end. And this is hardly surprising, for the whole evolution of black music is the evolution of the rhythm of the consciousness of freedom—a consciousness that unceasingly overflows all restrictions. To be sure, many black revolutionists whose political positions are not traditionally nationalist have nonetheless declared themselves nationalists, largely out of revulsion against the puerility, chauvinism, and racism of the "white left." It is almost a truism that nationalist demands will continue to be made by blacks until the last vestige of racism is thrown off by the whites. More than ever the right of self-determination must be energetically defended. But here as elsewhere the revolution admits no easy labels. Malcolm X said in one of his last interviews: "If you notice, I haven't been using the expression [*black nationalism*] for several months. But I still would be hard-pressed to give a specific definition of the overall philosophy which I think is necessary for the liberation of the black people in this country."

With bop, the "secret society" always latent in jazz begins to assume a fuller development. With its background in African and Caribbean traditions, and drawing from underground traditions of black nationalism, its immediate need of occultation was doubtless as a defense against the encroachments of many and varied predators and parasites. Most of these, needless to say, have been white: the cockroach capitalists of clubs and record companies; the commercial imitators; the critics. The boppers' effort to keep out the public, to assure that their research would be innocent of concessions to existing "taste," was doomed from the start, as is poignantly suggested by an album such as *Charlie Parker with Strings*.

The bop musicians did not "sell out." One by one, in different ways, most of them were *crushed* by an inhuman culture that, though obviously dying, became increasingly murderous in its blind efforts at self-preservation. A series of deaths and defections brought about the eventual liquidation of bop as an independent movement. The ensuing reaction, "cool" jazz (led by that glacial genius, Miles Davis), in essence an accommodation to the climate of the Cold War, was quickly adopted by the white middle-class intelligentsia, who found the soothing, muted, sterile sounds of Stan Getz and Chet Baker well suited to their own "existentialist" frigidity. In this regard a deathbed declaration of Charlie Parker, that "too many of the young cats" did not know the *blues*, takes on a symptomatic significance, for the blues, as Bird added, "is the basis of jazz." It was entirely in the nature of things that the next revolution in jazz, after bop, would have among its leaders many whose grounding in blues had been deep and enduring.

Sowing the seeds of an urgent promise, bop yielded an incomparable harvest on the other side of despair. Charlie Parker's achievements in music are on the same plane as Rimbaud's in poetry, or Picasso's in painting, with this difference: Bird, unlike Rimbaud and Picasso, did not allow the last years of his life to detract from his earlier grandeur. Let it never be forgotten that Charlie Parker died of an overdose of American racism, exploitation, and complacency. But just as his indomitable spirit remains a symbol of unblemished courage and lucidity, so too the revolution in consciousness to which he devoted his life is not a lost cause. On the contrary, it gains new ground each day.

The substance of Parker's courage and lucidity permits us to define the *quest* of bop as a heroic and in large part victorious effort *to expand the field of improvisation*—that is, to expand the prerogatives of the imagination over memory's fixed forms. All the "technical" problems of jazz (displaced accents, "irrational" rhythms, contrast of sonorities, the gradual eclipse of the clarinet and triumph of the saxophone, the breaking up of time, the excursions beyond the four-bar unit of construction, the negation of melodic and harmonic barriers, etc.) are inseparable from this quest.

The authentic heirs of bop, who have taken up these and countless other problems, have been the passionate pursuers of this quest. Picasso's celebrated motto, "When I run out of red, I use blue," has its jazz equivalent in Charlie Mingus's remark: "There are no wrong notes." It is not that "anything goes" but rather that "anything goes for those who know." The tendency toward occultation, which the post-bop jazz currents have greatly developed, involves an experience of nothing less than *initiation*. The surrealists have long recognized this principle (see Breton's *Second Manifesto*) that not only keeps out the uncongenial—by means of what Joseph Jarman calls "a web to keep the eyes of those who will never understand away"—but also strengthens and develops the faculties of those who share the secret.

Between the noun *entrance* and the verb *entrance* the experience of initiation concentrates the darkness into a magic flame that immolates every resistance and reveals a ladder of air to that "point in the mind" at which the real and the imaginary cease to be perceived as contradictory. Let us waste no words on those who confuse this revolutionary moral rigor with the masochistic chastisements of religion, or on those who seek the philosopher's gold at the currency exchange. The removal of opportunists, stragglers, fence-sitters, and others who are *morally disqualified* is a necessary correlate of the uninterrupted pursuit of what Breton called "the light that will cease to fail." That several of the greatest black musicians have independently arrived at similar conclusions is further evidence of the profound unity of their aspirations and ours.

∾

If Charlie Parker is comparable to Rimbaud and Picasso, then Cecil Taylor with his *Jazz Advance* (1956) has given us a veritable surrealist manifesto in music. If this were a history it would be necessary to chronicle the specific and in some cases enormous contributions of Thelonious Monk, Miles Davis, John Coltrane, Charlie Mingus, Eric Dolphy, Sun Ra, Ornette Coleman, and others. But *Jazz Advance*, and particularly its interpretation of "Sweet and Lovely," seems to me a landmark of such magnitude and brilliance that it can serve here, without distorting the course of events, as a definition (insofar as a "definition" is possible) of what has been called variously the "new music," "Great Black Music," the "new thing" in jazz, and—taking its name from the title of an Ornette Coleman/Eric Dolphy album that was one of the first to echo the implications of Cecil Taylor's achieve-ment—*free jazz*.

All the old controversies over Monk's "depersonalization of the chord," and his alleged "excess" of dissonances, remind us today of such historic examples of ineptness as Paul Valery's question, addressed to André Breton: "How is one to distinguish cubist A from cubist B?" And there is no longer any doubt that it is largely thanks to Cecil Taylor that a death blow has been dealt to every equivocation of this sort. The decisive lessons of Taylor's work seem to me as follows: that the emancipation of what has been known as jazz could be achieved only by rigorously following through the profoundest essence of this music; that salvation could not be found in any compromise or eclecticism; that the victory of the "jazz revolution" required *absolute fidelity to its own means*—namely, the *definitive triumph of improvisation*, pursued (as it could only be pursued) in conditions of *moral asepsis*.

Paraphrasing Breton's famous statement about words in auto-matic writing, I suggest this formula: With Charlie Parker, the sounds stop fooling around; with Cecil Taylor, the sounds start making love.

When Cecil Taylor presses chords on the piano, his fingers touch keys that open doors on the electric pulse of a luminous freedom waking in the murmuring eyelids of a vertigo scaled like the innermost cliff overlooking the boundless main of a vision thirsty for the troubled waters of an externalized fear—absolute fear, the supersession of which, as Hegel argued in his *Phenomenology of Mind*, leads to mastery over the entire objective reality. If the history of jazz is the history of such successive supersessions, with each turn the stakes have grown higher;

today, thanks to Cecil Taylor and those closest to him, they are rapidly approaching a vengeful apex.

The expression *free jazz* signifies freedom not only in the negative and destructive sense (freedom *from* European values and other restraints) but also freedom in the affirmative: freedom *to* re-create the audible universe according to desire. The continuing exploration of Cecil Taylor and of several others who have taken the same path—or cleared new paths in the same direction—prove that the revolution in black music has not ceased to deepen and to extend its sway; that it shows no sign of loosening its grasp of historical truth. Such advances, in the face of the abominable social conditions enforced by an Ubuesque government and a no less Ubuesque "cultural establishment," can be made only by those whose uncompromising ardor and creative integrity permit them at first sight to distinguish essence from excrescence, true life from hopeless mirage.

Cecil Taylor's effort has been reinforced, in recent years, by a number of musicians mostly living in Chicago: Muhal Richard Abrams, Fred Anderson, Joseph Jarman, Roscoe Mitchell, Henry Threadgill, and others who, refusing to stand still on previously conquered terrain, confirm our conviction that today nothing is closed off to jazz—that the jazz revolution is indeed *permanent*.

Improvisation, once decried by respectable authorities as a regrettable "primitive" vestige, has long been an accomplished fact, even among modern European composers who expressly disavow interest in jazz. But for them it is only an isolated technical device, or a tarnished insignia of academic virtuosity, or, in the case of John Cage, an irredeemable promissory note glued to the shadow of Marcel Duchamp.

For those, however, who recognize in jazz a door opening on the Golden Fleece, improvisation is not such a trifle. There are, perhaps, an infinite number of ways to pull the wool over the eyes of the sleepless dragon, but each adventurer must find his own way, at the risk of his very life.

Pursued in the sense that Cecil Taylor exemplifies, collective improvisation in jazz, as in the written or drawn "Exquisite Corpses" of surrealism, introduces us into the communism of the Marvelous. In *Unit Structures*, how admirably the piano's vines of phosphorous polyphony, dripping with crystal whispers from a moat of serpentine surprises, climb through the fine blue branches of altoist Jimmy Lyons's split-second solos, drawing forth the nectar of their inmost reserves, bringing us intermingling auras of black truth on the magnetic fields of a momentous expectation, always multiplying that *higher vigilance* and urging us up the asymmetrical stairway out of the quotidian deception to the outer reaches of thought in amorous pursuit of its object!

With Cecil Taylor improvisation becomes *absolute* in a trance that transfigures the very ground of what has been regarded heretofore as humanly possible. Nothing else in music resounds with this irrepressible *golden tremor* that will yet make a deafened world jump forward into the excited rediscovery of its own ears. Already his works have permitted many listeners to return from the brink of one or another untold disaster—to return with a confidence that can come only from inspiration truly global in origin as well as in implications. Works such as Cecil Taylor's, which catapult us to a new and profound sense of the terrifying fragility of existence, and at the same time inspire our awareness of how the conditions of this existence can be changed—works, that is, that are capable of overcoming the stultifying skepticism of all modern miserabilism, and restoring to men and women the consciousness of the possibilities of a life of exaltation—such works are themselves irrefutable testimony that their creator is doing *exactly what is called for, exactly at the right time.*

For the new musicians it is no longer a question of music alone, of music as an "isolated discipline." Rather, without in the least betraying the magnificent tradition of black music for which they all have deepest veneration, the new musicians have increasingly tended to take up the problems of human expression in all its forms.

It could be argued that, just as surrealism is not a "type" of poetry but, on the contrary, alone represents authentic poetic activity in our time, so the music of Cecil Taylor and Joseph Jarman can no longer be regarded as a "type" of music. It has become, rather, the most important element in the *refoundation* of music—or, perhaps it would be more accurate to say, the *axis* around which serious research into sound, as a vehicle for expressing the "real functioning of thought," has come to revolve. As jazz has sloughed off, bit by bit, all superfluous elements, the purity sought and won has been less musical, perhaps, than *magical*. Free jazz does not mean "pure music," in the sense of a sterilized aesthetic. Its purity signifies rather the removal of everything that interferes with the expression of liberated desire. When the British critic Max Harrison complains, in *Jazz on Record*, that Coltrane's *Ascension* "seems more a ritualistic than a musical experience," he proves only that he got the point and missed it too. The surrealist painter Max Ernst published a book in 1934 called *Beyond Painting*. The position of the new jazz musicians could be defined as Beyond Music.

Thus, the "occult" preoccupations of some jazz musicians seem to me closer to the *high tone* of a work such as John Dee's *Hieroglyphic Monad* than to any of the pseudo-esoteric tinklings so fashionable today. Similarly, those musicians who find inspiration in astronomical and mathematical lore have ventured into the domain of Pythagoras for motives completely distinct from, and even opposed to, the hyperhygienic vanity of the so-called computer composers. Moreover, the scope of jazz has been expanded to such an extent that its applications are as limitless as its inspirations. It is in this sense that one should regard the brave assertion of Sunny Murray: "If some avant-garde jazz musicians played outside a hospital they'd say they were going to kill the patients or make them sicker because the patients weren't in tune to that sound. But maybe it was them working so hard not to hear natural sounds that contributed to putting them as patients into the hospital in the first place. And maybe the sound we make could touch and unloose something in those patients and make them want to live again. You see, the intensity of this music can really change things; the elements we live in, the air and the water."

By circuitous and unexpected paths we have rediscovered problems not unlike those that concerned Charles Fourier, whose "passional calculus" allowed him to announce that with the establishment of Social Harmony there would be thirty-seven million poets equal to Homer.

Today, however, in the English language, there are hardly even thirty-seven poets—a fact that sums up the ever-greater precariousness of the human condition. The present social order is inflexibly hostile to poetry, and vice versa. This is why, since the dawn of Romanticism, which coincided with the consolidation of the bourgeois revolution, authentic poets have tended toward a more and more conscious revolutionary attitude. As champions of the triumph of the human spirit, the new musicians also have necessarily tended toward the criticism and overthrow of the obstacles to this triumph. We could paraphrase Benjamin Péret's pronouncement on the poet and say that the creative musician today has no choice but to be a revolutionary—or to cease being a creative musician.

It is worth emphasizing that the bourgeois revolution can truly never be consummated; that bourgeois society is always and everywhere unstable. Long periods of relative quiescence cannot do away with the fundamental and irreconcilable contradictions between the creative masses, who produce all the wealth, and the handful of leeches who control it. The working class, by definition (to the extent that it is conscious of itself as a class), struggles for the abolition of wage slavery and therefore for real freedom; the capitalist class, however, in direct proportion to the class-consciousness of the workers, slides inexorably into fascism. Especially at those historic moments when the question of workers' power is most seriously posed, all the feudal and pre-feudal atavisms unresolved by bourgeois rule reenter the stage of history as active factors on the side of counterrevolution.

The overestimation of the immediate exchange-value of language (which gives bourgeois culture its wholly *prosaic* character) nourishes these unresolved atavisms and directly enforces the passivity and apathy of the working class. With the vacuous and degraded language held in check by the commodity economy, workers are unable to formulate the ardent images of revery and revolt indispensable to the development of revolutionary consciousness. And it is precisely to the extent that they are unable to formulate bold and emancipatory images, as the emblems of their deepest desires and the heralds of decisive actions, that the workers fall victim to the regressive and repressive images of reaction.

The task of the revolutionary poet, therefore, is to restore language to its essential poetic function, to promote the elaboration of a specifically poetic climate of sensibility, which I have defined elsewhere as a *climate of readiness for the actualization of the Marvelous*: the only climate in which revolutionary consciousness can take root and flower.[1] The task of the revolutionary poet is to assist in the destruction of all repressive myths and ideologies and to assist in creating the situation whereby all will become poets.

If the term *revolutionary poet* has obviously become practically synonymous with *surrealist*, it should be no less obvious that the musicians of "free jazz" are not mere allies but, objectively, active participants in the surrealist revolution. The works of surrealist poets, painters, photographers, and sculptors and the free jazz musicians belong as unshakably to the revolutionary future as 99 percent of what passes for literature, art, and music in our society belongs to the reactionary dead weight of the past. The legion of false poets, false painters, and false musicians invoke a fear of the future and a masochistic accommodation to "nostalgia." They are hired to embellish and conceal the decay of bourgeois culture, to disguise and reinforce everything that deserves to perish. And just as reactionary politicians have not hesitated to plunder the works of revolutionary theorists to concoct new confusionist demagogies, neither do reactionary litterateurs or artists (to say nothing of advertising agents) hesitate to plunder surrealism and black music for commercial and confusionist purposes. But this requires only that the social and surrealist revolutions be deepened and carried through all the way, to *expropriate the expropriators*.

The intrinsically revolutionary and communist character of surrealism and free jazz is exemplified by their disdain for the vile conception of private property, including the stupid notion of "talent" that is the hideous hallmark of bourgeois cultural ideology. Moreover, the surrealists' and free jazz musicians' emphasis on automatism (improvisation)—not only individually but collectively—and their research into chance, collage, and other means of "forcing inspiration," contribute substantially to breaking down the barriers of "specialization": the alienated, atomized framework characteristic of an exploitative society. Such a struggle clearly exceeds the old categories, implying the supersession of art, literature, and music. "We have nothing to do with literature," the first surrealists declared in 1925, and the new musicians could say the same today of music, "but we are quite capable, when necessary, of making use of it like anyone else."

If, with very few exceptions, recent poets writing in English had nothing to say about jazz—apart from some dismal journalistic asides and condescending whimpers—it is because they were not true poets. A poet who is false in poetry is necessarily false all along the line, true only in his consistent falsehood. How could the false poets, whose bad breath is only the exhalation of their bad faith, respond with anything but hostility or hypocrisy to the revealers of sounds whose echoes know only the brightest promises of the future?

For the false poets jazz is entirely *foreign* and therefore regarded suspiciously as something to be suppressed outright or, at best, treated as a bit of exotic flora, used to brighten up their colorless estates. Jazz, for these literary colonialists in whom is concentrated all that is rottenest in European culture, is at best a "background" against which they can rattle the ice cubes in their cocktails. Morally, and in every other sense, they have compromised themselves into a coward's corner, from which point all they can do is grovel before the icons of existing dishonor.

The failure of American poetry throughout this century is inextricably linked to the "mysticism" that has been said to afflict certain musicians: Coltrane, Sun Ra, Pharoah Sanders, and others. Mysticism flourishes in direct proportion to the defeat of poetry and revolution. If one considers the unrelieved wretchedness of existence that most black musicians have been forced to endure—the horrors of exploitation and poverty intensified a thousandfold by racism and philistinism—the wonder is not why some musicians succumbed to mysticism but rather how so many avoided it.

The task of poets in this regard was and is to provide the "untrammeled immediacy" of jazz with the concrete situations of revolutionary poetic action, to inspire confidence in the destiny of dreams, to make the spiritual air breathable, to defend the adventure of love against all ravages of the Reality Principle. And here the dialectic of history has performed one of its noblest acts of revenge: in the absence of an ongoing poetic climate, several major figures of the jazz revolution have themselves become poets. Without the slightest hesitation I would say that five lines of any text by Cecil Taylor, chosen at random, are superior in all respects to the whole pseudo-poetic production of any and all of the contemporary "poets" represented in Donald Allen's *New American Poetics*. This is because Cecil Taylor, as everyone must know who has ever heard him play, is deeply aware of the whole range of the crisis of consciousness in our time, sensitive to all that is urgent, all that is *looking ahead*. In contrast, Donald Allen's troupe of literary eunuchs are capable, with but one or two partial exceptions, only of squealing and squirming before the collapsing court of christian/capitalist confusion.

A qualitative advance in communication between the long-isolated vessels of poetry and music required the intrusion of an authentic poetic praxis. That this praxis is now elaborated not only by poets but also by musicians who are poets means that the old barriers are being broken down from both sides.

The disintegration of all prevailing aesthetic values—values that, in painting, poetry, and music, have been only the emblems of man's inhumanity to man—is the essential precondition for the reintegration of all modes of expression signified by surrealism, which replaces all obsolete notions of beauty with what Breton designated *convulsive* beauty. Convulsive beauty is, of course, inseparable from the social convulsions of this epoch, which announce the disintegration of old values and the myths of which they are a part; the disintegration, indeed, of the entire social order, *an entire civilization*, that upholds such values and myths and is upheld by them. These convulsions announce also the formation of new values and a new myth—revolutionary values derived from a liberatory and poetic myth, the collective dream of those whose poetic way of life contributes to resolving the contradictions between dream and action as well as between collective and individual.

In his own speculations on the forms this new myth might take, Breton posited the Great Invisibles: harbingers of all that transcends the human condition, temptations to all that is "larger than life." Although his specific discussions of this theme begin only in the 1940s, hints toward it are not lacking in his earlier writings, as in this passage from the *Second Manifesto*: "The fact is that the preparations are, roughly speaking, 'artistic' in nature. Nonetheless, I foresee that they will come to an end, and when they do, the revolutionary ideas that surrealism harbors will appear to the accompaniment of an enormous rending sound and will give themselves free rein."

I have always felt that this "enormous rending sound" marked the *movement* of the Great Invisibles toward visibility, and that the character of the sound is suggested by the great jazz musicians, just as the visual manifestations of these secret beings are suggested by the surrealist painters. Those who venture into the unknown have neither maps nor models; they must *improvise*. If their improvisation draws on knowledge acquired in the "old world," their aspirations nonetheless are entirely *elsewhere* and so is their direction. The surrealists and the new musicians ultimately are concerned not with a new art but with a *new life*. The new myth is the hidden door to this new life.

Black music, jazz, has its place—a prime place—in the formation of this new myth and of the new life that it announces. The new musicians have proved already that the Great Invisibles are also the Great Inaudibles, whose potential audibility depends on the resolution of the contradiction between inner and outer music, which in turn is a function of the *becoming of freedom*.

25

Buster Keaton

First published in "Surrealism and Its Popular Accomplices," special issue of *Cultural Correspondence*, guest-edited by Franklin Rosemont, nos. 10–11 (Fall 1979): 47.

———

Joseph Francis Keaton (1895–1966) got his nickname from his godfather, Harry Houdini, when, as an infant, he fell downstairs without getting "busted." Raised in the whirl of vaudeville, he had more arduous adventures before he reached the age of two than most people know in a lifetime. Once he was picked up by a cyclone and sent flying for hundreds of feet through town. Almost from birth he was performing regularly in his parents' comedy routines. His father would hold him by his ankles and sweep the floor with Buster's hair (he was billed as "The Human Mop"), then hurl the lad across the stage or into the audience. Almost before he could walk, Buster Keaton knew how to fall without getting hurt. He was, indeed, something of a *specialist* in falling (throughout life, he almost never used stuntmen). This is by no means as easy as it might appear. The art of falling requires not only an incredible coordination and equilibrium but also a certain way of looking at things—a certain "attitude" akin to the experience of *satori* in Zen, or to the "pure psychic automatism" of surrealism. "Because I find it easy to scratch my left ear with my toe," Keaton once said, "you may think me incapable of having opinions on poetry or music. But after all, learning how to scratch your ear with a toe requires strong muscular discipline, and every discipline implies another, cerebral discipline."

Keaton's marvelous resiliency, in any case, underscored his perfect tranquility. His "Great Stone Face" surely is the most expressive blank stare of all time. Magic lamps burn in each of his eyes, signaling the intense *passion* that seethes beneath this mask of Spinoza's imperturbable calm. There is nothing superfluous in Keaton's movements. His indomitable grace owes much to the subversive directness of his gestures. Entering a workplace, he notices a sign that says "Punch Clock"; with the merest glance at this instrument of degradation, he puts his fist through it (*The Playhouse*, 1921).

In all his films Keaton is a man with *things to do*. He has tasks to accomplish, obstacles to overcome, aims to fulfill. With his unique kinesthetic/poetic energy, he supersedes the mossgrown distinctions between acrobatics, athletics, and dance and gives us a profound sense of the truly *inspired* human body exceeding all known limits.

His comic method consists in creating situations, to use an expression of Marx, from which all turning back is impossible. A past master in the art of keeping cool in a crisis, he accepts all challenges, and always in his own way: *with the greatest of ease.* He lights his cigarette with a bomb thrown by an anarchist, and then blithely tosses the bomb into a throng of police (*Cops*, 1922).

It is significant that, unlike Chaplin, who consistently mistrusts machines, Keaton finds that machines can be sources of pleasure and play. Ample evidence of this exists in nearly all his films, but it is shown with particular force in two of his greatest: *Sherlock Jr.* (1924) and *The Cameraman* (1928), both of which are movies about movies. Camera and projector are seen here not as intrusive impersonal devices in opposition to human activity, threatening the individual's autonomy as alien forces, but rather as vehicles of an exalted subjectivity: elements, like everything else, of a dream within a dream within a dream.

These two films best exemplify Keaton's revolutionary/poetic worldview. When he passes through the looking-glass, he is not content merely to see what is on the other side: he braves his way through a whole succession of looking-glasses, each behind the other, and each reflecting only the meagerest hint of what we call "the real." And what motive could possibly underlie such feverish wanderings back and forth through the interpenetrating spheres of the pluriverse? The answer is crystal clear: Keaton's audacity is in the service of *sublime love.* His agility is always radiant with a lover's grim determination. There is no risk that he will not take for the woman he loves. Only Buster Keaton, moreover, can sustain a single kiss for two years (*The Paleface*, 1921).

We do not know to what extent Keaton was aware of the magnitude of his achievements. Always modest, devoid of pretense, he spoke little of his intentions or deeds. We have his autobiography, *My Wonderful World of Slapstick* (1967), and a number of interviews—all warm, informative, helpful, yet somehow strangely reticent. There is no doubt that he knew much more than he ever cared to express in words. It is interesting to note, in this regard, that when he made the remark about scratching his ear with his toe, in 1929, he was reading a volume of selected writings by Karl Marx.

It was in his silent films that Buster Keaton said everything he wished to say, and he said it with such brilliance and verve as to preclude all misunderstanding. Nothing could be plainer than the fact that every one of his films is implacably against war, alienated labor, law 'n' order, sentimentality—against all the rotten values and institutions of bourgeois/christian civilization.

In dozens of marvelous films, Buster Keaton lives as the embodiment of a quality all too rare: an exemplary *total freedom*. An intrepid foe of the inhuman, he is never a mere superman and always much more than a "humanist." Overreaching himself at every turn, he urges us to try to overreach ourselves. For many of us, he is one of the few who have made life worth living in the twentieth century.

26

Modern Dance

First published in Mari Jo Buhle, Paul Buhle, and Dan Georgakas, eds., *Encyclopedia of the American Left* (New York: Garland, 1990), 476–82.

Emerging as a new art in New York in the late 1920s, modern dance was born of the quest to discover the real capacities of the human body as a means of expression, which in turn implied a revolt against the stifling conventions of ballet. The principal initiators of the new movement were Doris Humphrey, Martha Graham, and Helen Tamiris. Although there have been many male dancers of significance, the central and innovative figures of modern dance have been women, exemplifying an important aspect of feminist culture that not only persisted but flourished after the eclipse of organized feminism following the passage of the Nineteenth Amendment in 1920.

Emphasizing that modern dance began as a movement of, by, and for women is the fact that its chief forerunners were two maverick matriarchs. At the turn of the century Isadora Duncan had boldly proclaimed a strong feminist dimension of her own dance, inspiring at least two generations of women—and not only women—to take risks for the sake of freedom and self-fulfillment. An enthusiastic supporter of the Russian Revolution, Duncan left a legacy of wholehearted rebellion.

The less radical Ruth St. Denis also played a liberating role, spearheading exploration of the possibilities of non-Western dance. As it happened, the vaudevillian St. Denis influenced the course of modern dance more directly than the "Divine Isadora," largely because Duncan lived in Europe while modern dance was slowly taking shape in her native land. Duncan's dance, moreover, was the spontaneous and unique result of her own intuition and, as such, unteachable by anyone but her. Of course there were, and still are, some worthy proponents of one variety or another of "Duncan dance": the line of descent from Isadora through Julia Levien to Annabelle Gamson, the outstanding interpreter of Duncan's dances in the 1980s, is straight and unmistakable. Dance à la Isadora was featured at the anarchist Modern School in Stelton, New Jersey, and the "Natural Rhythmic Expression" taught by the little-known Bird Larson at New York's socialist Rand School also owed much to Duncan's example. But the fact that there are so many different versions of Duncan dancing raises doubts about how much of Duncan survives in any of them. Few of the founders of modern dance ever saw Duncan herself dance, and they tended to be unimpressed by what they did see of Duncan-style dancing, which, in any case, has been peripheral to the development of the modern movement.

St. Denis, by contrast, was engaged in the day-to-day business of giving practical, technical dance instruction to pupils who intended to earn their living by dancing. For more than fifteen years, first in Los Angeles and later in New York, she directed (with Ted Shawn) the Denishawn School of Dancing and Related Arts.

St. Denis's own variety of theosophy was an important part of the Denishawn curriculum. Instilled with her belief that Dance (with the capital *D*) was a mystical mission, the best students were expected to remain with the company, not only as teachers but also as propagators of the Denishawn faith on extensive tours. Such a self-effacing regimen was not for everyone, and it is hardly surprising that the most gifted dancers eventually broke away.

Among the graduates of Denishawn were two dancers who, by 1929, were recognized leaders of a "revolution" in dance. A direct descendant of Miles Standish, Martha Graham (1893–1991) was born and raised in a Pittsburgh suburb and moved to California with her parents in 1908. After seven years with Denishawn she set out on her own. By decade's end the very titles of her performances—"Revolt," "Immigrant," "Poems of 1917," "Heretic"—seemed to confirm *New York Times* critic John Martin's remark that her effect "has not been one of warmth and elevation, but rather of tension and disturbed thinking."

Doris Humphrey (1895–1958), who was born in Oak Park, Illinois, and grew up in Chicago, went west in 1917 to enroll in Denishawn, in whose company she remained for eleven years. In 1925–26 she took part in the Denishawn tour of Asia. An outstanding theorist as well as practitioner of dance (her classic treatise *The Art of Making Dances* was published posthumously in 1959), Humphrey played a role in the formation and elaboration of the modern movement equal to that of the more publicized Graham, and not a few dancers and critics have regarded her as the greater choreographer.

Helen Tamiris (1905–66), a third major figure in the formative years of modern dance, started out as a student of classical ballet in New York City, where she was born. Remarkably versatile, she later choreographed Broadway musical extravaganzas and Hollywood films such as *Show Boat* and *Annie Get Your Gun*. In the late 1920s she was one of the first modern dancers to identify herself with the revolutionary workers' movement. "The validity of the modern dance," she argued, "is rooted in its ability to express modern problems and, further, to make modern audiences want to do something about them."

Although critics applied the term "revolutionary" to any and all modern dancers, Tamiris's avowedly activist orientation was not shared by Graham or Humphrey, who remained aloof to the political turmoil of the Depression years. Graham's biographer, Don McDonagh, notes that "her vision was directed to unlocking the fetters that bound the spirit, not those twisting the social fabric." In a period of mass labor organizing, Humphrey refused to join a union, fearing that such membership might somehow limit her freedom.

The apoliticism of some of its leading personalities notwithstanding, modern dance began as an integral part of the American Left milieu and was universally regarded as such. "I never heard of a modern pro-fascist dance," wrote Margaret Lloyd, dance critic for the *Christian Science Monitor*. The new movement was repeatedly denounced in the conservative press and, for a time, was treated unkindly in mainstream liberal papers as well. The modern dance audience, moreover, consisted almost entirely of young people who thought of themselves as radicals and revolutionists.

Tamiris welcomed the objective link between social radicalism and the new dance, while Graham and Humphrey can be said to have resigned themselves to it. All three, however, agreed that dance could not and should not be reduced to any sort of propaganda or even to a narrowly "social" aesthetic. For her part, Tamiris clearly felt that a certain amount of red-flag-waving was permissible, as in her "Revolutionary March" of 1929, and even Graham and Humphrey sometimes touched on "social" themes. But the heart of their work lay elsewhere. Most of their dances—such as Humphrey's "The Shakers" and "Square Dances," Graham's "Frontier" and "Letter to the World" (inspired by Emily Dickinson), and Tamiris's "Circus Sketches," "Prize Fight Studies," "Negro Spirituals," and "Walt Whitman Suite"—were rooted in myths, poetry, folklore, and other magic-laden byways of the American past and present. Left critics tended to be sympathetic to this effort. Recognizing in such dances something of the Left's own striving toward a radical reinterpretation of the American experience, they embraced the new movement as an important component of an emerging revolutionary culture.

For an increasing number of student dancers, however, this vague association of modern dance and social radicalism was not enough. These youngsters, many of whom were members of the Communist or Socialist parties, sought to place the whole modern dance movement at the service of the revolution. Eager to make dance itself play a role in the overthrow of capitalism, they choreographed dances to serve the workers' everyday struggle against the bosses. The Communist Party's ideological tightening-up at the turn of the decade hastened this process. With slogans of "Bolshevization" and the "Third Period" quickening their pulses, young dancers took their cue from manifestoes for "proletarian culture" and proclaimed that "dance is a weapon."

Tamiris, the most politically radical of the elders, was a natural leader of these boisterous troops. Ironically, however, Graham's and Humphrey's students made up much of the active core of such militant groups as the Red Dancers, organized in 1929, the Rebel Dance Group, New Dance Group, Theatre Union Dance Group, Office Workers Dance Group, and nearly a score of others that formed over the next few years. Several of Graham's students, celebrated dancers in their own right in later years, were especially prominent. Jane Dudley danced "In the Life of a Worker" (1934) and "Song for Soviet Youth Day" (1935); Anna Sokolow danced an "Anti-War Cycle" (1937); and Sophie Maslow offered her comrades "Two Songs About Lenin" (1934) as well as a "May Day March" (1936). Eleanor King, a Humphrey student who later established her own school in Seattle, choreographed "A Song About America" (1939), featuring homages to the abolitionists and the Haymarket martyrs; sponsored by the Communist Party, the performance took place on the fifteenth anniversary of the death of

Lenin. There were dances to poems by Communist Mike Gold and Socialist Arturo Giovannitti, and others inspired by the Scottsboro and Tom Mooney cases. Is it necessary to add that most of these dances were ultraserious, even somber? Here and there, however, humor was allowed to hold the stage, as in the Red Dancers' "Sell-Out" (1934), choreographed to a parody of "The Man on the Flying Trapeze" and first performed at a textile workers' union meeting in Paterson, New Jersey.

Of the quality of the dancing itself little is known, for these dances long ago disappeared from the repertories, and few if any were filmed. Critic John Martin was probably not far from the mark when he wrote, in *America Dancing* (1936): "In the early stages of the movement, dancing ... consisted of choosing some literary slogan in conformity with orthodox radical political thinking, and of showing with what energy the dancer or dancers involved agreed with the sentiments thus conveyed. The power of expressional movement, the real stuff of the dance, was not seen to exist."

Undaunted, however, by criticism from anyone other than workers or comrades, the movement spread like wildfire, and the modern dance audience, once a mere coterie, grew enormously. The young radicals performed at the New School for Social Research and other educational institutions as well as at trade union picnics, strike meetings, and political rallies. It was said that Graham and Humphrey had a hard time scheduling performances for the first of May because so many of their dancers were away giving performances of their own at May Day gatherings.

The proliferation of radical dance groups around the country inevitably suggested a federation. The Socialist Party's Rebel Arts included several dance groups, but the Workers' Dance League, politically allied with the Communist Party, was much larger and more influential. Organized in 1932, the league had more than a dozen affiliated groups in New York City, plus others in Yonkers, Newark, Passaic, Boston, Washington, DC, Philadelphia, Pittsburgh, Detroit, Chicago, and Los Angeles. Individual dues were twenty-five cents a year. Its "aims and functions" included: "Building a dance art vital and clear, a dance art that is inspired by and useful to workers. Organizing dance groups in working class neighborhoods.... Broadening the dance audience by performing wherever workers gather.... Educating dancers and audiences to the problems of the working class.... Cooperating with artists in other fields of revolutionary cultural activity."

Working conditions in the dance world were generally poor—long hours and low wages prevailed—and the *Workers' Dance League Bulletin* (later *New Dance*) regularly covered dancers' struggles to improve their lot. In November 1934 league members, with Tamiris in the forefront, helped form the New York Dancers' Union, open to all dance workers. A year later *New Dance* reported that the burlesque dancers were organized but that the effort to line up the taxi-dancers had thus far met with limited success. An ad hoc Dancers' Emergency Association was set up to organize the unorganized dancers but, like many other organizations of "cultural workers" spearheaded by Communists in those years, the "dancers' union" proved ineffectual and ephemeral.

Unemployment during the Great Depression was a serious problem for dancers, and many, including those in the Workers' Dance League, looked to President Roosevelt's New Deal relief programs to solve it. Meanwhile, significant changes were taking place in the Left dance scene. With the advent of the Communist Party's Popular Front line in 1935, the Workers' Dance League quietly became the New Dance League, and the shrill rhetoric of its early days was toned down in the process. The accent was no longer on class war and impending revolution but rather on the need to support the Congress of Industrial Organizations and to combat race discrimination and fascism.

This policy doubtless facilitated the administrative involvement of a number of party members and sympathizers in Works Progress Administration (WPA) projects. Tamiris helped organize the Federal Theater Project and, by means of a visit to Roosevelt's adviser Harry Hopkins, saw to it that dance was an integral part of the program. Late in 1935 the Dance Project was started in New York, with a hundred dancers; a unit began in Chicago the following year. WPA productions, some of which had impressively long runs, provided work for many unemployed dancers and incidentally introduced modern dance to a substantially larger audience. This experiment in government-subsidized dance proved short-lived, however, for Congress put a stop to it in July 1939. In New York, according to ballet critic Anatole Chujoy's *Encyclopedia of Dance* (revised edition, 1967), the Dance Project "petered out" even earlier "due chiefly to improved theater business." Other commentators, including many dancers active in the project, maintained that Congress acted in response to prodding by the recently formed House Un-American Activities Committee (HUAC).

If Popular Front strategy eased the entrance of Communist-oriented dancers into the larger society, it also diminished the necessity for an organization made up exclusively of Communist-oriented dancers. In addition to the Workers' Dance League and Rebel Arts there were numerous dance groups linked to unions; the International Ladies Garment Workers Union in New York had an extensive dance program involving more than two hundred participants. The National Dance Congress in May 1936 brought together the whole range of American professional dancers and prepared the way for the amalgamation of the league and other groups to form the American Dance Association a year later. The Congress was organized by Tamiris, who became the first president of the new association. Communists, liberals, apolitical dancers, and perhaps even a few conservatives were now united under one umbrella.

There were many reasons why the explicitly revolutionary political phase of modern dance was of such short duration. The free-spirited young women who made up the great majority of modern dancers could hardly have felt at home for long in any male-dominated political apparatus. A tension that must sometimes have been overwhelming existed between these dancers' well-meaning social aspirations and their fundamentally avant-garde sensibilities. A few may have abandoned dance to work full-time for the party, but most of them preferred to abandon the party. By mid-decade, when it became more widely known how severely modern dance was frowned on by the official ballet-loving "socialist realist" aestheticians of the Soviet Union, the romance between dancers and Communists was already declining. Most dancers, in any case, were interested in politics as it affected dance more than in politics as such. "These young rebels," wrote Eleanor King many years later, "were as much against abstraction and mysticism in dance as they were against fascism, exploitation of the workers, and poverty."

It is notable that the decade of "red" dance produced no enduring body of Left dance criticism—a failure all the more striking in view of the pioneering role of socialists in this field. Back in the 1910s, two of the most prominent personalities of *The Masses*—novelist-essayist Floyd Dell and painter John Sloan—had commented insightfully on the dance of Isadora Duncan. In the same years Louis C. Fraina,

Marxian economist and a founder of the Communist Party, edited and wrote much of *Modern Dance* magazine; although this publication focused on social dancing, Fraina also wrote of Duncan and other forerunners of the new dance of the late '20s. Another periodical, *Dance Lovers Magazine*, which started in 1923 and evolved into today's *Dance Magazine*, was edited for its first four years by an outspoken leftist, Vera Caspary, best known as the author of the film scenario *Laura*, based on her own detective novel. These promising beginnings, however, were not fulfilled. The Communists' *Daily Worker*, *New Theater* magazine, and especially the *New Masses* (the Socialists' equivalent was *Arise*) included much material on dance, but most of it was mere reportage, and the rest tended to be trite superficialities or propagandistic bombast.

As dancers' faith in the Soviet Union diminished, so did their sympathy for the cause of socialism. "There are no reds in modern dance today," Margaret Lloyd wrote in 1948, but in fact the radical dance movement was already over by the start of World War II. The antiwar dancers of the 1930s did not perform their antiwar dances once war had begun. By the end of the decade the character of the entire modern movement had changed beyond recognition. Activist dance largely disappeared: the postwar strike wave and the struggle against Taft-Hartley had to get along without dancers' support. Showing just how far the pendulum had swung, in 1954–56 the once-red-baited Martha Graham, whose company had included so many emphatically pro-Communist dancers, made several overtly anticommunist overseas tours organized by the US State Department, which touted her as America's "Ambassador of Dance." The sole survivor of the Workers' Dance League, the New Dance Group School in New York, took up nonobjectivism and existentialism. Developed especially by Merce Cunningham, this tendency paved the way for the minimalist and conceptualist dance of the next generation. As dance shrank from real human problems, its audience shrank with it. Modern dance was "no longer a revolutionary emancipating principle," wrote John Martin, but rather "an academic tyranny as binding as that of the traditional ballet against which it originally rebelled."

Exceptions to the rightward trend took unexpected forms that didn't fit any of the existing styles of American radicalism. Perhaps the most innovative and imaginative dancer of the post-1940 years, Chicago-based Sybil Shearer, defied all existing values with the insouciant extremism of a William Blake or a John Muir; baffled critics could not decide whether she represented a return to the simplicity and naturalness of Isadora Duncan or a plunge into the troubled waters of surrealism.

Another nonconformist was Californian Bella Lewitzky, who had been born in Job Harriman's Utopian socialist Llano del Rio colony in the Mojave Desert and was a member of the Los Angeles New Dance League in the 1930s. Her refusal to testify before HUAC in 1951 ("I'm a dancer, not a singer," she quipped) provoked a barrage of obscene and threatening phone calls, but she remained a familiar sight at protest meetings and on picket lines. In dance as in life, revolt and freedom have always been her favorite themes, as in "Tierra y Libertad" (1941, choreographed by Lester Horton), "Warsaw Ghetto" (1949), and "Leyendas de Mexico" (1953, based on the Indians' struggle against the conquistadores), danced in an extravagantly antirealistic idiom that had nothing in common with the agitprop of earlier years.

Esther Junger, a student of Bird Larson's who in 1935 had scandalized Boston as the star dancer and choreographer of the Theater Guild's Communist comedy *Parade*, was yet another dancer who bravely resisted the downhill slide of modern dance from poetry to prose. One of the most singular personages of the modern movement, she was for a time choreographer for the Ringling Brothers/Barnum & Bailey Circus. Her dances inspired by jazz, wild animals, Gauguin's paintings, and the lore of indigenous cultures added something new and unsettling to a dance scene increasingly dominated by the predictable.

Black modern dance also challenged the prevalent academicism and Cold War disengagement. Independent of the main currents of the modern movement, Chicago-born Katherine Dunham and Pearl Primus of Trinidad, both with doctorates in anthropology, developed a powerful dance idiom rooted in Afro-Caribbean folklore. Dunham, director of the Chicago WPA Dance Project's Negro Unit and later of the New York Labor Stage, also was choreographer for several Hollywood films devoted to black Americana, including *Stormy Weather* and *Cabin in the Sky*. Primus, widely regarded as the world's foremost authority on African dance, choreographed several Negro spirituals. In recent years the Association for the Advancement of Creative Musicians has featured several innovative dancers in its celebrations of "Great Black Music."

A modest resurgence of radical dance accompanied the social ferment of the 1960s. The Living Theatre of Julian Beck and Judith Malina drew more or less equally on Antonin Artaud's dance-based "Theater of Cruelty" and anarchist-pacifist-Industrial Workers of the World traditions to produce the Left's most influential dance-theater of those years. Expressive movement has also been central to Peter Schumann's Bread and Puppet Theater. Agitprop resurfaced primarily in mime, most effectively in the popular San Francisco Mime Troupe. A student of Lewitzky's, surrealist Alice Farley, one of the few contemporary dancers to champion the cause of social revolution, has performed extraordinary stilt-dances in New York antiwar parades. At the close of the century dance radicalism survived in widely scattered individuals and companies such as these, isolated in the outermost margins of the dance/theater world. But its heritage was a vital one and always capable of renewal.

PART IV

Labor History and Culture

27

T-Bone Slim and the Phonetic Cabala

First published in "Surrealism and Its Popular Accomplices," special issue of *Cultural Correspondence*, guest-edited by Franklin Rosemont, nos. 10–11 (Fall 1979): 22–23.

———

The greatest writer of the Industrial Workers of the World (IWW)—and one of the most curious figures in American literature—was the man known as T-Bone Slim. Little is known of his life. Of Finnish descent, he was born Matt Valentine Huhta around the turn of the century, probably in or near Ashtabula, Ohio. He died in New York, where he had been employed as a barge captain, in 1942.

The IWW's most persistent columnist, T-Bone Slim wrote regularly for One Big Union papers and magazines for some twenty years. Three of his songs—"Mysteries of a Hobo's Life," "I'm Too Old to Be a Scab," and "The Popular Wobbly"—remain among the best-loved lyrics in the famous *Little Red Songbook*. In 1922 his only extended work, a thirty-eight-page pamphlet titled *Starving Amidst Too Much*, was published by the IWW's Foodstuff Workers Industrial Union no. 460. An impassioned critique of the food industry, it also is a classic of black humor.

Humor as black as midnight is, in fact, the hallmark of all of T-Bone's writing, and it was heightened by a remarkably acute sensitivity to the *hidden ways of words*. It is this that gives his work a special *flavor* that is unlike anything else in our literature. He veered constantly toward the extreme limits of language, to the disquieting no-man's-land of puns, palindromes, malapropisms, and slang. For T-Bone, the words "stiff without a brother" equal "ship without a rudder." "Betterments," he tells us, "should be better meats." His work is strewn with sparkling neologisms—*Brisbanality* (after the top columnist on the Hearst papers, Arthur Brisbane), *Saphroncisco, civilinsanity, inexhorrible, sarcasthma*—and incomparable maxims: "Half a loaf is better than no loafing at all." "Wherever you find injustice, the proper form of politeness is attack." "Juice is stranger than friction."

Slang and wordplay always have been characteristics of popular literature, as well as principal vehicles by which the expressiveness of language is continually enriched. The best-read authors have drawn heavily on puns and the "language of the streets," often with marvelous results. When we read, for example, in *Boxiana*, by Pierce Egan (1772–1849), an oft-reprinted work by one of the most widely read authors of his day, such lines as "the numerous GILLS he has *punished* ... the LUSTY COVES he has *milled* ... the SAUCY SWELLS he has *pinked*"—all of which translate into "the fighters he has vanquished"—we may appreciate the remark by a writer in *Blackwood's Magazine* (1820) that "the man who has not read *Boxiana* is ignorant of the power of the English language."

In T-Bone's case, however, wordplay assumes a significance that is deeper and darker. This revolutionary hobo—a conscious member of that class "with nothing to lose but its chains"—realized, perhaps more than any of his American contemporaries, that language is not ours to facilitate aesthetic, literary, or moralistic pursuits but rather *to be unfettered* so that it can help extend the universal unfettering known as Revolution.

In Jack London's tale "Local Color," a curious digression tells us that the words *hobo* and *oboe* derive from the French *haut bois* (high wood): "In a way one understands [the word *hobo*] being born of the contempt for wandering players and musical fellows." This is especially suggestive in view of the alchemical scholar Fulcanelli's contention (in *The Mystery of the Cathedrals*, 1925) that the expression "gothic art" has nothing to do with the Goths, as so many have believed; rather, "gothic art (*art gothique*) is simply a corruption of the word *argotique* (slang) which sounds exactly the same. This is in conformity with the *phonetic law*, which governs the traditional cabala in every language and does not pay any attention to spelling." Moreover, Fulcanelli continues, "dictionaries define argot as 'a language peculiar to all individuals who wish to communicate their thoughts without being understood by outsiders.' Thus it is certainly a spoken cabala." And he goes on to point out, "In our day, cant is spoken by ... the poor, the despised, the rebels calling for liberty and independence, the outlaws, the tramps and the wanderers. Cant is the cursed dialect, banned by high society, by the nobility (who are really so little noble), the well-fed and self-satisfied middle class, luxuriating in the ermine of their ignorance and fatuity. It remains the language of a minority of individuals living outside accepted laws, conventions, customs, and etiquette."

For Fulcanelli, finally, "Argot (cant) is one of the forms derived from the Language of the Birds ... the language which teaches the mystery of things and unveils the most hidden truths.... To [the ancient Incas] it was the key to the double science, sacred and profane."

It is worth emphasizing how perfectly Fulcanelli's perspective coincides with the discovery by philologist/philosopher/poet Fabre d'Olivet (1768–1825) that the word *poetry* does not derive, as is still commonly believed, from the Greek word meaning *maker* but rather from the Phoenician word signifying the *highest principle of language*.

That the quest for this highest principle of language should be pursued by those held to be of the "lowest" class is one of those exhilarating priorities of dialectic that help clear a "humid path" through the ice of ideology, and thus help to make us masters rather than victims of the bottomless bag of tricks that Hegel called "the cunning of history."

T-Bone's theory and practice—"humor," he wrote, "is the carefree manhandling of extremes"—situates him at the juncture of traditional phonetic cabala and the surrealist image. The sureness of his poetic *direction* is exemplified in a brief-sketch, teeming with alchemical implications, wherein he announced "T-Bone Slim's Golden Discovery," a *"motion mirror"*: "You throw a dead cat in front of it, and it shows the cat tearing up a live buzzard."

When he remarked, moreover, that he wrote "using a cross between a Chinese and a Hebrew grammar," this may not be a plain "fact," but it is surely more than a "joke." Does it not suggest T-Bone's consciousness that "Something Else" circulated "between the lines" of his penciled notations—that his "grammar" exceeded the accepted boundaries of discourse and carried on a kind of "double monologue," or rather a monologue *to the third power*?

We may thus reinterpret Shakespeare's celebrated remark about puns being the lowest form of wit. In the light of Fulcanelli and T-Bone Slim, it would seem that "lowest" here means *deepest*—that is, that wordplay penetrates to the *physical* foundations of language. The embarrassment provoked by puns in "polite" society suggests that they do indeed touch something vital and hidden, as has been amply shown, of course, by psychoanalysis.

T-Bone takes us to the very heart of this elusive domain—to the erotic spaces *between words*. He shows us the wild dances of suffixes and prefixes, the explosive matter and antimatter of homonyms, the gambols of etymological roots, the magnetic attraction of syllables.

"Words make love," said André Breton. Who better than T-Bone Slim has shown us the infinite variety of *verbal foreplay*? Without even trying, he left us the prolegomena to a veritable *Kama Sutra* of language on the loose.

28

Juice Is Stranger than Friction: T-Bone Slim

Selections from "Mysteries of a Hobo's Life," introduction to *Juice Is Stranger than Friction: Selected Writings of T-Bone Slim* (Chicago: Charles H. Kerr, 1992).

> *Out of work, our only joy is poetry:*
> *Scribble, scribble, we wear out our brains.*
> *Who will read the works of such men?*
> —Han Shan

Edgar Allan Poe urged seekers of true genius to ignore biographies of "the good and the great" but to pay special attention to the residents of lunatic asylums and prisons.[1] Had he lived a few generations later, I like to think Poe would have added the hobo jungle and the old-time union hall. Such, in any case, have been the environments of some of the most resoundingly nonconformist voices in modern American literature. Wildest of them all, in many ways, was the man who called himself T-Bone Slim.

A working stiff, a hobo, and an irreconcilable revolutionist—that is to say, utterly lacking in qualifications for literary respectability—T-Bone Slim won for himself a total exclusion from academic histories and textbooks of American literature, a distinction legions of lesser writers, before and since, have found it nearly impossible to attain.

Yet he was by no means an unknown. Indeed, he contributed some of the brightest pages to the American labor movement's all-time best seller: the *Little Red Songbook* of the Industrial Workers of the World. First published in 1909 and now in its thirty-fifth edition [a thirty-sixth edition was published in 1995], this pocket-sized compilation of songs "to fan the flames of discontent" has been cherished over the years by an incalculable number of workers "on the road, in the jungles and in the shops."[2] Three of the best-loved IWW lyrics—"The Popular Wobbly," "Mysteries of a Hobo's Life," and "I'm Too Old to Be a Scab"—were written by T-Bone Slim.[3]

Another favorite of his was "The Lumberjack's Prayer," often included in the songbook but also kept in print for decades on wallet-sized cards. Swedish-born Wobbly Pete Johnson recalled it many years later as "a poem that thousands of workers memorized," but distinguished representatives of the propertied class noticed it as well.[4] On January 12, 1924, for example, a San Francisco agent of the Federal Bureau of Investigation typed it out in full and included it in his report on "IWW Matters" to FBI director J. Edgar Hoover.[5]

Second only to Joe Hill as the IWW's most popular songwriter, T-Bone Slim incontestably was the Wobblies' greatest "man of letters." For two decades readers of IWW publications recognized him as the union's "most noted columnist."[6] His contributions to its publications would fill several large books. America's finest hobo wordsmith and a remarkable aphorist, he also merits a place among the great American humorists.

The aim of the present volume [*Juice Is Stranger than Friction*] is to make available for the first time a representative selection of work by an important author who has suffered undeserved neglect. Every message of pure revolt deserves to be heard, and T-Bone Slim's is one of the purest. His writing at its best has a remarkable flair, a deep and dazzling humor, a profound awareness of the sensuous alchemy of words. It also happens to be unlike anything else in the world.

The gaps in the story of T-Bone Slim are larger than the known story. Born Matt Valentine Huhta, he was an Ashtabula (Ohio) Finn, evidently American-born.[7] Nothing is known of his parents beyond the fact that they belonged to the working class; in his infancy his mother, a washerwoman, took him with her on her rounds.[8]

As a young man he married a woman named Rose, with whom he had four children: a son, Paul, who died at about age twenty-one, and three daughters—Anna, Florence, and Edna.[9] He and his wife separated and were divorced when the children were young. His youngest daughter, Edna, says that after her father left Ashtabula she "never heard from him again." His sister Ida married a man named Ekola and lived for a time in Erie, Pennsylvania.[10]

T-Bone Slim drowned in May 1942—the exact day is not known, but his body was found on May 15—in New York, while working as captain of the Hudson River barge *Casey*, employed by the New York Trap Rock Corporation. At the time of his death he was, as were many Wobs, a "doubleheader" or "two-card" man: a member of Barge Captains' Local 933-4 of the International Longshoremen's Association, affiliated with the American Federation of Labor, as well as a member of Marine Transport Workers Industrial Union 510 of the IWW.[11] His daughter Edna was notified that he had "no property or money when he died."

And that is about all we have in the way of standard biographical information. We do not know the date of his birth.[12] We know nothing of his family background or childhood. We do not even know when he joined the IWW.

We do know that his songs first appear in the IWW songbook in the seventeenth edition (1920) and that by spring of 1921 his contributions to *Industrial Solidarity* were appearing in almost every other issue. Eventually it would be almost weekly; the occasional lapses were generally because of illness, noted as such by editors. His column— sometimes published under recurring heads such as "T-Bone Slim Discusses," "Boneyard," or simply "T-Bone Slim," but most often titled anew each time it appeared—ran continuously till his death.

T-Bone's writings also appeared regularly in the weekly organ of the IWW's western branches, the *Industrial Worker* (which absorbed *Industrial Solidarity* in December 1931), and frequently in the IWW magazines: *Industrial Pioneer* in the 1920s and the new series of the *One Big Union Monthly* in the '30s. His twelve-page, pocket-size pamphlet *Power of These Two Hands* was issued by the IWW's General Construction Workers' Industrial Union 310 in 1922. The following year IWW Foodstuff Workers' Industrial Union 460 brought out his forty-page pamphlet *Starving Amidst Too Much*, a savagely humorous critique of the food industry.

To the best of our knowledge, T-Bone wrote only for the IWW press. It appears, however, that T-Bone Slim was not his only nom de plume. Like many Wobs, he sometimes used his IWW membership card number as a signature. The poems and articles signed "Card No.

198308" have all the qualities of the texts signed T-Bone Slim, and at least one article, a 1927 *Industrial Solidarity* column, contains revealing personal references. Overflowing with characteristically T-Bone-type wordplay, starting with its opening line, it closes with "'Nuff sed,' as Fellow Worker Casey would say"—*Casey*, of course, being the name of T-Bone's barge, often invoked by him as a living personage.[13]

His writings tell us all that T-Bone Slim wanted us to know about himself. Datelines or other indications in his columns, for example, give us an idea of his extensive wanderings. Working on the harvest in Kansas and the Dakotas, as a logger or camp cook in the Northwest, passing through Seattle's Skid Road, dropping in for a visit at the IWW Work People's College near Duluth, frequenting the hobo jungles clustered on the outskirts of downtown Chicago, or strolling along the Bowery in New York—T-Bone Slim, for much of his life, was a man on the move. "He traveled rather a lot," as one Wob writer put it, "but would stay in one place only a short time."[14] According to Fred Hansen, a fellow member of 510, T-Bone had a way of disappearing for weeks and even months at a time. Troubling shadows hovered over his life. We see him only in a glimpse here, a glimpse there—the rest is too often a blur, or darkness.

It is from his comments on the large and small events of his time— his accounts of his adventures, real and imaginary; his polemics; his songs; his wonderful rambling poetic playfulness—that we get a truer measure of the uniqueness and grandeur of T-Bone Slim. A few scattered lines "in passing" sometimes convey something deeper than biography. "Babe Ruth is America's greatest statesman," he once wrote, "Jack Dempsey the brightest scholar, Barney Google the most eminent scientist. The greatest writer? Modesty forbids our naming him."

Another time he plaintively asked: "Will some kind or unkind reader lend me a couple eggs till payday?"

Illustrating the obscurity in which he lived, his obituary in the *Industrial Worker* appeared five months after his death. "While there have been few workingclass writers of our time better known than T-Bone Slim," the article said,

> little was known about the man himself, even to those with whom
> he worked or who crossed his trail and stopped for a chat with him

in his frequent tours of observation about the country. He is said to have two children somewhere in Ohio. Beyond this, even rumor says little or nothing about his personal relations.... Having lived almost a full lifetime in anonymity, Fellow Worker Huhta died that way. We have an idea that's the way he wanted it to be.[15]

In his lifelong anonymity T-Bone exemplified a characteristic of hoboes in general and Wobblies in particular. Hoboes tended to be known by their monikers; their etiquette frowned on inquiring about one's "real" name.[16] And no revolutionary or labor group in US history was so antithetical to the "cult of personality" as the IWW. They took Karl Marx at his word: "The emancipation of the working class is the task of the workers themselves."[17] Their implacable disdain for the pretensions of all "leadership" was legendary. T-Bone was virtually the archetypal Wobbly: inspired, footloose, daring, brimful with creativity and humor, and at the same time a thoroughgoing rank-and-filer, who kept himself resolutely out of the limelight. Few people, even in the IWW, knew that Matt Valentine Huhta was T-Bone Slim.[18]

Fortunately, we do have a few recollections by some IWW old-timers who knew him. However fragmentary, these anecdotes and impressions help substantially to fill in our image of this elusive figure.

Fred Thompson, who edited the *Industrial Worker* on and off for several years during T-Bone's lifetime, tells us that he

> was largely a "loner," hoboing alone, rustling a job alone, and often seeking and getting the kind of job that kept him by himself, such as barge captain which he was for many seasons in the New York City port. This is not because he was unsocial— he periodically sought and enjoyed company and conversation or listening to the sound of people talking. But I think he had a sort of built-in recording system for it, and liked to spend ten hours reviewing and digesting these sounds for every hour spent picking them up.[19]

Thompson especially recalls T-Bone's "writing habit": "a pad in his pocket, and every now and then a sentence or two added to whatever he had there. In IWW halls, even at socials, lectures, etc., he tended to sit off by himself, without being particularly hermitlike, and now and then added to the material he had there."

Thompson emphasizes too that T-Bone "wrote his inspirations in a fine script that editors gave to the printer without typing or editing."

"I doubt whether T-Bone was familiar enough in Finnish to be funny," Thompson adds, "though he could speak it.... No, he was not a soapboxer.... I don't recall his ever holding a union post, or for that matter carrying job delegate credentials."

Charles Velsek, onetime secretary of the IWW's Agricultural Workers' Industrial Union 110 and many times a member of the union's General Executive Board, recalled T-Bone as a "dyed-in-the-wool hobo, traveling about the country doing what hoboes usually did: work when he could and panhandle when broke. His songs in the IWW songbook pretty much describe his lifestyle."

Anarchist Wobbly Sam Dolgoff remembers seeing T-Bone frequently in his last years at the IWW's Marine Transport Workers Industrial Union 510 hall on Broad Street in New York, where he sometimes "played pinochle with the boys" while discussing union affairs. Often, however, he would just "sit silently gazing out of a window in the hall." Dolgoff describes T-Bone as "a modest, quiet guy who kept to himself," a man who disdained notoriety, who "spoke very little, and never about himself."

T-Bone's quiet and reticent nature has been emphasized by everyone who encountered him. Frank Cedervall, one of the IWW's great orators, says that T-Bone "would drop in at a meeting once in a while— and be gone. I never could get into much talk about his personal life." Fred Hansen writes:

> I knew T-Bone for a few years in the early '30s. When I say that I knew him I mean that I saw him around and talked to him occasionally, but nobody, that I know of, ever "knew" him. T-Bone was a loner. He never participated whenever we would have a group discussion in the hall. He would walk back and forth in the hall with a notebook and pencil in his hand. I tried many times to engage him in a general conversation. He would lead it back to the current article he was writing.... He would, at times, read out loud some part of an article and ask us what we thought of it. He was, at that time, mostly unemployed and spent a lot of time in the [IWW] Marine Transport Workers' Hall on the waterfront.

Anna Shuskie recalls seeing him often in the late 1920s and early '30s at the Tarmo Club at 2036 Fifth Avenue in New York, a Wob-run restaurant with an upstairs hall where the union held meetings and affairs. Concurring that T-Bone was far from talkative, she did point out that his conversation could be quite humorous: "He had his moments. But he was very shy with women. I mean, he respected women. He never talked dirty around women, or told dirty jokes.... He never talked about his family or himself. Mostly we talked about union matters."

Asked who T-Bone's closest friends were, Anna Shuskie replied without hesitation: "the other barge captains," many of them also Wobblies. She and Sam Dolgoff also mentioned that our Finnish-American hero and hobo was a good friend of Ben Fletcher, the great African American leader of one of the IWW's largest and longest-lived constituent unions—the longshoremen's local of IU 510 that held job control on the Philadelphia waterfront for a decade ending in 1925. According to Dolgoff, T-Bone was also "on good terms" with the prominent Italian American anarchist agitator and editor, Carlo Tresca.

Archie Brown gives us a sense of the high esteem in which T-Bone was held by youngsters in the movement:

> I met him at Work People's College during the first year I was there [as a student], 1932–1933. T-Bone Slim came in one afternoon and Fred [Thompson, who taught there] invited a bunch of us to meet him. We met in the library.... We were impressed with his knowledge of current events and his stinging remarks about the system. He was quite caustic when we asked questions about the Depression, the handling of problems, and the stupidity of politicians. He was rather softspoken.... I was thrilled to see him, and it probably amounted to hero worship. He came to Duluth by boxcar, I suspect, and it was the dead of winter.... I didn't see him after that evening.

Carl Keller who, like Fred Thompson, edited the *Industrial Worker* when T-Bone was its most prominent writer, recalled that for T-Bone the normal proletarian mistrust of—and hostility toward—capitalists, cops, and preachers assumed an almost paranoid intensity; that he had something of a "persecution complex," especially during sojourns in the cities; that he felt, by contrast, completely at ease riding freight trains through the open countryside.[20] Such has been the outlook of countless generations of penurious wanderers, from gypsies through the Beat Generation to the homeless legions of today, and it is hardly surprising to find it shared by a card-carrying member of a revolutionary union that gave US capitalism the biggest scare it has ever known.

The hobo life, and especially the Wobbly hobo life, is certainly the stuff of which legends are made, and it is not surprising that some old-timers' reminiscences of T-Bone have a strong savor of legend. Consider this eulogistic testimony from Guy B. Askew, who called himself Skidroad Slim: "I knew T-Bone Slim for many years during the IWW harvest drives in North Dakota and Montana. His mind was far above the average of the wage slaves but strictly rank and file. He was highly intelligent, generous and kindly towards his Fellow Workers, always neat and clean in appearance, and was considered by many as handsome. When I knew him he was strictly sober at all times. He was a powerful, prolific writer and journalist."[21]

According to Skidroad Slim, T-Bone as a young man had been "a top writer and reporter for the Duluth Daily *News-Telegram*."[22] Sent by that paper to cover an IWW mass meeting, T-Bone submitted "a good factual write-up favorable to the IWW"; predictably, however, the editor "misquoted him and balled up his article," whereupon "T-Bone Slim quit his job as crack reporter for that paper and lined up in the IWW."

Sketchy and difficult to verify, this is the only account we have of how T-Bone happened to join the IWW.

After recalling that T-Bone could make "the finest and tastiest Swedish hotcakes of any chef in the USA," Skidroad Slim leaves us this concluding portrait: "He was known, highly respected, and well-liked by thousands of home-guard and migratory wage slaves all over the country. If he wasn't working on some job, he was a damn good bum on the Main Stem in restaurants, rich homes, offices, and elsewhere. T-Bone made friends among the wage slaves wherever he went and was always active and agitating for the IWW on the job, picket lines, boxcars, and everywhere else."

The passage from history to legend is also evident in some remarks made by folksinger-composer Aunt Molly Jackson, commenting on a song she recorded for the Library of Congress Archive of American Folk Song:

This is the story of T-Bone Slim. He told me how he got put in jail for a year and a day. He said he had tried to get a job for two months, and had been picked up as a vagrant different times till he had become desperate. He had not eat a bite in two days, he said, and it had been ten weeks since he had lain in a bed. He was so cold and hungry he said he was desperate. When he saw this old "big shot," as he called him, he just knocked the big shot down, and took his suit of clothes, watch, money and all. Just as he was taking off the old man's shoes he saw some men coming and he ran off with the fine suit on and a high top hat, and when they saw him with his old ragged shoes and that high silk hat and that fine suit of clothes, they grabbed him and pulled him before the judge. He said when they turned him out ... he did not have a cent and ... could not get a job for food and rent. He said he did not want to steal and rob; he said he began to wonder how he could find a job. He said he was almost out of his mind when he went down on the waterfront and joined the seamen's picket line. I was leading the picket line and I met him there. In the seamen's union hall he told me this story. I remembered it all, and a few days later I composed this song. Old T-Bone Slim got sunk in a ship when World War II come along. He was a good union seaman, but he is dead and gone.[23]

Note that the river barge has become a seagoing ship, and that T-Bone's death is linked to the war.[24] As a Wobbly and hobo, T-Bone Slim hardly could have avoided occasional brushes with "law 'n' order," and his writings indicate his familiarity with the insides of jails, but none of the IWW old-timers with whom I have spoken or corresponded knew of this incident with the well-dressed "big shot"; most of them doubted that he had ever been in prison.[25] However, as Anna Shuskie pointed out, "lots of the boys didn't like to talk about those things."

In "Poets and Pearls: A Rhapsody," T-Bone cites Robert Burns as "the brilliantmost star in poesy's constellation." Elsewhere he avows his interest in or admiration for writers as varied as William Blake, Edgar Allan Poe, Mark Twain, Oscar Wilde, George Sterling, and humor-columnist Bugs Baer. He was clearly familiar with the principal works of Marx and Engels, and his writings include several mentions of Freud. Apart from a few such passing references, we know nothing of his sources of inspiration, nothing of what he read.

It is certain, however, that the two major influences on his life and work were much more than literary: his proletarian Finnish background and the IWW.

In considering the influence of his cultural background, it is worth recalling the extent to which Finnish culture has been affected by the struggle over language.[26] For hundreds of years after Sweden conquered and christianized Finland in the twelfth century, the Finnish language was banned for all except peasants. Even when Finland was taken over by Russia in 1811, it continued to be culturally dominated by Sweden.

The publication in 1830 of the *Kalevala*—an epic cycle of Finnish folksongs and tales, which demonstrated the poetic richness and versatility of the native tongue—inspired a powerful nationalist current that grew until Finnish was made the official language. It was not long before Finland enjoyed a particularly high literacy rate; the Lutheran Church, maintaining that all good christians must be able to read the Bible, made literacy a prerequisite for marriage. Meanwhile, however, another official policy—giving the church half of what farmers and sharecroppers produced—provoked mass hostility to religion.

The Finnish General Strike of 1905 forced the czar to grant universal suffrage; previously only property owners could vote. Thus Finland became the third nation in the world where women could vote (preceded only by Australia and New Zealand).

It would seem, then, that the many thousands of Finns who came to the United States in the late 1800s and early 1900s—including the parents and other relatives of T-Bone Slim—were already largely predisposed toward radical ideas. Finnish immigrants, indeed, played a role in the American labor movement all out of proportion to their numbers. T-Bone's Finnish background is therefore inextricably intermingled with his life in the IWW.

The IWW's foreign-language sections have received too little attention from historians.[27] Of these sections the Finns were by far the largest. A 1920 issue of the *One Big Union Monthly* lists thirteen foreign-language IWW publications: one each in Russian, Hungarian, Spanish, Italian, Bulgarian, Lithuanian, Romanian, Czech, and Yiddish, and *three* in Finnish. And whereas most of these appeared weekly or monthly, the Finns alone had the distinction of publishing an IWW *daily*. Long after all the others had folded—long after the five English-language papers had collapsed into a single monthly—the Finnish *Industrialisti* came regularly out of Duluth, three times a week well into the 1970s.

The Finnish immigrants, with their sturdy egalitarian tendency, did not suffer from any sense of "cultural inferiority." They regarded even the summits of culture as accessible to all. The division "highbrow" and "lowbrow" simply did not have the hold on them that it did—and still does—on English-speaking Americans. Finns brought with them a large measure of cultural self-confidence, a legitimate pride in their own achievements, and a recognition of the wonders that could yet be achieved through united mass action.

T-Bone Slim shared this general cultural outlook characteristic of the immigrant Finns. And perhaps too his Finnish background—with its omnipresent echoes of the *Kalevala*—stimulated a particular alertness to language, an awareness of the power of *words* in the shaping of a nonconformist and revolutionary sensibility.

"Fond of unusual twists that could be given to words," as Thompson remarked, T-Bone filled many of his columns with three-, four-, and five-line samples of his extraordinary wordplay. In addition to coining many striking neologisms—*Saphroncisco, oleogarchy, holidaysical, silksockracy, ghoulhash, sarcasthma, Perhapsbyterian*, and dozens more—he was a prolific creator of multiple puns as well as an adept of orthographical oddities, and even of what has been called "phonetic cabala."[28] His *Industrial Worker* column of October 30, 1926, opens with these curious reflections:

> What's in a name? Sherman without the S spells Herman; Herman hyphenated registers Her-man; without the r Her-man spells He-man; bring back the s and she's a she-man; give him both s and r and he's a Sherman.

For T-Bone Slim, a "stiff without a brother" equals a "ship without a rudder." He speaks of "wry bread," calls Hearst's *Herald-Examiner* the *Hairoil-Eczema*, insists that "pie à la mode" should be pronounced "pile-o-mud," and calls our attention to the rather esoteric fact that "Edison spelled behindward spells No side." He transforms the old saying "Truth is stranger than fiction" into a provocative new saying ["Juice is stranger than friction"].

Several of T-Bone's texts—"Electricity," for example, which appeared in the Chicago-based *Industrial Pioneer* in 1925—would not have seemed out of place in the pages of *La Révolution surréaliste*, published in Paris at the same time. Some of his sayings ("Mazuma is the rutabaga of boll-weevil") have the flavor of Marcel Duchamp's "Rrose Sélavy" puns. Other texts ("Don't Bomp Your Bomp") foreshadow the riotous exuberance of Jack Kerouac's "spontaneous prose." Still others ("31,680 Hotcakes per Mile") radiate a slapstick poetic goofiness—a vernacular surrealism—all his own. T-Bone Slim was one of the very few American authors of the 1920s and '30s who realized that the abolition of wage slavery requires the abolition of mental slavery—that the unfettering of the imagination is the revolutionary writer's first and essential task.

T-Bone's surrealist affinities, moreover, are by no means merely "stylistic." His conception of humor as "the carefree manhandling of extremes" is comparable to the views set forth by André Breton and his comrades, who have been inspired not only by Freud's theories but also by Hegel's dialectical notion of *objective* humor, and by a formidable tradition of *poetic* humor extending from Swift and Sade to Tex Avery and Leonora Carrington.

T-Bone's notion of "bringing the sublime and the ridiculous into a compromising proximity" corresponds to such surrealist practices of derangement and rearrangement as Gherasim Luca's cubomanias, Anne Ethuin's "coated collages," and Martin Stejskal's "interpretive cycles," in which one image is transmuted into another.

That T-Bone not only practiced humor but also interested himself in its theoretical ramifications makes us realize that he was very much a man of ideas, esteemed by Covington Hall and other Wobblies as the union's outstanding "philosopher."[29] At a time when the arteries of revolutionary thought seemed to be hardening into lifeless dogmas, when few radicals were humorists and even fewer appreciated the central role of humor in Marx's outlook, he approached the recurring questions of the labor movement—reform versus revolution, political versus direct action, leadership versus rank-and-file initiative, etc.—from new and unusual angles, light-years away from the traditional Left's notorious *esprit de sérieux*.[30] With his "cracked" humor, as Carl Cowl has called it, and his proto-hipster linguistic fire-works, T-Bone had a knack for presenting the IWW's revolutionary program again and again in ways that were unforgettably fresh, enticing, convincing.

Original too were his polemics against labor's enemies. Ridicule of flag-waving patriots, politicians, warmongers, cops, charity, the "free" press, and pro-capitalist labor "leaders" rolled freely from his proletarian pencil. With gusto and glee he turned many a Fourth of July platitude inside out. His off-the-cuff reflections on history, morality, militarism, economics, politics, and the seemingly most trivial incidents of daily life are an exemplary blend of revolutionary criticism and rip-roaring comedy. His definitions ("*Tear gas*: The most effective agent used by employers to persuade their employees that the interests of Capital and Labor are identical") read like excerpts from a Wobbly edition of *The Devil's Dictionary*. Some of his sparkling aphorisms ("Wherever you find injustice, the proper form of politeness is attack," "Half a loaf is better than no loafing at all") are worth a hundred ponderous volumes.

Far more than most radicals, Wobblies sensed the vast scope of the revolution required to overcome the repressive misery of capitalism, and T-Bone Slim sensed it more than most Wobs: "Let us not lose sight of the fact that we are at grips with 'the noble white man' that made agony both ingenious and scientific, and relegated life's possibilities to the select few and life's 'garbage' to the many." Elsewhere he wrote:

> Christian civilization (exploitation of man by man). Western civilization (exploitation of man by man). European civilization (exploitation of man by man).
> Etc., far into the night.
> The whole spells *capitalism*.

Other texts leave no doubt that he also opposed the exploitation of woman by man. He was admirably extreme for a European American radical of his time, and his many and well-aimed barbs against racism, xenophobia, and masculine egotism reflect an unequivocal affirmation of the revolutionary principles of equality and solidarity that is rare even today. Unlike most American humorists of the 1920s and '30s, he used ethnic and dialect gags very infrequently, and never in a pejorative way. The fact that he used such vaudeville-type material at all serves to remind us that he was, after all, a self-taught hobo, and that not even the most advanced revolutionary intellectuals, hobo or otherwise, can transcend all the conventions of their time.

Few writers, in any case, have defied as many conventions as he did. Flaunting his fearless fondness for unexpected, irrational images, and all the other boisterous manifestations of his characteristically runaway humor, T-Bone's work exemplifies American revolutionary writing at its undomesticated best: infinitely stronger stuff than the insipid imitations of Zola's novels that so many middle-class Communists and Socialists tried to pass off as the only true "proletarian literature" in those years. That he was aware of the radical originality of his project, and knew it would be regarded as "crazy" by the self-appointed guardians of literary sanity, is suggested by his jocular remark that he wrote "using a cross between a Chinese and a Hebrew grammar." On another occasion, acknowledging that his "stuff seems very jumbled, scrambled," he added: "so is the capitalist system. Us great writers must conform with prevailing aggravations."

A vigorous protest against the bourgeois devaluation of language as a medium of exchange, T-Bone's writing reflects an authentically surrealist ambition to expand the limits of human expression—to exceed the accepted boundaries of discourse by putting language in a state of exhilarating effervescence.

Unafraid of play—indeed, head over heels in love with it—he went for a stroll with words all the way through the trick mirrors of competitive ideology, and he had such a good trip that he never returned to a "normal" existence. Along the way, he gave us some of the most merciless and hilarious social satire of modern times. But here and there he also left us an even rarer treasure: a strong dose of pure, let-go-for-dear-life, anything-is-possible *poetic nonsense*.

His whole work looks ahead to what Lautréamont called "poetry made by all"—that is, a poetry realized in everyday life—a poetry *lived* by individuals who are no longer alienated and fragmented but freely associated and made whole at last in the course of transforming an enslaved society into a true human community (a community, moreover, that is no longer at war with other communities, or with the earth they all share with myriad other living beings). T-Bone surely qualifies as a prophet—one of those "moralists who roamed the villages starving" that Lautréamont evoked in his *Poesies*. But his morality was the revolutionary morality of a class-conscious hobo poet whose dream of the unlimited possibilities of an emancipated humankind made him unwaveringly oriented toward a truly anarchist (stateless) and communist (non-exploitative) future. Living in what he termed "hoarse and bogey days," his confidence in what *could be* remained boundless: "We haven't seen anything yet."

A writer with unusually important things to say, and with his own unusually inspired way of saying them, this lonely troubadour of class war was one of the freest spirits of our age. "Freedom," he once said, "is what makes life worth fighting for." T-Bone Slim's work is an impassioned appeal for—and a splendid prefiguration of—a future worth living in.

29

Joe Hill

Selections from Franklin Rosemont, *Joe Hill: The IWW and the Making of a Revolutionary Workingclass Counterculture* (Chicago: Charles H. Kerr, 2003), 146–47, 167–72.

As Ben Williams, editor of *Solidarity*, put it: "No victim of class injustice in times has exhibited such unswerving courage under fire [as Joe Hill]."

That the Joe Hill defense campaign drew such unexpectedly widespread support shows the magnitude of the popular sympathy for Hill's cause, and profound sympathy in turn suggests that Hill's personality had struck a responsive chord in America's and the world's popular consciousness. The depth of this resonance is further indicated by Hill's funerals. The first, in Salt Lake City, was attended by "several thousand" people, a staggeringly large number in a town with a population of fifty thousand, especially in view of the anti-Red hysteria promoted by the "powers that be" throughout the state.[1] Among the speakers was Utah congressman Emil Lund, who called Hill's execution "legal murder."[2]

The second funeral, on November 25, 1915, Thanksgiving Day, in Chicago, was the city's largest since the Haymarket anarchists' funeral of 1887, and was in fact organized with the help of a younger generation of Chicago anarchists, including Russian-born Boris Yelensky. To this day Joe Hill's Chicago funeral remains the largest funeral anywhere of any individual in the US labor movement. It was not its size alone, however, that distinguished it from other funerals; its whole character was different. Hill's mourners clearly took his last words to heart and thought of themselves very much as organizers. This least funereal of funerals was rather an immense workers' demonstration—a *singing* demonstration.[3]

The West Side Auditorium was filled to capacity hours before the services began, so that the great majority of the crowd had to remain outdoors. Inside, the program began with an IWW quartet singing Hill's "Workers of the World Awaken!," the audience joining in the chorus. Next came the noted soloist and IWW member Jennie Woszczynska (a student of Mary Garden), who sang Hill's "The Rebel Girl." Short addresses by Bill Haywood and Jim Larkin were followed by a longer oration by Hill's appeals attorney, O.N. Hilton. After Hilton concluded his talk, the crowd quietly marched into the streets to the strains of Chopin's Funeral March, played on the piano by IWW composer Rudolf von Liebich.

In the streets, stretched out for blocks, tens of thousands of work-ingmen and -women sang Hill's own songs of proletarian humor and defiance in many languages. At Graceland Cemetery, where the body was taken by elevated train to be cremated, short speeches were made in Swedish, Russian, Hungarian, Polish, Spanish, German, Yiddish, Italian, and Lithuanian. These were followed by yet more songs backed up by music provided by the Russian Mandolin Club and the Rockford, Illinois, IWW Band. Far into the night Hill's friends stayed on, singing his songs of working-class revolt and revolution.[4]

These funerals, moreover, were planned "to be continued." Hill's ashes were put in pocket-size envelopes, many of which were distributed to delegates to the union's 1916 convention. Other packets were sent to IWW locals in every state but Utah (in keeping with Hill's telegram to Haywood), and every country in South America, as well as to Africa, Asia, Australia, and New Zealand. On May Day 1916, fulfilling Hill's last will, his ashes were scattered to the winds all over the world, in mass meetings that again involved singing his songs.[5]

In Chicago, Hill's ashes were scattered at Waldheim Cemetery (now Forest Home), the final resting place of the Haymarket martyrs and—as years went by—of many other labor radicals, including several who in various ways were linked to the Joe Hill story: Bill Haywood, Elizabeth Gurley Flynn, Ammon Hennacy, and Fred Thompson.[6] In the 1990s, when the cemetery was sold, one of its new officials was quoted as saying: "We have no record of a burial or ash-scattering for anyone named Joe Hill, but we get more inquiries about him than about any other individual."[7]

In IWW locals, "In November We Remember" memorials were annual events, honoring the Haymarket anarchists, Joe Hill, Frank Little, Wesley Everest, and other murdered working-class fighters. Socialist and anarchist groups often held their own November memorials for Hill and others, and memorialized him in their press. The frontispiece of the December 1916 issue of the *International Socialist Review* (mailed the preceding month), featuring a photograph of Hill and his last will, was headed "In Memoriam—Joe Hill—Murdered by Capitalist Class, November 1915" and closed with the class-war battle-cry: "Don't mourn for me—organize."

Humor and spontaneity were among Hill's strongest traits. In her reminiscences decades after Hill's judicial murder, his sister, Ester Dahl, recalled his "teasing" kind of humor as a teenager, when he made up gently sarcastic songs about his younger siblings.[8] He would also read aloud from the newspaper, "taking a line here, a line there, resulting in the strangest news events"—a procedure later discovered and developed by surrealists.[9] Edward Mattson, a fellow worker who knew Hill in Seattle and San Pedro, remembered especially Hill's incredible ability to improvise lyrics as he played. When Hill was later asked to repeat a certain song, according to Mattson, he (Hill) would invent entirely new lyrics.[10] The man we know as the Wobbly bard was—at least within the circle of his friends and fellow workers—a stand-up improv comedian who also happened to be an accomplished musician. The fact that he had his listeners rolling in the aisles suggests that the spontaneity of his lyrics made them all the more effective. Many of his songs, including "The Preacher and the Slave," "Mr. Block," "Coffee An'," and "The Tramp," are real classics—not only of IWW humor but also of American and world humor.

In most of Hill's songs, what makes us laugh are the incidents in the story, and the punch lines at the end of each stanza. In others—such as "Casey Jones, the Union Scab," "Everybody's Joining It," and "Nearer My Job to Me"—the nervous, rattling rhythm of the lyrics heightens the humorous effect. More rarely he slips in a bit of wordplay. His little-known poem "Let Bill Do It"—a gentle gibe at fellow workers who sit around the union hall all day and refuse to do their share—is dedicated to those who "have nothing to lose but their chairs."

The same hard-hitting wit and imaginative agility that served Joe Hill so well as a writer of songs is also very much in evidence in his visual art. As it happens, the period in which most of his surviving artwork was made was the heyday of American vaudeville. Between 1910 and 1914, a comedy trio known as the Three Marx Brothers was creating havoc on stages big and little all over this land. The same decade also marks the dawn of the slapstick silent film comedies of Mack Sennett and Charlie Chaplin. Hill and other makers of the IWW counterculture took generous helpings of all that was best in the popular arts, but the end product was always distinctively their own: not only funny but also anti-capitalist and revolutionary. The Wobbly counterculture could in fact be defined in large part as *popular culture liberated and fortified by the IWW Preamble.*

In all of Hill's cartoons the accent is on a rollicksome hobo humor, relentless in its free-for-all sarcasm and satire. His no-holds-barred class-war militancy gave pride of place to proletarian laughter. These cartoons ridicule—and expose the boundless hypocrisy of—the whole gamut of bourgeois values. One of his hand-drawn cartoon postcards is at once a refutation of the myth that "all are equal before the law" and a protest against the brutal treatment of migratory workers—hoboes. From the 1910s through the '30s, cops, private detectives, railroad bulls, gangsters, and even the US Army routinely pursued roving workers with pistols, rifles, and high-powered military weaponry, killing and maiming hundreds if not thousands. Many thousands more were arrested and forced to work on chain gangs or at other unpaid labor. Hill's postcard drawing (fig. 43) shows a 'bo (perhaps himself) being kicked off a speeding freight train, as a waiting cop, brandishing a billy-club and grinning, prepares to march the "vagrant" off to jail or workhouse. Postmarked San Pedro, September 2, 1911, and addressed to Charles Rudberg at the Sailors' Union Hall in San Francisco, this picture postcard also includes the artist's brief commentary, a veritable poem on the perils of a hobo's life:

> The song of Mauser bullets
> may be exciting
> and the rattle of machine-guns
> may also have its thrills—
> but Oh you hoboing!

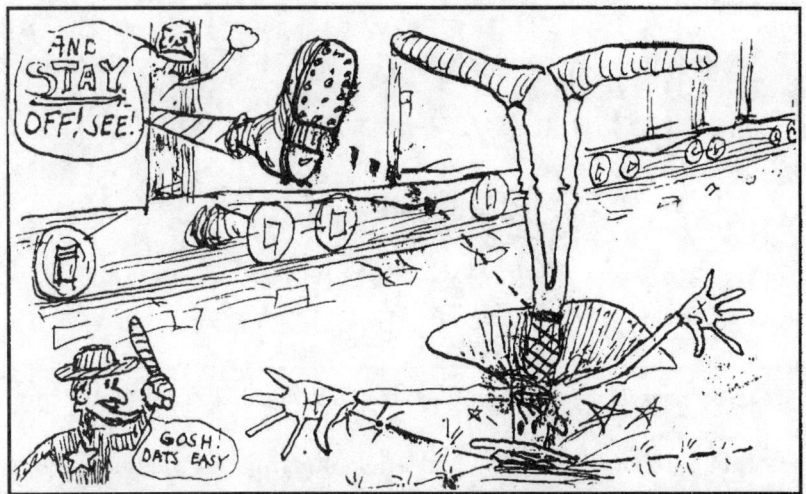

Fig. 43. Joe Hill, "Oh You Hoboing." Hand-drawn cartoon postcard to Charles Rudberg, September 2, 1911.

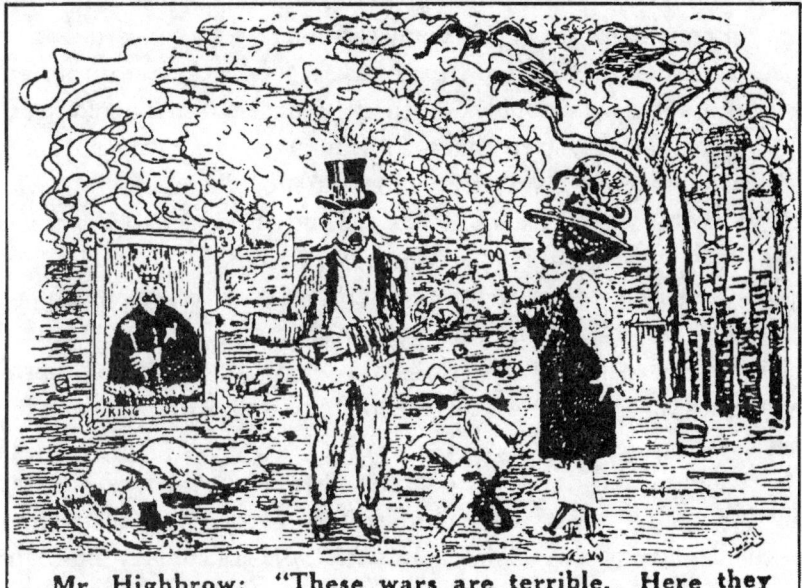

Fig. 44. Joe Hill, "Mr. and Mrs. Highbrow," *One Big Union Monthly*, November 1919.

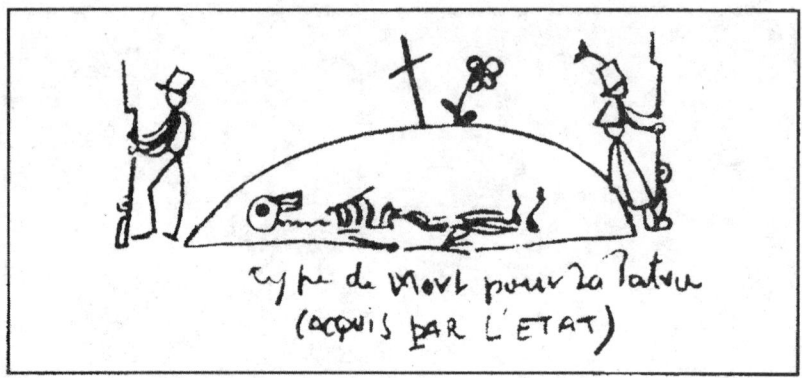

Fig. 45. Jacques Vaché, "Died for the Fatherland, Acquired by the State," 1917.

Another cartoon shows us a battlefield strewn with the dead, dying, and wounded (fig. 44). In the center, coldly oblivious to the horror and suffering around them, Mr. and Mrs. Highbrow are concerned only with the slight damage done to a painting of "King Loco."

Interestingly, this is Hill's only cartoon directly concerned with "art." I am sure his French contemporary Jacques Vaché, the great forerunner of surrealism, would have sensed its kinship with the subversive and protosurrealist spirit that he called umor—*humor* without the *h*. There are, moreover, strong affinities—in mood, temper, and tone—between this war cartoon of Hill's and the cartoons Vaché himself was drawing in the days of his celebrated *War Letters* (fig. 45). Vaché's subtle and ironic "desertion from within" reflected a sensibility quite distinct from Hill's openly proclaimed Wobbly revolutionism, but it is charming to see how similarly these two very different nonconformists expressed, in "scribbling," their absolute contempt and loathing for the first imperialist world war.

Laughing darkly, Hill also let his merciless pen reveal the utter futility and misery of petit bourgeois "cockroach capitalism" and parliamentary "slowcialism," along with the sorry but silly efforts of self-deluded wage slaves in pursuit of desirable but forever-elusive jobs. Hill's humor, like the best of T-Bone Slim's—and Wobbly humor generally—tends to be *black*, never pink or baby blue. In his art and writing as in his social philosophy, he favored direct action. Hill's cartoons, as Evert Anderson wrote of his songs, were "designed to jab, to shock, to wake the American wage-slave into an awareness of his class position."[11] The abominations of war, the brutality and injustice endured by the whole working class, the thoroughly fraudulent character of "free enterprise": Joe Hill, revolutionary industrial humorist, shows us all this and more. Wasting no time on polite euphemism, he goes straight to the point: *From top to bottom, the system stinks, and workers' solidarity is the only solution.*

As cartoonist and as songwriter, Hill never stops at mere social criticism; he is first and last a revolutionist. Always, however, he is a revolutionist with a well-developed sense of humor. He especially enjoyed creating images of capitalism being wrecked, either by its own imbecility and inertia or by working-class direct action. Sabotage, striking on the job, workers expropriating the bosses' stolen goods, *workers helping themselves*: these are the grand themes that warmed the cockles of his Wobbly hobo heart. His double-panel comic, "As It Was, As It Is," portrays literally a rebel worker helping himself to some of the "good things of life" that capitalists traditionally have reserved for themselves. Here is Joe Hill's own "Rise and Fall of Wage-Slavery" in two tableaux (reading time: six seconds).

His song lyrics pursue the same themes and resound with the same humor. Such songs as "Casey Jones, the Union Scab," "Everybody's Joining It," "John Golden and the Lawrence Strike," and that saboteurs' marching ballad "Ta-ra-ra Boom De-Ay" radiate the unrestrained irreverence, hilarity, audacity, and rowdiness of the wildest Felix the Cat cartoons, with IWW solidarity and direct action providing the basic plot and continuity. Albeit more subtly, Hill's eight-line poem "The Rebel's Toast" also captures this "all-hell-can't-stop-us" rebellious spirit:

> If Freedom's road seems rough and hard,
> And strewn with rocks and thorns,
> Then put your wooden shoes on, pard,
> And you won't hurt your corns.
> To organize and teach, no doubt,
> Is very good—that's true,
> But still we can't succeed without
> The Good Old Wooden Shoe.

Joe Hill's special blend of bitterness and glee is at its explosive best in the magnificent cartoon that appeared in *Solidarity* in 1914 under the double headline: "CLASS WAR NEWS/I.W.W. Submarines

Are Annoying the Enemy Everywhere." An IWW wooden-shoe-shaped submarine fires a "Direct Action torpedo" at the battleship *Capitalism*, captained by a smug and corpulent capitalist—labeled "Plute" (for Plutocrat)—who, as anyone can see, is hogging "All Necessities of Life" for himself. Of course, this supercilious representative of the employing class doesn't have a clue to what is going on "below." The cartoon's main action takes place under water because the work of proletarian saboteurs is clandestine and unexpected.

This single-panel drama of revenge and redemption hearkens back to David and Goliath, Robin Hood, and *The Three Musketeers*, but it also looks ahead to Tex Avery, *Little Lulu*, and a class-conscious *Calvin and Hobbes*. It is an old story that is nonetheless always new, and always worth retelling in ever-new ways: against seemingly impossible odds, those who have been exploited, oppressed, and made to feel small and weak band together and rise up to liberate themselves and their class. With Hill's delightful little touches—the astonished fish and sea-snake (or is it an eel?) looking on with wonder, and *five* speech balloons, no less—this is surely his single finest cartoon, and exemplifies his knack for expressing complex revolutionary ideas simply and enticingly. Wasn't it Michelangelo who said "Trifles make a masterpiece"?

The *Little Red Songbook*, moreover, includes *many* masterpieces by Hill: songs so irresistibly funny that even hardened scissorbills often caught the drift and joined up (thereby ceasing to be scissorbills). Masterpieces though they undoubtedly are, however, these songs have been systematically excluded from studies and anthologies of American humor. From Constance Rourke (1931) and Max Eastman (1936) to the later and more comprehensive (or at least more copious) tomes of Jesse Bier (1968), Walter Blair and Hamlin Hill (1970), and Russell Baker (1993), professional students of laughter have maintained an almost religious silence regarding Joe Hill or, for that matter, any other Wobbly. This exclusion has been so alarmingly thorough that it makes one wonder whether there might not be a little-known law requiring FBI pre-publication approval of all books on humor.

Discrimination along class lines is, of course, a well-recognized national disgrace. True, it is only one of a million or so national disgraces, including the presidency and the prison industry and the appalling fact that shameless commercialism makes it practically impossible to hear the wonderful music of David Boykin, Hamid Drake, and Nicole Mitchell on the radio in Chicago. That is the way things happen to be at the moment, and in this degraded era of multibillion-aires and postmodern postmortems for revolutionary change, there appears to be no immediate relief in sight.

But here is a handy tip that should save you a lot of time and trouble. Next time you come across a book purporting to be about "American humor," check the table of contents and index. If you don't find the names *Joe Hill* or *T-Bone Slim*, you have definitive proof that the book you've found is phony: it is *not* a book about American humor but only—and at best—about American *middle-class* humor.

PART V

Play and Humor

30

Rats Live on No Evil Star: A Selection of Palindromes

First published in *Free Spirits: Annals of the Insurgent Imagination*, no. 1 (1982): 153–54.

———

A palindrome is a word, phrase, or sentence that can be read forward and backward—that is, either from left to right or from right to left. According to historians of literary curiosities, palindromes are among the most ancient forms of wordplay. They are supposed to have been produced in abundance in Rome throughout the Decadence. It is also said that during the Middle Ages, numerous monks went insane in a relentless quest for palindromes.

A very few have become well known, such as the statement attributed to the defeated Napoleon: "Able was I ere I saw Elba."

Strangely disquieting in their utter detachment, their total gratuitousness, palindromes forbid access to all forms of interpretation. They are as distant from conscious intention as from psychic automatism. They might seem to be qualifiable as oneiric—surely they can be as haunting or as hilarious as any dream image—but palindromes are completely devoid of latent content. Composed as they are of letters and words "meaningfully" arranged, they would seem indisputably to belong to language. But just what it is they do mean remains entirely elusive. In terms of "expression," palindromes are perhaps closer to geometry or probability theory than to what we ordinarily regard as language. They are invariably solitary and exceptional; nothing can disguise their emphatic otherness.

And it is this unique otherness that gives palindromes their appeal and their importance. In our day, when the human sensibility has long been nourished by wordplay at its most extravagant—let it suffice to cite the work of Raymond Roussel, Marcel Duchamp, Samuel Greenberg, T-Bone Slim, and movements such as futurism, Dadaism, and surrealism—who could deny the possibility that palindromes may yet reveal answers to some of life's most troubling questions?

The following selection has been drawn from various sources. The concluding five examples, it should be noted, are the original work of Dmitri Borgmann of Oak Park, Illinois, one of the greatest palindromists of modern times.

∾

Rail at a liar.

Name no one man.

Snug & raw was I ere I saw war & guns.

No lemons, no melon.

Stiff, O dairy-man, in a myriad of fits.

Too far, Edna, we wander afoot.

Draw pupil's lip upward.

Emil asleep, Hannah peels a lime.

I roamed under it as a tired, nude Maori.

No sot nor Ottawa law at Toronto, son.

Desserts I desire not, so long no lost one rise distressed.

Paget saw an Irish tooth, Sir, in a waste gap.

Trash? Even interpret Nineveh's art.

Dog as a devil deified lived as a god.

Stop, Syrian, I start at rats in airy spots!

No, it is opposed; art sees trade's opposition.

Eureka! till I pull up ill I take rue.

Wonders in Italy: Latin is "red" now.

Straw? No, too stupid a fad. I put soot on warts.

'Tis Ivan, on a visit.

Egad! A base tone denotes a bad age.

Marge lets Norah see Sharon's telegram.

Eva, can I stab bats in a cave?

No mists reign at Tangier, St. Simon!

Deer flee freedom in Oregon? No, Geronimo, deer feel freed.

"Do nine men interpret?" "Nine men," I nod.

31

Humor: Here Today and Everywhere Tomorrow: A Short Introduction to the Next Revolution

First published in *Arsenal/Surrealist Subversion*, no. 4 (1989): 81–84.

It is obvious that the role formerly played by *religion* in society—as a set of allegiances (prejudices) rooted in neurotic faith and fear; a self-ordained, hierarchically structured, "omniscient" arbiter of taste; the definitive "spiritual" authority (i.e., the dominant mode of ideological manipulation); and a more or less compulsory guide to everyday conduct—has been largely replaced, in this century, by *advertising*.

Much less acknowledged, however, is the extent to which traditional religion has itself *merged* with advertising, forming a new repressive synthesis that helps define the epoch of computerized cretinization. Christianity, of course, as well as Judaism and Islam, have been "Big Business" for centuries, but modern technology has vastly enlarged their commercial and exploitative possibilities. Commodity fetishism is *par excellence* a system of authoritarian mystification, a field in which theologian, priest, and evangelist are old hands. Today's up-to-the-minute pope poses for his picture sipping Coca-Cola instead of the blood of Christ; and the imperial scumbags of the Ku Klux Klan now thump not only their Gideon Bibles but also their IBM software. The age-old patriarchy has gone high-tech to save its soul.

If the traditional omnipotent father-of-the-family and his celestial reflection, God (a.k.a. "Him"), are forgotten relics of a bygone age, both still turn up—somewhat the worse for wear, but still functioning serviceably as the same old repressive symbols—twenty-four hours a day on radio and TV, as well as in the pages of a thousand newsstand magazines and newspapers, and on billboards from coast to coast, urging us one and all to drink this, smoke that, eat this and buy, buy, buy, buy, buy, buy, buy. Religious mysticism's main-stays—sexual repression, guilt, and fear, together with an endless variety of saleable innuendo—are part and parcel of the mystique of management and moneymaking. The Oedipus Complex today can easily dispense with the two-hour church service but not with the sixty-second commercial.

When the things one buys constitute all the meaning life is allowed to have, one's choice of automobile, deodorant, soft drink, cigarette, sleeping pill, and vacation spot inevitably involve devotional exercises as elaborate and tortuous as anything that ever kept Loyola or Calvin awake at night. Thus the shopper long ago replaced the worshipper, just as the tourist replaces the pilgrim. The most visited tourist traps in the world today are Lenin's Tomb and Disneyland, the central shrine of the Russian Orthodox Stalinist church and American capitalism's gaudiest temple of "free enterprise." Our old friend Hegel would recognize the inanimate corpse of the old Bolshevik, and the oversized, rubberized, motorized, smiling caricature of a mouse that greets visitors to the cutest and most profitable of all utopias, as perfect embodiments of the innermost spirit of the two main varieties of state-capitalist miser-abilism today.

Of course the situation is rapidly changing: as the USSR gets increasingly Disneyized, US capitalism is trying at least the warmed-over hors d'oeuvres of "Stalinism" (à la Gorbachev). Recently *The Progressive* reported that a manufacturer who found that nobody was buying his Ollie North dolls converted the whole lot into Gorbachev dolls, which sold like hotcakes. Vacationers in Moscow may yet get to gawk at an oversized smiling Lenin, meaninglessly waving his white-gloved hands in the air, while Los Angeles tourists are allowed to file solemnly through a brightly colored fast-food tomb to gaze on the deathlike demeanor of an embalmed Hollywood mouse who died for the sins of Wall Street.

The crucial point is that modern moronization is *global* in scope, uniting all previous modes of repressive mystification into one all-encompassing mega-mystification that tends to be more and more monolithic *and monotonous*. One can no longer tell, merely by looking, whether a contemporary building is American or Russian or German or Brazilian or Japanese—or whether it is an apartment building or a bank or a hospital or a church or a prison: *they all look alike*. Totalitarianism has always been accompanied by the large-scale production of tawdriness and trivialization, of course, but today's minimalist have-a-nice-day version of fascism is something new in authoritarian abjection.

Typical of the latest fashions in the institutionalized death wish is the vilest form of advertising ever devised: TV news. Day after day, night after night, stupefied spectators *by the million* are "allowed" to buy—and at what cost, to themselves and the planet—addictive doses, and overdoses, of their own enslavement and misery. In view of today's *real* (and therefore suppressed) news—universal ecocidal devastation, genocide, war, torture, calamities without end (did you know that the building of *prisons* is America's number one "growth industry"?)—the regimented idiocy of worldwide "bureaucracy for bureaucracy's sake" affords a true picture of civilization-as-we-know-it: a panorama of *absolute horror*.

That it is perceived as such only by a tiny minority, mostly poets and others commonly called "crazy," is entirely in the order of things. No society, as such, recognizes its horror until the *hegemony* of horror—the combined power of Capital, Church, and State—has begun to crumble and to be replaced by rebellious counterinstitutions. As long as the perpetrators of horror are in a position to enforce their rule, and thus to blithely deny that the horror exists at all, the majority of society—and especially that monster known as The Public—almost inevitably accommodate themselves, willy-nilly, to the oppressors' legally sanctified pretenses. False consciousness is, above all, a form of negative hallucination. Most people today are as oblivious to the prevailing horror as people in the pre–Civil War United States were oblivious to the horror of chattel slavery—as oblivious as the people in the fable were to the fact that the emperor wore no clothes.

An example of people who are *not* oblivious is provided by the recent Hmong immigrants from Laos to the United States. As reported in *Natural History* in November 1983, thousands of these semi-tribal peasants, brutally uprooted from their traditional rural way of life by the catastrophic ravages of inter-imperialist rivalries, have been forced into a nightmarish exile in several large American cities, where many of them eke out an existence collecting soda pop cans and selling them (for half a cent a can) for recycling. The response of these peaceful, hardworking people to everyday life in America is instructive indeed: they have the highest rate of *sudden death* of any people on earth. As this phenomenon was unknown in their native land, it can only be a consequence of their new conditions of life in the United States. Clearly, these "backward," "primitive" people—people largely uncontaminated by the conventions of what T-Bone Slim called *civilinsanity*—perceive, with an immediacy and intensity that often proves fatal, things about American culture that most Americans learn early to shield themselves against by elaborate techniques of delusion and denial. That this is indeed the case is suggested by the striking fact that many victims of this "sudden death syndrome," as commentators have termed it, have died *while watching television*.

A rarely remarked chapter in Oliver Sacks's popular book *The Man Who Mistook His Wife for a Hat* offers another illuminating example: the response of a group of aphasiacs to a televised speech by President Reagan. Incapable of understanding words as such, but extraordinarily sensitive to intonation, inflection, facial expression, and gesture, these patients roared with laughter at the Great Communicator's emotional appeal. "One cannot lie to an aphasiac," Sacks explains.

> He cannot grasp your words, and so cannot be deceived by them; but what he grasps he grasps with infallible precision, namely the *expression* that goes with the words, that total, spontaneous, involuntary expressiveness which can never be simulated or faked, as words alone can, all too easily…. Thus it was the grimaces, the histrionisms, the false gestures and, above all, the false tones and cadences of [Reagan's] voice, which rang false for these wordless but sensitive patients. It was to these (for them) most glaring, even grotesque incongruities and improprieties that my aphasic patients responded, undeceived and undeceivable by words. This is why they laughed at the President's speech.

A patient of what Sacks calls "an exactly opposite kind," a tonal agnosiac—a woman who had *no* sense of expression or "tone," while retaining her comprehension of words—responded differently but no less tellingly. She was unmoved by Reagan's speech, Sacks says. "No speech now moved her—and all that was evocative, genuine or false completely passed her by. Deprived of emotional reaction, was she then … transported or taken in? By no means. [Reagan] 'is not cogent,' she said…. 'His word-use is improper. Either he is brain-damaged, or he has something to conceal.'"

"Here then was the paradox of the President's speech," Sacks writes in his conclusion, which is well worth reflecting on. "We normals—aided doubtless by our wish to be fooled—were indeed won and truly fooled.... And so cunningly was [Reagan's] deceptive word-use combined with deceptive tone, that only the brain-damaged remained intact, undeceived."

∿

Against all forms of oppression and horror, humor wreaks havoc. When oppression and horror become total, nothing less than total humor can do the trick. In the coming revolution the role of humor will be decisive, and the role of surrealism no less so, for surrealism is the *lever* of that humor.

Clearly the fundamental task of revolutionists today must be to find ways of freeing people, and especially working people, of their repressions, so that instead of denying the omnipresent horror they can recognize it and change the social system that perpetuates it. Humor alone can effect this revolution in consciousness on a large scale.

Attempts to achieve the same ends by "serious," rational means invariably prove self-defeating. Rational argument affects only a very small number of people a very small part of the time; if this were not the case, the world revolution would have been made long ago, and we would all right now be enjoying life in marvelous anarchy. But to try to convince someone, by rational means, to see something that is in fact unbearable, is doubly thankless: first, because no one *wants* to see how horrible everything really is, and second, because even if some could be *made* to see it, to do so would probably serve to paralyze them with fear rather than move them to action. To perceive the horror *directly* is more than anyone can stand and can lead only to suicide or madness. Humor, however, not only deflects the horror's full force by means of a powerful shield of *poetic intuition* but also provides, in self-defense, weapons of eros-affirmative action. In the world as it is today, humor has become a matter of life and death.

The overwhelming superiority of a humorous, irrational, eros-affirmative approach over sober, moralistic, and/or rational argument should be plain from everyday experience. People who *consciously* respect the police, admire their employer, and revere the church fathers nonetheless will laugh heartily at film comedies, songs, and comic strips that sadistically ridicule cops, bosses, and preachers. The "comic situation" allows the unconscious truth to erupt into consciousness in a spontaneously liberating way. To translate this laughter into revolutionary action may not always be easy, but it provides an indispensable point of departure that rational argument does not.

Surrealism intervenes precisely at that point. Our task, to paraphrase Marx, is *to create the comic situation that makes all turning back impossible.*

∾

Surrealism began historically by appropriating all the advantages of madness—that is, of the Mind functioning outside the confines of reified Reason—while avoiding its disadvantages. It was not without humor that the prerogatives of the hysteric, the paranoiac, the schizophrenic became the prerogatives of surrealists. Precisely because they have not been mad, surrealists have been able to use madness creatively, or rather dialectically, in the service of revolution. Had madness not come to the rescue, moreover, Reason would not have been reborn.

The opening salvoes of surrealist revolution ushered into an unsuspecting world *an entire community* of men and women who not only fought the good fight for a life of *marvelous freedom now,* as individual poets, artists, hoboes, and lunatics had done for ages, but also showed how this poetic struggle could broaden, deepen, and expand so as to truly transform society and change life for the benefit of all. For the first time in a world-historical sense, the human imagination reasserted its primacy and refused to take no for an answer to its defiantly utopian questions.

As surrealism has continued to evolve, from its original narrowly circumscribed sphere as the last of the poetic/artistic avant-gardes toward its historic fruition as the theoretical and practical basis for the revolutionary supersession of capitalist/christian civilization, this struggle has assumed new and ever higher stages of development. And, as is usually the case in decisive turning points in the history of revolutionary thought and action, humor's role has been pivotal.

After the Second World War the various cultural and political avant-gardes sank together into definitive oblivion. Only the surrealist movement—whose adherents, incidentally, had from the start detested the avant-garde label—survived this debacle, albeit largely underground, shunned by the major galleries and publishing houses, and discussed in books and magazines exclusively in terms of its now-marketable past. Characteristically, while the commercially contrived and short-lived pseudo avant-gardes concocted by speculators as "successors" to surrealism—abstract expressionism, Pop, Op, conceptualism, minimalism, etc.—all subscribed to a reactionary "High Culture" elitism, surrealism renewed itself instead at the majestic and fertile river of popular culture.

This had always been an important focal point for surrealist inquiry—as witness the surrealists' early enthusiasm for Buster Keaton, Charlie Chaplin, the Fantômas pulp novels and films, *King Kong*, and the Marx Brothers; this enthusiasm, indeed, was one of the things that distinguished them from other "artists" and "intellectuals." In the late 1940s, however, such preoccupations grew steadily more pronounced, and since the international resurgence of the "disquieting muse" in the 1960s the explosive dialectic of surrealism and popular culture has been central to the movement's revolutionary perspectives.

When one considers that horror and humor are the great extremes of popular expression, and that these extremes also meet at their highest tension in surrealism, it should become clear why this dialectic is indeed explosive. As I have had occasion to remark more than once before, "the barriers dividing poetry and the proletariat are being assaulted from *both* sides."

In the United States, for example, we surrealists have been pleased to discover, in the work of such very different figures as Tex Avery, H.P. Lovecraft, Todd Browning, Memphis Minnie, Ernie Kovacs, Dixie Willson, Simon Rodia, Mildred Wirt, Carl Barks, Charlie Parker, Fredric Brown, Harry Stephen Keeler, Bill Holman, Martha and the Vandellas, and T-Bone Slim, elements of a revolutionary poetic critique of repressive values and institutions, and hints of proposed alternatives, that complement our own.

Humor's next qualitative leap will be the result of a new and dynamic synthesis of the surrealist spirit and mass working-class self-activity—and above all the class-wide affirmation of *the right to be lazy*—on an unprecedented scale. This in turn will be the signal for the next revolution. *Beginning* with the living fusion of surrealism and its popular accomplices, this is one revolution that need *never end*.

This next revolution starts, quite simply, with *the concrete negation of the religion of advertising*. This signifies nothing less than pulling the plug from what Alfred Jarry termed the "Disembraining Machine"—the vast and terrible megamachine of ideology and culture that, as the founder of Pataphysics noted further, is "better than the Bomb with its big bang" as a means of enforcing an Ubuesque social order.

Against the bureaucracy's one-way information system ("Just follow orders! And don't ask why!"), which reduces each and every one to cogs in this deadly machine, the next revolution restores *language, dialogue, and communication* to human beings who, at first by *talking back* to those in power and then by talking to each other and themselves, will proceed to reinvent daily life the only way it can be reinvented: playfully, imaginatively, humorously, against all authority. Annihilating "The Public" as a manipulable ruling-class fiction, freely associated individuals will be able to decide, for the first time, what they want to do.

Initial and highly promising signs of the new humor—humor that tends to be activist, anonymous, collective, often black, illegal, and above all *objective*—are visible all through the warp and woof of social dissidence today: in workers' wildcat actions; in the outstanding strikes of recent years (P-9 at Hormel, Watsonville cannery workers, clerical and technical workers at Yale, etc.); in the widespread revival of sabotage and direct action by workers, students, environmentalists, the homeless; in new forms of expression such as *billboard revision*; in disruptions of state/corporate affairs by such groups as Greenpeace, the Animal Liberation Front, and Earth First! These last-mentioned disruptions also serve to emphasize that a militant anti-anthropocentric attitude is a key element in the new humor and the next revolution. A species that enslaves all others cannot itself be free.

The new humor need not be "funny," in the usual sense of the word. Poetry can exist and even flourish without poems, and humor can get along very well without chuckles and guffaws. "I do not know how to laugh," said Lautréamont, the new humor's most decisive forerunner.

Aggressively undermining the existing order's monopolization of the definition of reality, and refusing the musty compartmentalization of a timid traditional Left—the Left as represented by all and sundry condescending saviors, those whose sole ambition is to become the managers of what the German Dadaist Raoul Hausmann once called "the proctatorship of the Dilletariat"—the new humor opens fire in all directions with the only effective weapons of the next revolution: the free development of rambunctious shenanigans, the ceaseless unfettering of the revolutionary imagination, new ways of saying no to the whole stinking mess of capitalist-christian civilization.

According to Hegel in volume 1 of *Aesthetics* (Clarendon Press, 1975, 609), objective humor that develops in objectivity necessarily leads to "action and event." By its very nature the new humor tends to exceed individual limits and to become a *social* force.[1] When the new humor, globally conceived, reaches its critical mass, we shall all enjoy the Bastille Day of the next revolution.

Never before has the fate of humankind depended so much on the outcome of humor. Verily it should be shouted from the rooftops, or at least whispered to strangers on streetcorners, that the future of our whole planet depends on the present generation's ability to exemplify, here and now, the objective humor of a livable, desirable future. "How funny it'll be, don't you see," declared Jacques Vaché, "when this real New Spirit breaks loose!"

In modern mythology, no one is more exemplary of this world-historical *becoming* of the new humor than the inexorably disorienting dialectician, Bugs Bunny. In the activity of this perennial pilferer of carrots from Fudd's garden, what Hegel called humor's "conscious disintegration" of existing social relations attains a subversive *excess* that can only be described as *absolutely enticing*. If there can be said to be a *model* for the next revolutionaries, it would be difficult to think of a better one than the World's Greatest Rabbit.

As an inscription in a surrealist publication I received from abroad some years ago put it: "Bugs Bunny world! Bugs Bunny life! These two commands are for us but one."

Until further notice, the watchword of the next revolution remains: "What's up, Doc?"

32

Revolution as Play

Reprinted from Franklin Rosemont, *An Open Entrance to the Shut Palace of Wrong Numbers* (Chicago: Surrealist Editions, 2003), 151–54.

———

Every Wrong Number is a problem encounter. It poses the question "What is to be done?" in the most immediate personal terms, for the Voice of the Unknown is not speaking to anyone else but the recipient. Curiously, instead of accepting this experience as a welcome stimulus to imaginative spontaneity—an invitation to join the game—it is scorned as an unpleasant occurrence. The explanation lies less in the particular phenomenon of the Wrong Number itself than in a more generalized phenomenon, of which antipathy to Wrong Numbers may be considered a part: *the fear of play.*

All children know what play is without having to look it up in the dictionary, but adults have a much harder time with it. In most people the sense of play seems to fade away long before high school. Those in power regard knocking play down as a prerequisite of growing up. In advanced industrial or postindustrial society, "responsible adults" are those who obey the biblical injunction to put "childish things" behind them.

No country in the world is as playless as the United States, and this stark playlessness is surely at the root of the deadly, aggressive cynicism that defines the sewer-like moral climate of late capitalism. And nowhere is the fear and loathing of play more horrifyingly evident than in the appalling industry known as sports.

Contrary to widespread misconception, sports are not forms of "organized" play, for nothing of the spirit of play survives in these highly aggressive, super-authoritarian, and hyper-commercialized corporate-bureaucratic gladiatorial spectacles. Sports in our time have even less connection with play than wage slavery has with non-alienated labor. The so-called players, in any case, are decidedly secondary, for sports are above all *competitive performances for spectators*.

Today's athletic performances, wrongly called games, are basically fast-moving images symbolic of the permanent war economy, specially packaged in huge arenas for the most satiated and therefore most frustrated consumers on earth. One of the most addictive forms of capital's increasing domination of leisure, sports are the biggest and most dangerous drug on the market.

Also antithetical to play are 99 percent of what is called play in US schools and by far the larger part of the activities imposed on children in the dreary playgrounds of metropolitan parks, those mini-gulags for tots. As for video and computer games, I won't even bother to comment.

In bright contrast, real play is not only a way of using up surplus energy or a means of amusement or an escape from reality—it is one of life's most exhilarating, pleasurable, self-developing, and liberating experiences. The essence of play is *the creation of imaginary situations and active participation in them*. Spontaneous, collective, unselfconscious, dynamic, unconventional, non-competitive, uninhibited, and wildly adventurous, play is a consciousness-expanding *initiation* into a real community, the vital *process* by which individuals become truly *social*.

Neva Leona Boyd was one of the outstanding theorists of play. A coworker of Jane Addams at Chicago's Hull House in the 1910s, she was a quiet, unpretentious individual who avoided the limelight. Her radical theory and practice, however, became highly influential through her students. Pearl Pachaco Williams, founder of the African American "little theater" movement in Chicago, acknowledged Boyd as a major inspiration. Boyd also inspired Viola Spolin's *Improvisations for the Theater*, which in turn prompted the formation of the Compass Players, Second City, and the whole still-burgeoning movement of improv comedy.

Boyd regarded play as "a vacation from one's everyday life," an imaginary trip as far as possible from monotony and regimentation. In her view, true play always releases the repressed elements of one's self and is thus a natural antidote for debilitating routine: work, sports, school, church, and other morbid and alienating chores. Play, as she conceived it, is collective improvisation—a pleasurable activity in which strain and conflict are dissolved and heretofore unknown potentialities are set free. Creative and therapeutic, play is the withering away of the state of anxiety and therefore the best form of social education. Free play also provides the only firm basis for an eros-affirmative morality and the most stimulating environment for creative and intellectual originality.

Although Boyd does not appear to have identified herself with the revolutionary movement, the implications of her theory and practice of play are unmistakably anarchist, and there is more than a slight touch of surrealism in them as well. The emancipation of play, as she describes it, seems to me to be synonymous with the realization of the dream of the global "festival of the oppressed" known as revolution.

The emancipation of play, of course, can be accomplished only by players themselves. Our task, then, is clear: to overcome, by any means necessary, that fear of play that prevents the workers of the world from being players—that is, revolutionists.

Clearly Wrong Numbers have been given to humankind to make surrealist use of them—and that means first of all to *play* with them, to see how they fit into the story we happen to be telling ourselves when the Wrong Number arrives, and then to see what possibilities open up.

It was through play that my own perception of Wrong Numbers began to deviate more and more radically from the long-entrenched norm. Regarding these calls playfully and then—albeit tentatively at first—actually playing *with* them, I found that I could no longer think of them as pestiferous interruptions; rather they were chance meetings that could, from time to time, lead to "interesting things." The more I played, the more I discovered, the more I wanted to play. My experiences led directly to my attempt at a systematic study, which in turn suggested the larger project: to rehabilitate the Wrong Number in public opinion—or, more specifically, *to render Wrong Numbers attractive*. Strategically, accenting the creative and emancipatory potential of Wrong Numbers seems to be the surest step toward enlisting their aid, first in the general provoking of inspiration, then in the radical redefinition of the relations between poetry and everyday life, and henceforth in the solution of the fundamental problems of human existence.

I was encouraged to find that the alchemists of old considered play to be an essential symbolic phase in the elaboration of the Great Work. In Elias Ashmole's *Theatrum Chemicum Britannicum* (1652) we read:

This very place is called by many names,
As *Imbibition, Feeding, Sublimation,*
Clyming high Mountaines, also *Children's Games;*
and rightly it is termed *Exaltation.*

I was also charmed to learn that Neva Boyd described her own life's work with children in unmistakably alchemical terms: "If play is thought of as comparable to the irradiance of a brilliant jewel it will be given a truer interpretation than were a [formal] definition attempted."

With a tip of the hat to the alchemist Fulcanelli, explicator of "phonetic cabala," we can follow the transmutation of the Wrong Number from a simple *nuisance* into a veritable complex of unantici-pated *nuances* that, in turn, evolve into an excitingly *new sense* of things and life, and at last into a playful *new science* of transforming the world.

"Kid stuff"? Yes, but it is also the Wisdom of the Ancients, restored and revised. The Wrong Number may open with "Hello" and close with a *click*, but it is a New Pearl of Great Price all the same.

PART VI

Ecology

33

Radical Environmentalism

First published in Mari Jo Buhle, Paul Buhle, and Dan Georgakas, eds., *Encyclopedia of the American Left* (New York: Garland, 1990), 623–30.

A direct descendant of the older conservation movement, contemporary environmentalism became conscious of itself as traditional conservationist goals were redefined and expanded in the course of large-scale public health and workplace-safety struggles in the early 1960s. A specifically left-wing environmentalism—generally known as radical environmentalism or the "ecology movement," influenced by the late '60s New Left, counterculture, and radical American Indian and women's liberation movements—came into prominence in the mid-1970s and early in the next decade was recognized as an important force in the movement.

Conservationism could count an impressive number of poets, artists, and philosophers among its ancestors—including Henry David Thoreau, George Perkins Marsh, and painters John James Audubon, Thomas Cole, and George Catlin—but its beginnings as an organized movement can be credited above all to the indefatigable efforts of the "Yosemite Prophet," John Muir (1838–1914). Born in Scotland, Muir grew up in rural Wisconsin and lived most of his later life in California, much of it in the mountains. A highly original thinker as well as one of America's most inspired and popular writers on nature—his books include *A Thousand Mile Walk to the Gulf, Travels in Alaska*, and *The Mountains of California*—he led the successful struggle to protect the Yosemite Valley against mining, lumbering, and other exploitation by having it officially declared a national park in 1889. Three years later he helped cofound the Sierra Club and was elected its first president, an office he held for the rest of his life.

Though influenced to some extent by the aesthetic socialism of John Ruskin and the single-tax theories of Henry George, Muir's writings elaborated an indictment of industrial civilization that was almost wholly his own, based on his prolonged and profound experience of the American wilderness. Many of his most revolutionary pronouncements appeared in his journals and remained unpublished until long after his death—those, for example, touching on his rejection of Christianity (because of its supercilious disdain for nature), his militant anti-anthropocentrism, and his scorn for capitalism, which he called "the gobble-gobble school of economics"—but these fugitive jottings show that Muir was far more radical than the conservation movement he did so much to found. Not too surprisingly, these uncompromising private musings proved to be a powerful inspiration to later radical wilderness activists, especially since the mid-1970s.

In Muir's view, the human experience of the natural beauty of wilderness was the decisive key to solving the ills of society; he regarded mountains and forests as sacred places of freedom, where alone people could learn not only the truths of nature writ large but also the truth of their own nature, so suppressed and disfigured by the artifices of an acquisitive, exploitative civilization. "Pollution, defilement, squalor," he wrote, "are words that never would have been created had man lived conformably to Nature." The "hope of the world," he was sure, lies in "the great, fresh, unblighted, unredeemed wilderness [where] the galling harness of civilization drops off, and the wounds heal ere we are aware."

The "Muir tradition" of radical conservation—maintained through the years by small bands of devoted amateurs, ardent with the love of wildlife and wilderness for their own sake, independent of human use—contrasts starkly with the conservative, professionalized, much larger and better known wing of the movement, typified by Gifford Pinchot, founder of the US Forest Service and associate of Theodore Roosevelt. Pinchot's concern was not the wonders of nature but the scientific "management of resources." For him, a forest was "a manufacturing plant for the production of wood." The goal of conservation, as he conceived it, was not to save wildlife or wilderness, as such, but rather to save these *crops*, or *commodities*—that is precisely how he saw them—for future exploitation. While Muir boldly challenged anthro-pocentrism and affirmed the equality of species (he championed especially those animals most feared and hated by modern society, such as wolves and grizzly bears), Pinchot upheld the Western world's traditional notion that man is the "lord of creation" ordained by God to exercise stewardship over the planet and the creatures God made for his use. The task of conservationists, Pinchot argued, was to limit destructive excesses committed by overly rapacious, unscientific industrialists.

The glaring disparity between the two wings of the movement was not perceived by the broad public, and adherents of Muir and Pinchot were able to work together on many issues. The fact that both wings consisted almost entirely of white native-born Anglo-Saxon Protestant males made the movement as a whole vulnerable to the charge of "elit-ism" frequently leveled at it by opponents on the Right as well as the Left. In John Muir's last great and unsuccessful crusade, to prevent the damming of California's beautiful Hetch Hetchy Valley, Pinchot took an emphatically pro-dam stand, but even the minor concessions he was willing to make to the Muir forces were too much for Texas congress-man Martin Dies, who denounced Pinchot as a "radical." (In the 1930s and 1940s, Dies would head a congressional committee notorious for its persecution of socialists and pro-labor radicals.) Notwithstanding Pinchot's demagogic, populist-tinged motto, The Greatest Good for the Greatest Number, his overall view reflected a conservative eastern mugwump Republicanism. After the collapse of the short-lived "Bull Moose" party, Pinchot's closeness to Theodore Roosevelt—who himself, as president, enjoyed a largely undeserved reputation as a champion of conservation—bound the movement to the Republican Party to such an extent that it was not until the New Deal that the Democrats attracted any conservationist following.

Prior to the 1930s, a number of Left writers had attempted to develop a specifically socialist conservationism, or at least a social-ist approach to the questions conservationism raised. As early as the 1890s Edward Bellamy, especially in his weekly, the *New Nation*, and in his last book, *Equality* (1897), laid bare the links between the triple exploitation of nature, women, and labor, positing a socialist utopia in which humankind and nature were no longer at odds, and in which the massive restoration of wilderness was a central element. Ernest

Thompson Seton, Bellamy-influenced socialist author of best-selling natural-history books for children; "single-taxer" and outdoorsman Dan Beard; Chicago socialist muckraker William Kent, an abolitionist's son and associate of Jane Addams's Hull House; and anarchist novelist J. William Lloyd—to cite four very different figures, widely separated by ideology and temperament—also gave voice to a radical dimension in the conservationist cause, a voice heeded by many in the pre–World War I years, which witnessed the rise of a widespread "back to the land" movement.

The Marxist wing of the socialist movement in those years gave scant attention to this whole question, inhibited as its protagonists were by well-established social-democratic traditions supporting increased productivity and technological progress at all costs. But there were some notable exceptions. Articles urging forest preservation and other conservationist subjects could be found in the popular socialist monthly *Wilshire's* and elsewhere in the Socialist Party press. Even more significant, *International Socialist Review* editor Algie M. Simons translated a treatise of radical ecology, *Germs of Mind in Plants*, by Austrian biologist Raoul Francé, illustrated by Ralph Chaplin—who, a few years later, would be a leading poet-artist-editor of the Industrial Workers of the World (IWW)—and published in 1905 by Charles H. Kerr's socialist cooperative in Chicago. This book, which has gone through numerous printings and has remained in print ever since, included a militant preface in which Simons avowed that it was because he was "both a socialist and a nature lover" that he translated it. Kerr also published *The Universal Kinship* and other works by socialist and vegetarian J. Howard Moore, whose conception of "earth-life as a single process ... every part related and akin to every other part" and whose recognition that "all beings are *ends* [and] no creatures are *means*" made him an important precursor of the environmental ethics of the 1990s.

Conservation issues, however, remained tangential to the broad socialist movement, and not until the 1970s did such concerns figure significantly in any Left party platform. Ironically, the mainstream Marxists—the Socialist Labor Party, Socialist Party, Communist Party, and Trotskyists—notwithstanding their voluble opposition to business-union bureaucrats and "robber barons," shared the latter's reified view of wildlife and wilderness to an astonishing degree. It was among the heterodox and libertarian Left, the anarchist movement, and above all the IWW that elements of a radical conservationism developed most freely in earlier years.

The Wobblies, in fact, often exceeded the limits of conservationism as such and took up the whole gamut of questions later subsumed under the heading "radical environmentalism." The IWW press featured articles protesting the devastation of forests by the lumber industry—"strong conservational action" was demanded by IWW Lumber Workers Industrial Union 120—but also provided its readers with information on the problem of noise in American cities, on the use of poisons in manufacture (in hat-making, for example), and other texts on capitalism's destruction and pollution of the planet.

The IWW in its heyday was largely a union of the foreign-born, which may help explain its environmentalist tendency. While upper-class conservationists not infrequently blamed recent immigrants for "ruining" the American landscape, evidence suggests that the adoration of "Mother Nature" expressed, for example, by Italian immigrant anarchist martyr Nicola Sacco in his prison letters reflected an attitude by no means uncommon among foreign-born radicals. Indeed, immigrant radicals, whose regular activities included picnics in the country and long hikes in the woods, tended to be much more conservation-conscious than their native-born comrades.

However tenuous the links between the socialist and conservation movements, the fact remains that they rose to prominence together during the 1910s and faded together in the 1920s. Significantly, the next major resurgence of militancy within the conservation movement itself—the formation of the Wilderness Society in 1935—was spearheaded by two longtime socialists: Benton MacKaye and Robert Marshall.

MacKaye (1880–1975) was a Connecticut Yankee, the son of actor-playwright Steele MacKaye and a classmate of John Reed's at Harvard, where he went on to teach forestry for a few years before going to work for the US Forest Service. An associate of Oscar Ameringer, "the Mark Twain of American Socialism," MacKaye joined the Socialist Party in the heyday of Eugene Debs.

The much younger Bob Marshall (1901–39), of New York, joined the much smaller Socialist Party of Norman Thomas but was even more outspokenly radical than MacKaye and considered himself a Marxist. Son of a founder and leader of the American Jewish Committee,

Marshall, who had a PhD from Johns Hopkins, was one of the first non-WASPs prominent in conservation. Passionately attracted since childhood to "blank places on the map," he was a zealous mountain climber and an eloquent defender of everything wild against the ravages of capitalist "development." Finding the United States to be "a civilization remote from nature, artificial, dominated by the exploitation of man by man," he affirmed the essential unity of working-class socialism—"production for use and not for profit"—and "the freedom of the wilderness." His best-selling *Arctic Village* (1933) recounted a year's sojourn in a small community in the mountains of Alaska, two hundred miles north of Fairbanks, where he found "the most complete liberty one can imagine" and "the happiest folk I had ever encountered." In *The People's Forests*, the first major work of socialist conservationism in the United States, also published in 1933, he called for the socialization of wilderness to assure its protection from the insatiable greed of private industry.

MacKaye and Marshall were two of the four men who conceived the Wilderness Society, and it was they who drew up its "Platform," proclaiming, "The time has come, with the brutalizing pressure of a spreading metropolitan civilization, to recognize the wilderness environment as a serious human need rather than a luxury and a plaything." The first real fusion of socialism and the Muir tradition, the society immediately attracted the most radical-minded conservationists in the country, including Aldo Leopold, whose classic *Sand County Almanac* (1949) would become the most influential conservationist text since Muir. (Although he was generally regarded as "apolitical" by his friends and commentators, it is notable that Leopold voted for Norman Thomas throughout the 1930s and 1940s.) Deliberately restricting its membership to unequivocal supporters of wilderness for wilderness's sake—"We want no straddlers," Marshall insisted—the Wilderness Society, and its journal, the *Living Wilderness*, represented the most radical wing of the conservation movement well into the 1970s.

Meanwhile, the radical insurgency of the Depression years affected older conservation groups as well, including the group widely regarded as the oldest: the Audubon Association, which, though its history had in fact been discontinuous, liked to trace its origins back to an earlier New York-based Audubon Society formed in 1886. Feminist Rosalie Edge, a onetime suffragist who became the foremost woman in conservation, led a spirited revolt against the association's corrupt leaders, who had, among other things, rented the group's Louisiana bird sanctuary to hunters and trappers. Largely as a result of her prolonged efforts, assisted by civil libertarian Roger Baldwin, a member of the association's board of directors, the association was substantially reorganized in the mid-1930s. (In 1940 it changed its name to the National Audubon Society.)

President Franklin Roosevelt's New Deal incorporated elements of conservation, provided jobs for conservationists, and did much to establish conservation as a respectable mainstream current. However, as with all movements for social betterment, conservation invariably declines during wartime, and the movement lapsed into quiescence in the first half of the 1940s. The 1945 publication of Lizzie Marsh Wolfe's Pulitzer Prize–winning biography of John Muir, *Son of the Wilderness*, which led to new editions and collections of Muir's own writings, inspired a notable revival, but not for another decade and a half would a conservation-oriented mass movement emerge, for the first time, in the United States. Rachel Carson's best-selling *Silent Spring* (1962), an exposé of the lethal dangers of pesticides, especially DDT, by a marine zoologist who had been one of the first women to hold an important position in the US Fish and Wildlife Service, provoked enormous controversy in the mass media and prompted a vast number of related studies—on smog, asbestos poisoning, black lung disease, cancer-producing substances in food, and so on. Never before had so broad a public been confronted by such urgent life-and-death questions of health in a specifically conservationist context. Out of the widespread agitation sparked by Carson's book, bolstered by the already large opposition to nuclear weapons testing, the environmental movement was born.

From Upton Sinclair and Mary Marcy in the early 1900s to Linus Pauling and Barry Commoner half a century later, socialists had been leading spokespersons of public health issues, but their efforts had not led to any broad-based ongoing organizations focused on such concerns. In the absence of such a grassroots movement, the groundswell of popular protest aroused by *Silent Spring* found organizational expression in the existing conservation groups, which were willing to fill the breach. Of course, these groups were themselves changed in the process: they grew larger, their outlook broadened, and, at least for a time, they tended to become more action-oriented. By implementing the aggressive strategies of David Brower, for example, the Sierra Club, which, during most of its existence, was a narrowly West Coast mountaineering group with a membership of two thousand or three thousand, became a major social force, national in scope, with a membership of well over one hundred thousand by 1970 and nearly a half million in the next decade. Wilderness preservation remained its prime focus, but its perspectives were enlarged to include the entire environment, the whole planet; together with the popular wilderness photo albums by Ansel Adams and Elliot Porter, Sierra Club Books took up the problems of overpopulation, air pollution, and nuclear power.

Central to the transformation of old-time conservationism into contemporary environmentalism was the concept of *ecology*, the science of the interrelations of the various components of the natural world. The word had been coined by German biologist Ernst Haeckel in the 1860s, popularized (albeit in a restricted sociological sense) by Robert E. Park and the "Chicago School" of sociology in the 1920s, and used in its current sense by Aldo Leopold and Robert Marshall in the 1920s and 1930s, but did not enter everyday usage until the 1960s, when the emerging environmental movement made it one of its watchwords and even a battle cry.

The new movement's vociferous opposition to what its spokespersons called "corporate greed," and its strong links to the antinuclear and antiwar movements, gave the impression that environmentalism was solidly on the Left. But in fact the alliance between social radicals and environmentalists began uneasily, with considerable mistrust on both sides. Old and New Left ideologists frequently accused environmentalism of being a "bourgeois" fad to divert public attention from other, supposedly more fundamental issues; for many, this charge seemed to be confirmed by President Richard Nixon's adoption of environmentalist rhetoric and his administration's support of "Earth Day" in 1970, a one-shot day of nationwide environment-related events largely sponsored by Coca-Cola and other multinational corporations that in fact had long-standing anti-conservationist policies. Many environmentalists in turn found the Left quarrelsome, sectarian, and indifferent to wildlife and wilderness concerns. Nonetheless, many radicals recognized the revolutionary implications of the ecological critique, and many more environmentalists perceived that the enemies of their movement and of the environment itself were the traditional enemies of the Left. In the larger milieus beyond groups and factions—in the widespread if short-lived "underground" press, for example, and the broad "counterculture"—the New Left and the new environmentalism mingled and to a great extent fused.

All through the 1970s, as professionalization and bureaucratization diluted much of the militancy and impact of the 1960s environmentalist upsurge and steered the movement's energies toward conventional electoral politics and lobbying, new and more radical revivals of the Muir tradition began to emerge. Pointing out that more wilderness was destroyed in the decade following the passage of the 1964 Wilderness Act than in the preceding five decades, and that most of the funds collected by the established environmental groups went to the advertising agencies that conducted their fund-raising drives, younger eco-radicals developed a new and specifically environmentalist activism that increasingly expressed itself in civil disobedience and direct action. Even before the end of the 1960s, *ecotage* (i.e., sabotage of equipment or property owned by industrial destroyers and polluters of the environment) was recognized as a major problem by industry trade journals; many tens of thousands of rural billboards were destroyed, for example, by "ecoteurs" who regarded such advertising as a hideous disfigurement of the landscape. For several years the daring exploits of a Chicago-area masked man known only as the Fox repeatedly made headlines nationwide, as when he invaded the executive headquarters of US Steel and poured on the office rug buckets of the same dangerous chemical waste the corporation was dumping into Lake Michigan. Greenpeace, founded in 1971, attained worldwide renown almost overnight as a result of its bold, brave interventions in defense of whales, dolphins, seals, and other species endangered by commercial exploitation. Such dramatic actions fired the imaginations of a broad public and contributed mightily to the development of a new surge, and a new "style," of environmental radicalism from the mid-1970s on.

Activist first and foremost, the new radical environmentalism appreciably expanded and deepened conservationist theory. Muir, Thoreau, Bob Marshall, Aldo Leopold, and David Brower remained the brightest stars in the new movement's philosophical firmament, but the younger generation also found much to be learned in the works of

a wide range of social critics not previously regarded from a conservationist perspective. Many loose ends of American radicalism—including
strands of utopianism, anarchism, feminism, the IWW, and heterodox Marxism—have been picked up and developed by proponents
of radical ecology. Ralph Borsodi's and Lewis Mumford's critiques of
technology and urbanism, dating from the 1920s and 1930s, challenged
the centralist assumptions of classical liberalism and Marxism and
stimulated a growing interest in decentralist solutions to social problems. This direction was also pursued, in his later years, by longtime
socialist Scott Nearing, who linked his decentralist vision to vegetar-
ianism and a new back-to-the-land movement, as well as by a former
Trotskyist, Murray Bookchin, in several works relating ecology to anarchism, starting in the 1960s. Frederick Turner's *Beyond Geography:
The Western Spirit Against the Wilderness*, Roderick Nash's *Wilderness
and the American Mind*, Gary Snyder's *The Old Ways*, Ursula Le Guin's
ecotopian novel *Always Coming Home*, and the works of Paul Shepard,
Peter Matthiessen, Bill Devall, and the Canadian Farley Mowat are only
a few of the most influential contributions to radical environmentalist
theory.

Perhaps the most representative of the new radical environmentalist groups, and certainly the purest contemporary expression
of the Muir tradition, is the movement known as Earth First! (the
exclamation point is an essential part of its name), whose motto is No
Compromise in Defense of Mother Earth! Founded in the Southwest in
1980, by the end of the decade it had locals all over the United States
as well as in many other countries and had become by far the largest
and most influential specifically radical environmentalist group in
US history. Not content with demanding the preservation of all existing wilderness, Earth First! calls for the vast *re-creation* of wilderness.
Its avowedly extremist orientation and tactics—hammering spikes
into trees, for example, as an "immunization against logging"—have
sparked heated controversies in the environmental movement and
broad Left. Like the old IWW that it has repeatedly acknowledged as
its major "philosophical forebear," Earth First!'s decentralized ranks
include an impressive number of poets, artists, cartoonists, songwrit-
ers, and musicians—its *Li'l Green Songbook*, like its ecotage manual,
Ecodefense, has gone through many editions—and its direct actions
tend to be guerrilla theater strongly marked by humor. Earth First! has

also been influenced by Kropotkinian anarchism, by anarchist-inclined novelist Edward Abbey, whose ecotage novel *The Monkey Wrench Gang* (1976) provided the movement with much of its original style, and more recently by the theories of "deep ecology" advanced by Norwegian writer Arne Naess, author of studies on Spinoza and Gandhi.

Ideological diversity remains a hallmark not only of Earth First! but of the whole spectrum of radical environmentalism. New Left, IWW, anarchist, feminist, and even Marxist influences are discernible and, indeed, openly avowed, but so are the very different influences of Taoism, Zen Buddhism, and indigenous (so-called primitive) cultures, as well as a radical poets' countertradition extending from William Blake and Emily Brontë to Robinson Jeffers and Philip Lamantia. These latter influences have helped inspire radical ecology's deepening critique of the values and institutions of Western civilization, which in turn has been a growing influence on social radical thought in recent years, resulting in any number of ideological hybrids. Radical environmentalism today includes many distinct currents—it is a long way from the pragmatic Citizens' Clearinghouse for Hazardous Waste to Keith Lampe's visionary *Green Hippie*—and such tendencies as bioregionalism, ecofeminism, deep ecology, and anti-technological neoprimitivism, which only a decade ago appeared esoteric, now claim a substantial number of adherents. Notable, too, is the growing trend toward the involvement of organized labor in environmental struggles; the United Farm Workers union, for example, has been in the forefront of anti-pesticide agitation.

The continuing and, indeed, worsening problems of acid rain, pollution, the greenhouse effect, overpopulation, toxic waste disposal, nuclear power, rainforest destruction, extinction of plant and animal species, and other calamities suffice to assure the vitality and growth of radical environmentalism in the coming years. Efforts to import the ideology and style of the European "Green" movement to American shores have thus far met with small success, but cross-pollination between radical ecology and the more traditional forms of American radicalism will doubtless continue, and it does not require a prophet to predict that ecological concerns will be central to the new New Left of the future.

PART VII

Autobiography and Reminiscences

34

Autobiographical Kaleidoscope

First published in Franklin Rosemont, *The Morning of a Machine Gun* (Chicago: Surrealist Editions, 1968), 63–64.

———

I myself shall continue living in my glass house where you can always see who comes to call; where everything hanging from the ceiling and on the walls stays where it is as if by magic, where I sleep nights in a glass bed, under glass sheets, where who I am will sooner or later appear etched by a diamond.

—André Breton

I was born the second day of October (the same day as Nat Turner) in 1943 and grew up in and around Chicago, home of the blues, non-cinematic gangsters, the Haymarket anarchists, the Industrial Workers of the World, the Water Tower, and the Maxwell Street Market. Armed with Zen lunacy, Nietzsche, Rimbaud, and the first glimmers of the surrealist adventure, I dropped out of high school and hitchhiked west through the giant bones of the Rocky Mountains, the bleeding deserts of Arizona, and the ectodermic forests of California to those clouds of medieval radiance that are San Francisco ...

Chicago is the lever that stands San Francisco on its head; it is the dialectical hammer and veritable pulse of all the American dreams. The latitude, longitude, and temperature of this emotional, temporal, and geographical chaos lead one to the conclusion that, as far as the human imagination is concerned, here and now, it is a question of the Fox Indians, Albert Parsons, Nelson Algren, J.B. Hutto and his Hawks, and the surrealists (a signal enumeration!) against urban renewal, Mayor Daley, capitalists, cops, and the hideous *Tribune*. Urbanism is a problem for poetry and for revolution that sociology only conceals. Insurrection and revolutionary arson are the only "urban renewals" that matter.

I was an IWW organizer from September 1962 to November 1965; during this period I discovered the arcane proletarian revelations of T-Bone Slim (d. 1942). I studied anthropology for two years and went to Mexico in 1963, wandering through the streets of Tenochtitlan for personal illumination. If I believed in reincarnation, in former lives I would have been an Alaskan timber wolf at least once, certainly a Hopi Indian, and perhaps a comrade of Florian Geyer and the Black Troop in the sixteenth-century Peasants' War.

My poems and drawings erupt and flow automatically from my own psychophysical and biomythological totality, and are offered for consideration as modest presentations of the true, delirious, electromagnetic river of surreality. I am a revolutionary mammal, an alchemical atheist, and an aquatic-aerial anarchist as well as a poet. From the past I feel closest to Paracelsus, Han Shan, Blake, Fourier, Nat Turner, Emily Brontë, John Brown, Lautréamont, Marx, Rimbaud, Lewis Carroll, Rosa Luxemburg, Charles Fort, André Breton, Benjamin Péret, Emiliano Zapata, T-Bone Slim, José Guadalupe Posada, Arshile Gorky, Simon Rodia, the blues singers Robert Johnson, Elmore James, and J.B. Lenoir, the Durruti Column, the Kwakiutl Indians, and Marilyn Monroe. I am irresistibly attracted to the Krazy Kat cartoons of George Herriman, the analogies of Malcolm de Chazal, and anything having to do with rabbits, Hegel, Black Hawk, Shays' Rebellion, Nat Turner, the Ferris Wheel, Zoroaster, cocaine, and the Cthulhu Mythos elaborated by H.P. Lovecraft and his circle. In fantasies I often see myself as Bugs Bunny or a zebra. I play rhythm 'n' blues piano and harpsichord. I take this opportunity to spit on the president of the United States and his ignominious war against the Vietnamese.

I live with my woman, Penelope, in the Lincoln Park area of Chicago, a few blocks from the zoo, where several times a week (though less in the winter) we visit the African porcupines, the timber wolves, the nilgai, the gazelles, the secretary bird, the penguins, the elephants, the bushbabies, the giraffes, and the Giant Anteaters. The revolution will liberate these beasts who will collaborate in the reintegration of the waking dream-life of man.

In December 1965 we went to Paris to meet with André Breton and the comrades of the surrealist group. Presently we are issuing an English-language periodical agitational news-poster, *Surrealist Insurrection*, and preparing a surrealist theoretical journal and other publications and actions, including the establishment of a Bureau of Surrealist Research to coordinate the diverse interventions of the marvelous in everyday life, to assist in the elaboration of a liberating mythology, and in general to promote the convergence and synthesis of the real and the imaginary, waking, and dreaming.

In poetry as in life I am for freedom and against slavery: for the Indians against the European invaders and the American exploiters; for the black insurrections against the white power structure; for guerrillas against colonial administrators and imperialist armies; for youth against cops, curfews, school, and conscription; for wildcat strikers against bosses and union bureaucrats; for poetry against literature, philosophy, and religion; for mad love against civilized repression and bourgeois marriage; and for the surrealist revolution against complacency, hypocrisy, cowardice, stupidity, exploitation, and oppression.

35

My Three San Francisco Renaissances

Reprinted from Franklin Rosemont, *An Open Entrance to the Shut Palace of Wrong Numbers* (Chicago: Surrealist Editions, 2003), 34–42.

The San Francisco poetry Renaissance of the late 1950s and early '60s, when the city became the "capital" of the Beat Generation, seemed entirely in the order of things to me. Growing up in Chicago I heard much more about San Francisco than about the city in which I was born and raised. My father loved to tell us stories of his own child-hood on the family's small farm in Mill Valley, and at their printing office, Rosemont Press, at 21 Rosemont Place, a block-long street in the city's Mission District. Even before I started school I knew that we were descendants of refugees from religious persecution in England who had started emigrating to North America around 1640, and settled in such New England villages as Ashby, Boscawen, Hingham, and Winchendon: names that rang the bells of wonderland for me. I knew too that a large part of the New England branch of the family went on to become California pioneers; the first of them, Alexander Putney, had been "One of Fremont's Men" in 1848–49, according to the inscription on his headstone.

I also knew San Francisco was far, far away—"out west," as my father put it—but that did not prevent its holding stage center in my real and imaginary worlds, and it affected just about every phase of my formative years. The first oil paintings I ever saw—I was four or five—were still lives of roses painted by my great-grandmother, Juliet Josephine Petremont, and it was those two dark canvases in black wooden frames that sparked my love of painting, or rather of certain paintings that have, at critical moments in my life, leaped to my eyes.

Around the same time I also discovered the prairie—a struggling remnant of the grand prairie of old but still a magnificent sea of tall grass and wildflowers, gloriously populated by vast numbers of birds, spiders, insects, snakes, rabbits, and thirteen-striped ground squirrels. The prairie was just a little west of our house, but that was enough for my five-year-old mind to link it to San Francisco.

Chancing upon my great-grandmother's paintings and wandering into the wilderness were my earliest experiences of *enchantment*.

Besides being an artist, Petremont—known in the family as "Mamère"—also taught French and "deportment" to children of the Forty-Niners. Physically small to the point of daintiness (her dancing slippers were size three), she was nonetheless considered a "powerful presence" and perhaps just a wee bit eccentric, for she sported a man's silk top hat and smoked cigars. She died thirty-two years before I was born, but she has remained a powerful presence for me. Her husband was a musician and music printer, and for many years their music store at Kearny and Sutton was one of the largest purveyors of sheet music west of the Mississippi. They named their son (my grandfather) Ludwig von Beethoven, but with characteristically Far West informality Grandpa Rosemont shortened it to L. Budd. Unpretentious, reckless enthusiasm seemed to me to describe their whole way of life, and I was especially charmed by what I heard of the immense freedom enjoyed by the next (my father's) generation of California Rosemont children. When the printing business on Rosemont Place (later it moved for a time to Sycamore) kept my grandparents at work in the city for extended periods, most if not all of their eight youngsters—ranging in age from mid-teen to toddler—often stayed at the farm for weeks at a time, caring for the horse, cow, chickens, geese, and above all the many dogs, for the California Rosemonts were also active in the purebred dog business and organizers of major dog shows. With their penchant for mutual aid, group singing, in-house plays, family meetings, and making their own ice cream and root beer, the children carried on much like the characters in Louisa May Alcott's *Little Women*—which, by the way, was a family favorite.

The young majority tended to rule the roost even in the house on Rosemont Place, in the city. Although tradition has it that in earlier years Mark Twain had been a guest for a week or two, the family dwelling-place—which took up a sizeable chunk of the block—was never exactly a boardinghouse. It was home, however—for a night, or a week, and sometimes much longer—for countless visitors, most but not all of them the children's friends. As my father told it, rare were the evening suppers without at least two or three newcomers sitting in; Grandpa Rosemont's standard query, "And *whose* are you?"—always asked in a genial, welcoming way—signified "Which of my children invited you to join us at our table?"

Even my mother, daughter of Polish immigrants and a lifelong Chicagoan, added appreciably to this rampant Rosemontian San Franciscoism. As a professional musician (accordion, piano, vocals), and leader of the Sally Kaye Trio, one of her gigs involved entertaining a whole trainload of conventioneers and their wives on a two-week trip to and from—yes, San Francisco! According to family legend, that trip occasioned my first experience with the phone. There I was, not quite five, listening to my mother—the onetime "Boop-boop-a-doo Girl" of the Chicago Theatre and star of "The Streets of Paris" at the 1933–34 Chicago World's Fair—talking *and singing* to me on the telephone, long-distance from San Francisco.

All this genealogical, autobiographical preambling is meant to drive home the point that, in at least one little house on Chicago's western extremity during the dark and dreary close of the 1940s, the spirit of Old San Francisco was still young, and that at least one adventurous preschooler took it to heart. My "knowledge" of the place, of course, consisted almost entirely of fantasies, only lightly seasoned with facts. Between the ages of four and twelve, my "image" of San Francisco—which amounted to a personal myth—blended elements of many worlds: the Wild West, Hopalong Cassidy, the *Cinnamon Bear* radio saga, *The Wizard of Oz* movie, the *Foodini* show on early TV, Dixie Willson's story "The Train That Went Traveling," tales of pirates and buried treasure, towering mountains, vast giant redwood forests, music, painting, and all the arts, a freewheeling communal way of life, printing with moveable type, red roses everywhere, and (by no means least) little or no school. For me, the city "out west" was a kind of children's utopia characterized by freedom, wilderness, creative eccentricity, lots of dogs to romp with, and cable cars to ride on night and day.

Rather disconcertingly, my visualizations of this mythic realm, drawing on my father's rambling stories, old snapshots and postcards, fleeting scenes in incomprehensible movies, and photos from *Western*

Kennel World (mailed to us each month direct from Rosemont Press), also incorporated images of the late Middle Ages and early Renaissance: Uccello's Florence and Dürer's Nuremberg. I suspect this confabulation resulted from my father's attempt to explain to his five-year-old son the origins and meaning of the name "San Francisco." In any event, for me, the boundaries between "out west" and "once upon a time, long, long ago" remained blurred for many years.

Having grown up in a household that quietly but steadily celebrated a miniature San Francisco Renaissance all its own, I continued even as a teenager to think of myself as a kind of San Franciscan in exile. All along I knew in my bones that someday I would head out west and visit my ancestral "home away from home." By 1960, as a discontented high schooler learning the fine art of hitchhiking, I decided that now was the time. A few miles west of Chicago I stuck out my thumb; seventy-two hours later I reached the West Coast.

In 1960 San Francisco was in the midst of a Renaissance so boisterous that it made headlines around the world. As a militant partisan of the Beat Generation at Proviso High, and a regular reader of *Big Table* and *Evergreen Review*, I had followed every twist and turn of this Renaissance since 1958, and naturally—despite the fact that I lived a mere two thousand miles away—I considered myself a participant. When I finally got there, my experiences of déjà vu were so many and close between that I almost felt like an old-timer; I was in fact sixteen, but most of the people I met, especially those close to my own age, were new to the city and knew nothing of its history or traditions. Dizzy with the joy of discovery, and full of enthusiasm for the future, I spent most of my time wandering the streets, sitting and reading in the old easy chairs at City Lights Books, and talking with poets and jazz people at the Co-Existence Bagel Shop.

As it happened, most of the poets I had hoped to meet in San Francisco (including Bob Kaufman, Philip Lamantia, and Gary Snyder) were either far away or laying low. One evening I was pleased to run into Lawrence Ferlinghetti at City Lights, but business was brisk and we spoke only for a few minutes. The friends I made at that time, however— Shig Murao and Dick McBride at City Lights; Robert Stock, who tended bar at the Bagel Shop; and several whom I knew only by their first names, most notably a young African American philosopher-poet, Tyrone—fully embodied the practical utopianism and spirit of improvisation that figured so prominently in the one-house San Francisco Renaissance of my Chicago childhood. The sense of community, solidarity, creativity, and mutual aid in the North Beach Beat scene seemed to me to reflect, on a grand scale, all that I had heard of the collective vitality and adventurousness of the California Rosemonts of the 1890s through the early 1920s.

In the 1960 San Francisco Renaissance, the "experimental life" flourished as nowhere else, and part of the experimentation involved herbs and substances that the US government had declared illegal. As is so often the case when a new free spirit is in the wind, the local police were notorious for their brutality, which they largely directed against peaceful "beatniks" and jazz musicians. Although "possession or sale of illegal drugs" was a frequent pretext for that brutality, the real reason was well known: North Beach was a racially integrated community and, as such, an affront to the white supremacist cops.

During the two months that I lived there, drug use was a rather minor pursuit among the people I knew. LSD and mescaline were often discussed, but nobody ever seemed to have any. From time to time, someone passed around a reefer. A few folks had prescriptions for dexedrine (which never attracted me; I was frantic enough already).

The really dangerous, deadly drugs were commonly called "over-the-counter" and "legal" drugs, for the simple reason that they were on sale at drugstores everywhere. One of these legal drugs, known as Asthmador, was an alleged treatment for asthma. For a few weeks in the fall of 1960, among a small minority of young North Beach poets and assorted cognoscenti, Asthmador was something of a fad: a "guaranteed" provoker of "weird" and "interesting" hallucinations. It was readily available at a special low price at a drugstore of dubious virtue known as The Hub, which was open all night and frequented by many North Beach residents looking for legal "highs."

As a zealous reader of Rimbaud, I decided to see what Asthmador could do. Because I was six feet tall and weighed 160 pounds, it was suggested that I take twice the recommended dose. Because I was sixteen and didn't know any better, I took a triple dose.

For half an hour, nothing happened. It was early evening, and I was out walking, impatient for something to happen and wondering whether I should take yet another dose. And then, out of nowhere, a friend from the Bagel Shop appeared, coming from the opposite direction, and we stood there and talked for a few minutes before going our separate ways. Something about this conversation struck me as a little odd, and when I turned around, my friend had disappeared.

"Uh-oh," said I to myself, "the Asthmador must be working at last." Fortunately, I had a place to stay. A jazz bass player friend had a pad on Laguna Street paid up to the end of the month, but he had to go home to Sonora for a few days, maybe longer, because of illness in the family. He had given me his key and told me that as long as I came in after dark and left early in the morning, there'd be no hassle with the building manager. I hurried off to the Laguna Street pad, third floor, hallucinating all the way.

The hallucinations were not only "interesting" and "weird," they were also terrifying and overwhelming. An endless noisy procession of demons, devils, monsters, composite beings, and phantasmagoric characters worthy of *Bugs Bunny and the Magic Sneeze* cavorted all over the ceiling, walls, and furniture—appearing, disappearing, constantly changing. With my eyes open or shut all I saw was nightmare after nightmare. A lamp that had changed into a lizard went on to become, in rapid succession, a bird of prey, the MGM movie lion, and Francis Marion, the "Swamp Fox" of the Revolution. Anything and everything kept changing into anything and everything else. Time was in flux, or in reverse—the "world" I was in had a lot in common with the fifteenth century. This Renaissance was not, however, that of Raphael or Leonardo, but rather of Hieronymus Bosch, with a dash of Tex Avery thrown in.

At one point I opened the closet and beheld the brass monkey trio—See No Evil, Hear No Evil, Speak No Evil—three feet tall, giggling, and thoroughly evil. Horrified, I shut the door quickly, lay down on the bed, and tried again (unsuccessfully) to sleep. Several times in the course of that terrorsome night I looked in the closet again and was barely able to suppress a scream when I found those malevolent monkeys still there, still giggling. Hours later, when I looked yet again, I was just as scared to find them gone!

Interspersed with these visions of gloom, foreboding, and cosmic terror were many calm encounters with people I knew. Aside from the fact that these visitors were not really there, our conversations were not particularly extraordinary. I hallucinated several friends from the Co-Existence Bagel Shop and other hangouts, and for the most part we talked about matters at hand. Here was poet Robert Stock, who assured me that the "state" I was in wouldn't last forever, that it would subside before too long, that soon I would be able to look back on it all and laugh. And there was Shig from City Lights, telling me that this sort of thing happens to all poets—that I should just relax and chalk it up to experience. My friend Tyrone also showed up in these visions and contributed a few characteristically sagacious words of his own. And here too was Lawrence Ferlinghetti himself, not saying a word, but smiling—exactly as he had smiled at City Lights that busy evening when a fellow I had met the day before had said "Well, we meet again" and I replied, idiotically: "It's the smallest of all possible worlds." Now, in the sheer hell on Laguna Street, third floor, this bon mot of mine took on a new and cataclysmic meaning.

Late that night, around 2:00 a.m., looking out the window, I was astonished to see Hedy Lamarr (looking as she did in her 1940s films) sitting on a tree limb just a few feet away and beckoning to me. I opened the window and climbed out onto the tree's largest limb. By then, Ms. Lamarr herself had vanished, but a large, framed photograph of her had been left in her place. As I ventured a little closer toward it, someone yelled: "Hey, what the hell do you think you're doing?" I knew that this was an intrusion of "reality"—that those words were intended for me—even before the shouter added: "Get out of that tree or I'll call the police!"

So there I was, out on a limb in a tall tree in the apartment court-yard at 2:00 a.m., inching my way back to the third-floor window. As I climbed into my room, I felt cold, exhausted, and, truth to tell, a little sorry for myself. Closing the window, I glanced back and noticed that the photo of Hedy Lamarr was gone.

For a few minutes I thought that the voice from the "real world" and the cold air had brought me out of the nightmare and that I was now "back to normal" at last. Alas, in no time at all the multiplication of unusual creatures in the room persuaded me that the hallucinations had started up again, with a vengeance.

And so it went for another agonizingly long night and day. By the third day, I was convinced that I would never recover; that I was doomed to keep hallucinating for the rest of my life; that the Asthmador had destroyed large areas of my brain; that I had stupidly messed up my whole life—in short, that all was lost.

And then, suddenly, the telephone rang!

I must have jumped at least three feet in the air. But as it rang and rang, again and again, I persuaded myself that this was probably just another auditory hallucination, so I slowly sat down on the bed and did my best to ignore it. Staring at the phone and pretending not to hear it, I listened to it ring for two, maybe three years. I wondered what to do. Feeling as I did like an alien from an unknown planet, I wasn't sure I wanted to talk with anyone from Earth.

For some reason, I eventually picked up the phone and said "Hello?" No matter who it was, I was determined to bluff my way through.

Amazingly, it was my friend the bass player—the guy whose room I was staying in. The fact that no one else knew I could be reached at that number had not occurred to me.

"Hey, man," my friend said. "What's happening?"

I stammered back that I was feeling a bit "out of it," but that basically I was all right, sort of, more or less.

"You sound a little funny," he said.

"I *feel* a little funny," was my snappy reply.

"Oho!" he replied. "I think I know what you're saying. You haven't been over to The Hub, have you?"

"Well," said I, "I don't really want to go into all that right now."

"Okay, man," he said, laughing a little, "but are you sure you're okay?"

When I insisted I was fine he said "Be cool" and hung up.

Oddly enough, I did in fact feel much better. After that unexpected call, the hallucinations—with a few minor exceptions—went away and stayed away. For me, life started all over again.

A couple hours later I called home to Chicago and did what I considered a fairly good imitation of a normal human being. Neither of my parents seemed to think I sounded "funny," and they really put me to the test with a barrage of questions. Yes, I had been to Rosemont Place and Chinatown and Muir Woods and had ridden cable cars and crossed the Golden Gate Bridge several times; and yes, I was fine, had a nice place to stay, and even had a job of sorts, selling the weekly *San Francisco Star*, an early "underground" paper. By the time I hung up, I realized that my sense perception was fully restored, and in fact heightened by a strong feeling of *elation*, which, by the way, lasted for days. In my own personal *renascence*, the nightmares were over.

The active ingredient in Asthmador was belladonna, also known as nightshade, the powerful medicinal and hallucinogenic properties of which have been known for ages. Some scholars have argued that Hieronymus Bosch, as a member of the Brotherhood of the Free Spirit, which used the drug in certain rituals, was familiar with it. The opening sentence of the second canto of *Les Chants de Maldoror* refers to Maldoror's mouth "full of belladonna leaves." For generations it was a standard household remedy. One of the youngest characters in *Little Women*, coming down with "headache, sore throat, and queer feelings," takes belladonna for relief.

In my three-day nightmare journey, belladonna was clearly the active element, but the telephone—its passive accomplice—played a critical role as well. My friend's call, however innocuous, served as the "Voice from Outside" that is so important in vision-seeking and other shamanic experiences. This was not a Wrong Number, but an unhoped-for call that allowed me to escape from a whirlpool of wrongness.

Simply by dialing his own number (which was no longer his), my friend unwittingly provided an example of a "wake-up call" in the truest and most prophetic import of the word: a sudden, simultaneous reawakening of the senses, mind, and spirit. In the wink of an eye I emerged from the pit of despair and soared to the heights of ecstasy. I felt not only renewed but also *reborn*.

The whole experience—vision quest, descent to the underworld, and rite of passage—marked a decisive turning point in my life. For three days that seemed centuries, in a state of agonizing intensity, fearful anguish, and total despair (I was sure I was going to die at any moment), I lived and dreamed the wildest Transcendentalist abandon, an *Argonautica*, a *Season in Hell*, and I emerged from these despondent wanderings a new person: *another* "I" that superseded all my previous I's.

Afterword

Paul Buhle

Franklin Rosemont (1943–2009) is widely remembered as a key reanimator of a historic but seemingly discontinuous surrealist movement. This dramatic avant-garde impulse, embraced in the 1920s by leading artists and writers, diminished considerably in its visibility and art world prestige by the 1940s. Critics, especially hostile critics, treated surrealism as a force both spent and transcended. The rise of fascism and the Second World War had seemingly overwhelmed all previous and vastly hopeful visions of the fantastic. Circles of artists and activists seemed to disappear from public sight.

By the time the 1960s came around, a generation or so later, the contemporary rise of market-friendly "youth culture" and new age mysticism together seemed to reintroduce parts of the language of surrealism's founders but mostly in the most misleading ways. The terms *surrealism* and *surrealistic* appeared widely as vague adjectives or consumer appeals. Against all this, Franklin Rosemont devoted himself to reviving and expanding the aims and practices of the original. He continued this work for the rest of his life, in a wide variety of ways, as poet, historian, artist, editor, and group leader.

Rosemont did something remarkable along the way. He gathered around himself and coworker and partner Penelope (Penny) a series of collaborators sharing the same vision and, just as important, reestablished lines of communication and solidarity with old-timers, former members, or sympathizers around the world. Thereby, he reestablished a tradition and encouraged newer generations of surrealists to emerge, an accomplishment that has become more clear and vital since his passing, especially in the Global South.

He did something else as well. Drawing deeply on his childhood fascinations, making discoveries of many kinds from obvious and erudite sources alike, Rosemont patterned his own vision of what may be called "popular culture from below." His overall contribution in this vein eludes any synthesis, no doubt because the subject matter is vast, as vast as the categories of this anthology and still larger. An underlying way of thinking and understanding is nevertheless clear. In some way or other, actually in many different ways, the thirst for freedom and free expression, and the presence of these in creative individuals and groups, permeates everything that he admired and sought to explain to readers.

His own very personal experience revolved, in crucial ways, around Chicago, his lifelong residence. Home to a huge and infinitely diverse industrial working class, rich with ethnic and racial cultures, Chicago was naturally the birthplace of the Industrial Workers of the World, the home of post–World War II blues music, and a thriving community of artists and intellectuals largely outside of academia or other institutions.

Chicago, massively exploitative, wasteful, and brutal, fell onto hard times even before industry moved elsewhere during the 1970s and 1980s. The rich became richer as working-class influence diminished and nonwhites in particular met the worst of the so-called American Dream. The very sense of a city of diverse communities suffered badly. The assorted rebellions of young people and others in the dynamic moments of the 1960s found Chicago at the center, with the protests at the Democratic National Convention of 1968 as an apex. And then capital took its revenge, anticipating and playing a large part in the neoliberal era to follow.

Franklin Rosemont dearly loved the older Chicago and recorded, as keenly as anyone, the significance of its passing. He was perfectly placed to do so by virtue of his parents, a noted print-trade union-ist father and a mother active in public arts. His instinctive feelings for the almost but not quite vanished older Chicago cultures could be described as symbolically marked by the presence of the IWW's national headquarters, with old-timers somehow holding on as waves of younger people drifted in and out. The *Rebel Worker* (1963–66) might be described best as a bridge between old and new but also as an expression of his own personal exuberance and commitment.

Much of what appears in this volume possesses an immediate, ardent feeling for the material, a feeling all too rare in academic life. It is closer in tone, perhaps, to writings of the older generations of journalists, a few of them columnists for Chicago newspapers in days of yellow press glory, or, alternatively, closer to that of radio inter-viewer Studs Terkel, a Chicago personality very much on the local scene from Franklin's youth to middle age. Discovering the odd facets of urban life, the precious details of small hopes or rebellions, gave Rosemont a veritable universe of interests. If one looked for a more mainstream, twenty-first-century counterpart, one might suggest the socialistic comic artist Ben Katchor, whose books have imaginatively re-created city scenes and a city language of greater New York, redolent of pungent, hilarious details.

Rosemont wrote about his favorite comic strips, for instance, with the vigor of a grown child who could return to boyhood favorites and find something that no one else had seen so insightfully. He thus anticipated the scholars, for instance, of *Krazy Kat* and, further ahead, the twenty-first-century online journals of comic art that he did not live to see. He had no academic referees to evaluate his commentary, no restraints on the language of his appreciations and complaints. Sometimes his playful analyses covered strips already widely writ-ten about, like *Dick Tracy*. Just as often, he uncovered the obscure. If *Smokey Stover* has yet been analyzed closely by anyone else, it would be a surprise.

The same is largely true of his fondness for the heroes of anima-tion, a genre widely popular but little appreciated in critical terms until the 1970s and 1980s, beyond specialists and fan literature of limited circulation.

Something different but intimately related might be said about his fondness for blues, jazz, and modern dance. In each case, he deter-minedly sought to rescue modernism from its devotees and enemies alike. Here too, however, he also determined to mine the historical back-ground buried deep in the culture and in danger of being forgotten or misunderstood. Thus he found a precursor in the young revolutionary Louis C. Fraina, a key socialist intellectual of the 1910s and sometime editor of the short-lived magazine *Modern Dance*, who commented acutely that people, ordinary people, were becoming or seeking to become artists in their own lives. This observation glistened in an era of blue-collar youngsters newly "jazz dancing," of self-conscious bohe-mians reading *The Masses* magazine in a dozen cities and a handful associating themselves with the pre-surrealist Dada movement, and of Harlem arising as the center of the Black world civilization.

That Franklin Rosemont, if determinedly playful, was also a perfectly serious socialist and revolutionary becomes clear to readers with his studies of radical environmentalism. His sharing of his favorites' vision of freedom in nature showed his sensibility of freedom as both vision and practice.

But playfulness is the final note to strike here. Free play recalled to Rosemont childhood joys and a distinct way of seeing life's possibilities. This is a volume of his personal discoveries made available to others.

The visages of young Penny and Franklin Rosemont, in a comic story written by Penny and published as part of *Students for a Democratic Society: A Graphic History* (2008), offered an angle on popular culture not quite encompassed in Franklin Rosemont's ruminations. "My Life in SDS" carries the couple forward from their first meeting through the end of 1969 and beyond. With artwork by Gary Dumm, in a volume mostly written by alternative comics giant Harvey Pekar, it only hints at surrealism as an art form. In the anthology *Wobblies! A Graphic History of the Industrial Workers of the World* (2005), two stories arguably go further: "Wobblies in the '60s," written by Franklin Rosemont, with artwork by Mike Konopacki, and "College of Complexes," written and drawn by surrealist sympathizer Jerome Neukirch.

Memories of poet Philip Lamantia by Penny Rosemont and Nancy Joyce Peters in *The Beats* (2009), drawn by Summer McClinton, perhaps comprise the apex of surrealist-influenced graphic narratives, along with "The Janitor" by Jerome Neukirch, in the same book, about Chicago's College of Complexes. The portrayal of African American modern dancers Katherine Dunham and Pearl Primus in *Bohemians* (2014), by Lance Tooks, is also noteworthy in this regard.

Did it matter when surrealism itself became an object of popular culture creation? As editor or coeditor of the graphic histories just referenced, I think these are questions worth asking. Along with the fresh attention to surrealism in museum exhibits, in academia, and especially by artists in the Global South, they allow new interpretations of surrealism's past and its further trajectory. Here, it is fair to say, no orthodoxy rules, and a good thing: the inspiration is unconfined and, as the scholars have shown us, even the past is now reopened as its inspiration is renewed.

Notes

Introduction

1   Paul Buhle and David Wagner, untitled editorial statement, *Cultural Correspondence*, no. 1 (August 1975): 1. Buhle remained involved with *Radical America* until 1973.

2   Paul Buhle, "Introduction: The 1960s Meet the 1980s," in *Popular Culture in America*, ed. Paul Buhle (Minneapolis: University of Minnesota Press, 1987), xx.

3   Buhle, "The 1960s Meet the 1980s," xx.

4   Buhle, "The 1960s Meet the 1980s," xi.

5   Buhle, "The 1960s Meet the 1980s," xx.

6   Buhle, "The 1960s Meet the 1980s," xx.

7   Buhle, "The 1960s Meet the 1980s," xxii.

8   Franklin Rosemont and Charles Radcliffe, eds., *Dancin' in the Streets! Anarchists, IWWs, Surrealists, Situationists and Provos in the 1960s as Recorded in the Pages of "The Rebel Worker" and "Heatwave"* (Chicago: Charles H. Kerr, 2005), 40. Charles Radcliffe, who became friends with Franklin Rosemont in 1966, shared many of Rosemont's affinities for popular culture, as evidenced in Radcliffe's journal *Heatwave* (London), of which two issues were published, in July and October 1966. See also Charles Radcliffe, *Don't Start Me Talking: Subculture, Situationism and the Sixties* (n.p.: Bread & Circuses, 2018).

9   Abigail Susik, "Chicago Surrealism, Herbert Marcuse, and the Affirmation of the 'Present and Future Viability of Surrealism,'" *Journal of Surrealism and the Americas* 11, no. 1 (2020): 42–62. On "affirmative culture," see Herbert Marcuse, "The Affirmative Character of Culture," in *Negations: Essays in Critical Theory* (London: MayFly Books, 2009), 70.

10 Penelope Rosemont, interview with Susik, September 2, 2022.

11 Hal Rammel, email to Susik, September 30, 2022.

12 Penelope Rosemont, email to Susik, March 10, 2023.

13 Rosemont and Radcliffe, *Dancin' in the Streets!*, 6–8; and Kate Khatib, "Surrealism's America: Notes on a Vernacular Epistemology" (PhD diss., Johns Hopkins University, 2013), 13.

14 Penelope Rosemont, interview with Susik, February 8, 2020.

15 Penelope Rosemont, email to Susik, March 10, 2023.

16 Abigail Susik, *Surrealist Sabotage and the War on Work* (Manchester, UK: Manchester University Press, 2021), 188.

17 Joan Smith (Nyala) Cooper, "Rebel Worker About Change: Person to Nation," in *Rise of the Phoenix: Voices from Chicago's Black Struggle, 1960-1975*, ed. Useni Eugene Perkins (Chicago: Third World Press Foundation, 2017), 162–73.

18 Later in life, Rosemont became more critical of rock 'n' roll. Joanna Pawlik, "The Comic Book Conditions of Chicago Surrealism," in *Surrealism, Science Fiction and*

Comics, ed. Gavin Parkinson (Liverpool, UK: Liverpool University Press, 2015), 129–54.

19   Rosemont and Radcliffe, *Dancin' in the Streets!*, 17. On the subject of vernacular surrealism, see Joanna Pawlik, "Cartooning the Marvelous: Word and Image in Chicago Surrealism," in *Mixed Messages: American Correspondences in Visual and Verbal Practices*, ed. Catherine Gander and Sarah Garland (Manchester, UK: Manchester University Press, 2016), 67–84; and Khatib, "Surrealism's America," 29. On the rebel workers' attraction to the IWW culture, see Franklin Rosemont, "The Seismograph of Subversion: Notes on Some American Precursors," in "Surrealism in the Service of the Revolution," special issue, *Radical America* 4, no. 1 (January 1970): 50–63 [included as chapter 1 in this volume].

20   Rosemont and Radcliffe, *Dancin' in the Streets!*, 17 (emphasis in original).

21   Joanna Pawlik, *Remade in America: Surrealist Art, Activism, and Politics, 1940–1978* (Berkeley: University of California Press, 2021), 199.

22   Letter from Franklin Rosemont to Paul Buhle, April 20, 1968, Radical America Records, 1966–75, ms 271, box 3, folder 11, Wisconsin Historical Society, Madison.

23   Untitled tract ("Lisez/ne lisez pas") (1931), in *Tracts surréalistes et déclarations collectives: 1922–1939*, ed. José Pierre (Paris: Le Terrain Vague, 1980), 202, 454–55.

24   Abigail Susik, "Surrealism and Jules Verne: Navigating Context, Intertext and Subtext for a Collage by Max Ernst," in *Surrealism, Science Fiction and Comics*, ed. Gavin Parkinson (Liverpool, UK: Liverpool University Press, 2015), 16–39.

25   See, for instance, Robin Walz, *Pulp Surrealism: Insolent Popular Culture in Early Twentieth-Century Paris* (Berkeley: University of California Press, 2000).

26   Franklin Rosemont, "Humor: Here Today and Everywhere Tomorrow," *Arsenal/ Surrealist Subversion*, no. 4 (1989): 84 [included as chapter 31 in this volume]. See also Pawlik, "Comic Book Conditions," 145–47; and Pawlik, *Remade in America*, 211–13.

27   Penelope Rosemont, *Surrealism: Inside the Magnetic Fields* (San Francisco: City Lights, 2019), 24–25, 34–35, 40–41, 48–49.

28   Rosemont, *Surrealism*, 35, 48.

29   Rosemont, *Surrealism*, 27.

30   Claire Boustani, "Entretien avec Alain Joubert," in *Art et mythe*, ed. Fabrice Flahutez and Thierry Dufrêne (Nanterre, France: Presses universitaires de Paris Nanterre, 2011), 157.

31   Joanna Pawlik, "USA," in *The International Encyclopedia of Surrealism*, ed. Michael Richardson et al. (London: Bloomsbury Press, 2019), 139–48. See also Pawlik, *Remade in America*, 195–228.

32   Franklin Rosemont and David R. Roediger, eds., *Haymarket Scrapbook: 125th Anniversary Edition* (Oakland: AK Press; Chicago: Charles H. Kerr, 2012); Ron Sakolsky, ed., *Surrealist Subversions: Rants, Writings and Images by the Surrealist Movement in the United States* (New York: Autonomedia, 2003); and Ron Sakolsky, *Dreams of Anarchy and the Anarchy of Dreams: Adventures at the Intersection of Anarchy and Surrealism* (New York: Autonomedia, 2021).

33   Franklin Rosemont, *Joe Hill: The IWW and the Making of a Revolutionary Workingclass Counterculture* (Chicago: Charles H. Kerr, 2003). For an overview of surrealist activism, see Abigail Susik and Elliott H. King, "Surrealism as Radicalism," in *Radical Dreams: Surrealism, Counterculture, Resistance*, eds. Elliott H. King and Abigail Susik (State College, PA: Penn State University Press, 2021), 2–19.

34   See, for example, Paul Garon, *Blues and the Poetic Spirit* (New York: Da Capo

Press, 1979). We include in this anthology essays by Rosemont from the January–February 1976 edition of the journal *Living Blues* (no. 25), all of which were influenced by Garon, a cofounder of that publication.

35   Franklin Rosemont, Penelope Rosemont, and Paul Garon, eds., *The Forecast Is Hot! Tracts and Other Collective Declarations of the Surrealist Movement in the United States, 1966–1976* (Chicago: Black Swan Press, 1997); and Abigail Susik, "Subcultural Receptions of Surrealism in the 1960s International Underground Press: *Resurgence* and Other Publications," in *Cambridge Critical Concepts: Surrealism*, ed. Natalya Lusty (Cambridge: Cambridge University Press, 2021), 380–400.

36   Postcard from Franklin and Penelope Rosemont to Paul Buhle, 1970, Radical America Records, 1966–75, ms 271, box 3, folder 11, Wisconsin Historical Society, Madison.

37   Franklin Rosemont, "Free Play and No Limit: An Introduction to Edward Bellamy's Utopia," in "Surrealism and Its Popular Accomplices," special issue, ed. Franklin Rosemont, *Cultural Correspondence*, nos. 10–11 (Fall 1979): 7 [included as chapter 4 in this volume]. Pawlik also writes about Rosemont's Bellamy essay in "Comic Book Conditions," 150–51.

38   Rosemont, "Free Play and No Limit," 15.

39   Rosemont, "Free Play and No Limit," 12.

40   Rosemont, "Free Play and No Limit," 13.

41   Franklin Rosemont, "A Bomb-Toting, Long-Haired, Wild-Eyed Fiend: The Image of the Anarchist in Popular Culture," in Rosemont and Roediger, *Haymarket Scrapbook*, 203–12 [included as chapter 5 in this volume]. For another example of Rosemont's combination of surrealism with American popular culture, see "Rats Live on No Evil Star: A Selection of Palindromes," *Free Spirits: Annals of the Insurgent Imagination*, no. 1 (1982): 153–54 [included as chapter 30 in this volume].

42   Rosemont, "Wild-Eyed Fiend," 209.

43   Pawlik, "Comic Book Conditions," 131–32; and Sandra R. Zalman, "The Vernacular as Vanguard: Alfred Barr, Salvador Dalí, and the U.S. Reception of Surrealism in the 1930s," *Journal of Surrealism and the Americas*, no. 1 (2007): 44–67.

44   Pawlik, "Comic Book Conditions," 132.

45   Pawlik, "Comic Book Conditions," 132 (emphasis in original).

46   Rosemont, "Humor," 83.

47   Rosemont, "Humor," 83.

48   Rosemont, Rosemont, and Garon, *Forecast Is Hot!*, xxviii (emphasis in original).

49   Roland Barthes, *Mythologies*, trans. Annette Lavers (New York: Hill and Wang, 1972), 135–36 (emphasis in original).

50   Barthes, *Mythologies*, 135.

2   Notes on the Legacy of Cthulhu

1   A few years after Rosemont published "Notes on the Legacy of Cthulhu" in *Arsenal/Surrealist Subversion* no. 3 from 1976, he published another short essay on Lovecraft in which he briefly discusses Lovecraft's racism. Rosemont writes, "Elsewhere in the same letter he affirms his commitment to anti-fascism and the labor movement. He had long before outgrown the provincial racism and conservatism that disfigured some of his early 1920s letters. But in this last unfinished text we see how far the author of 'The Call of Cthulhu' had advanced on the road of revolutionary clarity." Franklin Rosemont, "Lovecraft, Surrealism and Revolution," *Cultural Correspondence*, "Surrealism and Its Popular Accomplices," guest-edited by Franklin Rosemont, nos. 10–11 (Fall 1979): 17.

4 Free Play and No Limit: An Introduction to Edward Bellamy's *Utopia*

1   All quotations from Bellamy, unless otherwise specified, are from *Looking Backward* (Boston: Ticknor & Co., 1888), *Equality* (New York: D. Appleton & Co., 1897), and *Edward Bellamy Speaks Again!* (Kansas City, MO: Peerage Press, 1937). "The Religion of Solidarity" is included in Edward Bellamy, *Selected Writings on Religion and Society*, ed. Joseph Schiffman (New York: Liberal Arts, 1955).

2   Sylvia E. Bowman's *Edward Bellamy Abroad* (New York: Twayne, 1962) traces Bellamy's influence in twenty-eight countries. The bibliography lists eighty translations of *Looking Backward*, into twenty-three languages.

3   The best sources remain Arthur E. Morgan, *Edward Bellamy* (New York: Columbia, 1944), and Howard H. Quint, *The Forging of American Socialism* (Indianapolis: Bobbs-Merrill, 1964).

4   Morgan, *Edward Bellamy*, 155.

5   Edward Bellamy, "How I Wrote Looking Backward." In *Edward Bellamy Speaks Again!* (Kansas City, MO: Peerage Press, 1937), 221.

6   W.D. Howells, preface to E. Bellamy, *The Blindman's Tale and Other Stories* (Boston: Houghton Mifflin, 1898), vi.

7   André Breton, "Le merveilleux contre le mystère," in *La clé des champs* (Paris: Éditions du Sagittaire, 1953).

8   Marjorie Louise Henry, *Stuart Merrill: La contribution d'un Americain au symbolisme français* (Paris: É. Champion, 1927).

5 A Bomb-Toting, Long-Haired, Wild-Eyed Fiend: The Image of the Anarchist in Popular Culture

1   Nhat Hong, *The Anarchist Beast* (Minneapolis: Soil of Liberty, c. 1978).

2   Hugh Henry Brackenridge, *Modern Chivalry* (Philadelphia: Peterson, 1857), 61. Part 1 of this work was completed by 1797.

3   J.W. Buel, *Russian Nihilism and Exile Life in Siberia* (St. Louis: Historical Publishing Co., 1883), 186.

4   Josiah Strong, *Our Country: Its Possible Future and Present Crisis*, quoted in David Brion Davis, *The Fear of Conspiracy* (Ithaca, NY: Cornell University Press, 1971), 174–75.

5   Richard T. Ely, *The Labor Movement in the U.S.* (New York: Thomas Y. Crowell & Co., 1886), 291.

6   Nina van Zandt, in August Spies, *August Spies' Autobiography* (Chicago: Nina van Zandt, 1887), 85.

7   August Spies, *August Spies' Autobiography*, 73.

8   Oscar Neebe, in Albert R. Parsons, *Anarchism* (Chicago: Mrs. A.R. Parsons, 1887), 73.

9   John P. Altgeld, *Reasons for Pardoning the Haymarket Anarchists* (Chicago: Charles H. Kerr, 1986), 46.

10 Paul Avrich, *The Haymarket Tragedy* (Princeton, NJ: Princeton University Press, 1984), 61.

11 Johann Most's *Science of Revolutionary Warfare* had predicted "that airships would one day be able to drop dynamite on military parades attended by emperors and kings." Avrich, *Haymarket Tragedy*, 165.

12 *Hartmann the Anarchist* was reprinted in the magazine *Forgotten Fantasy* in June and August 1971. An introductory note by the editor stated that many of the ideas expressed by Hartmann could be taken straight from the revolutionary speeches and writings of "today's radicals."

13   Much science fiction, however, is implicitly anarchist. See John Pilgrim, "Science Fiction and Anarchism," *Anarchy* (London), December 1963.

14   Philip S. Foner, "A Martyr to His Cause: The Scenario of the First Labor Film in the U.S.," *Labor History*, Winter 1983, 103.

15   G.W.F. Hegel, *Aesthetics* (Oxford: Clarendon Press, 1975), 607–9; Sigmund Freud, "Humor," in *Character and Culture* (New York: Collier, 1963), 263–69; André Breton, *What Is Surrealism?* (New York: Monad Press, 1978), 80, 154, 188–96.

16   Antonin Artaud, "The Marx Brothers," in Franklin Rosemont, ed., *Surrealism and Its Popular Accomplices* (San Francisco: City Lights, 1980), 48.

17   On anarchist elements in cinema, see Ado Kyrou, *Le surréalisme au cinema* (Paris: Le terrain vague, 1963); Robert Benayoun, *Le dessin animé après Walt Disney* (Paris: Jean-Jacques Pauvert, 1961); and Franklin Rosemont, "Buster Keaton," "Homage to Tex Avery," "Bugs Bunny," etc., in *Surrealism and Its Popular Accomplices*. Alan Lovell's *Anarchist Cinema* (London: Peace News, 1962) strangely ignores comedy.

18   The comments of "Mr. Dooley" on anarchism were appreciated by anarchists; see the letter from *Freedom* (London) quoted in *Free Society* (Chicago), October 20, 1901.

19   "George Herriman," in Rosemont, *Surrealism and Its Popular Accomplices*.

20   See "A Cartoonist of the People," *Wilshire's Magazine*, October 1902; B.O. Flower, "Frederick Opper: A Cartoonist of Democracy," *The Arena*, June 1905; and the introduction to Ernest Riebe, *Mr. Block: 24 IWW Cartoons* (Chicago: Charles H. Kerr, 1984).

21   See Dave Wagner, "Donald Duck: An Interview," *Radical America* 7, no. 1, 1973; Franklin Rosemont, "Carl Barks/Uncle Scrooge," *Surrealism and Its Popular Accomplices*.

22   A fine portfolio of Roberto Ambrosoli's Anarchik cartoons, with an article by Ambrosoli, was featured in the summer 1985 issue of the anarchist review *MA!*, published in Geneva.

7   The Rise and Fall of the Dil Pickle

1   Jack Jones, "The Bigotry of Bohemia," *The Dil Pickler*, no. 2 (1921).

2   Ben Reitman, "Notes on Dil Pickle History," two-page mimeographed circular, issued by Reitman in connection with his guided tours of Chicago Bohemia, 1935.

3   On pre-Pickle forums, in addition to Fagin's thesis, see Paul Ghio, *L'Anarchisme aux États-Unis* (Paris: Librairie Armand Colin, 1903); Hutchins Hapgood, *The Spirit of Labor* (New York: Duffield, 1907); and Paul Jordan-Smith, *The Road I Came* (Caldwell, ID: Caxton Printers, 1960).

4   On "Chicago Idea" anarchism, see Paul Avrich, *The Haymarket Tragedy* (Princeton, NJ: Princeton University Press, 1984); Bruce Nelson, *Beyond the Martyrs: A Social History of Chicago's Anarchists, 1870–1900* (New Brunswick, NJ: Rutgers University Press, 1988); and Dave Roediger and Franklin Rosemont, *Haymarket Scrapbook* (Chicago: Charles H. Kerr, 1986).

5   On the educational/cultural dimensions of the IWW, see Joyce M. Kornbluh, *Rebel Voices: An IWW Anthology*, revised and expanded ed. (Chicago: Charles H. Kerr, 1998). See also my *Joe Hill: The IWW and the Making of a Revolutionary Workingclass Counterculture* (Chicago: Charles H. Kerr, 2003), and the new introduction to Frank O. Beck, *Hobohemia: Emma Goldman, Lucy Parsons, Ben Reitman and Other Agitators and Outsiders in 1920s/30s Chicago* (Chicago: Charles H. Kerr, 2000), which also includes material on Bughouse Square.

6   Slim Brundage, *From Bughouse Square to the Beat Generation: Selected Writings*

of Slim Brundage, Founder and Janitor of the College of Complexes, ed. Franklin Rosemont (Chicago: Charles H. Kerr, 1997), 80.

10 Homage to Henry Darger

1 Here are the titles of the works shown: (1) *Young Rebonna Dorthereans. Blengins—Catherine Isles—Female—One Whip-Lash Tail.* (2) *Child-headed Whiplash-Tail Blengins. Blengiglom—Enean Island.* (3) *Crimecian Gazoonian. Venemous Calverinia. Hideous but a Very Gentle Creature. It Is However Exceedingly Ferocious Toward Enemies of Its Friends.*

12 Bill Holman (*Smokey Stover*)

1 A translation of this document is included in André Breton, *What Is Surrealism?* (New York: Monad Press, 1978), 320–21.

2 *Surrealism in 1978: 100th Anniversary of Hysteria* (Cedarburg, WI: Ozaukee Art Center, 1978). Catalog of the *Surrealism in 1978* exhibition at the Ozaukee Art Center.

14 Chester Gould (*Dick Tracy*)

1 Introduction to *The Celebrated Cases of Dick Tracy, 1931–1951* (New York: Chelsea House, 1970), xxv.

2 Lancelot Hogben, *From Cave Painting to Comic Strip* (New York: Chanticleer Press, 1949), 216.

15 George Herriman (*Krazy Kat*)

1 e.e. cummings, introduction to George Herriman, *Krazy Kat* (New York: Grosset & Dunlap, 1969).

2 Arthur Asa Berger, *The Comic-Stripped American* (Baltimore: Penguin, 1973).

3 Robert Warshow, *The Immediate Experience* (New York: Doubleday, 1962).

4 On the notion of "Jes Grew," see Ishmael Reed, *Mumbo Jumbo* (New York: Doubleday, 1972), which is, by the way, dedicated to George Herriman.

5 Quoted in Herriman, *Krazy Kat* book, 168.

6 A ballet version of *Krazy Kat*, with music by John Alden Carpenter, was choreographed and staged by Adolf Bolm for the Chicago Grand Opera Ballet in 1920, and by Walter Camiyn in 1948.

7 Rumors of Herriman's Afro-American ancestry persist; if true, this would appreciably substantiate these speculations.

18 Dream-Conscious Times: Surrealism and Early Cinema

1 Matthew Josephson, *Life Among the Surrealists: A Memoir* (New York: Holt, Rinehart and Winston, 1962), 123.

2 Philippe Soupault, *Charlot* (Paris: Plon, 1931), cited in Josephson, *Life Among the Surrealists*, 123–24.

3 Michel Leiris, *Brisées = Broken Branches*, trans. Lydia Davis (San Francisco: North Point Press, 1989), 181. Other surrealists who wrote about Chaplin include Jacques Brunius and Ado Kyrou.

4 André Breton, *Nadja* (New York: Grove Press, 1960), 37.

5 André Breton, "As in a Forest," in Paul Hammond, *The Shadow and Its Shadow: Surrealist Writings on Cinema* (London: British Film Institute, 1978), 42–46.

6 Linda Williams, *Figures of Desire: A Theory and Analysis of Surrealist Film* (Berkeley: University of California Press, 1992).

7 Louis Aragon, quoted in Michel Sanouillet, *Dada à Paris* (Paris: J.J. Pauvert, 1965), 102.

19 A Short Treatise on Wobbly Cartoons (1988)

1 See, for example, George Milburn, *The Hobo's Hornbook* (New York: Washburn, 1930); John Greenway, *American Folksongs of Protest* (Philadelphia: University of Pennsylvania Press, 1953); Barrie Stavis and Frank Harmon, eds., *The Songs of Joe Hill* (New York: Oak, 1960); and Archie Green, "John Neuhaus: Wobbly Folklorist," *Journal of American Folklore* 73 (1960), 189–217.

2 Pierre Couperie and Maurice Horn, *A History of the Comic Strip* (New York: Crown, 1968) was the first major scholarly work on the subject. It was originally published in French in 1967 in conjunction with an international exhibition of comic art at the Louvre. Earlier US books on comics were either anecdotal surveys, such as Martin Sheridan's *Comics and Their Creators* (Boston: Hale, 1944), or sociological studies, such as David Manning White and Robert H. Abel, eds., *The Funnies: An American Idiom* (New York: Free Press of Glencoe, 1963).

3 See, for example, Max Eastman, *Enjoyment of Laughter* (New York: Simon & Schuster, 1936), 72–74; Oakley C. Johnson, *Marxism in U.S. History Before the Russian Revolution* (New York: Humanities Press, 1974), 144–49; and Richard Marschall's superficial and misinformed "Twelve Angry Men," in *Nemo*, no. 24 (February 1987): 46–61. Nick Thorkelson, "Cartooning," *Radical America*, March/April 1979, sketches the development of US political cartooning from Nast and Davenport and *The Masses* artists through Herblock, Mauldin, and the "undergrounds," but the only IWW cartoonist he mentions is Ernest Riebe. For a historical overview of American labor cartooning, see Franklin Rosemont, "Labor Cartoons: A Living Legacy of Humor, Struggle and Protest," in *Bye! American: The Labor Cartoons of Huck and Konopacki* (Chicago: Charles H. Kerr, 1987), 110–12; and Paul Buhle, ed., *Labor's Joke Book* (St. Louis: WD Press, 1985).

4 Sal Salerno, *The Early Labor Radicalism of the IWW* (PhD diss., Brandeis University, 1986), 13–14.

5 Thomas J. Hagerty, "Some Objections to Socialism," *The Comrade*, September 1902, 267.

6 Franklin Rosemont, *Joe Hill: The IWW and the Making of a Revolutionary Workingclass Culture* (Chicago: Charles H. Kerr, 2003), 158–59.

7 Joe Hill, letter of August 15, 1915, in Philip S. Foner, ed., *The Letters of Joe Hill* (New York: Oak, 1965), 50.

8 Chaplin discusses his career as an artist in his autobiography, *Wobbly: The Rough and Tumble Story of an American Radical* (Chicago: University of Chicago Press, 1948).

9 Franklin Rosemont, introduction to Ernest Riebe, *Mr. Block: 24 IWW Cartoons* (Chicago: Charles H. Kerr, 1984); Douglas Haller, "IWW Cartoonist Ernest Riebe" (master's thesis, Wayne State University, 1982).

10 Recent revivals of *Mr. Block* are noted by Carlos Cortez in "Power of the Unspoken Word," *Industrial Worker*, October 1982.

11 *International Socialist Review*, December 1915, inside front cover.

12 In the table of contents of the *International Socialist Review*, October 1915, Machia's first name is given as Arturo.

13 Minnie F. Corder, "Ray Corder" (obit.), *Industrial Worker*, January 1969, 2.

14 See Art Young's autobiographies, *On My Way* (New York: Liveright, 1928), and *Art Young: His Life and Times* (New York: Sheridan House, 1939), as well as *The*

Best of Art Young, with an introduction by Heywood Broun (New York: Vanguard Press, 1936).

15   "A Cartoon with a Thought," *Industrial Pioneer*, August 1924, 21; Young, *Art Young: His Life and Times*, 454.

16   Art Young, *Thomas Rowlandson* (New York: Willey, 1938), 26.

17   See the news story on Ellis in *New Majority*, August 2, 1919, 5.

18   Johnson, *Marxism in U.S. History*.

19   A.D. Condo and J.W. Raper, *The Outbursts of Everett True* (Vestal, NY: Vestal Press, 1983). A short biographical sketch of Condo appeared in *The Comic Buyer's Guide*, August 5, 1983, 9–10.

20   Riebe, *Mr. Block*, 19.

21   "The John Baer Story," *Electrical Workers Journal* 66, no. 1 (January 1967): 53–55; Bill G. Reid, "John M. Baer: Nonpartisan League Cartoonist and Congressman," *North Dakota History* 44 (Winter 1977): 4–13.

22   See Zinn's letter to the editor, "Dislikes Articles on Lumber Workers," *Industrial Worker*, February 28, 1948, 2.

23   An obituary for Olday appeared in the *Industrial Worker* for July 1977. A "Tribute to John Olday" was published as a special supplement to the English anarchist paper *Freedom*, September 3, 1977 (vol. 38, no. 17).

24   "Show Your Appreciation," *Industrial Pioneer*, June 1926, 23.

25   An edited transcript of an oral history interview with Ern Hanson is included in Bert Russell, ed., *Hardships and Happy Times* (Harrison, ID: Lacon, 1978), 86–129.

26   Carlos Cortez, *Wobbly: 80 Years of Rebel Art* (Chicago: Gato Negro Press, 1985), 26.

27   "Eugene Barnett, Cartoonist," *Industrial Pioneer*, February 1924, 18; "A Rebel Worker's Life" serialized in *Labor Defender* from January 1927 through January 1928; Ralph Chaplin, *The Centralia Conspiracy* (Chicago: General Defense Committee, 1924), 28–29; Harvey O'Connor, *Revolution in Seattle* (New York: Monthly Review Press, 1964), 193.

28   Editorial note on bottom of page, *Industrial Pioneer*, January 1925, 44.

29   For biographical information on Henkelman I have relied on recollections by Richard Ellington of Oakland, California, and Jenny Velsek of Chicago; see also Cortez, *Wobbly*, 18.

30   "Cartoonist X13," *Industrial Worker*, June 1971; correspondence with Nicolaas Steelink; Cortez, *Wobbly*, 32; Guy Louis Rocha, "The IWW and the Boulder Dam Project," in Joseph Conlin, ed., *At the Point of Production: The Local History of the IWW* (Westport, CT: Greenwood, 1981), 218–19.

31   Cortez, *Wobbly*, 22; interview with Jenny Velsek, Chicago, October 1987.

32   Cortez, *Wobbly*, 38.

33   Cortez, *Wobbly*, 40; Clif Bennett, "Resistance in Prison," in *Retort*, Winter 1949 (more accessible in the special *Retort* anthology published by *The Match!* [Tucson, AZ, 1987]).

34   Interview with Carlos Cortez, October 1987. The MOMA exhibit *Committed to Print* (1988) includes one of Cortez's woodblocks.

35   Tor Faegre, "Organizing Blueberries," *Rebel Worker*, no. 2 (Summer 1964): 6–9.

36   *Permanence du regard surréaliste* (Lyon, France: ELAC, 1981), 61; Edouard Jaguer, preface to Robert Green exhibition catalog, Platypus Gallery, Evanston, 1983; Adam Biro and René Passeron, eds., *Dictionnaire général du surréalisme et de ses environs* (Paris: Presses universitaires de France, 1982), 155.

37   As quoted here in *Rebel Voices* [Joyce M. Kornbluh, *Rebel Voices: An IWW Anthology* (Chicago: Charles H. Kerr, 1988)], 71.

38   Gelett Burgess, "The Wild Men of Paris," *Architectural Record* [New York], May 1910, 400–414.

39   Kenneth Rexroth, *An Autobiographical Novel* (Wheybridge, Surrey, UK: Whittet Books, 1981), 145.

40   The poster is reproduced in color in John Canemaker, *Winsor McCay: His Life and Art* (New York: Abbeville, 1987), 176.

41   Penelope Rosemont and Joseph Jablonski, "Miserabilism and Anti-Miserabilism in 1986," *International Surrealist Bulletin*, September 1986, 3–6.

42   Dave Foreman and Bill Haywood, eds., *Ecodefense: A Field Guide to Monkeywrenching*, 2nd ed. (Tucson, AZ: Ned Ludd Books, 1987), 231–32.

43   On the popular imagination, see André Breton, *What Is Surrealism? Selected Writings* (New York: Monad Press, 1978); Franklin Rosemont, ed., *Surrealism and Its Popular Accomplices*, originally published as a special issue of the journal *Cultural Correspondence* (Providence, RI, 1979) and reprinted as a book the following year (San Francisco: City Lights, 1980); Paul Garon, *Blues and the Poetic Spirit* (New York: Da Capo, 1979); *Free Spirits: Annals of the Insurgent Imagination* (San Francisco: City Lights, 1982); and Paul Buhle, ed., *Popular Culture in America* (Minneapolis: University of Minnesota Press, 1987).

44   Quoted in Stewart Bird, Dan Georgakas, and Deborah Shaffer, *Solidarity Forever: An Oral History of the IWW* (Chicago: Lake View, 1985), 68.

45   A useful introduction to the IWW around the world is the postscript to Patrick Renshaw, *The Wobblies* (Garden City, NY: Doubleday, 1967), 221–38.

46   Maurice Horn, *World Encyclopedia of Comics* (New York: Chelsea House, 1976), 518–19. Nicholls, incidentally, is the only cartoonist for the IWW included in this 789-page reference; his IWW connection, however, is not mentioned.

47   Franklin Rosemont, "A Bomb-Toting, Long-Haired, Wild-Eyed Fiend: The Image of the Anarchist in Popular Culture," in Dave Roediger and Franklin Rosemont, eds., *Haymarket Scrapbook* (Chicago: Charles H. Kerr, 1986), 203–12 [included as chapter 5 in this volume].

48   The Australian poster (signed DI-NO) is reproduced in Ian Turner, *Sydney's Burning* (Sydney: Alpha Books, 1969).

49   The importance of the ethnic minorities' contribution to the IWW, and to American radicalism generally, is stressed in Salerno, *The Early Labor Radicalism of the IWW*; and Paul Buhle, *Marxism in the USA: From 1870 to Today* (London: Verso, 1987).

50   Philip S. Foner, *Organized Labor and the Black Worker, 1619–1973* (New York: International, 1978), 107–19.

51   Richard Ellington, "Guy B. Askew: A Reminiscence," unpublished article.

52   Trina Robbins and Cat Yronwode, *Women and the Comics* (Guerneville, CA: Eclipse Books, 1985). Trina Robbins discusses comic art and her own work in "Interviews with Women Comic Artists," *Cultural Correspondence*, no. 9 (Spring 1979): 10–12, and in *Comics Journal*, no. 100 (July 1985): 135–39. Her "Triangle Fire" appeared in Avis Lang Rosenberg, *Pork Roasts: 250 Feminist Cartoons*, catalog of an exhibition at the UBC Fine Arts Gallery in Vancouver, 1981.

53   According to records at IWW headquarters in Chicago, Gloria Nelson joined the IWW in September 1970; her cartoons are all signed "G. Nelson." Leslie Fish signed up in June 1971.

54   Roger Lewis, *Outlaws of America: The Underground Press and Its Context* (Baltimore: Pelican, 1972), noted, "Many of the old-timers around the IWW relate to the new youth movement in a very positive way" and added, "Many underground papers are printed under the IWW union label."

55 Ann Schofield discusses some early woman-related IWW cartoons in "Rebel Girls and Union Maids: The Woman Question in the Journals of the AFL and IWW, 1905–1920," *Feminist Studies* 9, no. 2 (Summer 1983): 335–58.

56 Details of the history of the UCWA were provided by Denis Kitchen and Manuel "Spain" Rodriguez.

24 Black Music and the Surrealist Revolution

1 "The New Argonautica," in the surrealist section of Lawrence Ferlinghetti, ed., *City Lights Anthology* (San Francisco: City Lights, 1974).

28 Juice Is Stranger than Friction: T-Bone Slim

I have footnoted every reference for which a published source exists. With few exceptions, I have *not* footnoted quotations or information gleaned from my interviews and correspondence with several dozen people who knew T-Bone Slim or had details to communicate about him; instead, I have cited such sources in the text itself. [F.R.]

1 Edgar Allan Poe, "Marginalia [June 1849]," in *Essays and Reviews* (New York: Library of America, 1984), 1460.

2 Richard Brazier, "The Story of the IWW's 'Little Red Song Book,'" *Labor History*, Winter 1968, 91–105; Archie Green, "John Neuhaus: Wobbly Folklorist," *Journal of American Folklore* 73 (1960): 189–217.

3 Recent editions of the IWW songbook have dropped most of the hobo songs, including Joe Hill's and T-Bone's, but the three songs mentioned, plus three others by T-Bone, are included in a reprint of the 1923 edition: *IWW Songs—1923 Edition* (Chicago: Charles H. Kerr, 1989). Bruce "Utah" Phillips, Joe Glazer, Pete Seeger, Faith Petric, and others have recorded several of T-Bone's songs.

4 Bert Russell, ed., *Swiftwater People: Lives of Old Timers on the Upper St. Joe and St. Maries Rivers* (Harrison, ID: Lacon Publishers, 1979), 282.

5 Thanks to Steve Rosswurn for obtaining this piece of paranoid Americana under what's left of the Freedom of Information Act. On the photocopied documents, the FBI agent's name has been carefully blocked out by present-day Justice Department functionaries.

6 Fred Thompson, *The IWW: Its First Seventy Years* (Chicago: IWW, 1976), 199.

7 Thompson, *IWW*, 199. In "Even Breaks," in the *Industrial Worker* (July 16, 1921), T-Bone states: "Unfortunately, I was born in this country."

8 *Industrial Worker*, March 14, 1923.

9 These details of T-Bone's marriage and family were reported by his daughter Edna and communicated to me by her friend Edna Zalimeni.

10 This information is included in a file of ten documents in the possession of the New York City Medical Examiner's Office, classified as Case No. M42-2690 (May 1942). Thanks to Ellen Borakove, current director of public affairs for the New York City Medical Examiner's Office, for locating this file and informing me of its contents.

11 New York City Medical Examiner's Office, Case No. M42-2690. See also the obituary "T-Bone Slim, IWW Humorist, Passes Away," *Industrial Worker*, October 24, 1942, 1. Though unsigned, this article was almost certainly written by the editor, Carl Keller. In the late 1940s or early '50s, the Barge Captains Union was absorbed by Local 333 of the ILA.

12 I asked five of T-Bone's acquaintances to estimate his age. According to their guesses he was between forty-five and sixty-two at the time of his death. This would place the year of his birth between 1880 and 1897. "Approximately

fifty" was the estimate given by the physician for the New York City Medical Examiner's Office after T-Bone's death in 1942.

13 Card No. 198308, "Brisbanalities," *Industrial Solidarity*, January 11, 1928, 4. According to a letter from his sister Ida, in the records of the New York City Medical Examiner's Office (Case No. M42-2690), T-Bone also used the name Joseph Hilgor. This may be the name he gave employers, flophouse proprietors, and other representatives of the "established order."

14 Unsigned article, "T-Bone Slim," in the Hungarian-language IWW weekly *Bermunkas* (Cleveland), October 31, 1942, 1.

15 "T-Bone Slim, IWW Humorist, Passes Away."

16 Nels Anderson, *The Hobo: The Sociology of the Homeless Man* (Chicago: University of Chicago Press, 1923).

17 Karl Marx, "General Rules of the International Working Men's Association" (1871).

18 "T-Bone Slim, IWW Humorist, Passes Away."

19 Fred Thompson, quoted in Joyce Kornbluh, ed., *Rebel Voices: An IWW Anthology* (Chicago: Charles H. Kerr, 1988), 370.

20 Franklin Rosemont, "Who Was T-Bone Slim?," *Industrial Worker*, December 1975, 7.

21 Guy B. Askew, "Reminiscences of T-Bone Slim," *Rebel Worker*, no. 7 (January 1967): 24, 33.

22 Although no *News-Telegram* was published in Duluth, one of the city's major papers in the 1910s was the *News-Tribune*, which Askew evidently conflated with another daily published just across the river, the Superior, Wisconsin, *Evening Telegram*.

23 Quoted in John Greenway, *American Folksongs of Protest* (New York: A.S. Barnes, 1960), 264.

24 Jimmy Glavin, an early and maverick member of the National Maritime Union (NMU), in a recent interview with Thomas Walker, also expressed his belief that T-Bone's death was war-related. I am grateful to Thomas Walker for communicating this information to me.

25 Aunt Molly's anecdote, as quoted above, is an excerpt from her interviews with John Greenway during 1950–52. In *American Folksongs of Protest* the story prefaces a song she recorded in 1939 under the title "Crossbones Scully" (Library of Congress AAFS 2539B, 2556A). The lyrics appear in the book with the title "T-Bone Slim," but in the appendix (page 313) it is given as "Crossbones Scully Slim." Adding to the confusion, in a series of interviews in 1957–58, Aunt Molly told Archie Green that her brother, Jim Garland, had named the song "T-Bone Scully." Reiterating that she had met T-Bone Slim, she added that she did not know why her brother had changed the name of the song; she was, however, according to Green, "characteristically vague" about the matter. In a memo dated February 1, 1992, Green notes that nothing in Aunt Molly's song, or her comments on it, really points to T-Bone Slim or the IWW. With Aunt Molly, Jim Garland, and John Greenway all deceased, the mystery of crossed identity seems unlikely to be solved. However, we may be able to learn whether there really was a man known as Crossbones Scully.

26 The following discussion of Finnish history and Finnish-American radicalism is largely drawn from Sirkka Tuomi Lee, "The Finns," in "The Origins of Left Culture in the U.S.: 1880–1940," special issue, *Cultural Correspondence*, nos. 6–7 (Spring 1978): 41–49.

27   Sal Salerno's *Red November, Black November: Culture and Community in the IWW* (Albany: State University of New York Press, 1989) is a refreshing exception and a major contribution to the reevaluation of Wobbly history. My awareness of the enormous role of the Finns in the IWW owes much to my conversations and correspondence with Jenny Lahti Velsek, Harry Sütonen, and Abraham Wuori.

28   For a short survey of the terrain, see "T-Bone Slim and the Phonetic Cabala" in my *Surrealism and Its Popular Accomplices* (San Francisco: City Lights, 1980) [included as chapter 27 in this volume].

29   See, for example, the heading of T-Bone's column in the *Industrial Worker* for October 13, 1923: "Notes of the Class Struggle by Our Own Philosopher," and Covami [Covington Hall], "You Said It, T-B.S.," *Industrial Worker*, May 1, 1926, 3.

30   Robert Paul Wolff, *Moneybags Should Be So Lucky: On the Literary Structure of "Capital"* (Amherst: University of Massachusetts Press, 1988). Forty-eight years earlier, as Wolff points out, Edmund Wilson—in his *To the Finland Station*—argued that Marx was "one of the great masters of satire" and "certainly the greatest ironist since Swift."

29   Joe Hill

1   Barrie Stavis, *The Man Who Never Died: A Play About Joe Hill* (New York: Haven Press, 1954), 99.

2   Friends of Joe Hill Committee, "Joe Hill: IWW Martyr," *New Republic*, November 15, 1948, 18–20.

3   Ralph Chaplin, "Joe Hill's Funeral," *International Socialist Review*, January 1916, 400–405.

4   Chaplin, "Joe Hill's Funeral," 404.

5   Philip S. Foner, *The Case of Joe Hill* (New York: International, 1965), 99.

6   Joe Powers and Mark Rogovin, eds., *The Day Will Come: Stories of the Haymarket Martyrs and the Men and Women Buried Alongside the Monument* (Chicago: Published for the Illinois Labor History Society by the Charles H. Kerr Company, 1994). Note that half of Haywood's ashes were buried in Chicago; the other half were buried in the Kremlin Wall.

7   Thanks to Mark Rogovin for communicating this anecdote.

8   John Takman, "Joe Hill's Sister: An Interview," *Masses and Mainstream*, March 1956, 26.

9   See Jehan Mayoux, "Correspondence," in *Le Surréalisme au service de la révolution*, no. 5 (1932): 42. "Latent News," a surrealist game similar to Hill's playful "rewriting" of the newspaper, is described (with examples) in Ron Sakolsky, ed., *Surrealist Subversions* (New York: Autonomedia, 2002), 204–5.

10   Ture Nerman, *Joe Hill: Mördare eller Martyr?* (Stockholm: Pogo Press, 1979), 36.

11   Evert Anderson, "Joe Hill, IWW Rebel, Is Honored in Sweden," *Industrial Worker*, May 20, 1964, 4.

31   Humor: Here Today and Everywhere Tomorrow: A Short Introduction to the Next Revolution

1   Humor is the decisive component of the "transitional object of a new type," or "transitional event," discussed in my "Introduction to the Reading of Benjamin Paul Blood," *Arsenal/Surrealist Subversion*, no. 3 (Spring 1976): 75.

Index

Page numbers in *italic* refer to illustrations. "Passim" (literally "scattered") indicates intermittent discussion of a topic over a cluster of pages.

About the Author and Editors

Franklin Rosemont was born in Chicago in 1943. His father, Henry, was a labor activist, and his mother, Sally, a jazz musician. He edited and wrote an introduction for André Breton's *What Is Surrealism? Selected Writings* and edited *Rebel Worker, Arsenal/Surrealist Subversion, The Rise and Fall of the Dil Pickle,* and *Juice Is Stranger than Friction: Selected Writings of T-Bone Slim.* With Penelope Rosemont and Paul Garon he edited *The Forecast Is Hot!* His work was deeply concerned with both the history of surrealism (writing a foreword for *Max Ernst and Alchemy: A Magician in Search of Myth*) and of the radical labor movement in America. For several decades he and Penelope Rosemont combined such interests in helming the venerable radical publishing house the Charles H. Kerr Company. He died in 2009 in Chicago.

In her wide-ranging research devoted to modern and contemporary art history and visual culture, **Abigail Susik** focuses on the intersection of international surrealism with antiauthoritarian protest cultures. She is the author of *Surrealist Sabotage and the War on Work* (Manchester University Press, 2021), editor of *Resurgence! Jonathan Leake, Radical Surrealism, and the Resurgence Youth Movement, 1964–1967* (Eberhardt Press, 2023), and coeditor of the volumes *Surrealism and Film After 1945: Modern Mysteries* (Manchester University Press, 2021) and *Radical Dreams: Surrealism, Counterculture, Resistance* (Penn State University Press, 2022). Susik is a founding board member of the International Society for the Study of Surrealism and an associate professor of art history at Willamette University.

Paul Buhle is the author or editor of more than three dozen books, including historical graphic novels such as *Wobblies!* (2005), a centenary celebration of the Industrial Workers of the World created with the participation of Franklin and Penelope Rosemont. He founded the SDS journal *Radical America* and the Oral History of the American Left archive at New York University's Tamiment Library. He is coeditor of the *Encyclopedia of the American Left* (1990) and is a former senior lecturer at Brown University.

ABOUT PM PRESS

PM Press is an independent, radical publisher of critically necessary books for our tumultuous times. Our aim is to deliver bold political ideas and vital stories to all walks of life and arm the dreamers to demand the impossible. Founded in 2007 by a small group of people with decades of publishing, media, and organizing experience, we have sold millions of copies of our books, most often one at a time, face to face. We're old enough to know what we're doing and young enough to know what's at stake. Join us to create a better world.

PM Press
PO Box 23912
Oakland, CA 94623
www.pmpress.org

PM Press in Europe
europe@pmpress.org
www.pmpress.org.uk

FRIENDS OF PM PRESS

These are indisputably momentous times—the financial system is melting down globally and the Empire is stumbling. Now more than ever there is a vital need for radical ideas.

In the many years since its founding—and on a mere shoestring—PM Press has risen to the formidable challenge of publishing and distributing knowledge and entertainment for the struggles ahead. With hundreds of releases to date, we have published an impressive and stimulating array of literature, art, music, politics, and culture. Using every available medium, we've succeeded in connecting those hungry for ideas and information to those putting them into practice.

Friends of PM allows you to directly help impact, amplify, and revitalize the discourse and actions of radical writers, filmmakers, and artists. It provides us with a stable foundation from which we can build upon our early successes and provides a much-needed subsidy for the materials that can't necessarily pay their own way. You can help make that happen—and receive every new title automatically delivered to your door once a month—by joining as a Friend of PM Press. And, we'll throw in a free T-shirt when you sign up.

Here are your options:

- **$30 a month** Get all books and pamphlets plus a 50% discount on all webstore purchases

- **$40 a month** Get all PM Press releases (including CDs and DVDs) plus a 50% discount on all webstore purchases

- **$100 a month** Superstar—Everything plus PM merchandise, free downloads, and a 50% discount on all webstore purchases

For those who can't afford $30 or more a month, we have **Sustainer Rates** at $15, $10, and $5. Sustainers get a free PM Press T-shirt and a 50% discount on all purchases from our website.

Your Visa or Mastercard will be billed once a month, until you tell us to stop. Or until our efforts succeed in bringing the revolution around. Or the financial meltdown of Capital makes plastic redundant. Whichever comes first.

The Big Red Songbook: 250+ IWW Songs!

Edited by Archie Green, David Roediger, Franklin Rosemont, and Salvatore Salerno with a Foreword by Tom Morello and an Afterword by Utah Phillips

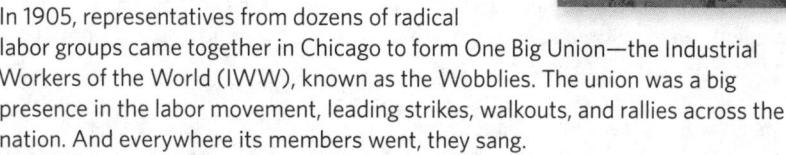

ISBN: 978-1-62963-129-5
$29.95   560 pages

In 1905, representatives from dozens of radical labor groups came together in Chicago to form One Big Union—the Industrial Workers of the World (IWW), known as the Wobblies. The union was a big presence in the labor movement, leading strikes, walkouts, and rallies across the nation. And everywhere its members went, they sang.

Their songs were sung in mining camps and textile mills, hobo jungles and flop houses, and anywhere workers might be recruited to the Wobblies' cause. The songs were published in a pocketsize tome called the *Little Red Songbook*, which was so successful that it's been published continuously since 1909. In *The Big Red Songbook*, the editors have gathered songs from over three dozen editions, plus additional songs, rare artwork, personal recollections, discographies, and more into one big all-embracing book.

IWW poets/composers strove to nurture revolutionary consciousness. Each piece, whether topical, hortatory, elegiac, or comic served to educate, agitate, and emancipate workers. A handful of Wobbly numbers have become classics, still sung by labor groups and folk singers. They include Joe Hill's sardonic "The Preacher and the Slave" (sometimes known by its famous phrase "Pie in the Sky") and Ralph Chaplin's "Solidarity Forever." Songs lost or found, sacred or irreverent, touted or neglected, serious or zany, singable or not, are here. The Wobblies and their friends have been singing for a century. May this comprehensive gathering simultaneously celebrate past battles and chart future goals.

In addition to the 250+ songs, writings are included from Archie Green, Franklin Rosemont, David Roediger, Salvatore Salerno, Judy Branfman, Richard Brazier, James Connell, Carlos Cortez, Bill Friedland, Virginia Martin, Harry McClintock, Fred Thompson, Adam Machado, and many more.

"This engaging anthology features the lyrics to 250 or so Wobbly songs, rich with references to job sharks, shovel stiffs, capitalist tools, and plutocratic parasites. Wobbly wordsmiths such as the fabled Joe Hill, T-Bone Slim, Haywire Mac, and Richard Brazier set their fighting words to popular tunes of the day, gospel hymns, old ballads and patriotic anthems."
—San Francisco Chronicle

Joe Hill: The IWW & the Making of a Revolutionary Workingclass Counterculture, Second Edition

Franklin Rosemont with an Introduction by David Roediger

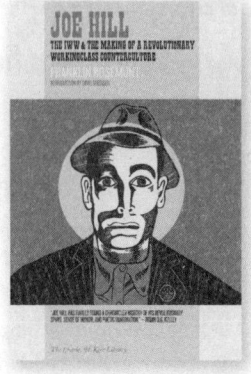

ISBN: 978-1-62963-119-6
$29.95   656 pages

A monumental work, expansive in scope, covering the life, times, and culture of that most famous of the Wobblies—songwriter, poet, hobo, thinker, humorist, martyr—Joe Hill. It is a journey into the Wobbly culture that made Hill and the capitalist culture that killed him. Many aspects of the life and lore of Joe Hill receive their first and only discussion in IWW historian Franklin Rosemont's opus.

In great detail, the issues that Joe Hill raised and grappled with in his life: capitalism, white supremacy, gender, religion, wilderness, law, prison, and industrial unionism are shown in both the context of Hill's life and for their enduring relevance in the century since his death.

Collected too is Joe Hill's art, plus scores of other images featuring Hill-inspired art by IWW illustrators from Ralph Chaplin to Carlos Cortez, as well as contributions from many other labor artists.

As Rosemont suggests in this remarkable book, Joe Hill never really died. He lives in the minds of young (and old) rebels as long as his songs are sung, his ideas are circulated, and his political descendants keep fighting for a better day.

"Joe Hill has finally found a chronicler worthy of his revolutionary spirit, sense of humor, and poetic imagination."
—Robin D.G. Kelley, author of *Freedom Dreams*

"Rosemont's treatment of Joe Hill is passionate, polemical, and downright entertaining. What he gives us is an extended and detailed argument for considering both Hill and the IWW for their contributions toward creating an autonomous and uncompromising alternative culture."
—Gordon Simmons, *Labor Studies Journal*

"Magnificent, practical, irreverent and (as one might say) magisterial, written in a direct, passionate, sometimes funny, deeply searching style."
—Peter Linebaugh, author of *Stop, Thief!*

Rebel Voices:
An IWW Anthology

Edited by Joyce L. Kornbluh with
a Preface by Daniel Gross and an
Introduction by Fred Thompson

ISBN: 978-1-60486-483-0
$27.95   472 pages

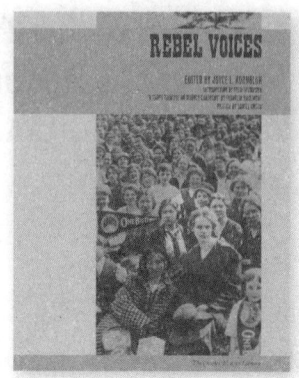

Welcoming women, Blacks, and immigrants long
before most other unions, the Wobblies from
the start were labor's outstanding pioneers and innovators, unionizing hundreds
of thousands of workers previously regarded as "unorganizable." Wobblies
organized the first sit-down strike (at General Electric, Schenectady, 1906),
the first major auto strike (6,000 Studebaker workers, Detroit, 1911), the first
strike to shut down all three coalfields in Colorado (1927), and the first "no-fare"
transit-workers' job-action (Cleveland, 1944). With their imaginative, colorful,
and world-famous strikes and free-speech fights, the IWW wrote many of the
brightest pages in the annals of working class emancipation. Wobblies also
made immense and invaluable contributions to workers' culture. All but a few
of America's most popular labor songs are Wobbly songs. IWW cartoons have
long been recognized as labor's finest and funniest.

The impact of the IWW has reverberated far beyond the ranks of organized
labor. An important influence on the 1960s New Left, the Wobbly theory and
practice of direct action, solidarity, and "class-war" humor have inspired several
generations of civil rights and antiwar activists, and are a major source of ideas
and inspiration for today's radicals. Indeed, virtually every movement seeking
to "make this planet a good place to live" (to quote an old Wobbly slogan), has
drawn on the IWW's incomparable experience.

Originally published in 1964 and long out of print, *Rebel Voices* remains by far
the biggest and best source on IWW history, fiction, songs, art, and lore. This
new edition includes 40 pages of additional material from the 1998 Charles H.
Kerr edition from Fred Thompson and Franklin Rosemont, and a new preface by
Wobbly organizer Daniel Gross.

*"Not even the doughtiest of capitalism's defenders can read these pages without
understanding how much glory and nobility there was in the IWW story, and how
much shame for the nation that treated the Wobblies so shabbily."*
—*New York Times Book Review*, on the 1964 edition

*"The IWW blazed a path in industrial history and its influence is still felt today.
Joyce Kornbluh has performed a valuable service to unionism by compiling this
comprehensive anthology on the more militant side of labor history."*
—*Southwest Labor*

Ben Fletcher: The Life and Times of a Black Wobbly, Second Edition

Edited by Peter Cole with a Foreword by Robin D.G. Kelley

ISBN: 978-1-62963-832-4 (paperback)
        978-1-62963-862-1 (hardcover)
$24.95/$60.00   352 pages

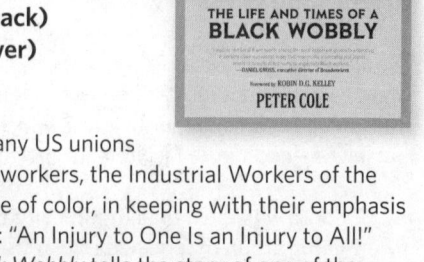

In the early twentieth century, when many US unions disgracefully excluded black and Asian workers, the Industrial Workers of the World (IWW) warmly welcomed people of color, in keeping with their emphasis on class solidarity and their bold motto: "An Injury to One Is an Injury to All!" *Ben Fletcher: The Life and Times of a Black Wobbly* tells the story of one of the greatest heroes of the American working class.

A brilliant union organizer and a humorous orator, Benjamin Fletcher (1890–1949) was a tremendously important and well-loved African American member of the IWW during its heyday. Fletcher helped found and lead Local 8 of the IWW's Marine Transport Workers Industrial Union, unquestionably the most powerful interracial union of its era, taking a principled stand against all forms of xenophobia and exclusion.

For years, acclaimed historian Peter Cole has carefully researched the life of Ben Fletcher, painstakingly uncovering a stunning range of documents related to this extraordinary man. *Ben Fletcher: The Life and Times of a Black Wobbly* is the most comprehensive look at Fletcher ever to be published. It includes a detailed biographical sketch of his life and history, reminiscences by fellow workers who knew him, a chronicle of the IWW's impressive decade-long run on the Philadelphia waterfront in which Fletcher played a pivotal role, and nearly all of his known writings and speeches, thus giving Fletcher's timeless voice another opportunity to inspire a new generation of workers, organizers, and agitators. This revised and expanded second edition includes new materials such as facsimile reprints of two extremely rare pamphlets on racism from the early twentieth century, more information on his prison years and personal life, additional recollections from friends, greater consideration of Fletcher from a global perspective, and much more.

"This stirring collection gives us the drama, largely in his own exciting words, of the life and work of black radical labor leader Ben Fletcher. It is a story of suffering, fighting, and organizing but also of thinking deeply and writing clearly about the social power of labor, and particularly of maritime workers, and the possibility of a world beyond racial division and class exploitation."
—David Roediger, University of Kansas, author of *Class, Race, and Marxism*

The Society of the Spectacle (PM Edition)

Guy Debord
Edited and translated by Ken Knabb

ISBN: 979-8-88744-056-9
$19.95   160 pages

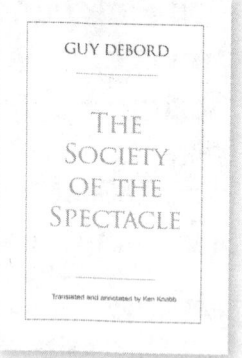

The Society of the Spectacle is a carefully considered effort to clarify the most fundamental tendencies and contradictions of the society in which we find ourselves—in order to facilitate its overthrow.

Guy Debord was the founder of the Situationist International, the notorious avant-garde group that helped trigger the May 1968 revolt in France, which brought the entire country to a standstill for several weeks. His book *The Society of the Spectacle*, originally published in Paris in 1967, has been translated into more than twenty other languages and is arguably the most important radical work of the twentieth century. Ken Knabb's meticulous new translation is the first edition in any language to include extensive annotations, clarifying the historical allusions and revealing the sources of Debord's quotations and "détournements."

Contrary to popular misconceptions, Debord's book is neither an ivory-tower philosophical discourse nor a mere expression of "protest." This makes the book more of a challenge, but it is also why it remains so pertinent more than half a century after its original publication, while countless other social theories and intellectual fads have come and gone.

It has, in fact, become even more pertinent than ever, because the spectacle has become more all-pervading and glaringly obvious than ever. As Debord noted in his follow-up work, *Comments on the Society of the Spectacle* (1988), "Spectacular domination has succeeded in raising an entire generation molded to its laws." Debord's book remains the best guidebook to understanding that mold and breaking it.

"I read The Society of the Spectacle *again and I thought, 'This is a fucking amazing book!' I had forgotten how terrific it was, and it was actually quite different to how I remembered it. I insist that the key chapter is not the first one, on the spectacle itself, but the second to last—the chapter on détournement. To me, that concept is the great gift of the Situationists. They realized that one can exploit this critically—one can copy and correct in the direction of hope."*
—McKenzie Wark, author of *A Hacker Manifesto*, in *Los Angeles Review of Books*